Such a Refuge

Children of the heav'nly Father
Safely in his bosom gather.
Nestling bird nor star in heaven
Such a refuge e'er was given.

Carolina Sandell (Ernst W. Olson, trans.)

Such a Refuge

A History of the
Children's Shelter of Cebu

Paul Healy

In loving memory and appreciation

Cebu Friends

Romulo Alejado

Laura Atillo

Gloria Navasquez

Ronald R. Duterte

Rebecca Pellajera

Mateo Martinez

Rufa Mae Obiedo

Vivian Briones

Felipa Davin

Carlo Paña

Elma Paña

Rebecca Deliña

CSC Kids

Micah Maluping 1982

Arnold Borres 1989

Sonny Boy Briones 1990

Agnello Tanjay 1991

Ronnie Llaban 2001

Samantha Nunez 2002

Darvie Davidson 2004

Luke Baisic Barcelona 2006

Jacob Danny Collamat 2019

Junrey Ruta

Hendre Ibañez

U.S. Loved Ones

Former Residents

Rene Dreiling

Jamin Melton Dodd

Jeffrey Ray Eidson

John Leone

Ian Noel

Friends

Ray Burke

Jackie Cherne

Cliff Danielson

Arman Eicher

Robert Wesley Hagen

Warren Hagfors

Marie Hagfors

Jerry Healy

Millie Healy

Kathy Johnson

Al Sannerud

Contents

Preface

BLESSED ARE THOSE WHOM GOD CALLS, and blessed are those who listen and respond!

Almost fifty years ago a young woman in Minnesota heard, listened, and convinced her (maybe) soon-to-be fiancé to accompany her to explore a need in the Philippines. A home in Cebu was rented. Children were rescued from the streets, and the Children's Shelter of Cebu was born!

After over four decades of response and service, Paul and Marlys Healy have retired as founders and directors of CSC. During this time God has used them and others to transform the lives of many hundreds of young Filipino children and their "forever families" around the world.

This book chronicles CSC's magnificent journey. Through many times of challenge and many times of joy, God has used CSC to change lives.

We thank God for His faithfulness and the faithfulness of Paul and Marlys and many others in answering His call. Your hearts will be blessed and your lives enriched as you read of this journey.

Dr. Paul Sanders
Cambridge, Minnesota

Dedication

THIS BOOK IS DEDICATED to the memory of Ronald Duterte, the best friend that any staff or ministry could ever have. He took us under his wing in Cebu when we started in 1979; bailed us out often; opened doors that would otherwise have remained closed; gave us credibility; taught us about the Philippines; and suffered our sad attempts at assimilation, language learning, and government relations. As long as Ron was on our side, we didn't have to worry about many things. He was always there.

In addition to being the president of CSC in the Philippines for much of our history, he was our friend. He took us out to eat, came to CSC or the Children of Hope School for every important program, let us use his beach house, and brought some of us golfing at courses where he was a member. And while his golf game was nothing to emulate, everything else about him was.

Ron died of liver cancer in 2005. We are not the same organization without Ron. Sometimes we flounder. Sometimes we feel alone when walking into a government building or applying for a license or permit. Often we wish we had his advice or his companionship. Every day we miss him in one way or another.

Ron was a man of many interests and talents. He was a good speaker, having learned that skill in law school and on the campaign trail as a politician. He was a highly regarded lawyer in Cebu City. He had received an undergraduate degree in law from Columbia University in New York and a graduate degree from the University of Madrid. He and his father, also an attorney and later a judge, built a successful law practice and engaged in some landmark cases. Ron was a good singer and played the piano. I remember him favoring us with songs when we had him over for an evening. His favorite song was "Born Free." He was also a good dancer and performed Philippine cultural dances with CSC board member Lisa Saavedra and CSC staff member Gloria Deliña on occasion.

Ron was a member of the KBL political party of President Ferdinand Marcos. Virtually every office holder in the country in those days was affiliated with Marcos. In 1986, when the Marcos dynasty collapsed and he was deposed and left the country for exile in Hawaii, all government officials who were seen to be Marcos allies were summarily kicked out of office and replaced with someone loyal to Cory Aquino, who had run for president against Marcos and won. Ron had the strange experience of going to Manila for a meeting as Cebu's mayor and, while he was away, finding that people from Aquino's group broke into his office and installed a new mayor. Those were turbulent times for the Philippines and for Ron personally. In the coming years he would again run for office, this time for Philippine Congress. He lost that election and his political career—which had included

stints on the Cebu City Council, as vice mayor of Cebu, and eventually as city mayor—was over.

When this part of Ron's professional life ended, he went to work as president of the University of Southern Philippines, his alma mater. He helped improve the curriculum of that school and establish a law program in the graduate school.

Throughout his career in politics and higher education, Ron dedicated himself to helping CSC and our staff. His contacts in government opened doors for us. His legal knowledge helped us in applying for licenses and permits. He represented our children in court for abandonment and custody hearings and gave us invaluable advice about Philippine culture and how to navigate a society that was very different and sometimes inscrutable for us. I remember a few instances where he bailed us out of difficult situations:

Kim Eicher, the daughter of Dennis and Sharon, long time CSC supporters and the adoptive parents of three of our boys, was in Cebu as a summer volunteer. While driving around the Fuente circle, she hit another car. As is the custom in Cebu, both vehicles stopped where the accident occurred and waited for the police to come to the scene. Kim called me and I hurried to the accident scene. I don't remember who was at fault, but the driver of the other vehicle was undoubtedly ready to give a rendition of the event that would put the blame on Kim. She was not prepared for this kind of confrontation and was emotional while waiting for the police to arrive. Luckily, Ron was driving by at that time and recognized our vehicle, so he stopped. (Ron wasn't actually driving his car as he, being mayor, had an armed driver and a bodyguard with him.) Ron stopped just as the police arrived. I remember the "oh-oh" look on the face of the other driver when he saw the mayor get out of his car and give Kim a hug. Ron had a word with the officer and, much to the dismay of the other party, the policeman said it looked like Kim was the victim and sent her on her way.

On another occasion we received a container van with donated medical supplies from Minnesota, and I went to the Customs Bureau to claim the freight. As is typical in the Philippine government bureaucracy, I was sent from one desk or office to the next. Finally I was told that they would not release it until it was inspected again and duties were collected. We were really worried because the container had already been opened, and because the Customs Bureau was notoriously corrupt, we suspected that the contents would be raided. I was made to sit and wait and worry. I didn't want to bother Ron with something like a customs problem, but I eventually called him when I realized we were at a stalemate. His office was close to customs, so he said he'd be right over. Fifteen minutes later we were walking out the door with all the paperwork we needed to claim the equipment. I was shaking my head when I asked Ron what he had done. He laughed and said that many of the people in the customs office were his relatives, so it was easy! Years later, when we had our Bikes for Tykes program and imported bikes from Minnesota for sale in Cebu, Ron again helped move things through the corrupt Cebu Customs Bureau, saving us thousands of pesos and tons of hassles.

Another time we took in two boys for temporary care who had been kidnapped and abused by a man who was apprehended by the police and was in jail awaiting trial. The boys were from Manila but were in Cebu to testify in the trial. One of them needed medical attention and was admitted to Cebu Doctors Hospital. One afternoon Ron came to visit the boy, and we were talking about what had happened to him at the hands of the accused man. One of us, full of emotion, said something like "they oughtta ____ the guy for doing that." Ron looked at us and said, "Hey, I can arrange that with one phone call." It was said jokingly but it drove home to us that this was an influential and powerful official who cared for the kids we were caring for and didn't want them, or us, to suffer.

Once while Marlys and I were on furlough in Minnesota, Ron made a trip to the United States to attend an international conference and made a side trip to Minnesota to visit us. It was a big secret, and he had arranged it through Marlys's dad, Cliff Danielson. We were sitting around in some-one's house visiting when Ron suddenly walked in! Years later Ron went to Minnesota to speak at our CSC banquet, and we were so happy to show him around and return a little of the hospitality he had shown to us and hundreds of visitors to CSC and Cebu over the years.

Ron was a big help in us securing the land in Banawa Hills for our new residences. When we finally procured the land, he went there every day to plant trees. Visitors would be amazed to see the mayor of Cebu on his knees under the hot sun digging in the soil.

When he was mayor, Ron was treated with deference and respect wherever he went. Once we went to Cagayan de Oro in Mindanao for a trip to the DelMonte golf course, taking the overnight boat from Cebu to Cagayan. When we arrived in the early morning, a team of porters grabbed our bags and golf clubs and took them off the ship to a waiting limo. We piled in and were driven up the mountain to the golf course for breakfast before starting our round of golf. A few years later, after the Edsa revolution, when Ron was out of office and an ordinary citizen, we made that same trip to DelMonte. This time we arrived to no fanfare. I remember struggling over the gangplank, carrying golf clubs and travel bags,

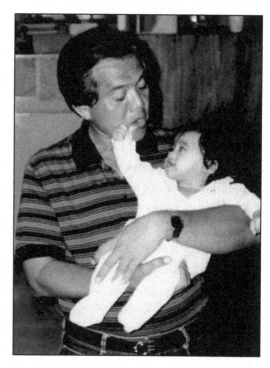

fighting the crowd, and looking for a jeepney to take us to the course. Ron laughed when we teased him about "how far the mighty have fallen."

Our newest residence in Banawa Hills is named the Duterte Home. With only a few exceptions, the children now living at CSC never knew Ron. Those who lived at CSC when he was alive and were adopted probably have only a limited sense of what a unique and remarkable person he was; what he might have risked politically and socially to be associated with us; or, most importantly, what an impact he made on CSC.

The Duterte Home

Clarification

THE MINISTRY CHRONICLED IN THIS BOOK has had various names over the years, and the reader might be confused by them. On the stateside end, we progressed from being the DelAdlawan Foundation, coined by combining the names of our first two Filipino partners in the ministry, to taking the name Cebu Christian Shelter Community for Children (CCSCC), and, finally, Children's Shelter of Cebu. In Cebu, we were initially known as the Corpus Christi Foundation, then Children's Shelter of Cebu. Filipinos will not know anything of DelAdlawan or CCSCC because they were never used in the Philippines. Conversely, Americans will not recognize the Corpus Christi name.

To make things even more confusing, the Canadian organization initiated to help fund the ministry has its own name. Thankfully, they have never changed it. They are the Cebu Christian Shelter Society of Canada.

I have tried to use the names in the order in which they were the legal names of our organizations. Sometimes, in reflecting back on an earlier era, I have chosen to use Children's Shelter of Cebu for the organzation, though it might have been operating under a different name at that time.

I have used the following abbreviations:

CHS   Children of Hope School
CSC   Children's Shelter of Cebu
DSWD   Department of Social Welfare and Development
        (Philippine government agency)
DepEd   Department of Education (Philippine government agency)
ICAB   Inter-Country Adoption Board (Philippine government
        agency)

Introduction

CSC HAS DONE WHAT MANY ministries have failed to do: We have endured and thrived for over 42 years. Through decades of challenging tests and in a world of shifting needs and values, we have persevered. And we have done so without well-trained leaders, a sizeable endowment, or a mother ministry to show us the way to go. We have grown from an idea in the heart and mind of a young woman from Minnesota into a thriving ministry that cares for up to 100 children and has had up to 14 U.S. staff, 130 Filipino workers, and impressive facilities across two acres of land in the middle of Cebu City in the Philippines.

I am incapable of writing a strictly historical tome about CSC. Though I will undoubtedly include important historical data, like who did what and when (and maybe even why), it's the personal stories of people doing amazing things at just the right time, the miracles that have occurred, and the great kids, staff, and friends that have made CSC work for all these years that will form the basis of this history. And I want to include a sort of "intellectual history" of CSC, important lessons we have learned throughout our history, lessons that have kept us on the right path over the years. Although this book will not be a recipe for how others might start an orphanage, it will be a testimony to how God "helps those who help his little ones." That is the statement I hope will be the thesis for this book.

We know most of the people who have contributed in significant ways. But there is much we don't know: the anonymous friends who gave at just the right time, those on fixed incomes who included a prayer with their gift that God would multiply it, those who prayed when prompted by the Holy Spirit or shared the ministry with a friend or church to help extend the network of support for CSC.

The risk in any history of an organization is that someone's contribution might get overlooked. That will almost certainly hold true of this one, and I apologize to anyone who was unintentionally omitted.

Marlys and I have had the pleasure to be involved in the first 42 years of CSC's life. We have often reflected on what a great ride it has been. To be involved in something that is so important to the lives of many people, and to be in leadership in a ministry that God has chosen to bless so richly over the years, is exciting and humbling. We have asked a lot of people to join us along the way, and many have done so—as staff, volunteers, prayer supporters, and donors. To each who has contributed, we want to take this opportunity to say thanks. Our prayer is that the emotional and spiritual returns God has bestowed on us will also be yours. Because this ministry gives great rewards!

CSC is God's ministry. He has used lots of people, and they have done amazing things throughout our history. But the sum of their contributions and accomplishments would not be enough to explain the impressive history of the ministry. I have tried to keep that in mind while writing this book. As we celebrate the people who have done good things, we acknowledge the God who has done great ones.

I wrestled with the idea of "voice" in this book. Initially I shied away from using the first person to tell the story of CSC. I wanted to avoid the problem of making things appear to be centered on me, my contributions or perceptions. But as I started writing, I came to recognize that I can only see things through my own eyes, from my own point of view. Although I discussed the ideas contained in this book with many people, it is ultimately based on my opinion of what is noteworthy and significant. Others involved in the same event might see it differently than I do. So I chose the first person with prayers that I will be able to present a history that is fair, open-minded, and generous.

One shortcoming of the English language can work against attempts to "share the credit" for the accomplishments of CSC. The possessive pronoun "our" does not distinguish between an inclusive and an exclusive sense. For example, if I say, in speaking about the benefits of helping abandoned children, that our blessings have been many, I want an inclusive sense of "our." Indeed, those blessings go beyond the staff to include, possibly, those of you reading this.

Because "our" is a flexible term, it might not always be clear just who is included: all of us, or some of us. In the Visayan language, which we speak in Cebu, there are separate words for the inclusive (atong) and exclusive (among) uses of "our," which helps provide a more accurate description of the people and events of our history.

One last issue I have thought a lot about is how to handle negative things. Over 43 years of ministry there have been fumbles, foibles, and follies. Some people have let us down. Great ideas ended up being disappointing mistakes. Personal needs sometimes got in the way of the children's needs. Some CSC kids struggled in their adopted families. Financial downturns happened. Fundraising methods were sometimes unsuccessful or ill-advised. Frankly, there have been a lot of heartbreaks to go with the high points over the years.

Many tears have been shed. Children have died, sometimes unexpectedly. Staff members and workers have left. Fire and natural disasters wreaked destruction on our property. At times unity was difficult to come by among the different elements of CSC. Kids we wanted to place for adoption were denied that opportunity because of government apathy or red tape. Government agencies acted in ways we felt were antithetical to the needs and best interests of our children. Court cases didn't go our way. Our photo albums contain pictures of happy-faced children playing, laughing, and enjoying good food, excellent facilities, and loving people, but no shots of crying staff gathered around the coffin of little Luke, contentious staff or board meetings, the look of our Bulacao home when the upstairs was destroyed by fire in 1983, or the fear in the eyes of our workers when the Covid 19 virus became a reality in Cebu.

Undoubtedly, the good has greatly outweighed the bad. We have had advocates, friends, contributors, and encouragers who have lightened our load and helped us move forward. And we have also had a few detractors, stumbling blocks, and hurdles. We are thankful for them, too, as they have refined us, made us stronger, and, in their own way, helped increase our resolve to continue with the ministry. My challenge is to keep the focus on these positive people and events while telling a truthful history of this amazing ministry.

As you will read in the chapters to follow, CSC began in the heart of Marlys Danielson. God touched her with the needs of Filipino children, and she responded. Out of her heart the ministry was started in 1979, and her heart was the engine that propelled us through the first 43 years of our history. I have a mental picture that epitomizes my view of CSC. It is a picture of Marlys standing over a hospital bed where a CSC child is suffering. Her eyes are filled with tears and worry as she absorbs the fear and pain of that sick child. It could have been any one of hundreds of kids she agonized with over the years. I can hear her voice reassuring the child, checking with the nurse to see that everything possible is being done, or talking on the phone to let the staff know about the diagnosis and enlist prayer support for the child.

From the voice of Marlys through that phone, to the ear of someone in our office or homes, to the keyboard of my computer, through fax, mail, email, text, or Facebook message, to the computer or phone of someone in Minnesota, to the phones or devices of our CSC prayer supporters, to their families, church congregations, or prayer networks—the needs of that child in the Cebu hospital bed are shared, disseminated, and raised in prayer around the world.

It is that kind of love, compassion, advocacy, and spiritual support that is at the heart of the story of CSC. I pray that you will be blessed by reading this book and seeing what can happen when one person, moved with compassion, responds to God's leading and has the courage and dedication to do as He asks.

A Ministry Is Born

"Don't ask us what happened. We'll never tell.
Just take these and get out of here tomorrow!"

A Burdened Heart

WHERE DOES A MINISTRY BEGIN? From one point of view, all ministry starts in the heart of God. Ministry is ordained of God as an expression of love to the people He has created. Those engaged in ministry are His instruments in accomplishing His will on earth. Because He uses people, we can trace the roots of ministry in their lives as God calls them, empowers them, and directs them to the people He would redeem.

In this respect, we can say that CSC began in the heart of one person, Marlys Healy, and spread from there. The first responders to her call to action were unlikely heroes: a recent high school graduate, a mystery person, an accident victim, and a ruined machinist. God used situations, relationships, and miracles to direct people in the way He wanted them to go. Such has been the history of CSC. Their stories form the basis of this book: ordinary people rendered exceptional by the hand of God on their lives.

In 1976, Eleanore Danielson passed away at Miller Hospital in Saint Paul, Minnesota. A pastor's wife, Eleanore had suffered with leukemia for a year. Her husband, Cliff, was the pastor of Constance Evangelical Free Church, then a small country church near what is now Andover, Minnesota. Marlys, Eleanore and Cliff's youngest child, was devastated by her mom's death. The family had experienced tragedy previously when Marlys's older sister, Lois, died in a car crash in 1971. Marlys and three friends were also in that car.

Cliff and Eleanore had been partners in the church ministry at Constance, and he found it difficult to go on without her. Cliff was acquainted with an evangelist, Aubrey McGann, whom he had met through McGann's involvement with the Evangelical Free Church. Cliff had helped organize crusades through the Tri-County Association in east-central Minnesota. He became aware of a need in the Aubrey McGann Association for a crusade director to help with advance work and logistics for crusades. Cliff resigned from Constance EFC in 1977 to join McGann.

One of Cliff's first assignments was to accompany Aubrey and his team to Hong Kong and the Philippines for a series of crusades. The other team members were accompanied by their wives, so Cliff invited Marlys to go with him. Marlys was working at a clinic as a medical assistant and doubted that she could get the time off. And she wasn't too excited about traveling across the world. Besides, she didn't have money for the expensive plane tickets. She talked to her boss, who offered her vacation days, but the money was still an issue. At this time, Constance Free Church had a farewell party for Cliff, and a freewill offering was enough for both their tickets.

All of these circumstances worked together to make it difficult for Marlys to say no. Her decision to go was monumental, and she felt that God was clearly leading her, though she had no idea why. So, Marlys joined the team and they headed to Southeast Asia. After several crusades in Hong Kong, they proceeded to Manila and eventually Cebu.

Cliff and Marlys Danielson

Cebu City is the second-largest city in the Philippines, with a population of more than two million. The Philippines is a country of great beauty contrasted by abject poverty, particularly in the urban areas. While touring the city, Marlys was shocked by the conditions of families and children. Coming from middle-class America, she had not experienced that kind of poverty. She saw hungry, homeless children begging and sleeping on the streets. Her heart was broken by their suffering. God was working in her.

While in Cebu the team stayed at the Montebello Hotel. Marlys befriended a hotel employee named Della Longakit and invited her to go around the city with her and explain some of the poverty that had troubled her. Della had grown up in relative wealth and ease in Cebu, and hadn't confronted some of the issues facing the poor. In a developing country like the Philippines, often the advantaged people, with poverty all around them, don't really absorb what is going on. They don't allow themselves to think about the disparities between themselves and the poor, to really see and feel the desperation of those who are sick, hungry, and hopeless. In seeing the streets of Cebu through Marlys's eyes, Della was moved to tears. God was also working in her life. Marlys invited Della to attend the evangelistic meetings in downtown Cebu City. She accepted Marlys's invitation and, at one of the services, responded to Aubrey McGann's invitation and gave her life to Christ.

Della Longakit

Marlys was doing a lot of reflecting and praying while in Cebu. Was God directing her to respond in some way to the suffering of children like those she had observed? She could not get them out of her mind when she tried to sleep at night. Their sad faces and pathetic living conditions were etched on her heart.

Marlys met a lot of people in Cebu, including a number of Free Church Filipino pastors whose churches were involved in the city crusades. One of them, J.A., was interested in Marlys's experiences and the growing desire in her heart to do something to help. She didn't get a chance to talk with many missionaries, but sensed that little was being done to reach out to homeless children in the city.

When she returned to Minnesota, the images would not go away. Unlike many tourists who have significant experiences during their travels but go back to their lives and put their experiences into photo albums or Christmas letters, Marlys wanted to share her trip with her friends. An idea was germinating in her mind to return to Cebu and start an orphanage.

One of her good friends was Kathy Norlien, who attended Constance Free Church and lived a short distance away. Kathy had recently been in a car accident where her hand was injured. She received an insurance settlement and began thinking about whether she might somehow use that money for God's Kingdom.

I was another friend, who had recently graduated from Bethel College and was working in a small machine shop in Saint Paul. Raised by educators, I was inept at tool and die disciplines and was wondering what was next for me. My B.A. in philosophy hadn't presented me with a lot of possibilities for employment. I was interested in what Marlys had to say.

Just a few days after returning to Minnesota, Marlys had a phone conversation with pastor J.A. To her surprise, he was interested in getting something going and encouraged Marlys to return to Cebu to make contacts and discover what it would take to start a ministry to homeless children. Although no specific ideas were discussed, the vague concept of an orphanage was developing. Marlys said she would see if another trip was possible, though she doubted it. But, unexpectedly, her boss gave her the green light and Kathy offered to pay for the tickets and expenses from her insurance settlement. What was going on here?

Marlys and Kathy made arrangements to go to Cebu, but as the date neared and they discussed the trip, they both felt it would be good to have a male along and decided to ask me, even though the trip was imminent. They decided it would be best to ask me right away, and went to my workplace that very afternoon.

I was working at a place called Micromold, housed in a rundown industrial building in the Midway area of Saint Paul. They had no idea whether I was even there, or if I could talk to them while on duty. They weren't even sure they had the right place, since there was no name on the building. But when they opened the door, there I was with my hand on the doorknob, just coming out of the building. My boss had asked me to drive the truck to pick up some wood, and I was just heading out for that job. Something was going on here.

They asked about my availability to go to the Philippines, and I was very interested. My heart had been touched by Marlys's accounts of her trip. I wasn't tied down at the time. But I was taken aback when I asked about the timing of the trip. "We're going tomorrow," they said. "Okay," I answered. (The freedom and spontaneity of youth.) In reviewing what I was committing to, I remember thinking that it might be a good idea to talk to my parents and my boss before too much longer. My boss was happy to see me go. I then headed for Bethel College, where my dad was a professor, for a cup of coffee and a bombshell.

"Dad, what do you think of my going to the Philippines with a couple of gals you don't know?"

"Uh, when will this take place?"

"Tomorrow, Dad."

Brief silence. "Does your mom know?"

"Not yet."

"Well you probably should let her know so she can prepare a few clothes for you. Oh, one more question. Do you have a passport?"

"Uh, no I don't."

"Well, that will be an issue."

But it seemed that Marlys and Kathy had anticipated that problem and had made a few calls. The only way that it would work was to go to San Francisco the next morning, where the passport office vowed they could issue a passport right away, even within a few hours. Marlys and Kathy had purchased tickets for early the next morning: Minneapolis, San Francisco, Honolulu, Manila, Cebu. So I rushed home to talk to my mom, look up the Philippines on a map, find my birth certificate, pack a suitcase, and get to sleep. Things were happening fast, but I had the strange sense that they weren't out of control.

The next day we flew to San Francisco, where a passport was indeed issued in a few hours. We grabbed a few hours sleep and left the next morning for an amazing adventure in the Philippines.

God was indeed in control of the people and circumstances that enabled us to make this trip. It would have been easy and perfectly under-standable if my parents had been negative about the trip. Who would have dreamed that I could get a passport in a day? And what about the circum-stances in Kathy's life that resulted in an insurance settlement and her willingness to use it for three tickets to the Philippines. Agreeable bosses, supportive families, available flights, the timing at Micromold—its almost too much to imagine. Unless. Unless God was putting the pieces in place for young Minnesotans to begin a ministry to his precious children in the Philippines. Even at this early stage, those involved in the dramatic early days of what was to eventually become CSC were learning a lesson that would characterize the history of the ministry. God loves the suffering children of the Philippines, and He blesses those who seek to bless them.

The Return to Cebu

WHEN MARLYS, KATHY, AND I arrived in Cebu on February 7, 1978, we were immediately confronted by significant differences from what we were used to in Minnesota. When we walked out of the airplane, we were greeted with a blast of hot air that was a preview of humid, sweaty days ahead. Della Longakit met us at the Cebu airport, and we rode a mini-cab to the hotel where we would stay. I folded my 6'7" frame into the front seat, while Marlys, Kathy, and Della squeezed into the back with the luggage.

As we crossed the Mactan bridge and headed into the city, we encountered some of the stark contrasts that characterize life in the Philippines: modern-looking commercial areas and large public markets; residences of the wealthy surrounded by squatter areas consisting of ramshackle huts; heavy, noisy traffic and the presence of hundreds of pedestrians walking in and alongside the city streets; and cars, taxis, buses, and jeepneys (miniature buses that are the principle means of public transportation for most urban Filipinos) sharing the roads with people, carts, bicycles, tricycles, and a variety of animals. The noise and smells were striking. The poverty was emotionally overpowering. Kathy and I were seeing it for the first time and were starting to realize some of what Marlys had experienced on her initial trip to the city.

In the next week and a half, we three Minnesotans would see a lot more of the city. Going out on the streets of Cebu in the evenings, we saw children sleeping and begging on the sidewalks. Some were badly malnourished. Some were there with their families, while others seemed to be totally alone. People walked right past them, hardly noticing their nakedness, protruding bellies, or hungry eyes. Accompanied by Della, we uneasily took pictures of sleeping children, some lying on cardboard, others right on the cement. We would return to the hotel and try to process what we had seen. Often there were no words to describe our feelings about what we were seeing.

We met with many people during our short stay in Cebu, including Filipino pastors, American missionaries, and government officials. We were surprised by the reactions of some we talked to concerning the things we had seen and our desire to help. The Department of Social Welfare representatives seemed more concerned with the long list of regulations for child welfare programs than with the actual needs in their city. A couple of the missionaries were discouraging, stating that in Philippine culture, families take care of their own and that many of the children begging on the streets were actually a part of a syndicate, with well-to-do parents or others who were exploiting them. One missionary said they were addressing these problems by planting churches, which would in turn reach out to those in their communities who were in need. We Minnesotans tried to balance what we were hearing with what we had experienced.

But our meetings in Cebu were not devoid of encouragement. Several missionaries, particularly those from the Evangelical Free Church, who had already met Marlys during the Aubrey McGann crusades, were inspirational. Several pastors expressed a willingness to help. We met with a lawyer who explained the process of becoming registered with the Philippine government and who offered to help. A support system was forming, though it did not seem to include the Philippine government, at least at that point. That would come later, but for now we Minnesotans were motivated by the faces of the children we had seen and the words of one pastor who told us, "I feel so lost about how to help the suffering children. I would be happy if you could come and help us."

Della Longakit was an important resource throughout the trip. As a young Christian, she was starting to turn her life over to Christ and wondering how all the interests and plans of the young people from Minnesota related to her and her future. She had a good job with the hotel and a bright future in the travel industry. Her family members were staunch Catholics and would not look positively on her leaving her employment to join a fledgling Protestant group that had no experience and no money. Who could blame them? But something was happening in Della's life. She expressed to Marlys a desire to be a part of a ministry that would reach out to suffering children in her city.

Della and Pastor J.A. were familiar with a piece of land in an area south of Cebu City that was for sale. We went to see it and talk to the owners. It was not an ideal location, being 30 miles south of Cebu City. The nearest municipality, CarCar, was a sleepy provincial town with no good medical facilities and limited phone and electrical services. While walking around the several-acre site, we drew a curious crowd of children, and some adults, who followed us wherever we went. This was something we would experience countless times in the coming days, as people in the rural areas were not accustomed to seeing Caucasians, particularly one who was a "higante" (giant). This piece of land in Vallodolid, CarCar, became the place where we imagined starting the ministry, and we left the details of negotiating the price and other details to the Filipinos.

One person we met while on our Cebu junket was Ronald Duterte, the vice mayor of Cebu City and a prominent lawyer. He had studied in New York and had married an American, and was very friendly and encouraging. Little did we know just how helpful attorney Duterte would be in the years to come, or what his friendship would mean to all of the team and the hundreds of people who would become involved in the ministry that was just being started in 1978.

The trip was over and the Minnesotans were left with a myriad of experiences, some encouraging, some not. But we emerged with a strong sense that taking care of homeless and destitute Filipino children was where God wanted us to be. We were young and naïve, but God had control of our hearts and lives, and we went back to Minnesota to share our hearts with friends and family. If we had known all that would occur in the coming months and years, we might have filed our experiences away and gone back to our previous lives. But God sometimes gives His children only a glimpse at what's in store for them, revealing his plan progressively as they are better prepared to deal with the challenges. In the coming months we would face opposition to our plans by some who saw it as their role to give us a "dose of reality." Others would be supportive. Some would combine support with asking hard questions that forced us to face issues such as the need for significant amounts of money for travel and the purchase of the CarCar property, procuring visas for the Philippines, and establishing a sending organization in Minnesota for immediate and ongoing support.

Home Again, Home Again

I PUT TOGETHER A NEWSLETTER that was sent to friends and family members telling of the birth of the DelAdlawan Foundation and our vision of starting a home for children in the Philippines. Some modest fund-raising efforts were undertaken, including candy and donut sales and a few church presentations in the Constance area. We were learning as we went, having no experience in fundraising or organization building.

During this time, Marlys, Kathy, and I made contact with Larry Hansen, an audiovisual expert who was in the business of making slide shows. My dad, Jerry, had done narration for Larry for several years and knew of his talent and willingness to help. Larry had a studio above the State Theater in downtown Minneapolis. We went to visit him and tell him of our dreams.

Larry loves to tell the story of us sharing our "crazy idea of wanting to start an orphanage in the Philippines." Being a slightly crazy guy himself, he heard us out and agreed to help. Little did we all know how significant that offer would be in the months and years to come.

Larry took the pictures we shot in Cebu and put together a media presentation that could be used in churches and civic organizations. The slide show, narrated by my dad, told the story of the needs of homeless Filipino kids that was at the heart of the DelAdlawan Foundation and the motivation for us to return to Cebu as soon as possible to begin caring for them.

Early support-raising efforts were hampered by the fact that the ministry was only a dream of ours. We had nothing to show, no track record. In fact, we had no formal training in childcaring or cross-cultural ministry. We were asking people to invest in our dreams. Only the Holy Spirit could have blessed these early efforts. People like Larry Hansen, the early board members, and the family and friends of the staff and others were led to help. Their encouragement and financial and prayer support were a Godsend as we attempted to put together an organization and raise funds for the creation of the ministry.

Fueled by our enthusiasm, drive, and conviction that God was calling us to this endeavor, we were moving ahead. This resolve was to be tested significantly in the days ahead as our inexperience and desire to get things going in a hurry would result in some sketchy decisions and poor outcomes, especially in the area of fundraising.

The DelAdlawan staff was concerned about the need to purchase land for the proposed home for children, and we knew that the parcel we had seen on our trip to Cebu would cost about $40,000. It seemed to us that the proceeds of candy sales and occasional offerings would not produce that kind of money, so the idea was born to have a large fundraising concert to raise a significant amount. We wanted to be able to purchase that lot and get ourselves over to the Philippines to begin the ministry. Somehow we came up with the idea to get in touch with B.J. Thomas to see if he would do a concert in the Twin Cities. B.J. was a fairly popular recording artist at the time (1978), with hits such as "Raindrops Keep Falling On My Head" and "Hooked on a Feeling." Most important, Thomas had recently professed faith in Christ, so he seemed like a good choice for a fundraising concert.

Kathy and Marlys got get in touch with B.J.'s agent and learned that it would cost $10,000 plus expenses for him to do a concert. A tentative date in August was discussed, and the agent agreed to send out a contract and a list of requirements. Even though we had no experience in promoting a major concert, we pushed ahead with the plan. We signed the contract, booked the Minneapolis auditorium, sent a down payment to Thomas's agent, and started making plans for an August concert. If we had weighed all the pros and cons of such an event, we might have decided not to pursue this plan, but we were strongly determined to "get the show on the road." We lacked business acumen but were motivated by the faces of the children we saw in Cebu and the desire to get over there and start helping them.

The concert was a disaster! As one friend of the staff commented, "People stayed away in droves." Only about 2,000 people showed up in a venue that seated 9,000. There was not enough money to pay the bills.

When Thomas and his band left their hotel the next morning, and we didn't have enough money to pay the hotel bill, Marlys was not allowed to leave the hotel until the bill was settled. I had to go out and find the money, since none of us had enough personal funds to pay the account.

While driving around the Twin Cities I thought of a friend, Tom Johnson, who was a star pitcher for the Minnesota Twins. Tom had been a youth pastor at Constance Free Church, so he knew Marlys and Kathy, as well as me. Tom had gone to Murray High School, where I had also attended, and was a good friend of my older brother, Dave. The next day Tom gave Marlys and me a check for $3,000, which paid for the hotel obligation and helped settle some other bills from the concert. These were not the days of multimillion dollar contracts for young baseball players. $3,000 was a lot of money, even for a major leaguer.

It took us several months to pay off all the bills from the B.J. Thomas fiasco. The momentum was gone. The focus had shifted from raising money for the homeless kids in Cebu to helping us dig out from the concert debt. It seemed like the dream was dead.

But this ministry was meant to be. Discouragement was short-lived. We spent time in prayer. We received a letter from Pastor J.A in Cebu in which he announced a plan to travel to Minnesota to assist in fundraising efforts in light of the failure of the concert. His brother agreed to help with his airfare.

A Breakthrough

DURING HIS TIME IN MINNESOTA, pastor J.A. met with lots of people. He and I made a trip to Chicago to meet with Virgil Olson, who was head of the Baptist General Conference's World Missions Department. Dr. Olson told us that the BGC was primarily, if not exclusively, involved in church planting and would not have a place for the type of ministry we envisioned. This was the same message we had received from other denominations and church missions committees. Doors seemed to be closing all around them. But things were to change soon.

One of the speaking opportunities that J.A. had while in Minnesota was to a group of Bethel College students who were interested in missions. They met regularly to talk about missionary enterprise and pray. J.A. told them of our desire to start a ministry in Cebu and asked them to pray for that. After the presentation, a member of that student group, Joe Lincoln, mentioned a trust fund that had been given to him and said he might be interested in giving some of it to DelAdlawan to buy the property in CarCar.

Several other important developments occurred during these days that would move the project along:

Jeff Snyder

1. We met a young man, Jeff Snyder, who was interested in the project in the Philippines, and wanted to become a part of the staff. Jeff was involved in the youth group at Coon Rapids Free Church and was seeking an avenue of service. He began meeting with us, joining us in praying and asking God to open doors for ministry in Cebu.

2. In January of 1978, Joe Lincoln wired $40,000 to Cebu for the property. There would also be enough money to purchase a house in the Bulacao neighborhood of Cebu City. God had performed a miracle in Joe Lincoln's heart, accomplishing in a few inspired moments what hundreds of hours of concert planning could not muster.

3. The DelAdlawan Foundation was incorporated in March. One member of Constance Free Church, Clyde Morris, was an administrator in a law office in Minneapolis. He offered to help us become incorporated in Minnesota and apply for tax-exempt status, which would be crucial for fundraising. Within a few months the tax-exemption was approved by the state of Minnesota, and an organization was born: the DelAdlawan Foundation, named after Della and Pastor J.A., our principal Filipino partners. The initial board members were family and friends of ours. They included my parents, Jerry and Millie Healy, Cliff, Al and Betty Sannerud (friends of Cliff), Kathy Johnson (friend of the Healys), John Priestley (my best friend), and Jim and Lorraine Roste (neighbors of the Healys).

4. Marlys met with her friend Sandy Swanson to see if she might be interested in joining the staff. Marlys had known Sandy since they were children attending Constance Free Church. They had traveled together to Florida and the Canary Islands. Sandy was working at Camp Shamineau in Motley, Minnesota. The ministry that was proposed in Cebu was of great interest to Sandy because of her love for children. Though she was not prepared to leave her position at Shamineau at that point, she began praying for the DelAdlawan staff and how she might be involved in the future. As evidence of our willingness to raise funds wherever the door was open even a crack, Marlys and I made a trip to Shamineau and sold minidonuts at family camp and put what I later classified as "a little bit of pressure" on Sandy to join the staff. Little did we know that God was already working in Sandy's life and the huge impact she would make on the ministry in the months, years, and decades to come.

Camp Shamineau

15

5. Marlys and I were becoming romantically involved. Our courtship was intertwined with our work with DelAdlawan and our desire to serve God in the Philippines. But we had come to love each other and began to

talk about marriage. On July 4, 1978, I asked Marlys to marry me, and a September wedding was planned. We were married on September 17.

As money came in, even modestly, we began thinking about when we might be able to go to Cebu to start the ministry. It was decided that Jeff Snyder would go over first, and Kathy, Marlys, and I would follow after a few months. The organization in Cebu, initially known as the Corpus Christi Foundation, was being incorporated at about this time, and J.A. and Della were anxious for things to get rolling. Jeff's going was, as much as anything, a symbol of our commitment to the ministry in Cebu, an appeasement for the Filipinos who were waiting for things to happen. Another reason was to show potential supporters that things were moving along and, though there was not enough money in the organizational coffers to send over and support four staff members, we were sending one person as a start. In short, we wanted to show that this wasn't just a crazy idea in our heads.

We determined that someone was needed to spearhead fundraising and promotion for the organization. Cliff Danielson had recently left the McGann Association and was available. On April 1, 1978, he became the first executive director of the ministry, establishing an office in his home in Constance. From there he wrote letters, made phone calls, put together newsletters, and arranged slide shows for presentations to whomever would grant him an audience. Cliff compiled a mailing list of friends, churches, and acquaintances he thought might be interested.

These fundraising efforts, like the donut sales at Camp Shamineau, met with limited success. We were asking people to give towards an idea, and a pretty rough idea at that. We were young and inexperienced. We had no denominational backing. In spite of this, several Minnesota churches got involved and began providing monthly support.

Central Baptist, my home church, and Constance Evangelical Free, Marlys's church, were the first to get on board. Offerings were taken and people signed up to receive our newsletter. Elim Baptist in Isanti, Minnesota, pastored by Truett Lawson, also began supporting the ministry-to-be, as did its neighbor church, North Isanti Baptist, under the leadership of Rev. Jonathon Larson. The early Baptist churches that got involved knew me through my dad, Jerry, who was a much-loved professor at Bethel College and a popular speaker in the Minnesota Baptist Conference and at Trout Lake Camp.

Some of Jerry Healy's faculty colleagues at Bethel also became charter members of the DelAdlawan support system. The Bethel faculty was much like a family in those days, so it was probably enough for some of them that I was Jerry's son and I was given the benefit of the doubt, at least initially.

The Team Unites in Cebu

ALTHOUGH MUCH HAD ALREADY HAPPENED to move DelAdlawan along, it was not until May 4, 1979 that the ministry began in earnest. On that date Marlys, Kathy, and I arrived in Cebu City. Like many experiences, this did not happen without some pain and drama. We arrived at the Twin Cities airport for our flight to Los Angeles and found that the plane had already left. We had not been informed of the change in schedule by the travel agent. So now we would not be able to catch our international flight. There was something of a carnival atmosphere at the airport, with many friends and family there to see us off. It was frustrating and embarrassing for everyone, and Kathy, Marlys, and I went to the Healy home in Saint Paul to make some phone calls and see if we could get another flight and whether we would have to forfeit the tickets we had already purchased, using most of the money in DelAdlawan's meager coffers.

While we were licking our wounds in Saint Paul, my dad and his good friend Howie Rekstad went to the Northwest Airlines office. Howie was a well-known Christian businessman in the Twin Cities and a long-time friend of the Healys. He and my dad came back in a couple of hours with new tickets for the next morning and big smiles on their faces. They would not tell anyone what they had said or done to get new reservations, but they had tickets in their hands and the staff had a new lease on life.

This remains one of the mysteries of the early days of the ministry but was just one example of people rallying around the cause, using their time and talents to move things forward. Howie's comment to me as he turned over the new tickets was classic: "Don't ask us what happened. We'll never tell. Just take these and get out of here tomorrow!" Did Howie and Jer have to pay for new tickets? Did they convince the airline ticket agents that they should refund the unused tickets and issue new ones without penalty? They were not talking.

When we finally arrived in Cebu, it probably should have seemed surreal to us that a little more than a year had passed since we were there before, considering all that had happened in our lives since then. Two of us had been married, two organizations had been incorporated, an executive director was working, fundraising was taking place, Jeff had been in Cebu for a couple months, and now we were finally fulfilling our dream of being in Cebu. But our group had the strong feeling that things were only then falling into place. Those few short months had seemed like a decade to us. But even in our restless spirits we had the strong sense that God was leading us, that the ministry we were in Cebu to begin was His, and that we were in for a great adventure as we followed Him.

THE FIRST YEAR

"Die, you disgusting creatures. You don't mess with us, vermin."

The Ministry Officially Begins

THE FIRST THING WE DISCOVERED when we arrived in Cebu was that some relational problems existed among the Filipinos who had incorporated as the Corpus Christi Foundation. So instead of jumping right in and starting the ministry, we had to deal with a lot of hurt and mistrust. We consulted an attorney to see what needed to happen to rescue the organization and establish a strong legal basis for it. That attorney was Ron Duterte, whom we had met on our first trip to Cebu. He was very gracious and helped us and the Corpus Christi board make some changes in the organization that helped restore order and confidence. This was the first of many times that Ron "saved the day" for us but probably the most important one.

Jeff and Della had made friends with a young Filipino named Sned Flora. He was a college student studying electrical engineering in Cebu City and had met Della at the Chi Alpha Student Center, a ministry of the Evangelical Free Church of the Philippines. Della introduced him to Jeff and a friendship began. Sned expressed an interest in helping the group get settled, and part of that involved fixing up the Bulacao house.

A House in Need of Repair

THE HOUSE WAS A REAL PROJECT! The only bathroom in the two-floor structure had a cracked tile floor. There was virtually no drainage and no window screens. Flies and mosquitoes were rampant, and the kitchen was tiny. Where to start? While the women fixed up the kitchen and cleaned the bathroom, Sned and I went to the hardware store to buy plastic screen, a few rudimentary tools, an assortment of nails and screws, coconut lumber, and some lath. We made a makeshift ladder and began fashioning screens. It was a slow process since we only had a small saw with no miter box. And it was hot! Nothing about Minnesota summer heat and humidity could compare with the weather of Cebu in May (the hottest month of the

The Bulacao House

year). Lots of learning was going on with the Americans while the Filipinos were learning patience.

Della, who had grown up in relative wealth, was adjusting almost as much as the Americans to the less-than-luxurious house. She was appointed cook for the group, though she had no experience doing that job. With a very limited budget to work with, Della prepared mostly fried rice and kamote (sweet potatoes) for the first few weeks. Meat was a luxury we could not afford, as most of our money had been used for house repairs. After a couple weeks of rice and camote, the fledgling staff decided it was time for a treat, so we sent Della to the public market to buy ground beef for a meatloaf. But we were in for a sad surprise when the meatloaf came out of the oven, as the meat smelled different than what we were used to and crumbled under our forks. Even copious amounts of banana catsup didn't help. The meatloaf tasted awful, and our hopes for a delectable feast were dashed.

Lessons Learned

IN THE FIRST FEW WEEKS, before screens were installed, we slept with mosquito nets around our sleeping bags on inflatable mattresses we brought from Minnesota. But it was hot inside the mosquito netting. Real hot. And we were in for some additional revelations. It was noisy. Dogs barked, motorcycle engines raced, music blared. Sleep was difficult, sound sleep impossible. This was part of the big adjustment we had to make to live in the Bulacao house and get started with the ministry we felt called to do. Although eating and sleeping constituted big changes for us, there was a strong sense of adventure and challenge among the group.

We had brought along big rubber boots for the rainy season. When the first big rain occurred, Sned and I went sloshing around Bulacao, caught a jeepney, and headed downtown. The daily rains were causing major drainage problems at our house, and we needed to make a canal so the water could flow out and connect with the canal that ran down our street. That one was almost always clogged somewhere along the line, so we worked with our neighbors to clean that canal. At times the water backed up into the house.

One day the septic tank overflowed and backed up into the bathroom. Sned and I discovered that there was a foot of water over the dirt floor, and on top of the sewage water swam hundreds of cockroaches that had been displaced from the septic tank. It was a breathtakingly disgusting sight, but we could only laugh and discuss a solution that did not involve any of the women having to go inside the bathroom. We deputized Jeff, found a couple of brooms and some large garbage bags, and started sweeping the cockroaches into the bags. There were occasional loud shrieks from the bathroom as some of the roaches became airborne and went for our faces when displaced from their roosts.

Nothing in any of our lives had prepared us for this morbid retrieval task. We filled up two large garbage bags with the vulgar vermin, tied them securely, and brought them into the living room. The beleaguered men took some measure of revenge for the roaches' aerial attacks in the bathroom, and our lapse of courage that had resulted in screams heard around the neighborhood, by taunting and trash-talking the captured foes: "Die you disgusting creatures." "You don't mess with us, vermin." "That's what we're talking about!" Our manhood again intact, we took the garbage bags outside and then began the task of unclogging the canals and cleaning up the bathroom. As disgusting a place as it was, it was the only bathroom for the six people living in the home—Paul, Marlys, Kathy, Della, Sned, and Jeff.

Clothes were washed by hand in those days, and everyone took their turn. With no clothes dryer, the clothes were hung on clotheslines in the back yard. We began noticing that blue jeans were disappearing from the lines just about every day. Thieves were scaling the hollow block wall in the back and taking jeans. We had to start hanging the jeans inside the house to dry. Eventually, that back wall was replaced with a ten-foot structure with glass on the top, as most other houses had, to discourage thieves. This did not solve the problem totally but greatly diminished the denim thievery.

Della was learning to cook a wider range of meals, so our diet came to include fish, mussels, roast pork, eggs, green beans, and white potatoes. We boiled our drinking water for 20 minutes because of impurities in the well. We purchased a new aluminum water tank that was a big expense but much needed for bathing, washing clothes, and cleaning.

We Minnesotans had only brought a small amount of money with us, so we were reliant on the stateside organization, through Cliff, to wire money as it was available. Often, not much was available. I opened up an account with a downtown bank, and when money was sent I went to the bank and withdrew most of it for our needs. Though some wire transfers took only a few days to arrive in Cebu, sometimes they were much slower. I spent many hours sitting in the bank, hoping money would arrive and be credited to our account. Often it didn't arrive as planned, and I had to go back to Bulacao empty-handed.

When money did arrive, I exchanged it for pesos and put it in a small wooden box that we kept on a shelf in the kitchen. The rule was that any staff member could take money as it was needed for any aspect of the ministry, but we needed to write down on a log sheet how much we took and when. There was no auditing, and everyone trusted the rest to use the money only for important expenditures.

Excerpts from letters sent to the stateside board show a variety of activities and challenges during these days:

> We have been fixing up the house in which we live, painting, screening, building cupboards and shelves, doing yard work and bathroom repair. This has kept us busy and has made the house livable. So far we've been able to do everything ourselves, but some major plumbing, gutter and roof work might require outside (competent) assistance.

A second priority has been to learn Visayan, the language spoken in Cebu. Jeff and I have been studying daily with a tutor, and Marlys and Kathy have lessons during the evenings. We are finding that it is hard work, but with the help of Sned and Della, we are learning.

As the house was becoming more livable, I started making inquiries with the Department of Social Welfare and Development about getting licensed to take in children. I learned that there would be many hoops to jump through, which would take quite a while. The easiest way to get started seemed to be for Marlys and me to apply to be foster parents and have children placed with us. We envisioned having a group home where everyone would assist in the tasks of daily living and in caring for the children that would be placed.

In the meantime, we were meeting lots of people in the community. One of the earliest contacts was Rebecca Deliña, who was working with the local government as a nutritionist. Her job was to go around the poor communities that surrounded our house and weigh babies with a portable scale. Through these weighings, she identified malnourished kids who needed assistance. She provided nutritional support and education for mothers. She was well known and loved in the community of Bulacao, and was a dedicated Christian who had a huge heart for the children she served.

Reaching Out in Bulacao

MARLYS, KATHY, AND DELLA occasionally went with Rebecca Deliña on her rounds in Bulacao. Sometimes they encountered children with medical needs that Rebecca could not address out of her limited budget. Rebecca would refer these children to us for assistance. Although the DelAdlawan staff had very limited resources, we were able to help a few of these kids. We learned a lesson in those early days: Many children suffer and even die for lack of basic medications and access to doctors and hospitals. Poor people living scarcely more than a stone's throw from our home in Bulacao were malnourished and dying. A second, painful lesson was that we could only help a few. Our hearts were big but our ability to help was small. This was a reality that would follow us constantly in the days, months, and years ahead, as we were awed by the forest of needs around us, even as we concentrated on a few individual trees we could save.

One child we were able to help was Jericho, a badly malnourished boy who had a hand missing from a birth defect. He was dying in the hospital and needed antibiotics and a blood transfusion. Rebecca knew his mother and was very concerned. Marlys gave blood, she and Kathy bought a vial of antibiotic, and Jericho was on the road to recovery. Rebecca continued to monitor his weight and offer help with food, and a partnership was established that would last for years to come.

Another child was referred to us around that time. Jessie Martinez, a two-week-old baby, was also a bad shape, struggling for his life in the small, dark shanty they called home. His mom, Eksyon, had many other mouths to feed. Eksyon was a friendly, hard-working woman with an outgoing personality and a huge heart for her children. But she had no money for medicine that Jessie needed for his pneumonia. Like Jericho, he was dying, destined to become another statistic in the logbook of infant deaths in Bulacao. We sent Rebecca to buy an antibiotic and Jessie started to recover almost immediately. We brought him to a doctor who said he needed blood. Sned donated blood, which was a really big stretch for him. But he wanted to do his part and joined the rest of us in thanking God for the opportunity to be his hands and feet in reaching out to the "least of these' in Bulacao. In the years to come, the Martinez family would become intertwined in the ministry, attending Bible study and worship services at the DelAdlawan home and, as the years went by, providing several workers from their family. Eksyon's husband, Teo, worked as a guard and maintenance man in the early 1980s.

While visiting Jessie in the hospital, we met another desperate mother watching her child die. The little girl, Jolyn, was so emaciated that it didn't seem possible she could be alive. While talking to the mother, Bernie, we learned that she had three other children at home, all very sick. Her husband, Ernie, was unemployed and trying to care for the sick kids at home, but they were extremely sick with pneumonia.

One night when Ernie came to the hospital to see how his wife and child were doing, Sned and I decided to go with him to their home to have a look at the sick kids. We rented a jeepney and headed out into the night. Nothing would prepare us for what we experienced when we found that tiny shack in a squatter area in Mandaue City. Sned went in first, with Ernie. Before I could climb the wobbly steps, Sned came barreling out of the shack, trying not to vomit until he got to the ground. He partially succeeded but ended up losing all of his supper. The smell inside that shack was like nothing any of us had ever experienced. The kids were deathly ill and needed immediate attention. We somehow got them to the government hospital and were able to purchase some antibiotics, and by the grace of God they survived. When they were discharged from the hospital, we found them a house in Bulacao where we could keep a close eye on them. Eventually we let them live on the property in CarCar that we purchased, serving as caretakers and raising their children in a more comfortable and safe environment.

We looked for other ways to minister to the community near where we lived in Bulacao. We built a makeshift puppet stage and began doing puppet shows at the home as well as in the squatter communities nearby. We wrote our own scripts, used our crude language skills (with expert interpretation by Sned or Della), and drew a crowd wherever we went. A letter from someone on the staff reflected some of the excitement we felt with these shows and the number of kids we were able to reach:

"What a sight! Jeff is walking towards the house with about 50 kids jumping and giggling behind him coming to the puppet show."

A Wednesday night service in Bulacao

We wanted to have a spiritual impact on the adults in our community, as well. We opened our home for a Wednesday night service of Bible study and singing. Friends we had met through Rebecca Deliña and others in the neighborhood were invited, and several came regularly. The Martinez and Deliña families were regular attenders, but others not previously known to us became interested. Dominga and Wilfredo Wenceslao were among this group. Fredo had a small barbershop out by the highway, and Minga sold pastries at their home. With a few others, these families formed the basis of the group that met every week in the home.

Pastor Lucas

ANOTHER FRIEND WE MADE in our first few months in Bulacao was Pastor Lucas, a man from India who pastored an Assembly of God church in the city of Minglanilla, about 10 miles south of our home. Pastor Lucas grew up in an orphanage in India and was raised by an American missionary named Mollie Baird. Mollie eventually transferred to Cebu and found a woman for Lucas to marry, so he followed her to Cebu and married Anna. Because of his background, Pastor Lucas had a big heart for the ministry of Corpus Christi and became a great friend to all of us on the staff. We would invite him over to the Bulacao home with his wife, and we had lots of good times visiting and laughing together.

Pastor Lucas

28

Pastor Lucas had hilarious stories of trying to navigate Philippine culture with minimal language and cultural skills. Though his wife helped when she could, he found himself in many situations that he didn't have a clue how to handle, and, invariably, he made mistakes. He was notorious for telling jeepney drivers to turn off their music, assuming incorrectly that other passengers shared his disdain for loud disco music blaring from the speakers. Several times he reached over and turned the volume down when the driver would not, and on more than once occasion he was told to get out of the vehicle.

One day Pastor Lucas was supposed to come to the Bulacao house for lunch, but when he didn't come we went ahead and ate. Several hours later he showed up with a bloody forehead and a story of having been in an accident. The jeepney he was riding had swerved to avoid a pedestrian and tipped on its side in the ditch. Lucas had been sitting next to what he described as a "fat lady" who, in the tipped-over jeepney, was now sitting on his head. He could not breathe. "Sister, sister," he implored, "please move! Please let me get up, sister." Eventually, someone helped disengage the portly passenger and free the near-dead Lucas. Even though he was shaken and bloody, we had all we could do to keep from laughing as Lucas described what had happened in his matter-of-fact tone. For decades afterwards we would beg Lucas to tell the story of the accident.

A Trip to Manila

ON JULY 15, 1979, WE MADE A TRIP TO MANILA, the capital of the Philippines and the center for commerce, industry, and government. Our purpose was to visit some childcaring institutions, meet with the Department of Social Welfare and Development regarding licensing, and receive some training. At least that was the plan that had been arranged for us by the government agency. We took a 24-hour boat ride to Manila, rode a jeepney and a taxi to our destination, and discovered that the people we were supposed to meet weren't prepared for us. After some hurried planning and negotiating, we were given a place to stay and a few meetings were set up. While Sned, Jeff, Della, and Kathy visited a government orphanage in Quezon City, Marlys and I met with the director of the Bureau of Child Welfare in Manila.

Flora Eufemio was a very professional, no-nonsense woman who had a forbidding aura. We were to learn later that she was the feared "Iron Lady" of the DSSD, and many people over the years had gone slinking out of her office after being lectured and intimidated. Marlys and I experienced

something of that. Mrs. Eufemio asked us some very pointed questions about what we intended to do in Cebu. She reminded us that we would need to have a license to operate a home for children and that her agency was the one to issue such a license. She concluded the meeting by telling us that she didn't think another orphanage was needed in the Philippines at that time and we should be open to other types of programs.

As we slunk out of her office, we were greeted by two women who were welcoming and sympathetic. Marilyn Manuel and Lyra del Castillo were social workers with the Bureau, and they had a pretty good idea what we'd been told by Mrs. Eufemio. They were very understanding and told us they would work to help us get the license we needed. What they offered us was kindness and hope that we would be able to navigate the bureaucratic maze that exists in government agencies in a country like the Philippines. They saw beyond our inexperience and recognized our compassion and dedication to the idea of reaching out to children that didn't have families. These two women were to become longtime friends of the ministry. Later, both of them left the government service and became directors of NGOs working with dependent children.

The meeting with Mrs. Eufemio was difficult but was a great learning experience for us, and by extension, the whole staff. She asked questions that needed asking. What type of "children's home" did we intend to have? What type of children would we serve? Who would serve on our local board? What sort of qualifications did any of us have? Who did we think we were? These questions were helpful for us in the days and months to come as we began to refine our thinking about our fledgling ministry and think about the future and how the Corpus Christi Foundation might handle the challenges of carving out a ministry in Cebu. We did not lose heart when faced with these challenges but knew we would need to work hard to enlist the support of people in Cebu and the States, and make sure that our plans and schemes were God-inspired and not just our own desires.

The trip to Manila ended on a sour note. We had not accurately estimated how much it would cost. Food and transportation costs were much higher in Manila than in Cebu. We were just about out of money and needed to purchase our boat tickets back to Cebu. The only people we knew in Manila were government officials, and we didn't want to admit our lack of planning and financial acumen to them. The only option was to ask Bob Carey, our Free Church missionary friend, if he could wire us some money, which we promised to pay back upon our arrival in Cebu. Bob graciously agreed and sent us 700 pesos (about $100), more than enough for our needs.

Marlys and I went to the business district in Makati City to get the money from the bank. It was overwhelming for us as we walked among the modern office buildings and five-star hotels, not knowing exactly where to go, not speaking the language of Manila, and not entirely sure how much money would be waiting for us. We wondered how there could be such wealth in a country with gruesome poverty all around. We wondered if things would always be like this, not knowing what we were doing, always being short of money, having to rely on others. We felt like "rubes" that day in Makati; we were uncomfortable and wanted to leave. But we needed that money, so we asked directions to the bank, waited several hours until it arrived from Cebu, and headed back to meet the rest of the staff in Manila and catch the boat home.

While we were away we entrusted the care of the Bulacao home to two friends, Lina and Gloria. We asked them to give medicine to Juni, one of the little boys we had befriended in the neighborhood. Marlys had left a note for Gloria and Lina to give Juni a pill every morning for primary complex tuberculosis. Somehow, Gloria and Lina got confused by the letter and, when a cat showed up at the door, decided that he was Juni. They fed him a pill every morning that we were gone.

When we got back, we asked how Juni was doing and whether he came by the house to get his pills. The girls reported that he had come every day but that they had a hard time getting him to swallow the pill. When their mistake eventually came to light, everyone had a good laugh. Marlys and Kathy went to find Juni and re-start him on his pill regimen. Meanwhile, the cat was tuberculosis free and confused as to why his pills stopped being given.

Back to Work

IN LATE SEPTEMBER the Corpus Christi Home for Children received its first referral: Mary Ann, a little girl who had been living in a Catholic orphanage that could not provide for her medical needs. The child had Potts Disease (tuberculosis of the spine) and needed lots of medicine, medical consultations, and, possibly, surgery. She was seven years old. Our excitement was high. Finally we would be doing what we felt called to do. All the preparation, travel, fundraising, legal work, house repair, language study, and license applications had been for this.

A few days later there was another referral, this time a one-day-old baby. We were thrilled that the government was entrusting us with children but were not prepared for a baby that young. (We were learning a valuable lesson in working with the government: Communication was not going to be smooth. In this case, nobody called to tell us they would be coming with a newborn baby.) When the social worker brought little Lloyd

32

Mary Ann was the first child we took in. Seven years old when she arrived, she had been living at a Catholic orphanage. Ann had Potts Disease, tuberculosis of the spine, which manifested in a hunched back.

Ann was a bright and loving girl who responded well to the love and care she received. I brought her to Manila to be examined at the Philippine General Hospital, where she underwent x-rays and blood work. Later we had her examined by Dr. Felix Vicuna at Cebu Doctors, who determined that she would need a halo pelvic devise to "stretch out" her spine so it could be surgically reinforced. Dr. Vicuna was sorry to tell us that the procedure and surgery could not be done in the Philippines at that time.

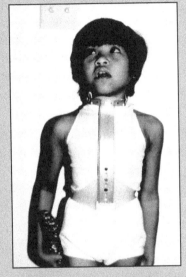

We began looking into options for sending her to Minnesota for surgery. Cliff Danielson made inquiries at Gillette Children's Hospital and found that she could be operated on there under the care of Dr. Winter, a well-known orthopedic surgeon. Two friends from the U.S. were visiting Cebu at this time and agreed to escort Ann to Minnesota.

A family in Isanti, MN, expressed an interest in adopting Ann. We were able to get a passport and U.S. visa with minimal effort in Cebu. All systems seemed to be "go" for Ann until, on the way to the airport, we stopped at the Department of Social Services to get a travel clearance, a requirement for Ann to travel internationally. The regional director had consulted with the Bureau of Child Welfare in Manila, but the BCW director, Mrs. Eufemio, was not in favor of giving Ann permission to travel. Everything came to a screeching halt.

In our enthusiasm, inexperience, and naivety we hadn't considered the legal aspects of the case. We called Ron Duterte, Cebu City vice mayor and a good friend of the Corpus Christi staff. He came to the DSSD right away and called Mrs. Eufemio. A few minutes later he came outside the office and gave us the thumbs up. Somehow he had convinced her that the surgery Ann needed could only be done in the U.S. and that her situation needed immediate attention. He might have told her a few other things, but he never shared the whole conversation with us. Ann was cleared and was soon on the plane to Minnesota, where her life would change in amazing ways.

to the Bulacao home, we all took turns holding him. When he started crying we looked at each other and said, "What do we do now?" So the women headed into the city to buy milk, bottles, pacifiers, and blankets while the men took turns holding little Lloyd. It was on-the-job-training for everyone.

Other children were placed with us in the coming months, most of them with health problems. It seemed like the government was placing kids with us that no other agency would accept. One boy had epilepsy, another cerebral palsy. A girl needed her cleft lip and palette surgically repaired.

During the early months of the ministry, a romance developed between Kathy Norlien and Sned Flora. They were married November 22 at Camp Bato, a Free Church camp in the mountains south of Cebu City. It was a beautiful wedding, attended by the staff and children of Corpus Christi.

Later in November, Sandy Swanson arrived to join the staff. She traveled to Cebu with Cliff Danielson. Sandy's background in child development and her experience working at Camp Shamineau were great training for her work in Cebu, and she made an immediate impact on the ministry. Cliff's three-week visit was encouraging to us, especially Marlys, and he brought great reports on the growth of the stateside organization and the work of the board. Cliff took lots of pictures to be used in promoting the ministry and met with the Cebu board of directors to establish a connection between the two organizations.

Sandy Swanson arrives in Cebu.

First Christmas

WE WERE PREPARING FOR CHRISTMAS, which we knew would be a fun time with the children but a difficult time to be away from our families. For all of us it would be our first Christmas away from home.

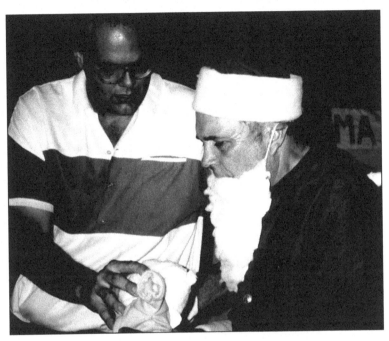

Uncle Wes was the first of many CSC Santas.

A letter from Jeff, published in the *DelAdlawan News*, told about Christmas, 1979:

> Even though we missed our loved ones back home, our first Christmas in Cebu was filled with a special love and warmth we had never experienced before. On Christmas Day we closed our door and didn't even bother to leave the house. We were just one big happy family: Paul and Marlys, Della, Sandy, Kathy and Sned, the children, Lloyd, Ann Ann, Roy, Ralph, Maria, and myself.

THE 1980s

"Well, I guess I'll have to call my friend, Vice Mayor Ron Duterte, to get out of bed and come down here and find out why there is nobody here willing to help this child."

1980

AS 1980 ARRIVED, the stateside organization was making strides to better support our efforts in Cebu. On January 26, the first annual meeting was held at Central Baptist Church, with 180 people in attendance. In just a few short months Cliff had been able to spread the word such that people were supporting the ministry and interested to hear what was going on in Cebu.

The annual meeting featured a message by Jerry Healy, board chair, in which he spoke of "a year of blessings: an established work in Cebu City, a dedicated staff, little children whose lives have been enriched, a strong financial base for the work, a spirit of joy and excitement as we review the past and look forward to 1980." Joe Lincoln gave a greeting; Al Sannerud gave a financial report indicating that income for 1979 exceeded $25,000; and board members Kathy Johnson, Jane Olsen, and Jim Roste gave testimonies. Stacy Thompson sang, pastors Garvin McGettrick and Ron Eckert (Central Baptist) led in "Children of the Heavenly Father," and Jack Sowers, pastor of Constance Free Church, gave the benediction. The evening featured a slide show produced by Larry Hansen.

Things were moving forward, even though they weren't always sources of pure joy. In January, Lloyd left for adoption, the first Corpus Christi child to depart for placement. He was adopted by a missionary couple living in Cebu, the Henrys, who were close friends of ours. It was a day of joy and sadness as the Henrys came to the Bulacao home to get little Lloyd. We were learning that there are tremendous emotional swings in a ministry like ours, and we needed to learn how to handle them. Specifically, we needed to learn how to love the children under our care but do our best to minimize the attachments that made it so painful to give them up. This was not an easy lesson for us.

During the early months of 1980, we began opening our home for Sunday afternoon services. Aside from the staff, 20-30 people would cram into the living room for these weekly services. Rebecca Deliña invited people from the community to attend.

Around this time Sandy Swanson's brothers, Jerry and Ron, owners of Socon, Inc. in Minnesota, made a donation of $2,000 for the purchase of a vehicle in Cebu, and we were able to get a shiny new green Ford Fiera. They also underwrote the cost of a telephone for the Bulacao house.

The Ford Fiera was usually filled to capacity.

In early 1980, the Floras took a short furlough to Minnesota. They spent time with Kathy's family (who had never met Sned), did some deputation, and met with the board. In April, Mary Ann left for the U.S. for surgery. This was a time of mixed emotions. As with the departure of Lloyd, there were many tears shed. We had invested so much love in Ann's life, and there was so much uncertainty in her future. We knew this was her big chance, something we had hoped and prayed for. But the tears fell like rain that day in April of 1980, as they would for many years to come as treasured children from the home would leave. It wasn't just a job for our young staff, not merely a home for children where they came and went and new ones came in. It was our life, and our relationships with the children were deep and meaningful.

In June our first short-term missionary came to Cebu to help the staff. Ruth Oliver was a Bethel student who spent her summer vacation in Cebu. Her job was primarily to play with the children, a short-term job description that has existed throughout our history. In those days we did not have many children, but they were sponges for the time and attention of staff, so having an extra person around was helpful.

A Lesson in Bureaucracy

IN JULY OF 1980, two Corpus Christi children, Roy and Johnny, were taken from our home by government social workers. We were told they would be going for adoption. In the early days of the ministry, we were not involved in placing our children. That was the sole responsibility of the government. But this situation had come up so quickly that there had been no time for emotional preparation for either children or staff. One day they were there and the next they were gone. Needless to say, we were not happy with this hasty departure, but there was not much we could do about it.

A few weeks after they were taken, I was visiting a new orphanage in Cebu, one that does not seek adoption for their children. I was shocked to see Roy and Johnny running around. "Surely it couldn't be them," I thought. "They were gone for adoption." But it was them! I was very angry and demanded to know what was going on. When I did not receive an audience with the orphanage director, I went immediately to the DSWD office to report the situation. I had a long meeting with the regional director and some other people who were involved in the case. They promised to look into it.

We wanted the boys returned to us so they would have a chance for adoption, and we enlisted help from Ron Duterte. It turned out to be a complicated and frustrating situation, as the other orphanage was Catholic and involved influential people. Although we never got the children back, we continued to advocate for their adoptive placement and were happy when they were eventually adopted. Roy went to the U.S. and Johnny to a family in Cebu.

This was a major learning experience for the staff. There were lessons we needed to absorb as we embarked on our work with children in Cebu. The government had some different procedures and priorities than we did. Political pressures and issues of influence sometimes ran counter to our view of the best interests of the children. We needed to work within the system that we sometimes disagreed with, learn to co-exist with the Church and the Philippine government agencies we were under, and try our best to cooperate with Catholic agencies and individuals who were influential and who had been working in child welfare a lot longer than we had. In our dealings with government workers, courts, and adoption authorities, we would sometimes lose our arguments and have to live with outcomes that we didn't agree with. It was part of doing business in the Philippines, and God gave us the patience, endurance, and grace to keep moving ahead for the sake of the kids we served.

Throughout our history, we tried our best to work within the system, respecting the authority of the Philippine government agencies we were under, even when we did not agree with their methods and policies. And we tried to cooperate with Catholic agencies and individuals, in spite of major differences in theology and priorities.

A Big Month

AUGUST WAS AN EVENTFUL MONTH for us. Jerry and Millie Healy spent a month in Cebu. It was a blessed time for Marlys and me, showing them the ministry and the beautiful scenery of the Philippines. They were able to travel to Baguio City in the north part of the Philippines and Mindanao in the south. Jerry and Millie were board members at that time. They were concerned about the condition of the Bulacao home, particularly the fact that the staff and kids shared one bathroom. They brought back a proposal that the board come up with about $1,000 to build another bathroom in the home. When Jerry shared his idea with Cliff back in Minnesota, he learned that an anonymous gift had just come in for $1,000. So the bathroom was covered!

Jerry Healy found time for some golf during his visit to Cebu.

Also in August, Jeff Snyder resigned and returned to Minnesota. His main reason for leaving was to attend Bible school, something that had been on his heart for some time. To replace Jeff, Gloria Navasquez was hired. She had been working with the Evangelical Free Church, helping manage the Chi Alpha Omega Student Center. Gloria was a good friend of ours and a faithful member of the

Central Free Church where we attended. She became Corpus Christi's community relations director. She was responsible for planning and supervising all evangelism, outreach, and follow-up work, and overseeing our medical outreach ministry that helped poor families in medical crises by providing medicines or temporary care.

At about that same time Kathy and Sned Flora returned to Cebu. They had enjoyed their "mini-furlough" in Minnesota. It was Sned's first exposure to the States, and he was excited about things he purchased. On their first night back they opened their suitcases and showed everyone their treasures, including new sneakers for Sned and motorcycle accessories for the bike he had shipped over from Minnesota. Sned had grown up in humble circumstances in Siquijor, a small island south of Cebu, so these were treasures, and everyone oohed and ahhed as he showed them off that night.

Gloria Navasquez has everyone's attention.

The next morning when we went downstairs, we discovered there had been a break-in during the night. Thieves had broken a window and gained entry to the living room. Sned's shoes and other items were gone. These were devastating losses for the Floras and a graphic reminder that we needed to be more vigilant about security and not let down our guard, even for one night.

In spite of small setbacks like this one, the ministry of Corpus Christi was moving forward, little by little. We were gaining experience in childcare and in dealing with the variety of medical and developmental challenges children were bringing. The DSWD was comfortable in placing more kids with us. The Floras were licensed as foster parents because the limit of children had been reached for our license. The church we started in the Bulacao home was growing.

A New Attitude

IT WAS DURING THIS TIME OF GROWTH, when things were falling into place and our dreams were starting to be realized, that a change of thinking started to take shape among the staff. The ministry, which had been more or less an adventure for us, was starting to change, and so was our attitude. We were beginning to assume that it would last. No longer was this simply a whim of several young people from Minnesota that would fizzle out as hurdles emerged and resources dwindled. We began believing in ourselves, and other people were starting to believe in us. This development in our attitude was fueled by several things: the Philippine government's cooperation, the increased influence we were gaining in Philippine society, and the fundraising success of our board in Minnesota.

But our change in thinking needed to be accompanied by a change on the stateside end, as well. Because of our youth and the fact that the board and early supporters of the ministry were made up primarily of our families and friends, the view of those in Minnesota was often of "the kids in Cebu." *We* were their kids. But the board needed to shift their thinking to embrace the staff's maturity and tested commitment, and to realize this was not a short-term venture. We were up to the task and the ministry was rolling. The board needed to grow as fast or faster than the work in Cebu.

More Kids!

WE HAD OUR HANDS FULL with more children coming to the home. Julio had epilepsy; Roggie also had seizures. Arlene had a cleft lip. Ernesto had cerebral palsy. Children were running around the living room, but there wasn't any yard at the Bulacao home. A small playhouse was built at the front of the house, and a swing set was donated by Ron Duterte. But things were getting crowded. Sned and I took the kids for a ride in the wagon around the neighborhood, and we brought them on outings to places that had playground or to the beach.

Every week Kathy made a schedule for who was "on duty." Everyone pitched in, caring for babies, toddlers, and older children. Schedules often needed to be changed, though, as children were brought to doctors or labs, or sometimes had to be admitted to the hospital. Children in the hospital needed to have a "watcher" at all times—someone to provide care, watch the i.v. bag, take temperatures, and give fluids. So if a child was admitted, our staff split up the watcher duties.

Our work with children in the Bulacao community was curtailed during these days because our focus was on children placed in our home. Rebecca Deliña continued to request help for families with sick and malnourished children, and we helped as finances allowed.

One night we heard someone at the gate calling "Maayo," which is the Cebuano custom of announcing your presence. It was 2 a.m. Rebecca had been at City Hospital helping a mother with her child who had been admitted there and was not doing well. Nobody on duty at the hospital was attending to them. The child would soon die if not given antibiotics and nourishment. With no money for public transportation, Rebecca walked the six miles from the hospital to the Corpus Christi home to ask for emergency help to save this little one's life. I was able to fire up the Ford Fiera, drive Rebecca to the hospital, and talk to the nurse on duty. The conversation went something like this:

Me (to the nurse on duty, who was asleep at the nurses station): "Ahem. Ma'am. Hello. I am here to see that this woman gets help for her baby."

Nurse: "We are not able to get the medicines at this time. Come back in the morning."

Me: "The child might be dead by then."

Nurse: "She shouldn't have waited so long to bring the baby in."

Me: "But the baby is here and needs help now. I'll buy whatever medicine is needed if you don't have it available here."

Nurse: "I need a doctor's order to give the medicine. No one is available at this time. Come back in the morning."

Me: "Well, I guess I'll have to call my friend, Vice Mayor Ron Duterte, to get out of bed and come down here and find out why there is nobody here willing to help this child. I'll call him right now."

Nurse: "That's not needed, sir. Just let me talk to the resident on duty."

Within 10 minutes the medicines were "found" and the baby was getting the help he desperately needed. We were learning how essential it was to have a friend like Ron to intervene on behalf of children we were helping. He was the difference between success and failure so many times. He knew the system in ways we never could. He had the authority to make things happen. But most of all, he had a heart for the kids and a respect for the staff who had given up much to leave our lives in Minnesota and travel to his country to take care of abandoned and neglected children. Ron was a major reason the ministry was able to take off in Cebu City.

Our efforts were strengthened during these days by items sent from Minnesota. Ruth Lonquist, a member of Constance Free Church and a life-long friend of the Danielsons, donated a Maytag wringer washing machine. Other friends helped pay for shipping it to Cebu. Clothes, shoes, toys, and hygiene supplies were also sent. When these care packages arrived, Marlys, Della, Sandy, Kathy, and Gloria unpacked and sorted everything. Those were exciting days for us and further evidence of the generosity and thoughtfulness of friends. It also showed the results of Cliff Danielson's work promoting the ministry. Cliff was the one to pack the boxes sent to Cebu, and it was always done with care and love. There was never any wasted space in a box. He even rolled up clothes and other items to put inside shoes to maximize space. It was always amazing for us to see how much Cliff could get in the boxes and how much love went into them.

To cope with the demands of cooking, cleaning, washing clothes, and caring for the children, we recognized the need to hire a few Filipino workers to help out. The first workers hired were LitLit and Perry Martinez, sisters of little Jessie, who were well known to us through the Bible study group in our home. As the ministry grew, additional workers were added.

We were learning so much about life and love and the grace of God. Two things were abundantly clear. First, the needs of children were an "easy sell." People respond to kids. Churches were starting to put us on their missions budgets. Individuals were touched by the newsletter or pictures we sent back to the States. People sent in money, collected items, and mailed them to Cebu, or prayed for the staff and children. Cliff was getting invitations from churches and civic organizations to make presen-tations. There was something compelling about the suffering of little children and our work to alleviate that suffering. People were gladly getting on board, supporting our efforts and answering the prayers of many.

The second lesson was about blessings: God blesses those who bless His little ones. This was clear in those early days of the ministry, and was proven true in the months and years to come. Jesus has a special place in His heart for children, and he bestows rich blessings on those who reach out to them in love. We saw those blessings evident in our own lives, as He opened doors, blessed relationships, gave strength and wisdom, and brought people into our lives who could move things forward with their gifts, talents, and encouragement. We were meeting people, both in Minnesota and the Philippines, whom we would never have met if it weren't for our ministry. Supporters reported emotional and material blessings that were direct results of their involvement with children through our organization. Parents told of their own children becoming involved in praying for our children and, in some cases, doing projects to raise money to help out. Others were considering growing their families by adopting a child or a sibling group. From an idea planted in the heart of Marlys Healy, love and blessings were radiating outward in the Philippines and across the ocean to people throughout the United States.

1981

THE YEAR ARRIVED with a sense of thanksgiving and hope. The second annual meeting in Minnesota was attended by 195 people, who gave an offering of $1450. Speakers included Drs. Robert Winter and John Lonstein, who explained the surgeries they performed on Ann, who blessed the group with several songs, including "Kids Under Construction," after which there was not a dry eye in the room.

Kids under construction.
Maybe the paint is still wet.
Kids under construction.
The Lord may not be finished yet.

Warren Johnson, a retired Baptist General Conference missionary who had served in Cebu, among other assignments, and Don Larson, a professor at Bethel and a recognized expert on the Philippines, gave short talks. CSC's treasurer, Al Sannerud, reported that income for 1980 was $41,343. Among other business items, the board introduced a new name for the organization: Cebu Christian Shelter Community for Children (CCSCC). The name DelAdlawan was hard to pronounce and for most people didn't have a recognizable connection to the work being done in Cebu. CCSCC was not exactly a catchy name either, but it did tell who we were, where we operated, who we were targeting for help, and the type of ministry we were offering.

On March 7, 1981, David Flora was born. This was a first for the Corpus Christi staff and necessitated big adjustments for the Floras. Since the staff and children lived together in the same house, finding privacy was always a challenge. And balancing family time with responsibilities with the kids in the home was challenging. As David grew he had lots of playmates in the home, but had to learn to share his parents with the other kids.

A Fire at Corpus Christi

WHILE THINGS WERE MOVING ALONG in a positive way, something happened that brought us crashing back to earth. On the evening of April 16, a Thursday, a fire broke out in one of the upstairs bedrooms of the Bulacao home. We were downstairs having a Bible study with neighbors and smelled smoke. The house was made of wood, so it didn't take long until two rooms were in flames and the fire was spreading fast. We hurriedly got the children out of the house. A neighbor saw the flames and called the fire department. In just a few minutes the fire truck arrived and the fire was extinguished. Two rooms were entirely gutted and another two were extensively damaged. It was a frightening night for everyone, but nobody was hurt. It could easily have been otherwise.

There was much damage to the house, and it was not livable. Friends of Corpus Christi heard about the fire and came to offer support. Lots of people were crowding around the house wanting to get in and see the damage, some of whom we didn't know. Teo Martinez, the husband of Eksyon, who was working as a guard for Corpus Christi at the time, took matters into his own hands when he announced, "Everybody out!" He said anybody who tried to get into the house would have go over him. It was a relief to know that people were looking out for our best interests that night and in the months to come.

After a brief meeting, it was determined that the staff and kids would go to the house of Rod and Camille Henry, missionary friends who were in California on a short furlough. We figured the Henrys wouldn't mind us taking over their house for a while. We drove up to the house, where we were greeted by the maid, who wasn't sure it was a great idea, but who knew how much the Henry's loved Corpus Christi, so she guessed it would be okay for a night. I promised to call the Henrys the next day and see what they thought of our leveraged takeover of their home. We got all the kids to bed, then spent time in prayer, thanking God for protecting the children and asking for his leading for the coming days.

The next morning I called Rod Henry and told him about the fire. He offered their home until they would be back from furlough in two weeks. I said, "Thanks Rod. We're already moved in!" In the midst of great stress and uncertainty, God had opened a door for Corpus Christi, as He had so often in the past and would continue to do in the months to come.

Later that day I went to see our insurance agent, Fred Cisneros, who looked over the policy and determined that we were covered for the repairs needed to restore the house. The work began almost immediately, and CCSCC provided money for new beds, cupboards, and clothes to replace the destroyed items.

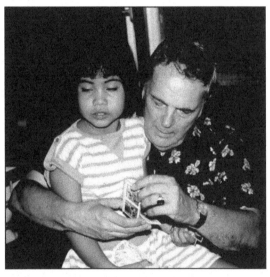

Wes Hagen finds a friend.

The Henrys returned to Cebu as planned, and the Corpus Christi crew moved to Happy Valley, to the home of Wes Hagen, our friend and fellow Minnesotan. Wes, a bachelor and an only child, and more than a little eccentric, was a retired volunteer with the Free Church mission and was renting a small house where he lived alone. He agreed to our moving in, probably not fully understanding what it would entail. Wes was gracious, but the children soon started getting on his nerves. He liked to listen to the radio, especially to J. Vernon McGee's program, "Through the Bible." He would sit with his ear cupped to the radio while babies cried or toddlers ran past him. He referred to the kids as "twinks," as in, "Can't you keep those twinks quiet while I'm listening to my program?" Wes had a great sense of humor and enjoyed the attention the kids gave him, even if he found them annoying at times.

The repairs on the Bulacao home took quite a bit longer than expected, so the situation was far from ideal for all concerned. On the day we loaded up the vehicle to return to Bulacao, Wes stood at the gate saying, "Good-bye twinks. Glad to see you going!" The feeling was indeed mutual, but we wondered what we would have done after the fire if not for the kindness of Wes Hagen and the Henrys.

Medical Needs

WITH A NEWLY REPAIRED HOME IN BULACAO, we could again concentrate on care of the children. Their medical needs demanded lots of attention and expense. With a limited budget, we had to maximize our funds by using less expensive doctors, labs, and hospitals. Dr. Blanco was our pediatrician. When someone needed hospitalization, Marlys applied for charity status at Velez Hospital or the charity ward at Cebu Doctors. We were beginning to realize how medical costs could dominate our budget. Unexpected medical expenses were forcing us to dip into limited reserves and, often, to request additional funds from the Minnesota organization. Since many of the children referred to us by the government had medical problems, the staff and Minnesota board developed a medical fund, separate from the regular budget, that could help pay for medical expenses. Some donors in the U.S. were motivated to give for medical needs, and the fund was a good way to match their interests with the needs of kids at Corpus Christi. It also reduced our agonizing decisions about the conflicting demands of medical needs and regular expenditures for food, utilities, salaries, and transportation.

In the June issue of the *CCSCC News*, Sandy Swanson wrote about a precocious little girl, Arlene, who entertained the staff with her antics:

One night we heard a noise upstairs that sounded like one of the children moving around. They were all supposed to be in bed, and since all but Junel sleep in cribs, I assumed he was up walking around. So I tiptoed upstairs hoping to catch him in the act. Instead, I saw little 14 month-old Arlene, who is one of the most mischievous of the children, crawl out of one room and into the next.

After further investigation I discovered she had kicked one of the slats from her homemade crib/playpen and crawled out the opening in the dark. She must have been out about a half hour because she had delivered three or four toys to each child in his or her crib, and all were playing happily.

Meanwhile, Cliff was making many presentations in churches, schools, homes, and places of business, getting the story of CCSCC to as many people as possible. Several churches were giving regular support for the ministry, including Elim Baptist of Isanti, Crossroads Covenant of Forest Lake, Central Baptist in Saint Paul, Constance Free Church, and others. During 1981, Cliff made 58 presentations. Lots of different groups were sending in donations: a high school honors society, Sunday School and Vacation Bible School groups, church women's groups, and civic organizations.

1982

BY FEBRUARY OF 1982, there were 12 children living at Corpus Christi. Roggie got strep throat and spent 19 days in the charity ward of Cebu Doctors Hospital. Marlys and I took turns as watchers, she during the days so she could talk to the doctors, and me at night. There was only a short wooden bench for me to sleep on, and lots of bugs and mice to deal with. I could hear the nurses chuckling at the sight of a lanky American curled up on that bench. It was a learning experience for us, as the medical personnel assigned to the charity wards were not always attentive or sympathetic. And watching mice scamper around the ward was something we were not accustomed to. Roggie did not respond to the antibiotics that were prescribed, so his recovery was very slow. The staff back in Bulacao had to cover for the Healys during this time.

In March, the staff was told that Roggie and Julio were ready for placement but there were no families available. Both boys had epilepsy. Through CSC's network of supporters, two families were identified who were willing to accept children with epilepsy. The Chernes of Minneapolis and the Rosdahls of Coeur d'Alene, Idaho, applied through their respective adoption agencies. The initial communication with the government adoption unit handling international adoptions indicated that the Rosedahls would adopt Roggie, but he was subsequently matched with the Chernes. More than six months later, the Rosdahls were informed that they were matched with Julio. It was a confusing time for the staff and families.

Furlough Time

MARLYS AND I WERE PLANNING to take a furlough in May, after three

51

years of service in Cebu. We needed a break and were eager to see our famiies and connect with friends and supporters. It was decided that we would have a one-year furlough. Sandy Swanson, who had been in Minnesota for a few months, was to return to Cebu to fill in for us. In addition, Joe and Kathy Grafft, a couple from Forest Lake, volunteered to go to Cebu to help out during the summer months. Kathy was an occupational therapist; Joe had taught industrial arts and was currently teaching emergency medical care and ambulance services in Spring Lake Park. They were well-trained young people who had much to offer the Corpus Christi staff.

There were tearful good-byes as we left for our furlough. We had invested much love in children's lives, and it was painful to leave. But we knew the staff would be able to handle the work. Sned would handle financial matters. Sandy and Kathy would collaborate on medical and childcare responsibilities, and Della and Gloria would continue their good work in cooking and community outreach, respectively. And everyone would pitch in to take care of the kids and do the administrative work necessary for keeping the ministry running smoothly.

We arrived at the Minneapolis airport to a host of greeters, including family and CCSCC friends. It was an overwhelming display of love, and we were emotionally drained by the time we got to the temporary quarters Cliff had arranged for us. On May 22, a couple days after our arrival, a welcome dinner was held at the Salem Covenant Church. Marlys and I showed slides and gave an update on the ministry, and there was a commissioning prayer for the Graffts. An offering was taken, amounting to a then-spectacular $4,718. We were more than sufficiently welcomed and were looking forward to making presentations on behalf of CCSCC and the work in Cebu.

We did not own a home, and CCSCC did not have sufficient funds to rent one for us, so we were all happy when an elderly member of Constance Church, Harold Thompson, allowed us to stay in his Ham Lake house for the year. Harold was living in a retirement home in Osseo. It was a small house with wood floors, a steep staircase to the upstairs, and a wood-burning furnace. I had never lived in the country before, so I needed a lot of help with simple maintenance chores. There was a pickup truck in the garage with a snow plow attached, which would have been a great help to anyone except me. Suffice it to say that we had some close calls that winter along the long driveway going in and out of Harold's property. Thankfully, one of Harold's relatives, Donny Stromgren, was a big help to us in keeping the truck running and learning how to use the furnace. I'm sure he and others had some good laughs in noting how little practical knowledge this missionary had for living in the country.

During their time in Cebu, the Graffts did a variety of tasks at Corpus Christi, including taking their turns at childcare. Kathy trained the staff to help Ernesto, a seven-year-old boy with cerebral palsy, who needed twice-daily therapy. Joe also did training for the staff, preparing them to handle basic emergencies in the home, and also offered this training to others in the Bulacao community. In addition, he supervised some remodeling projects around the home: screening in the front porch and expanding the nursery and kitchen, which doubled their size.

Joe and Kathy were a great inspiration to the staff, not only for the work they did but for the fact that CCSCC was able to attract people of their caliber to go to Cebu and help out.

The Graffts were the first of what came to be known as "short-termers": people with useful skills and experience for helping the children and staff. In the coming years, many such volunteers would follow the Graffts to Cebu City to meet needs both specific and general. They would include teachers, nurses, therapists, early childhood experts, and people who were content just to hold babies and play with the older kids. Some would go to Cebu for a few months, others for up to a year, especially if they were replacing staff members on furlough.

While we were in Minnesota, we talked with Greg Dirnberger, who was on the staff at Central Baptist Church, working with young adults. We hatched the idea for a team from Central to go to Cebu and help out. It seemed like a crazy idea because we'd never had a team visit, and it promised to involve a lot of money, which the church or the team would have to raise. I wondered who would want to go. But that seemed like the easy part, and Greg assured me that several college students would go if they were able to raise the money. Central Baptist was also new to this kind of thing, so the students would be on their own coming up with funds. We decided to proceed, albeit cautiously, with a plan for the group, which eventually became known as the Central 7, to go to Cebu in the summer of 1983.

Excerpts from Cliff's Mailbag

While on a trip we saw so many people spending money selfishly, including us, that we decided to double our pledge to Paul and Marlys.

Use this where your need is greatest. It is a memorial for our son.

Enclosed is a check. Our son asked that we give money in his name rather than Christmas gifts this year. Thank you for doing what we are unable to do.

Here is a little extra, so the staff won't be discouraged. The whole mission is in our prayers regularly.

1983

MARLYS AND I RETURNED TO CEBU on January 22 of 1983. It had been a good year for us, though a bit tiring. In order to make ends meet, Marlys worked at the Fridley Medical Center, where she was employed before going to Cebu. But we were able to make many presentations and meet people who were willing and able to become supporters. Still, I remember feeling like it was time to get home. Cebu had become home, and we intended for it to be such for many years. Although we knew that promoting the ministry was important work and that we were in a unique position to inspire people to give and pray, we felt so much more energized by actually doing the work than by telling about what we do. We were more thankful than ever for the work of Cliff and the board in raising funds for CCSCC.

In June, I escorted a baby, Edgar, to Minnesota for emergency brain surgery. He needed to have shunts put in his brain to drain fluid. Edgar was to be cared for by the Reedy family of Roseville prior to and after his surgery. Dr. M. Nagib was to do the surgery. Getting the United States visa for Edgar was a complicated process, but was made easier by cooperation of the Department of Social Services, especially Mrs. Lourdes Bulanon, who directed the Philippine Intercountry Adoption Unit. She coordinated with Crossroads Adoption Services for the Reedys to be approved to foster Edgar, and for eventual adoptive placement with them. This was to be the first of several placements with the Reedy family.

I will never forget the trip from Cebu to Minnesota with little Edgar. He cried a *lot*, which caused some irritation with other passengers. I got dirty looks and comments. Several women took it upon themselves to give me advice about how I should be caring for Edgar. "Have you fed him?" one asked. My inclination was to respond with, "Oh, you need to feed these things?" But most of the women meant well and some were sympathetic and offered to help me. I had been given instructions not to let people hold him, so that wasn't an option. One stewardess was very moved by Edgar's situation and asked if she could pray for him. He stared up at her with beautiful eyes and melted all the attendants' hearts. I felt so proud of him and grateful for having the chance to bring him to the United States for this life-changing opportunity.

When we got to Minnesota, the entire Reedy clan was there to greet us. Edgar was plucked from my grasp and passed around to waiting family members. I learned that Minnesota had experienced significant rainfall in the days preceding our arrival, so Lavonne Reedy decided that Edgar's name would become Noah. After having been with him nonstop for the past few days, it felt strange to suddenly be without him, even if I knew he was in good hands. He didn't need me any longer. It was like many other experiences we had and would have in turning our children over to adoptive parents. Most of the staff would eventually have the chance to escort our children for adoption and would get a taste of what I experienced that day at the Twin Cities airport.

The Central 7

IN JULY, THE CENTRAL 7 ARRIVED IN CEBU for a six-week assignment at CCSCC. The team was led by Greg Dirnberger and his wife, Laurie, and included Mitch Ohlendorf, Tammy Jo Nelson, Sue Gardner, Peter Nelson, and Karl Oase. Except for the Dirnbergers, all were college students and had spent several months preparing for the trip, working up songs and skits. They were full of excitement for their time in the Philippines and made an immediate connection with the staff and kids. The next six weeks would be filled with touring the city, playing with the children, doing presentations in churches, visiting Irv and Mary Stauffer, BGC missionaries serving on a neighboring island, and spending time with the staff. Little did we know how much that trip would impact our ministry in the future.

While in Cebu the entire team got sick with "stomach distress." They were staying in the apartment of Wes Hagen, the volunteer Free Church missionary who had opened up his home to the staff following the fire in

1981. The team members all were pretty sick and had to stay in bed day and night. The apartment had a tiny bathroom with a small toilet. The water tank that serviced the apartment was small and took a long time to fill. Sometimes a power outage meant the pump wouldn't work to fill the tank. With seven cases of diarrhea going on, that water was badly needed. And Mr. Hagen had announced early on that they were not to flush toilet paper but were to put it in the waste basket. What?!

For the several days they were sick, I would drive to their door, unload a case of toilet tissue, toss it in the door, and yell, "See you tomorrow. God love you." Greg Dirnberger was even hospitalized for a few days and never fully recovered while the team was in Cebu. It looked like the Central 7's trip would be a disaster. But they did recover, as tourists usually do, and were able to do most of the things we had planned for them.

One of those was a trip to Dumaguete City to do some presentations, including one at Silliman University. Our hosts were Irv and Mary Stauffer, church-planting missionaries with the Baptist General Conference. At Silliman, we sang a few songs, including a Beach Boys tune, "409." Afterwards we were at the Stauffer home and Irv was telling some of the church people about the concert. He mentioned that we sang some "really modern music." I guess Irv had been on the mission field too long and didn't know that the Beach Boys recorded that song in 1963, more than 20 years before we butchered it! But our friendship with the Stauffers was strengthened by the team's trip, and we appreciated the things Irv had set up for them to do.

In August we had 23 children in the home and had cared for 48 total since

It's crowded in Bulacao.

we began. We were absolutely full at the home in Bulacao and were wondering if there would come a day when we would have better facilities.

On October 27, our good friend Ron Duterte was inaugurated as mayor of Cebu City. He had served as vice mayor for several years and before that as a city counselor. This was the apex of his political career. His predecessor was promoted to a position in the Ministry of Health, and President Marcos selected Ron to follow him as mayor. In those days nothing happened without Marcos' approval. After being sworn in, Ron flew to Cebu and several of us were among the crowd there to meet him. It was a big day for Ron and, by extension, the ministry of Corpus Christi because we knew he would use his influence to open doors for us and the children he loved.

Goings and Comings

ON DECEMBER 13 JUNEL MONTEMOR left for France. This was tough for me because we were very close. Watching Junel's life change was one of the most poignant experiences of my life. With us he never went hungry. He wasn't on the B squad at Corpus Christi, where all the kids were varsity. We gave him something he had lost: his childhood.

Later that month Greg Swanson arrived in Cebu to spend Christmas with his sister, Sandy, and all the CSC gang. It was so much fun to have him there, and the kids loved playing with him and chasing him around the house and yard. Greg would make several trips to Cebu over the years, usually at Christmas time, and he served as Santa Claus on a few occasions.

The year ended with lots of joy and celebration of God's goodness. Income for the year was $67,000. We were caring for more children and more were being placed for adoption. Our number of supporters was increasing in response to this growth. This was a time of stability and advancement for the ministry. But political developments in the Philippines were causing concern for us and were the precursor to sweeping changes that would threaten that stability.

Political Dissent

PRESIDENT MARCOS WAS ELECTED IN 1965. He maintained power through intimidation and military might. He declared martial law in 1975, just a few years before our ministry began. In spite of a strong military

One day I received a call from Bruce Barnes, a missionary friend in Ormoc City, Leyte. He told me of a little boy who was starving to death in a squatter area near their home and asked if there was anything I could do to help. So that night I got on a ship and sailed for Leyte. Early the next morning I arrived in Ormoc and went to see Bruce, who brought me to meet Larry Junel.

When we got to the house where he lived we saw him sitting in the corner. Junel lived with his auntie. She had several children of her own and she was not happy to have Junel to take care of. She was not kind to him. When it was time to eat, her kids got to eat first. If there was any food, left she would let Junel eat. Often there was nothing for him to eat, so he became malnourished. The auntie was embarrassed about him, so she made Junel sit in the corner of their hut so no neighbors would see him. He was sick, sad, and very malnourished when I saw him.

I asked the auntie if we could take Junel to Cebu and take care of him. She said, "Sigi. Bahala na. (I don't care.) He is not my child."

So that night I took Junel to the boat. He was six years old but was so weak he could not walk. He had infections in his ears and they smelled bad. He had a white film on his eyes from not having the right vitamins, so he had a hard time seeing. I carried him on the boat and we sailed for Cebu, arriving in the early morning. Junel was asleep when we arrived at CSC, so I carried him up the stairs to his new bed.

The next morning when Junel woke up he heard the sound of children playing downstairs. He crawled out of his bed and down the stairs to investigate. Right away he went and sat down in the corner. Auntie Marlys said, "No Junel, you don't have to sit there. You can play with the toys." Junel thought the toys were for the other kids, not him. We brought him to the toy box and he stared a long time before picking a few to play with.

When it was time for breakfast, the kids went to sit at the table and Junel went back to the corner to sit. He thought he would have to wait to eat. Someone said, "No Junel, you can eat with the other kids." Junel was so excited to see the food, and he ate and ate and ate. The aunties said, "Junel, you might get sick if you eat too much. There will be more food at lunch time." Junel could hardly believe there would be another meal when he could eat.

In the next weeks and months Junel started to feel better. He made friends at CSC. He was kind to everyone and happy to be in a place of love and kindness. His favorite toy was a plastic film canister. He was given a few coins, which he put inside. He liked to shake the canister so he could hear his coins inside. It was the first toy he'd ever had. We could hear him all over the house when he shook that canister.

In a couple months the staff decided that Junel was healthy enough to start school. We enrolled him in the Lahug Christian Kindergarten school, which was run by a missionary named Millie Nelson. One day she told the students about children in Mindanao who were very poor. They had no shoes or slippers. Millie said that they would take an offering for these kids so they could buy shoes.

That day after school the CSC kids were playing in the house. The aunties were worried because they didn't hear Junel shaking his plastic toy with the coins. They asked the driver if he forgot Junel at school, but he said he was sure he'd brought Junel home. Uncle Paul called Junel's name. After a few minutes Junel came down the stairs. Uncle Paul asked him where his plastic toy and coins were. Junel smiled and said that Miss Nelson had taken an offering for poor children who had no shoes, and he had given all his coins in that offering to help those children.

We were all amazed at Junel. Those few coins were the only things he'd ever owned. He was so proud of them. But now, when he heard about poor children without shoes, he gave all of it in the offering. He had a big heart of compassion and love. We've never forgotten that heart of Junel and his generosity. We want everyone at CSC to have that kind of heart.

Years later we started the Junel's Box program to remember and honor him by helping a poor family every year at Christmas. We deliver food, household supplies, and building materials to a family our social workers select. Our kids put money in the box from their saved allowances to help the family. They are encouraged to be generous, and many of them give all their savings. Every year we tell the story of Junel and provide our kids an opportunity to emulate him by giving back some of the blessings they have been given.

presence in the country, it was a time of relative stability in Cebu. Dissent was squashed. There were no credible elections. The economy was controlled by Marcos. On August 21, 1983, opposition leader Benigno Aquino, Marco's principle political opponent, was assassinated as he arrived in Manila from exile in the United States. In spite of the government's sham of an investigation, most people in the Philippines believed that Marcos had ordered the murder. This ushered in an era of open dissent. Political demonstrations were common, and there was widespread dissatisfaction

Ferdinand Marcos

with the continued strong-arm government of Marcos. Big changes were coming, and we were nervous about what might happen.

1984

THIS WAS A YEAR OF CONTINUED PROGRESS for the ministry. Jerry and Millie Healy made another trip to Cebu. Although they were both board members, their primary purpose was to be with us, and we had lots of great times.

During the summer, Mitch Ohlendorf returned to Cebu to work with the staff. Not only had he gotten hooked on the ministry as a part of the Central 7 the year before, he had fallen in love with one of our childcare workers, Ruth Deliña (daughter of Rebecca). They had been involved in a long-distance relationship after Mitch went back to Minnesota. Mitch returned to Corpus Christi with two-fold enthusiasm.

Typhoon Nitang

IN AUGUST TYPHOON NITANG hit the Philippines with a vengeance. Although tropical storms are fairly common in the country, this typhoon caused extreme wind and flooding damage when it crossed the Philippines,

60

resulting in 1492 fatalities, one of the Philippines' worst natural disasters in modern times. A total of 480,000 were left homeless. Among them were the caretakers of our land site in CarCar, the Ochea family, whose house blew away during the storm. Four of our childcare workers lost their roofs. We were able to help all of them restore their homes.

We received word that the area worst hit by Nitang was the province of Surigao, in Mindanao, where our good friend Prisco Allocod was from. Their entire village was damaged, and the Allocod home was destroyed. I shared this information with Cliff and the board, and he informed some of our supporting churches. As a result, two of the churches took special offerings, and $2,000 was raised to help out Prisco's village in Surigao.

In 1984 Typhoon Nitang left 480,000 people homeless.

As soon as it was safe to travel, Prisco and I went to Surigao, purchased rice and building supplies, and began distributing these to families in the distressed village. We concentrated on restoring the Allocod house but were able to help 12 other families with nails, thatched roofing, wood, and other construction supplies, as well as 50-kilo sacks of rice. We had little idea of what we were doing; we just rented a jeepney in Suriagao City, purchased as much as $2,000 would buy, and headed east for Orbiz Tondo, Prisco's village.

It was a thrilling experience and a blessing to be able to help in this way. But it was very hard work, and the place we were staying had no electricity for the entire time we were there. It was a real introduction to me of how Filipinos are affected by natural disasters and how helpless most people are to rebuild. It was just the first of several such storms we would experience in the coming years.

Tragedies

LATER THAT YEAR, the staff experienced another first when little Micah died. He was a newly admitted baby who had serious health problems from the first day he came to us. He was a premature baby who probably would have lived if an incubator had been available. It was a devastating blow to us. Although there was nothing we could have done to save him, we somehow felt guilty. Other children would die in the years to come, but because this was the first, it hit us the hardest. It took us several months to recover.

Another tragedy occurred when Marlys was asked to drive a neighbor to the hospital in the middle of the night. He was an 18-year-old boy who was having an asthma attack. Marlys drove as fast as she could, but the boy was dead by the time they got there. Together with Micah's death, this situation reinforced that, in spite of our best efforts, there were things we simply could not prevent, even with our access to the best medical care available in Cebu.

In November, our board in Minnesota made a decision that was to have big ramifications for our future. They voted unanimously to proceed with an expansion of the ministry by renting a house in the city. The intent was to provide facilities for us to significantly increase the number of children we could take in. The board approved a budget of $7,000 to make improvements to a house and an additional $1,200–$1,300 a month for the expanded program. This was a bold move by our board and a leap of faith for a small organization like ours. For many months we had felt cramped in the Bulacao home. We were excited about the board's decision and eager to get started looking for a second home for Corpus Christi children.

The board's faith was certainly bolstered by increased success in Cliff's fundraising efforts in Minnesota. Our 1984 income was $91,608. New people and churches were getting on board the CCSCC express.

1985

THIS WAS TO BE ONE OF THE MOST SIGNIFICANT YEARS in our history, with earth-shaking developments in our program, in Philippine politics, and in one of the families closest to our organization.

In April, Della Longakit made a trip to the United States to visit friends and take part in the CCSCC banquet in Minnesota. It was her first time in the United States. Sandy Swanson left for furlough in April to rest and assist the stateside office with promotion and administrative duties.

In June, two young people from Minnesota—Caroline Clark, sister of AnnAnn, and her friend Kim Eicher—arrived in Cebu for a summer's involvement at CCSCC. They enjoyed helping out with the kids and being with the staff. Later that summer, we received tragic news from the Eicher family that a boating accident in Canada had claimed seven lives, including Kim's younger brother Arman, whom Dennis and Sharon Eicher adopted from an orphanage in Manila. He was just 10 years old. We spent time comforting Kim. Instead of going home to Minnesota, she remained in Cebu until her parents came to the Philippines in July.

A Second Home

AUGUST WAS A RED-LETTER MONTH for the ministry as we started a second home for the care of children. We had found a suitable house in Sun Valley, near the heart of Cebu City and much closer to the medical facilities we used and the courthouse and other government offices we frequently visited. It was a large house with a yard and a room suitable for an office. More important, it had a downstairs room that would work as an infirmary for sick kids. There was also a small apartment downstairs for house parents. We applied for and received a license from the Department of Social Services as a childcaring organization, which meant we could process our own referrals and handle case management of all our children.

To help us facilitate that, we hired a licensed social worker, Carmelita Baya. This was an important development for us because she knew how to write social case study reports and could more easily navigate government agencies. She was a hard-working, dedicated woman who, although short in stature, was strong and aggressive when it came to

Carmelita Baya

sticking up for the best interests of our children. This hire had far-reaching significance for us; Carmelita would serve for 31 years as our social worker. When we eventually hired additional social workers to help with the case load, Carmelita became the supervisor, training them into the system of social work done in a pre-adoptive childcaring agency. Carmelita was a pacesetter at CCSCC, helping us become more professional as an organization. We were no longer totally dependent on the government for referrals or case management, and we could work directly with the courts and the intercountry adoption agency for placing our children.

For the time being, we decided to call the new home the Jackie Cherne Mission Home, named after the adoptive mother of one of our children and a member of our stateside board, who died of brain cancer in 1984. She was a gifted woman with a huge heart for children and adoption. She and her husband, John, had been involved in helping Crossroads Adoption Services get started and had adopted non-CCSCC children from other countries and domestically. Before she died Jackie wrote a book, *This Encircling Chain*, published by Mini-World Publications. Profits from the book's sale were donated to CCSCC. The home in Bulacao would continue to be known as the Corpus Christi Home.

With the opening of the Cherne Home in Sun Valley, we were able to double the number of children we could care for. Gloria and Manny Deliña, who were married a year earlier, became the house parents of this home, and we started filling it up with children. A child with significant special needs, Luke Baisic, was the first child we admitted to the Cherne Home. At this time the Philippine board decided that we should change our name from Corpus Christi Foundation to Children's Shelter of Cebu.

Two CSC children were brought to the United States for medical work and were eventually adopted in Minnesota. Ernesto, who had cerebral palsy, was brought for evaluation for surgery on his hips and legs. He was later admitted to Gillette Children's Hospital. He was later approved for adoption by Hank and Lavonne Reedy, joining Noah (formerly Edgar) and

Robbie in that family. In September, Marlys brought Maricel to Minnesota for corneal transplant surgery. These were exciting days for us as our prayers were answered for these two to get the best medical care available in the world.

On September 2, we admitted two boys who both had serious staph infections. The new isolation room was a lifesaver. Marlys wrote in a letter to her dad, "Having an isolation room is a luxury we have not enjoyed until now. It is just one more benefit of our new home and a way we can do a better job of taking care of the great kids God is bringing to us."

On October 16 we took in our 100th child, Reynaldo. It had taken us six and a half years to reach that milestone. We would reach our next milestone, 200 children in 1988, just three years later.

Things were beginning to accelerate in Cebu and with the stateside organization. We were making the transition from being a foster home to a professionally run agency with more qualified staff and workers, and with the capacity to take better care of the children referred to us. With additional workers, we found ourselves having more administrative tasks, particularly in the area of human resources. Having Mitch Ohlendorf around was a big help in the administrative end of the ministry, and we looked forward to July 7, when he would officially join the staff. He helped us set up an accounting system that would help satisfy requirements of the Philippine government agencies that regulated us, as well as the needs of the stateside organization for financial accountability.

Political Turmoil

POLITICAL TENSIONS WERE LOOMING LARGE in the Philippines during this year of growth for CSC. Public outcry continued over the murder of Benigno Aquino, whom many believed had been killed on orders of President Marcos. Under intense international pressure, he talked of having a "snap election" the following year. There were frequent rallies held in Manila, and Cory Aquino, the widowed wife of Benigno, was gaining popularity as a possible opponent of Marcos. Things were calm in Cebu, though there were some demonstrations that called for Marcos to resign.

As a staff, we were too busy to spend a lot of time worrying about the country's political situation. And as foreigners, we did not want to align ourselves with either side. But our hearts longed for change in the

Philippines and a subsiding of the corruption that contributed to suppressing so many people, particularly the poor. We knew the opposition was linked with the communist movement in the Philippines, whether legitimately or not, and we were reluctant to encourage any suspicion that we were aligned with that group.

These were complicated times in the country, with lots of uncertainty. The Philippines media contributed to the confusion, publishing frequent rumors and conflicting accounts. What made things even more unsettling for us was the fact that Ron Duterte was a member of Marcos' KBL party. And although his affiliation with Marcos was more a matter of political expediency (no one served in government without his say-so) than ideology, we wondered what a change in government would mean for our friend and advocate.

Another development during these days was a decline in peace and order in Bulacao. Although we were not always sure of the information we received, we were hearing of attacks by the New People's Army, the military arm of the Communist Party. These were reportedly happening in Talisay, just a few miles south of our home. There were killings and intimidation, and we wondered about how safe we were, particularly the Americans. Additionally, traffic in Cebu City had become a serious problem, particularly between Bulacao and the city center. Although it helped to have the new residence and office in Sun Valley, we were still wasting a lot of time sitting in traffic along the south highway, either going into the city or going home. Even as we were still getting settled into the Sun Valley home, we began thinking about the possibility of selling the Bulacao home and buying or renting another house in the city.

It was not without some nostalgia that we considered giving up the Bulacao home. It was the place where we started the ministry. We had invested a lot of time and effort in fixing it up. We were well-known there, and many of our workers lived nearby. We had a nice playground that the landowner next door let us use. We had survived a fire and watched the house get rebuilt. And we had so many memories of kids we had taken care of there. But we knew that the house was small and poorly located, so we balanced that knowledge with nostalgia.

A Year to Remember

ALTHOUGH 1985 WILL BE REMEMBERED for the expansion of our work with the opening of the Jackie Cherne Mission Home in Sun Valley, many other notable things happened during the year. Four CSC board members visited Cebu: Greg Swanson came at Christmas time in 1984 and stayed into the new year; Elizabeth Healy, Paul's sister, who was serving as a short-term missionary in Okinawa, came in June to spend a few weeks working with us. In November, board members Al and Betty Sannerud visited.

It was encouraging for the staff to have these visitors and was an indication of how the world was shrinking as air travel continued to improve, making a trip around the world easier. In the coming years hundreds of people would visit Cebu: family, board members, short-term helpers, and adoptive families.

We made new acquisitions: a Mitsubishi car purchased from Rod and Camille Henry; a computer, in memory of Arman Eicher; a stove, beds, cribs, desks, living and dining room furniture, a filing cabinet, air conditioner, bicycle, playground accessories, hardware, software, kitchenware, underwear . . . .

I wrote an article for the *CSC News* that summarized the incredible year of 1985. In addition to highlighting the expansion, I added these words:

> One cannot focus on the new without remembering the old. When we think of new staff we always think of the "old" staff members who helped us pioneer this work. We think of Kathy and Sned Flora, Jeff Snyder, and Kathy and Joe Grafft, who gave of themselves, investing their lives in what we are doing here.
>
> When we think of the new house we think of the old one in Bulacao, and how God touched the heart of Joe Lincoln to donate the money that allowed us to get started here. We think of those early days fixing up the house. When we think of the 100th child we think of the first, remembering how God blessed our home with AnnAnn, and we wonder how all the children who have left our care are doing.
>
> When we think of new possessions we think of the many things people have given over the years. We think of Greg Swanson and the TV, Ron and Jerry Swanson and the Ford Fiera, Ruth Lonquist and the

Maytag, the hundreds of diapers and towels from the Edstadts, Stan Carlson and the tools, First Baptist Church in La Crescenta and the appliances, and hundreds of other things we have been able to buy as the result of people giving.

Yes, the past and the present are tied together in our work here. And I do not think that there will ever be a year, a month or even a week or day in the future when we do not look back and think about 1985 and what a great year it was!

1986

THE STAFF CONTINUED TO ADJUST to a changing landscape, necessitating different responsibilities. Instead of doing most of the work ourselves, we were training and managing a growing group of Filipino workers hired to cook, clean, wash clothes, and provide childcare. The house parents in the Cherne Home bought food, going to the Carbon market to buy fruits, vegetables and meat, and to the supermarket for canned and dry goods.

The Carbon market

In January, Tony Swanson, Sandy's nephew, donated three months of his time for building, repairing, and designing at both homes in Cebu. Accompanying him was Sue Hintz, a speech pathologist who worked with individual children and trained the staff on basic speech therapy techniques. This type of volunteer service was to become a regular and valuable part of the ministry. God provided the people with the right skills at the right times. Future volunteers for Cebu would include teachers, therapists, computer experts, photographers, and others who loved CSC and wanted to help make it a better place.

Tony Swanson

More Politics

THE POLITICAL CHANGES WE ANTICIPATED came about in a big way. The snap election that President Marcos called became highly divisive and threatened to cause civil war. The Marcos government proclaimed him the winner, while the international and domestic agencies overseeing the elections proclaimed Cory Aquino the winner. Filipinos were outraged and took to the streets in massive and unprecedented numbers to protest the election results and to proclaim Aquino as the rightful president. The People Power movement was born. Marcos vowed to squash the rebellion and used military might to try and quell the dissent.

Things came to a head in February when protesters and the military came together on a famous highway (EDSA) in Manila. The protesters were led by a group of nuns and a host of people from all walks of Philippine life. The whole world watched as People Power played out on television around the globe. In the end, the tanks that were roaring toward the marchers stopped. The military desisted and violence was averted. Several of the military leaders defected and threw their support to Aquino, effectively sealing Marcos' fate. He escaped by helicopter to an American air base north of Manila and eventually was granted asylum in Hawaii with his family.

These were tense days for everyone in the country, though most of the action was centered in Manila. Because of the country's geography, with ocean separating the many islands, we felt far removed from the action. But even in the relative safety of Cebu City, these were not times to be taken lightly. Whether we liked it or not, we needed to make contingency plans in case the situation dictated that our American staff should leave the country. We needed an exit strategy. Mitch and I met with pastors Prisco Allocod and Romulo Alejado, two of our most trusted Filipino friends, to see if they would be willing to take over the reins of CSC should we have to leave. They were clearly taken aback by the question, thinking, like many Cebuanos, that things were not all that serious. They were willing to help but could not conceive how things would be at CSC without the Americans around. We wondered, too, not knowing if it would be possible to send money to the Philippines if things were in crisis mode there.

This experience made us more aware than ever of the need to develop Filipino leadership and financial reserves that could fund the ministry in the scenarios we were thinking through in 1986.

With Cory Aquino's new administration, there was euphoria throughout the country. People danced in the streets, signaling an end to fear and intimidation as they anticipated the rebirth of democracy. In the coming months Aquino would establish her government, including commissioning a convention to draft a new constitution. Things were happening fast, and it was impossible not to get caught up in the spirit of hope.

Things were not so positive for our friend Ron Duterte. Acquino replaced all the government officials identified with Marcos, whether they had been elected or not. Ron made a trip to Manila, and when he returned to Cebu his office had been broken into and a new person had been established as mayor. In spite of having been a good official with a heart for the people, he was out on his ear.

New Influence

OTHER DEVELOPMENTS WERE MORE POSITIVE FOR CSC. The new Minister of Social Welfare and Development, Mamita Pardo de Tavera, wanted to make the department more responsive to people's needs by empowering nongovernment agencies like ours to be real partners in providing programs and services. Minister Tavera called a meeting of all the childcaring agencies working in adoption at their headquarters in Manila. I was there representing not only CSC but some other agencies that were not able to attend.

The meeting started with Minister Tavera asking us what changes we thought were needed in the Ministry's relationship with the private sector, specifically in the area of adoption. Many people spoke, though we were all fairly shocked by the question and the Minister's willingness to seek our opinions. This was not what we were used to in the largely contentious relationship between government and nongovernment agencies we had experienced during the Marcos years. It seemed the People Power revolution had ushered in a new way of doing government, at least in the MSWD.

The discussions were glorious, and people talked enthusiastically and emotionally. Minnie Dacanay, who represented the Kaisahang Buhay Foundation in Manila and who had been a great friend to me and CSC, was standing in the back of the room. I learned that she was supposed to leave for the airport and depart for Oregon to start a job with Holt International. She was torn between needing to leave and wanting to be part of this historic meeting. She stayed as long as she could, leaving the rest of us to answer the question posed by Minister Tavera.

After the impassioned discussion, Minister Tavera announced that she would form a task force to assist her with the Ministry's adoption program. She said we could decide who would be on the task force but that there should be representation from different areas: Metro Manila, the Visayas (the collection of islands in central Philippines) and Mindanao (the southernmost major island). For many years we had endured the largely "Manilacentric" approach of government, even in social services.

Things got even more unbelievable for me when my name was mentioned for being the Visayan representative. I didn't realize how many friends I had in that room because the next thing I knew, my name was written on the board, an unopposed candidate. I honestly could not believe what was happening in that room. Some of the other members appointed that day were Marilyn Manuel of the Kaisahang Buhay Foundation; Lyra del Castillo of International Alliance for Children (yes, Marilyn and Lyra were the two ladies who had befriended Marlys and me as we slunk out of Mrs. Eufemio's office seven years earlier); Louise Lynip, a veteran American missionary from Bethany Home for Children in Mindanao; Rose Garcia, of the Ministry of Justice; Mrs. Lopa, a friend of Minister Taveras; and two nuns, Sister Amor Samonte and Sister Mary Concepta, both of Heart of Mary Villa in Malabon.

These sisters were with the order of the Good Shepherd and became good friends of mine. They shattered any of my preconceived notions about nuns and their willingness to cooperate with Protestants. While we have had rather rocky relationships with some sisters over the years, these women were open-minded, cooperative, and supportive. Sister Amor is about four feet tall and loved to stand next to me and laugh. She appreciated my sense of humor, and we respected each other. Once when we had a task force meeting in their convent, I made a big deal out of not knowing where I would find a men's bathroom. The nuns looked at each other and laughed. One said, "Of course there is one. Where do you think the priest goes when he is here?" Ignorant Protestant!

The area where the convent is located, Malabon, flooded whenever there was a storm. Once Louise and I took a cab to Heart of Mary Villa, and the car was creeping along with water rushing by on either side. The driver didn't know where he was going and took a wrong turn, which put us in the middle of a canal, with water pouring in the doors. I thought we were dead but Louise voiced a quick prayer, told the driver to turn around, and, amazingly, we were okay.

A representative from the MSWD, Lulu Balan-on, was also included in our group. She was to become a good friend to CSC over the years as she rose in the ranks of the Ministry. Except for Louise, Mrs. Lopa, and me, all task force members were professional social workers with years of experience working in adoption both in and outside of government.

The task force was to last for four years. Louise and I attended whenever we could, but the others met almost every week. The group reviewed home studies of adoptive applicants and child study reports of children ready for placement, made policy recommendations to the Ministry, and put together guidelines for adoptive matching, something that had never been done, except within the Ministry. It was a lot of fun working with these women, and I was to experience something I would see many times in child welfare circles in the future: being the only man in the room. But being on the task force was a great learning experience for me, being so new to adoption work. And being on the inside was beneficial to CSC as well, giving us credibility where we previously had none. It was always understood that the task force would be coterminous with Minister Tavera, so we were not surprised when the new Minister disbanded the group upon her ascension to office.

More Changes

TWO WEDDINGS BROUGHT EXCITEMENT to the staff. On April 5, John Cherne took Della as his bride in a rain-soaked ceremony at the Sun Valley home. On June 7, Mitch Ohlendorf married Ruth Deliña in a small wedding at Central Evangelical Free Church. Both weddings had great significance for CSC at this crucial time in our history. The Cherne wedding marked the end of Della's service to us, as she would soon leave for Minnesota to establish residence at John's large home in Minneapolis. The Ohlendorf wedding made Mitch and Ruth a team that was to have a profound influence on the work of CSC.

In February, Maricel had a successful corneal transplant in Saint Paul, the surgery performed by Dr. J. Daniel Nelson of St. Paul Ramsey Hospital. LaVonne Reedy, who fostered Maricel before and after the surgery, wrote this in the April, 1986 *CSC News*:

> Dr. Nelson, who has been working with Maricel since her arrival, scheduled her for a corneal transplant in February. The outcome was questionable. She had been blind so long, and Dr. Nelson wouldn't

know the extent of the damage until the surgery took place. As we gathered in pre-op, Cliff Danielson offered a beautiful prayer committing this little one and her medical team to God's will and care. Did we then dare expect anything less than the news that came out of surgery three hours later?

Dr. Nelson found the retina and nerves in excellent condition and was able to complete the transplant successfully. God's will and God's care! On Friday morning Dr. Nelson lowered the lights and removed the bandages from Maricel's eye. She blinked several times and then looked around the room. She was obviously able to see. The look of wonder on her face was one of the most beautiful things I have ever seen and a moment I will never forget. Doctors and technicians who watched with us shared our joy—and our box of Kleenex.

In April, the 1986 CSC banquet in Saint Paul was a huge success, with 800 reservations and an offering of $17,000. The theme was "A Time for Miracles." Our good friend Rod Henry spoke, and a choir of former CSC kids and their siblings sang. Our banquets had certainly "come of age." They were not only a major source of income but also a gathering place for our supporters in the Minnesota area, and a chance to reinvigorate them for the work going on in Cebu. Cliff Danielson and the board did a great job of planning these events. Bethel College was proving to be good venue for the banquets, and the cost was manageable. Generous sponsors were recruited to offset the cost of the events.

Sandy Swanson returned from a nine-month furlough to her job as childcare director. She had become an integral part of our staff, and we were happy to have her back. Change was happening on the CSC board. Jerry Healy, who had been the board chair since the beginning, took a leave of absence, and Randy Stroman, a young businessman who knew Marlys and Cliff from Constance Free Curch, became the new board chair.

In October, Lynn Burke joined the CSC staff. Lynn, the niece of Ray and Phyllis Burke, volunteer managers of the Baptist General Conference Mission Home in Cebu City, got to know about CSC through them. She was a great addition to our staff and was willing to do anything to help out. During her time in Cebu, several staff members escorted children abroad for adoption. So Lynn had to fill in as both childcare director and medical director in her first year on the staff. Lynn has a great sense of humor and a zest for life that made everyone at CSC love her and feel better about the ministry. Lynn would serve on the staff for a year, and then again several years later.

Another benefit of Lynn's being on the staff was to help fill in for Marlys and me, as we were planning a furlough during 1987. It was to be our second furlough, and we felt confident of the staff's ability to fill in and do well in our absence.

From an initial program of caring for a couple children at a time, the ministry had grown significantly in just seven years. During 1986 we cared for 53 children, with an average of 33 at a time. Of those 53, 17 were surrendered, 20 were abandoned, and 16 were neglected. (These were the primary categories we used for describing the situations of the children admitted to our care.) Fourteen children went for adoption (two to Europe and 12 to the U.S.), and seven were returned to their families. The average age of children admitted during the year was 24 months. Our group of children included six with special needs, a percentage that would hold true in later years, as well.

Income for December was $38,111, helping us accomplish our goals for 1986. From the early years of the ministry, the pattern had been established that we would need strong giving in December to make our budget for the year. Our supporters invariably rallied and provided in magnificent ways. It was not rare for us to raise more than 20% of our yearly budget in December, much of that coming in during the week after Christmas.

1987

WE SAW SOME LESSENING OF POLITICAL TENSIONS as Cory Aquino established herself as president. There was still lots of uncertainty, however, as the military's stance towards her government was unclear. There were frequent rumors of military coups and some actual insurrection, which made everyone nervous. In a country like the Philippines, the military holds many of the cards in terms of government stability, and the Philippine military had many factions and alliances that made things complicated. It took time for the military brass to give support to Aquino.

The CSC board was working to find new sources of income in response to the growth we were experiencing in Cebu. While Cliff remained busy doing presentations in churches and with civic organizations, the board established a sponsorship program called Foster Friends whereby people could sponsor a particular CSC child or children. It became a solid part of our support system.

In 1986 and 1987, several staff members were able to escort CSC children to the United States and Europe. Gloria brought two children, Mitch escorted three to the East Coast, Marlys brought Maricel to Minnesota, and Sandy and I were also able to travel with children. Sandy described her escorting experience as "one of the greatest experiences of my life." She told of the joy of "placing 'our' little boy into the waiting arms of his overjoyed adoptive mother" and how he "cooperated nicely by giving his new mother a big smile, even though he was very tired and a bit upset after nearly 24 hours of travel. It's hard for us to say goodbye to our CSC kids, but what a privilege and a joy to see them in families of their own."

Marlys had similar sentiments in escorting a child to Norway:

When we arrived in Oslo [she was accompanied by another escort who brought a different child], our hands were shaking with excitement, so much so that we could barely fill out the immigration slips. A social worker from the agency there met us right away to bring us to the parents. We went way upstairs in the airport. Every turn we made we expected to see them. Finally we came to a private room with glass doors. Behind those doors someone cried, "There they are," and those anxious and tearful parents froze in their spots when they saw us. In a matter of seconds, though, they snatched up their children and everyone was crying tears of joy. It was truly thrilling to be on the receiving end of the adoption process, an experience I will never forget.

A Second Furlough

IN APRIL, MARLYS AND I LEFT CEBU for our second furlough in Minnesota. We moved into an apartment in Saint Paul and made the sometimes difficult transition to life in the United States. Like other staff members on furlough, we experienced withdrawal from the activity and challenges of working with the children in Cebu. For us, telling people about the ministry was great, but not nearly as enjoyable as actually doing the work. But we knew that having Cebu staff in Minnesota was a shot in the arm for fund-raising, and seeing our families was important to us.

The economics of CSC were such that Marlys needed to work again on this furlough for us to make ends meet. The salaries we were paid in those days were sufficient for our living expenses in the Philippines, but not enough for a U.S. lifestyle. Dennis Eicher, our good friend, adoptive parent, and CSC board member, did us a great favor by giving me a part-time job doing data entry work for his consultancy company. This gave us the extra income that we needed to complete our furlough.

Dennis explained the spreadsheets he wanted me to make, using a program popular in the 80s called Lotus 1-2-3. I had no experience with that software, so I just nodded and said I'd do my best. I knew that my best wouldn't be nearly good enough on that project, so I called up my friend, Warren Hagfors, a computer guy with lots of Lotus experience. He invited me over and gave me a crash course in spreadsheets, and I was able to get through the project (with some additional help from Dennis.)

Warren Hagfors

I reflected on my life and the lives of the other staff and how we had to learn so many things and develop so many skills on the fly in Cebu, and how that enabled us to learn things quickly when we came back to the United States, a place we hadn't seen much of in eight years. It was a survival skill that benefited us in both countries and allowed us to live the life of missionaries.

During this time Dave and Nancy Healy continued editing the *CSC News*. One feature of the newsletter was a list of memorial and honoraria gifts to CSC, and the list seemed to grow with every issue. These gifts were a great encouragement to me and the staff. It was heartening to know that people felt positively enough about CSC to honor the life of a loved one in this way. We had established a credible organization doing important work well. We didn't spend a lot of time reflecting on these laurels because the ministry demanded our immediate attention, but we were aware that a growing number of people were attracted to CSC and the work we were doing with homeless children in Cebu. Marlys and I got a renewed sense of that as we traveled around the U.S., presenting the ministry in churches and homes.

The CSC board in Minnesota did some reorganizing during 1987. The goal was to transform the board from a group of family and friends of the staff to a more diverse, professional group. They knew that would take time. The board at this time was composed of Jerry Healy, John Cherne, Kathy Johnson, Shirley Graham, Warren Hagfors, Hank Reedy, and Greg Swanson.

Filipino Visitors

IN JULY A DELEGATION FROM MANILA CAME TO MINNESOTA, led by Philippine Intercountry Adoption Unit Director Lulu Balan-on. Lulu had been instrumental in several of our children with special needs being able to go to the U.S. for medical care and eventual adoption. In addition to Director Balan-on, the group consisted of friends from the task force, Louise Lynip and Sister Amor, as well as an attorney from the Department of Social Welfare and Development, Nympha Ward. CSC sponsored a dinner for the group in Crystal, Minnesota, which gave our board a chance to meet them and exchange ideas about adoption.

We were all surprised and chagrined when attorney Ward announced that she was not in favor of inter-country adoption of Filipino children, something quite amazing since the delegation was in the United States to meet with adoption agencies that worked with the Philippines, and to do accreditation of the agencies. The rest of the group was embarrassed by Ward's comments and apologized to us, though none was needed. We always knew that not everyone in the Philippines was in favor of adoption but didn't expect that opinion to be expressed that night.

On October 10, Ron Duterte made a surprise trip to Minnesota to visit Marlys and me and our parents, whom he had met in Cebu. He also met some of our board members and supporters. Later that month Marlys and I returned to Cebu after six months in the U.S. In those days it was fairly common for Cebu staff to take furloughs of less than a year. Being gone from Cebu for longer made things difficult for the remaining staff. As our staff members acquired school-age children, short furloughs became more difficult, so later ones were usually a year.

In November, Lynn Burke completed her year in Cebu and returned to Seattle. Everyone was sad to see her go and maintained hope that she might re-join us sometime in the future. We have always joked that Lynn never officially resigned from the staff but instead took an extended furlough. This furlough reached more than a decade when she came back to Cebu to work with us in 2000.

During 1987 we cared for 54 children—33 boys and 21 girls. We had 22 admissions during the year and 21 left our care, with 19 being adopted and two returning to their families. Of the adopted children, 15 went to the U.S., two to Germany, one to Australia, and one to Norway.

Income for 1987 was $164,491, which was in excess of our budgeted amount of $146,181. Part of the reason for the windfall was the success of the Foster Friends program, which Cliff and Marlys and I promoted extensively during the year and which had been advertised in the newsletter.

1988

THOUGH JUST THREE YEARS OUT from the momentous year of 1985, new facilities and programs were instituted that allowed us to improve our services and reach out to new children in creative ways.

Leaving Bulacao

IT WAS TIME TO BID GOODBYE to the Bulacao home. We had been looking for another house somewhere in the city, near the Cherne Home in Sun Valley. Early in the year we found such a house in Singson Compound in Guadalupe. It had six bedrooms, which was its major attraction. It was not a well-made facility, and it turned out that the water supply was inadequate for our needs. It didn't have a yard but was near places where the kids could play. We moved the children from Bulacao to Singson on April 21. Sandy Swanson became the house mother for this facility.

I thought about Sned Flora the day we moved out of Bulacao. He and I had worked with Jeff Snyder screening that house, with precious little carpentry ability among us. I remembered taking kids on wagon rides with him around the neighborhood. I remembered the day we went to the nearby basketball court and I joined a pick-up game while he watched in horror as I "hot dogged" it, pretending I was a Harlem Globetrotter instead of just fitting in with the game.

Sned and Kathy Flora

I remembered his dad coming to visit and regaling us with his repertoire of Cebuano and English love songs, and how once he was joined by Ron Duterte, who knew all the same songs. I remembered Sned riding his noisy Suzuki motorcycle around the neighborhood and annoying one of the neighbors.

So many of my memories of that house and community were linked with Sned, and I had feelings of thankfulness for him and the others who helped us get started back in the early years but were no longer with us at CSC: Kathy, Della, Gloria, Jeff, Joe and Kathy Grafft, and others. I thought of the fire that could have destroyed that house and all of us, and how the Pardo Fire Department put it out in minutes. I thought of the Bible studies and worship services we had in that old house that paved the way for the Bulacao Free Church, and the people who came to know Jesus because of those efforts. I thought of the great kids we raised in that home, and those who were adopted into families around the world.

I cried that day for the innocence of four young Americans who came to Bulacao to do something bigger than all of us combined, who had the naivety to think we could make a difference in the world. I cried as I thought about the simple life we had in Bulacao, and what we gave up when we grew into a bigger and different kind of ministry. I cried as I thought about a group of wide-eyed, unqualified young people whose paltry loaves and fishes were multiplied by a loving, forgiving, omniscient God who called us, equipped us, and blessed us in Bulacao and beyond.

With the move from Bulacao, Marlys and I rented a house in Sun Valley, the very house that Wes Hagen used to rent, and the place we moved into following the fire. It was quite a transition for us after living in the Bulacao house with lots of children for nine years. In the coming years we would share the house with other staff, with short-termers, and eventually, with our daughters. But at first, it was just us, and the small house seemed like a mansion. We were just five minutes from the office in Sun Valley and ten minutes from the new place in Singson.

We were thrilled with a timely and much-needed donation of a brand-new Mitsubishi Sunshine coach van from Variety Clubs, International. We were able to get a dozen kids in there, and it was air conditioned. That van was to last us for several years and enabled us to haul hundreds of children around Cebu City and the entire province of Cebu. During a trip to Vancouver, Marlys and I were able to meet with some Variety Clubs leaders to thank them for the donation and to tell them what a blessing the van was to our ministry.

As of April we had 61 sponsors and 71 sponsorships in our Foster Friends program. At that time we had 37 children living in our two houses.

In May, Marlys and I made a trip to Minnesota to meet with the board to talk through some problems that had cropped up between the staff and some board members. This was the first such conflict that we'd had, and it involved differences of opinion about how the ministry should be promoted. We had some frank discussions and were able to find common ground. I returned to Cebu on the 25th, but Marlys remained in Minnesota for a few weeks to see Cliff through triple bypass and valve repair surgery

A New Venture

DURING 1988 WE HAD BEEN THINKING about how to complement our program by providing services to help mothers keep their children. One idea was a childcare center to enable single moms to support their families by our caring for their young children during working hours. There was no such center in the city, so we would be breaking new ground. Our goal was to help women keep their children rather than having to surrender them for adoption or neglect them while they were working or looking for work.

On September 6 we opened the Magbalantay Child Care Center in the heart of Cebu City. We chose a downtown location so it would be easily accessible to the mothers we would be serving. They could drop their children off in the morning and pick them up after work. We provided food, milk, vitamins, changes of clothes, books, and toys. Gloria Deliña became the manager, Pat Quijano was the teacher, and several women were hired as childcare workers. Our social worker held regular group meetings with the mothers, helping them solve problems and learn to trust God.

Around this time Mitch and I were working on a five-year plan for the ministry, the first long-range planning that had ever been done by CSC. With the cost of residential care being high because of its labor-intensive nature, we were thinking of expanding by adding additional childcare centers and feeding programs in poor communities.

Other Developments

• Kim Eicher started a one-year volunteer assignment in Cebu, doing childcare work in our two houses.

• We named the new house in Singson Compound the Arman Eicher Mission Home, after the adopted son of Sharon and Dennis Eicher, who died in a 1985 boating accident. Dennis and Sharon were in Cebu when we made that announcement. It was an emotional time for all of us and seemed like a great way to honor Arman's memory.

• We built a playground on a parcel of land right across from the Eicher home. The owner of that land graciously allowed us to put a fence around the site and make improvements to the lawn. We had a "grand opening" for the playground with the staff, the local board, the landowner, and the children in attendance.

With the move out of Bulacao and into Singson, with the opening of the Magbalantay Center and plans being made for future expansion, it was clear to everyone at CSC that the ministry was moving quickly ahead. But we all knew that for that to happen, new supporters would be needed back in the United States. And there were questions surrounding the stateside organization, with Cliff's deteriorating health. The year ended with a mixture of optimism and consternation as we approached the 10-year anniversary of CSC.

1989

BOTH STAFF AND BOARD WORKED to prepare for the big anniversary. There was much to celebrate. An article in the April *CSC News* highlighted the growth since 1979.

1979	1989
Income: $19,000	Budget: $193,000
One home	Two homes
Four children	36 children (180 cared for)
No vehicle	Three vehicles
100 on mailing list	4,300 receiving newsletter
No adoptions	Adoptions in 9 countries

Certainly these were not the only changes in 10 years. Our expenses had grown significantly, and 1989 was a time of economic uncertainty in the Philippines and the States. We started 1989 in a financial hole, with 1988 income of $167,797, well under our budget. Inflation in both countries was eating away our resources. The early months of 1989 were weak in terms of income, so some disbursements had to be curtailed.

With limited reserves on either side of the ocean, we were in serious financial difficulty. The headline in the August 1989 edition of the *CSC News* trumpeted "Crisis Time." In response, Cliff and the board had a phone-a-thon and sent out strong appeals to our constituency. Although the staff in Cebu wasn't privy to all the financial details in Minnesota, we knew things were tenuous. I wasn't gripped by fear, however. We had started with nothing, flying to Cebu with little more than the money in our pockets, representing a stateside organization that had only the money they could send each month and nothing else. We had learned a little bit about faith.

But our situation in 1989 was different because we had 36 children depending on us for their lives. That thought weighed heavily on my mind in those days, and every day since. Our responsibility was huge. We weren't just managing money and physical assets, but human lives. And it wasn't just the children living with us. We employed many workers, most of whom were the sole bread winners in their families. We had a web of dependencies, and needs didn't lessen during economic downturns.

So life went on, even during the crisis. One day we received a writ of habeas corpus from the Regional Trial Court. We had taken in a child whose birth mother was mentally ill, and we had heard that she was trying to get him back. Carmelita, our social worker, had done an assessment of her and found that she was living on the streets, existing day to day by begging. She simply could not care for the baby. We called up Ron Duterte and prepared for the next morning in court. When the hearing started, the judge read the complaint and told us to bring the child to the front. Ruth Ohlendorf was holding the baby and brought him up for the judge to see. Then, without letting Ron say a single word, he ordered us to return the child to the mother and even gave us an admonition about human rights violations. We were shocked. Ron was irate. However, there was nothing we could do but kiss the baby goodbye with a prayer for his safety.

A Faithful Response

MEANWHILE, OUR FAITHFUL SUPPORTERS in the U.S. were responding to the financial appeals. The deficit was made up and much hope was restored. We had been forced to send out what I considered to be "panic appeals," due to the severity of our situation. We didn't want to be like those organizations that regularly sent out such appeals, begging for money. We knew that people can get weary from such letters. But we hadn't done this before, and we had the credibility with our supporters that allowed us to be straightforward about our needs when it was appropriate. Everyone at CSC was thankful for the generous response of our donors. It certainly was not the last time we would have to present them with pressing financial needs, but it was the first time, and it was a learning experience for us, seeing how great our God is, and how responsive and generous our supporters were.

The financial vulnerability of CSC was perhaps more pronounced because of our expansion in Cebu. The Magbalantay Center was just a year old, and we had reached our capacity of clients. In addition, we hoped to open another center that would provide nutritional assistance to children in one of Cebu's largest squatter areas. The Kahangawa Center would be in Barangay Tejero, a neighborhood near where our social worker Carmelita Baya lived. The plan was to have a feeding program in the public school there, preparing the food at the center and having informational seminars for mothers about their children's nutritional needs. We conducted weighings in the school to identify the most needy children and hired another social worker to handle the program.

The one-year anniversary of Magbalantay was celebrated by mothers served by the center. Most of them took a day off work to attend the special program, and several gave testimonies how their lives had improved. Although there were many challenges working with these women, whose lives were difficult and complicated, and who often lacked the confidence to get ahead in the working world, there were enough success stories to inspire us to continue the program. We knew from the start that the two centers were not CSC's first priority, and should financial difficulties continue, they might need to be scaled back or discontinued.

Distress in Opol

IN JUNE WE ADMITTED A SIBLING GROUP of seven children, the largest sibling group we had ever taken in. We'd received a request from the children's uncle and from Roger Tompkins, a missionary friend of the family who was also close to CSC. They reported that the children's parents had been massacred by communist guerrillas in Mindanao and had been split up among their relatives.

I decided to go to Mindanao and see the situation before we made any decision about admitting them. It was suggested that I go to the village of Opol and talk to the grandfather. Some of the children were staying with him. My trip to Opol became an experience I never wanted to have again.

The village of Opol was about an hour and a half from Cagayan de Oro, a sizeable city in northern Mindanao. I had been to visit Bethany Christian Home in Talakag, Bukidnon, and their driver, Greg Longcob, was kind enough to drive me to Opol. On the way there I experienced some stomach discomfort and asked Greg if there might be a bathroom along the way. He looked at me like I was totally crazy, laughed, and said yeah, there were many opportunities, pointing to the side of the road. Ah, those opportunities. I said no thanks, and we continued towards Opol, with my stomach disorder getting more and more pronounced as we went.

When we got to Opol, I was in bad shape. The grandfather's hut was in the middle of a big field, and when I asked him if there was a bathroom there, he pointed at a small bush at the side of his house. I was starting to sweat and felt like I was close to exploding. I asked if any of his neighbors had bathrooms. He thought for a minute and said that I should follow him. He headed toward a group of houses about 50 meters away. I asked if he had any toilet paper. He said he did, went back to his hut, and came out with two pieces. I was now hunched over with intestinal pain and was sweating like a pig. I looked back and there were about 25 people behind me. I stopped to let them get by on the narrow path we were traversing. They also stopped, so it was clear that they were following me, not being used to seeing tall Americans with stomach discomfort.

Finally the grandfather stopped at a small hut and asked the owner if I could use his bathroom. He said sure, and took me to a small area behind his hut that was partially enclosed by bamboo slats. The wall was about four feet high. I looked back and the number of my followers had swelled to at least 50. I went inside the enclosure and started taking stock of my situation. I had to go desperately, and it was not going to be pretty. I had two squares of toilet paper. Everyone who wanted to watch me could, including children since the bamboo slats were not close together. But I didn't have any other options.

People surrounded the enclosure , four or five deep, their numbers now more than a hundred. There was an air of anticipation in the crowd. The "toilet" itself was a hole dug in the ground, with a ring of cracked cement around it. I could tell that it had been used, probably quite recently,

86

Arlene was one of our first children at CSC. She was a beautiful two-year-old who had undergone cleft lip repair before coming to live with us. She was an energetic and precocious child who enjoyed the attention she received in our Bulacao home. We called her Arlene Darling.

Another child in the home at that time was Julio, who had epilepsy and suffered from frequent seizures. When a seizure was coming on he had what is called an "aura," a kind of pre-sense that he would be having a seizure. He would omit a guttural groan that was almost as loud as a scream. We could always tell when Julio was about to have a seizure, and we would run to see that he was okay and wasn't injuring himself.

Arlene was a bright and observant child who noticed how Julio's seizures brought him lots of imme-

diate attention. One night we heard a loud groan from the kids' bedroom. We dashed upstairs to check on Julio and saw that he was fine. No seizure. We looked around the room and saw Arlene grinning in her bed. She had imitated Julio's aura to cash in on some of that staff attention for herself!

Twenty-eight years after Arlene left CSC for adoption, we heard from her. She had not been given information about where she lived prior to adoption, but had a picture that went along to her adoptive family showing her walking with me and four other kids outside our home in Bulacao. That picture was eventually made into the CSC logo.

All Arlene could remember about the Philippines was the name Auntie Sandy. She went online and googled "orphanages in the Philippines." The first one that came up was the CSC site, and she saw our logo and recognized it from the picture she had. "That's me," she cried out at her computer screen. She also found some information on Auntie Sandy, as well as our address in Cebu. She wrote us a beautiful letter, wondering if anyone remembered her. I think she was surprised to learn that she was very well-remembered. She told us she would soon celebrate her 30th birthday and would like to have it in Cebu with us.

by a number of people, possibly ten. Maybe more. I'll stop the story right there, for the sake of discretion. Suffice it to say that I was able to get through that humiliating situation and get back to what I had gone to Opol for in the first place. We ended up getting those seven kids, and I escorted them back to Cebu to live in the Cherne Home.

The Decade Winds Down

ALTHOUGH THE AQUINO GOVERNMENT had done much to improve peace and order, there were ongoing tensions, especially in Mindanao. In addition to the communist rebels who preyed on individuals and communities, Muslim separatists were fighting with the Philippine military, and there were many instances of hostage-taking in the region. Fortunately, our dealings in Mindanao were restricted to the northernmost provinces, which were relatively peaceful.

Sandy took a furlough in 1999 and escorted a child to Tennessee on her way home. While she was gone, Mitch and Ruth became house parents at the Eicher Home. Carlo and Elma Paña were hired to be the Cherne Home house parents. They had been teaching at a Bible college in Mindanao before coming to work for us. Nancy Bartiana was hired as the social worker to handle client mothers at the Magbalantay Child Care Center. She had been working with World Vision.

We had some very dear visitors during the year. Millie, Jerry, and Elizabeth Healy came for a few weeks. They were amazed at how things had changed in the few years since they'd been to Cebu, in our growth and in additional responsibilities we had assumed with the expansion. Other visitors were Warren and Marie Hagfors, who also visited the many friends they had made in Cebu managing the EFC Mission Home.

Cliff continued making presentations in churches. With the help of Larry Hansen, CSC produced several videos to promote the ministry and the Foster Friends program. Cliff could send these videos to places where he was not able to go, or show them as a part of his presentations. During the year he traveled to North Dakota, Connecticut, New Hampshire, and Massachusetts, as well as all over Minnesota.

In December one of our babies, Arnold, died. He had been sick, so Marlys brought him to our house for the evening. His condition worsened during the night, and he was fighting for every breath, so we rushed him to Cebu Doctors Hospital. He never recovered and passed away in the early morning hours. We were devastated, feeling helpless watching him die on that hospital bed. Was there something different we should have done?

In the morning Marlys went home to change, and I had the job of going to the Cherne Home to tell the workers and children that Arnold had died. It was an incredibly emotional time for them and for me. I will never forget when one of the childcare workers asked me who was with Arnold. I thought that she might not have understood that he had died. But she had. In Philippine culture, you do not leave the body alone. Even in the morgue someone from the family would be with him, and that would hold true in the funeral home, too. The workers probably thought we were heartless to have left him there, and a few of them hurried to the hospital to be with him.

This experience highlighted for me the cultural differences that separated us. Many times over the years we would be made aware of the vast differences in how we viewed life and death. Sometimes we were lured into thinking we were all the same, especially in a country as westernized as the Philippines, where many people speak English and enjoy American cultural exports like television, movies, and music. But we were often reminded that we are very different, too, and that we as Americans had much to learn and many adjustments to make.

As 1989 came to a close, several of the kids got very sick, including Luke, our child with significant special needs who had been in and out of the hospital since coming to us. At this time he was battling for his life. I called for a special prayer meeting for the staff and some missionary friends who were close to the ministry. We petitioned God on behalf of Luke and the other children. I wanted us to reflect on Luke's life and what we had learned from him.

Luke was a battler, having been near death several times. He was seven years old but had never had any voluntary movement of his arms or legs. He needed to be fed, changed, and dressed, and would need that for the rest of his life. God was using Luke to teach us many things, not the least of which was to be thankful for all that we had been given, the ability to walk and talk and take care of ourselves. As we prayed for Luke we thanked God for his life and for the chance we had been given to care for him. We really didn't expect him to make it through that night. But amazingly, when Marlys went to the hospital the next morning, he gave her a huge smile, as if to say, "I'm still here!"

A group from Cherry Hills Community Church in Denver sent Christmas gifts to us for all the children. This became a yearly blessing, not always from Cherry Hills, but other groups or individuals would step up to bless our kids at Christmas time. This year Warren Hagfors played the role of Santa Claus, handing out the gifts from Cherry Hills and getting a close look at the kids' smiles.

We were all learning important lessons every day. One was that there were many ups and downs in our work, which would always be the case. The same people and things that brought joy one day could bring heartaches the next. The children were a source of great joy, but sometimes we were brought to our knees by their problems and misbehavior. Our workers were the backbone of the ministry, but some of them caused headaches and administrative difficulties. We could be sailing along with seemingly no financial cares in the world, only to be grounded by economic downturns. We could think we had everything going in the right direction with the government agencies we worked with, and then something would happen to leave us shaking our heads in frustration.

Our work was a roller coaster ride, and we had to learn to take a step back from the ride and look at the bigger picture. Even during the difficult times of 1989, we needed to look at where God had brought us during the 10 years of our ministry. Our road had been both uphill and downhill. People we thought would be with us for the long run weren't, while others came along and filled the gaps. We had overcome typhoons, a fire, inflation, failed fundraising efforts, a People Power revolution with a near-complete change of government, heartaches caused by people who seemed to be working against us, cultural differences, and major medical problems with our children. But in spite of those setbacks, God allowed us to get started, to grow and develop, and to fulfill our goal of being a source of hope to children in need.

We were able to grow significantly in size and influence, place children with adoptive families around the world, start a church, and have a positive influence in three communities. And that was just the Cebu side of things. Stateside, we were able to build a solid support system, increase our income significantly by fundraising and friend-raising, develop a sizeable network of volunteers, establish an excellent staff and board of directors, create a successful annual banquet, and maintain integrity in our financial dealings. Truly, God had done much in and through us. And though I hesitated to use the term "miracle" to explain the ministry, His hand was clearly on the people and circumstances of our first 10 years in Cebu. We looked to the next decade with confidence and hope.

THE 1990s

During difficult times we fall back on the knowledge that
hundreds of people are with us in this work.

1990

THE YEAR BEGAN with the news that Cliff Danielson's health was not improving and that he had resigned as executive director. He would stay on as an ambassador of good will and would still make some presentations for CSC. Dennis Eicher agreed to serve as interim executive director while the board searched for a permanent replacement for Cliff.

Financial Challenges

THIS NEWS CAME while we were bracing for some major financial challenges. Income for 1989 had been $193,000, but our board adopted an aggressive budget for 1990. In addition to needing to raise additional funds for the two new centers, the board wanted to improve compensation for the Cebu staff. We had started our careers as essentially volunteers for the first few years. Salaries were increased in the mid-80s but at a very modest level. If CSC was going to last, we would need to be paid more than we were so that we could build up retirement income and have families and set up households. People had been generous to all of us when we were on furloughs, providing places to live, furniture, and transportation, but this could not continue indefinitely.

To fund a growing ministry and begin to provide better salaries, the CSC board adopted a 1990 budget of $351,000. What a step of faith that was. But with Cliff stepping down and nobody in place to take over his fundraising duties, things didn't look too rosy as we headed into the new year. Little did we know the amazing things that would happen in the coming months and years as God rewarded that faith and provided "exceedingly above all that we ask or think."

We began 1990 with a growing desire to build new facilities. With the two rented homes at or above capacity, there were several motivators for this desire: We were increasingly unable to admit children who really needed our care, and we were becoming convinced that the quality of care we desired for our children was compromised by the lack of space and the fact that our two homes were not close to each other. Our situation, with two separate small houses with little play space outside in either, was far from our initial vision of what our home for children would look like. And we were always worried about rents being raised or the properties being sold out from under us. We believed that if CSC was going to last and thrive into the future, we needed a place of our own.

A dinner honoring Cliff was held on February 24 at McGuires in Arden Hills. I was in the U.S. for the dinner because I had escorted a child to meet her adoptive parents in Chicago. I was able to share the love and appreciation the Cebu staff had for Cliff and all he had done to further the ministry. It was a good evening, highlighted by a video that included words of appreciation from staff and kids in Cebu, the primary beneficiaries of Cliff's stewardship of time and talent.

There were some positive things at work on the fundraising horizon. Sandy's furlough would include the first part of 1990, and Mitch and Ruth would follow, so they could do presentations and visit the supporting churches. We had faithful volunteers producing our newsletters and handling the mailings. Dennis Eicher was providing free office space, and our Foster Friends program was growing. But the budgeted amount for 1990 was daunting without a full-time fundraiser. By mid-year we were already behind our income goals by almost $40,000, in spite of being well ahead of where we were at that point in 1989.

But the work went on in spite of this. Mitch and Ruth began their furlough in April, and Sandy returned to Cebu in June. To help out in the Ohlendorf's absence, Ray and Phyllis Burke came for a four-month stint. They assisted me with office duties, and Ray filled in as a much-needed driver. Ray also served as the CSC photographer, which was his beloved hobby.

Warren and Marie Hagfors, whom the CSC staff met when they were guesthouse managers for the Evangelical Free Church mission, followed the Burkes for a few months to help in the office. Warren introduced us to the world of computers and even donated a portable Compaq to CSC. He taught us word processing and spreadsheets and gave us software (Wordstar and Lotus 123) to get us started. This was a huge step for us in managing information and communications for our growing ministry. Warren was generous with his time and talent, and patient in dealing with our group of computer illiterates.

CSC was growing fast, and in addition to computer use for record keeping, we purchased another vehicle. With the van that was donated by Variety Clubs, International, we had three vehicles to haul supplies, bring social workers on their trips to visit children's families, and bring CSC residents to school and to doctors visits.

Warren and Marie Hagfors

As a new decade started, because CSC's medical department was expanding its services, medical costs were a bigger part of our budget. In a given month we spent money for chest x-rays for all older children being admitted, immunizations, antibiotics, vitamins, dental visits, and hospital admissions. Because CSC was seeking adoption for most of our children, extensive medical reports were needed, which took up a lot of our time

During May eight children left for adoption, our biggest placement month by far. They were placed in Tennessee, Wisconsin, Illinois, Norway, and the Netherlands. The 11th annual CSC banquet saw 570 people attend and an offering of $14,331. The theme was "To God be the Glory," an important thought for all of us. As we were attempting to build a quality ministry, we needed to take time to bless the Lord of CSC, always giving Him the glory. Performers from the Cultural Society of Filipino Americans did several cultural dances, including the national dance, tinikling.

Buying Land

AROUND THIS TIME WE HAD A CALL from Arvid Olson, a short-term missionary with the Evangelical Free Church Mission (now Reach Global).

He told us that a friend of his, Harry Schmidt, was going to visit Cebu and that we should "roll out the red carpet for him." He said Harry was involved in building projects for ministries to children and was interested in CSC.

Jeannie Schotz, Marlys Healy, Harry Schmidt, Sandy Swanson

We did roll out that carpet! We spent a few days showing Harry around and sharing our dream of having facilities of our own to better care for our kids. On his last day in Cebu, Mitch, Ron Duterte, and I met with Harry at Ron's house. Harry asked what our plans were for putting up our dream houses. I told him we were thinking of having work teams come out from the states or Canada for the construction. Harry started shaking his head and finally said, "That is not a good idea." I will confess that I was thinking, "Who is this guy? He's here for a few days and is telling us how to do this building project?" My questioning mind was soon silenced when Harry said, "I will build your orphanage. If you can secure the property, my family will build." All three of us were dumbfounded. Nobody spoke for quite a while. Finally I croaked, "Aurrgaeeahaa. Harry, thank you so much. We'll get that land. "

So we started scouting for a piece of property in Cebu City. We looked at many sites, but they were all too expensive or not in a good location for a children's home. We wanted to be near the hospitals and government offices we patronized and close to where most of our workers lived. After months of scouting we finally settled on a piece of land in Banawa Hills. The property was owned by the family of Pastor Lucas's wife, Ana. Although not Christians, they were understanding of our needs and limitations. With Lucas's help, we negotiated a fair price. The property was 4,700 square meters, and we agreed to pay P500 per square meter, or around U.S. $84,000 for the lot. We didn't have this money, but we went ahead and put down a non-refundable deposit and started thinking and praying about how we would secure the balance.

Sonny Boy

ON JULY 22 OUR DEAR SONNY BOY DIED. He had put up an incredible fight for 72 hours, battling pneumonia, amoeba, and internal bleeding. He died in the intensive care ward of Cebu Doctors, surrounded by staff and child-care workers. Sonny was four months old when he died and had been at CSC for two of those months. Except for a few days, he was sick his entire life. Upper-respiratory problems and significant infections raged throughout his body. His mother had died shortly after giving birth to him.

In an article in the October *CSC News* I wrote about losing Sonny Boy:

> The grief in losing a little child is not so much for the life that we had come to love, although that is part of it. We grieve because he didn't live long enough for us to really know him. His whole life was spent crying in pain due to his various infections. He never had a chance to enjoy anything. Each time he looked at us, it seemed, there were tubes and needles sticking into him, or new ones being prepared to go in. It is hard to imagine why he would cling to such a painful life. Does this tell us something about the preciousness of life, or just about Sonny? Or does it tell us about both?

A Challenging Year

IT WAS PROVING TO BE A TOUGH YEAR in many ways. There was still a lot of political instability in the Philippines. The Aquino government was facing opposition from within, and there were rumors of military coups throughout the year. We were short-handed in the Philippines, with staff members having furloughs. Money was tight, as income lagged way behind expenses and reserves were few. Many children had been sick, and losing a child had been devastating. There was some discouragement among the staff and board members. Dennis Eicher, interim executive director—in an article in the *CSC News* entitled "Must We Turn Them Away?"—cited my June report to the board, where I wrote:

"We thank the Lord for each of you, and for the things you do to support this work. We are filled to overflowing with children, and we get more referrals all the time. There is a family of four children, malnourished and left to wander the neighborhood begging for food. We would love to take care of them, but we just don't have room." Dennis went on to write,

"I haven't been able to get that short paragraph out of my mind; and tears come again to my mind, even as I write this article.

"Having been privileged to visit the CSC Homes in Cebu several times, I have seen first-hand some of the many children who live alone or in small groups on the streets of the city. Coming out of restaurants or stores late at night, it's the norm to encounter groups of children who are struggling to survive, largely through what they can beg or steal.

"You and I, even together, cannot solve the problems of the countless malnourished children around the world. We can't even solve the problems in Cebu. In fact, while it hurts to admit it, judging from Paul's report, we are falling short of meeting all the needs that present themselves on our very doorstep. I don't mean for this realization to become a source of discouragement. I would rather wish that it would become a source of inspiration and challenge to allow God to guide us in the stewardship of the resources He has entrusted to us so that we might be used to meet the needs of at least a few."

In November, Gary Bawden began work as CSC's new executive director. Gary was with Midwest Challenge, an organization working with troubled youth. Concurrently, he was senior pastor of Grace Alliance Church in Forest Lake, Minnesota. Gary would work part-time for CSC while maintaining his other jobs. The plan was for him to travel to Cebu in January to meet the staff, children, and Philippine board to learn more.

In early November, super typhoon Ruping hit Cebu with high winds and extensive flooding. Many homes and businesses were destroyed, and 88 ships in Cebu harbor sank as a result of the wind and waves. Our property was not damaged significantly, but many of our workers lost their roofs and had water damage.

During this time one of our residents, Joemar, who was developmentally delayed, got dengue fever. As his platelet count continued to go down and was approaching critical levels, we were told he would need a platelet transfusion. Because of the crisis surrounding the typhoon, there was no blood available at the hospital or the Red Cross. Mitch and I called friends and other missionaries to see if someone had the right blood type and would be willing to donate for Joemar. One of our workers said he had a friend who would give blood, but he showed up drunk to the hospital and was rejected as a donor.

We were getting desperate. Someone suggested that we try the army camp, having heard that the soldiers are sometimes recruited for blood donating. We drove to the camp well after midnight and talked to the officer in charge. He agreed to our request and woke up the whole group and told them they would be leaving immediately on a mercy mission. They piled in our jeep and we brought them to the hospital for blood type screening. Only one of the soldiers had the right blood type. But when we got a 500 ml blood bag from the pharmacy, the sergeant said it was too big and that his soldiers could only donate 250 ml. The hospital pharmacy only sold 500 ml bags and they could not be used for smaller amounts of blood.

While the soldiers waited, Mitch and I went all over Cebu City in search of smaller blood bags, but we found none. We eventually had to bring the now angry group of soldiers back to their barracks. When we got back to the hospital, Marlys told us that Joemar's platelet count had started to go up so the transfusion would likely not be needed.

Cliff Danielson, who had been given the title executive director emeritus by the board, experienced major health problems and was hospitalized three times with congestive heart failure. Due to the typhoon, we were without power and phone service for several weeks, so Marlys was unaware of Cliff's hospitalization. One day, out of nowhere, she received a phone call from Warren Hagfors in Minnesota, telling her of Cliff's situation. It was the only call we had received for months, and after hearing from Warren we didn't get any calls for another month. God had provided a ten-minute window for him to reach us. So Marlys went to Minnesota in late November to help care for her dear dad. During that time Cliff moved to the Ebenezer Tower in Minneapolis to be closer to the doctors and hospital he would need during his recuperation.

At Christmas time in Cebu, a new tradition was started. The children were encouraged to save some of their allowance to buy gifts for needy families. Our kids come from histories of great need, so we felt it was important for them to think of others who live in similar circumstances. The children were very excited about this possibility and saved 2,000 pesos on their own. Rebecca Deliña chose six families in Bulacao she thought would benefit the most from the kids' generosity. Auntie Sandy brought six kids to the store to shop for the gifts for these families. She explained the shopping spree in a CSC News article entitled "A New CSC Tradition":

> The kids each had their own cart and tried hard to keep track of how much they were spending. The budget was limited to 300-400 pesos per family, depending on the family size. By the time we were finished (two hours later) the whole store was aware of what the kids were doing. One lady even bought a can of sardines for each of the families. We were able to buy enough for four or five meals for each family, plus some goodies. The kids were great shoppers, choosing each item so carefully.
>
> Some of the older girls made nicely decorated cookies and donuts for the families and for all of us, too. I was very proud of the kids. They really wanted to help those families to have a good Christmas. On Christmas Day we went out to Bulacao with all the kids and delivered the boxes and bags to each family in their homes. It was wonderful. The kids were blessed, the families were blessed, we were blessed. I was so proud of the kids!

1991

OUR OUTLOOK FOR 1991 WAS BOTH OPTIMISTIC AND PESSIMISTIC. The Gulf War was causing escalating prices of fuel and other commodities. Crop damage from Typhoon Ruping threatened the food supply and food prices in the Philippines. The local economy was shaky, with high inflation. The

U.S. economy was also under stress. Since the lion's share of our funding came from America, this was very concerning to our staff and board.

Our hope for 1991 was rooted in two things: our sense of calling and our confidence in our supporters. We knew that God had called us to be caring for His little ones in Cebu. Time and time again that calling had been recreated in our lives, helping us get back up when we fell. We knew that God did not call us to fail, nor to live in discouragement. So we moved on with confidence.

Support was another encouragement. As I wrote to the board at the start of the year, "During difficult times we fall back on the knowledge that hundreds of people are with us in this work. The evidences are many: the faithful and generous contributions; the prayers and letters of encouragement; the packages of clothing, medicines and educational materials that come regularly; and then the response to emergencies. The burdens we have are shared ones, thankfully." And our faith was buoyed by Harry Schmidt's incredible offer to build new homes for our children.

We had built a solid organization that could resist economic difficulties, loss of personnel, storms, fires, and even sickness and death. There would be further testing in the years ahead. That is what a children's ministry and organizational life, in general, is like. But 1990's challenges had made us stronger and better able to handle anything that might come along.

On June 15, Mount Pinatubo erupted, the second-largest terrestrial eruption of the 20th century. Complicating the eruption was the arrival of a major typhoon that brought a lethal mix of ash and rain to towns and cities surrounding the volcano. Predictions of the eruption led to the evacuation of tens of thousands of people from the surrounding areas, saving many lives. Still, 722 people died. The effects of the eruption were felt worldwide. In Cebu we received some ash but there was no damage from the volcano. But it was unnerving for us to consider the fragility of life and the dangers we faced regularly in the Philippines: typhoons, flooding, earthquakes, and volcanoes. On the neighboring island of Leyte, 8,000 people died in flash flooding resulting from a typhoon.

Because we had made a down payment on a parcel of land during 1990 and the balance was due in October, 1991, Marlys and I felt it would be good to go to Minnesota to spread the news and give people an opportunity to donate for that land. We probably wouldn't have considered investing in that trip if one of our supporting churches, Cherry Hill Community Church in Colorado, hadn't invited us to attend their Missions Conference and agreed to pay our airfare. So we met with people and shared our dreams for new homes for the children. And people responded! I think Harry's offer affected our fundraising in a positive way. It was like a matching gift of sorts, where a gift for the land helped make possible Harry's gift of the buildings. After a couple months we had the needed money, so we returned to Cebu.

We learned about the power of words and personal connections during 1991. Two examples proved to be huge blessings for CSC and the

Phyllis and Ray Burke

kids we served. Ray and Phyllis Burke, who were in Cebu to help out during the Ohlendorf's furlough year, returned to their church in Olympia, Washington, and shared about their time in Cebu with their adult Sunday School class. They told about the sibling group of seven kids who were living at CSC and our prayer that they might have a family some day. This touched the hearts of a couple who was there that day. After much thought and prayer, they decided to seek the adoption of all seven. They applied to the Philippine government through an agency in Washington. In God's providence the application was approved, and the seven kids were soon on their way to the upper Northwest.

The second example was when Arvid Olson shared the needs of CSC and our desire to construct new buildings for the ministry with his friend Harry Schmidt. Harry had asked if Arvid knew of any orphanages in the Philippines that needed help, and the result of their conversation would be beautiful new homes for our kids. In addition to all the sophisticated ways that CSC communicated with donors and potential givers, word-of-mouth advertising proved to be just as potent a force in getting out our needs.

The group of seven left with their adoptive parents on September 11.

For years we had been taking in sibling groups and placing them for adoption, but this was the largest group to date. As with any of our CSC kids, we are especially happy when they are adopted into Christian families, and that was the case with this group. These amazing people weren't ruled by the traditional values of American society. They had adopted internationally before taking in the seven. They wanted to make a difference in the lives of kids who otherwise might not have a chance at a family. Their willingness to adopt our seven was a reminder to us of God's greatness and His provision for CSC and our children by providing the right people for the right purpose at the right time.

On October 13, we had a groundbreaking service at the site we had only recently purchased in Banawa Hills. We had already completed the perimeter wall around the property, and it was time to break ground and ask God's blessing on the building of two houses and two other structures that would become Children's Shelter of Cebu's new home. I gave a greeting to the assembled group of friends and CSC family members. Prisco Allocod, our friend and the president of CSC Philippines, read scripture; Mitch Ohlendorf introduced the building program that was ahead; our CSC (Philippines) board chairman, Ronald Duterte, gave a challenge; the CSC kids sang; and Harry Schmidt, our benefactor, who had come from Canada for the event, spoke on "A Vision of CSC." Pastor Lucas, who had helped us procure the land, gave a rousing benediction to finish the program. Then the CSC kids pushed the large plow that began the groundbreaking process.

In the following days the earthmoving started in earnest. Harry Schmidt was around to observe and, although we had local engineers supervising the work, he had some strong opinions about how things should be done. Harry had overseen many projects in Canada and the northern United States, and his company, Harwood Industries, was well known for quality construction, particularly of affordable housing for people who might otherwise not be able to own their own home.

Harry and his friend John were watching the local guy working the bulldozer, and they weren't satisfied with his approach or his skill. I could see Harry shaking his head and yelling out suggestions to the guy. Finally, Harry jogged over to the bulldozer, ordered the poor guy down, and hopped up in the driver's seat and began doing the work himself!

So there were amazing things happening during 1991, both exciting and tragic. We had ridden the roller coaster of emotions from typhoons and volcanoes to the purchase of land and the promise of a new home for the ministry. As we prepared for Christmas, we realized that the celebration of Christ's birth is not tied to our temporal situations. The reality of Christ's presence in even the most difficult of life's situations is what gives it meaning. He is HERE in the midst of our problems and difficulties, and in our victories and miracles. He is Emmanuel, God with us. We celebrated that presence in a very special way at Christmas in 1991 by honoring Christ's birth. But there was no doubt that our celebration was tempered by the suffering of thousands of Filipinos living near us.

And to further emphasize the roller coaster ride that was 1991, our little Agnello died on December 26 after a valiant battle. He had spent three months in isolation at CSC, followed by two months in the hospital. While Agnello was fighting for his life on a ventilator, we gathered as a staff to consider turning off the life support and letting him go to heaven instead of continuing to suffer in the hospital. It was a gut-wrenching decision for us. We loved that little guy. Marlys and Sandy had been with him at doctors' offices, in the CSC infirmary, and at the hospital for many months. We had all watched him fight for his life. But we decided, prayerfully, that we should end his suffering and set him free.

When we announced our decision to the hospital staff, we were summoned to a meeting of the hospital's Ethics Committee. The hospital, Perpetual Succor, is a Catholic institution, so we sat down with a priest, two nuns, and a doctor and were told that it was not ethical or moral to do what we intended to do. Who gave us the right, they opined, to end Nelo's life? And we weren't even related to him in any way. It was an agonizing session, but it ended quickly when I said that we could not afford to keep him on life support and in intensive care indefinitely, so we would support the committee's decision as long as they took over the financial responsibility to keep him alive indefinitely. That pretty much ended the meeting, and sometime the next day the life support ended and Nelo's terrible struggles were over. We had faced the dilemma that thousands of Filipino families face every day, the agonizing interplay of ethics, economics, and emotions. Such was the reality of living and working in the Philippines.

But in the face of disappointments and even death, we were building our dream. Dave Healy's words in the December, 1991 CSC News reflected our feelings of joy and thanksgiving:

As a team of people called together from around the world—we build.

To meet the desperate needs of today—we build.

To meet the needs of children like Maria, Carlo, Amalia, and others like them who will flock to CSC in search of love and care—we build.

Thanks for building with us.

1992

"UP WE GO" WAS A HEADLINE in the Spring 1992 newsletter. Construction was going full bore as the new year began, under the supervision of Mitch Ohlendorf, architect Akoy Velasquez and engineer Gabriel Loqico, and with help from Gil Schotte, a friend of Harry Schmidt who was a veteran of many construction products and served as a consultant and quality-control supervisor. But it was Mitch who put in long hours seeing that materials were delivered on time, that we always had the crew of workers needed on a given day, and that money was available as needed for purchases and payrolls.

The estimate was that the buildings would be completed by April 1, so excitement was running high as the new year began. But the regular daily activities of CSC continued even during construction. Children left for adoption, new ones came to live with us, and remarkable things kept happening. Ruth Ohlendorf gave birth to a healthy baby boy, Anthony Scott. And Marlys Healy had a small growth removed, which we were thankful was benign. One of our little darlings, Belinda, went to the States to have intricate surgery on her brain and would stay in a foster home during her recovery. We didn't know yet whether she would eventually return to Cebu or if she would be adopted by the foster family and remain in the States.

During this time our newsletter was edited by Ruth Lindstedt, a retired missionary from the Philippines. Ruth and her husband, Marwin, were very kind to us when we first arrived in Cebu. Our whole crew was invited to their home for Sunday dinner when we were still in the homesick stages of our adjustment, and it was fun to have some American food and fellowship with this kind and experienced couple. We were impressed with Marwin's skill with the Cebuano language, and it challenged us to learn.

As we were anticipating completion of the house construction, the cost of which was fully underwritten by the Schmidt Family Foundation, we began estimating the cost of outfitting the homes and new infirmary, and equipment needed to maintain the property. We began making our donors aware of the need for kitchen appliances, beds, fans, a lawn mower, air conditioners, tools, phones, and other items to properly outfit our new homes. Marie Hagfors was busy making her artistic cross-stitches for the walls. Excitement was building.

The Jackie Cherne Mission Home

We were thinking about what to name our new homes as we watched them go up. We decided on the Jackie Cherne Mission Home for the house across the compound from the entrance gate. Jackie and her husband, John, had adopted one of our little boys, Roger. She was a teacher, author, and adopted mom to five children. She had been very involved in establishing the Crossroads Adoption Agency in Minneapolis and served on our CSC board. Jackie developed brain cancer and died in 1984.

The other home we decided to name after Arman Eicher. Arman had grown up in Manila and lived in the government's Reception and Study Center in Quezon City before being adopted by Dennis and Sharon Eicher. Arman and six others were killed in a tragic boating incident in Canada in

1985 while on a fishing trip with his dad, uncles, cousins, and grandfather. Arman was a great kid and had been loved deeply by his family.

On June 6th we moved the children into their new houses in Banawa. It was a dream come true for all of us, and the kids ran from the van to see their new places. They couldn't believe how much space there was for sleeping, eating, showering, and playing. It would be some time before the playground was completed, but that didn't dampen the excitement inside that compound that day. For 20 of the kids, school started on June 15. They had a fairly long walk, but one of our guards accompanied them to and from their new school in Banawa.

June 28 was the big day when the CSC buildings would be dedicated. Harry and Marlene Schmidt, their daughter Cara, and her friend Jay came from Canada and were among the 225 guests who gathered outside the Cherne Home to dedicate those amazing facilities to the God who provided them. Harry was pleased with the buildings and smiled through the whole program, except when he joined the rest of us in shedding tears when the kids sang "Thank You (For Giving to the Lord)."

> Thank you, for giving to the Lord, for I am a life that was changed.
> Thank you, for giving to the Lord, for I am so glad you gave.

Ron Dutertre, Pastor Lucas, the Canadian Ambassador, Undersecretary Valenzona from the Department of Social Welfare and Development, Cliff Danielson, who had gotten out of his sick bed to make the long trip to Cebu, and Prisco Allocod were all a part of the service of dedication.

During this time I was often asked whether I had ever dreamed that CSC would have a place like this. Whereas I was blown away by the beauty and size of the facilities, I had to answer that question "Yes." Our initial dream of building a home for children was big. I had imagined large houses with lots of kids in uniforms and knee socks and staff with clipboards and whistles. Maybe that was because we were young, idealistic Americans with lofty dreams and not a lot of understanding of what it would take to build and manage such a place. Now we knew. And we were so thankful to Harry and Marlene and all the people who sacrificed to make this day possible.

Even as we rejoiced in our new facilities, we were sad to have to stop our feeding programs and our Magbalantay Child Care Center because of budget shortfalls. We were helping a lot of people, including mothers and malnourished children. Our programs were well-run and successful. But we were struggling just to fund our CSC homes, our primary commitment, which had growing budgetary needs with the new homes and additional children and staff. Our budget for 1992 was $343,500. It was with heavy hearts that we closed down those programs. I felt especially bad for Carmelita Baya, our supervising social worker, who had helped us conceive, plan, and run those innovative and much-needed programs in the communities they served.

In retrospect, I think I was wrong in developing these programs. We really wanted to have a counter-balance to our work in preparing and sending kids for adoption, one that worked to keep families together. It was noble thinking, and, in a world of unlimited resources, something that we should have embarked on. If mothers who needed to work to feed their families could have been given that opportunity while their kids were safe in our center, it would have enabled some families to stay together. But CSC was not a social service agency to meet a variety of needs in the community with new and ever-changing programs. We were known and established as a residential home for children, and with the closing of these two programs, we realized the need to stay focused on what we were there to do. It is a problem with living and working in a city with so many crucial and unmet needs, with hearts that want to help but resources that are limited.

Late in 1992 the CSC Board made two important announcements. First, I was appointed president of CSC in addition to my role as field director. This meant that I would have increased responsibilities for planning, fundraising, and developing the stateside organization. With the resignation of Gary Bawden as executive director, the board announced that Pauline Bohachek would become CSC's director of development. Pauline, a pastor's wife, had been working as the director of Windsent, the fundraising arm of a Christian radio station in western Minnesota. She began at CSC on January 1.

The year closed with a sense of accomplishment and positive change and the realization that we had taken on a ton of new responsibilities. We were aware, both in Cebu and stateside, that our promotion and fundraising needed to accelerate to meet the growing needs of the ministry. And lots more changes and growth were around the corner!

1993

THE YEAR BEGAN WITH A NEW OFFICE FOR CSC IN MINNESOTA. We rented space in the basement of the Leaders store in Cambridge, Minnesota, which included the old Cambridge State Bank vault. It was a small space with no windows and a steep flight of stairs. The bank vault served as the storage area for brochures, newsletters, and office supplies.

Cambridge proved to be a good location for the office as it was nearer to where Pauline lived, and the town provided us with many loyal and hard-working volunteers to help prepare mailings. First Baptist Church let us use one of their Sunday School rooms for mailings. Other folks helped with clerical jobs in the office.

Kathy Hagfors began working as our administrative assistant. She knew everyone in Cambridge and surrounding areas and was a big help in transferring donor information from the old office to our new computer system. George Johnson of Cambridge kindly donated office furniture to help us get started.

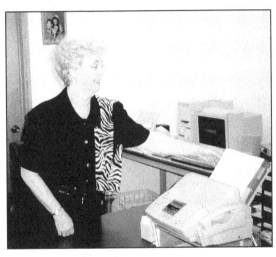

Kathy Hagfors

CSC has always had volunteers to help with mailings and other tasks. In the early days, when our office was in Cliff Danielson's trailer, a group of helpful people gathered at Constance Free Church to process mailings. When the office moved to Cambridge, new people took over. Their work helped CSC save a lot of money. On May 13, CSC had a volunteers appreciation dinner in honor of the many people who helped in various ways. A lasagna dinner was served and door prizes were given.

As has been said already but needs reemphasis, the history of CSC has been the right person coming at the right time to do the right job. Some came along to fulfill a staff function in Cebu. Some had a particular skill needed in Cebu or Minnesota. Some gave a gift at just the right time. And some offered a timely prayer or word of encouragement. God's miraculous hand brought all these people to us in his perfect timing to help CSC get started, grow, and develop into the quality organization and ministry that it is.

During this time an organization was established in Canada to help support the work in Cebu: the Cebu Children's Shelter Society of Canada. Canada had already had a big role in CSC through the Schmidt Family Foundation of Abbotsford, Canada. This organization was started by Arvid Olson, who had spent three years in Cebu with the Evangelical Free Church Mission and who was a friend of Harry Schmidt. (Arvid was the one who told Harry about CSC and our desire to build new homes.) And Variety Clubs International, which donated a new Mitsubishi van to CSC, has its headquarters in Canada.

In the following years, CCSSC grew and developed into a generous partner. Missionaries and leaders from CSC in Minnesota regularly attended and participated in their spring banquets, and CCSSC board members visited Cebu and funded projects, equipment, and vehicles. The Canadian organization operated strictly on a volunteer basis. Their board of directors did all the work of promotion and fundraising. They even recruited volunteers to prepare and serve the food at their desserts and banquets. They could honestly say that 100% of any donation went directly to Cebu, with no administrative costs incurred. The Canadian board always sent the money they raised directly to Cebu instead of routing it through our Minnesota office.

Almost immediately, CCSSC became an important part of CSC's support system and a great encouragement to our staff in Cebu and our stateside leadership. They provided vehicles, books, equipment for our special-needs kids, curricula for our school, and other important items.

In July, CSC's executive director emeritus, Cliff Danielson, left his earthly home and went to be with his blessed Savior. Everyone at CSC knew that our success, especially during the initial years, was a direct result of Cliff's hard work, his faith and determination. He had been sick for several years with congestive heart failure and had been in and out of the hospital. Thankfully, our family was home on furlough when Cliff passed away, so Marlys could be at his side, where she had spent a lot of time during his last days on earth. Marlys wasn't around to care for Cliff during much of the time he was ill, and she felt bad about that. But such is the reality of being a missionary in a faraway place. Other CSC staff experienced the same feeling of being torn between Cebu and the U.S.

Cliff Danielson and friends

Cliff started CSC's stateside operation out of nothing. In his initial promotions, he was talking to people about a ministry that did not yet exist. It was an idea in the head of his daughter and a few of her friends. He worked hard to put together a small mailing list; printed receipts, prayer letters, and a few simple brochures; and started calling his pastor friends to schedule church presentations.

Cliff was always excited about what we were doing in Cebu and deeply proud of his daughter. That love and intensity did not cease until he left this earth. He was an ambassador of good will long after he had to retire and a tireless prayer warrior. The CSC banquet was his baby, and he would call us in Cebu from a telephone outside Bethel's Robertson Center and report on the evening and the offering. He loved CSC with all his heart, and we would miss him greatly, especially Marlys.

CSC's Bikes for Tykes program was started in 1993. The idea was to get bikes donated in Minnesota, ship them to Cebu, fix them up, and sell them. We got a grant from the Wallestad Foundation of Minneapolis to cover shipping costs. Mitch Ohlendorf helped us get a grant from the Canada Fund to pay import duties. Volunteers collected the donated bikes from all over the Twin Cities. CSC board member Al Sannerud let us store them on his property in Ham Lake until his Kiwanis Club volunteers could load them into a 40-foot container and ship them to Cebu.

On the Cebu end we had to get the bikes from customs, bring them to our office in Sun Valley, sort them, repair the ones that needed it, and then put out the word and sell them for the best price possible. We were able to get lots of donations. It seemed like everyone had an unwanted bike in their garage. We especially wanted BMX and mountain bikes because those brought the best price in Cebu. Although we got some of those, many were very ordinary, or worse.

In the coming months we were involved in hiring and training new people to meet the demands of our growing ministry. Having new homes to maintain and more children to care for necessitated maintenance workers, nurses to assist Marlys with medical needs, guards, drivers, additional house parents, childcare workers, cleaners, laundry workers, and office staff. Of course, that meant more money was needed for salaries and additional HR functions in our office.

We were fortunate to have Joanna Talaid as our office manager. She came to us shortly after graduating from college and soon got her licensure

Joanna Talaid

in accounting. Later, Joanna studied law while still working with CSC and eventually passed the bar and began handling CSC's legal affairs. We added a second social worker to assist Carmelita with the paperwork of our growing population. Ruth Ohlendorf, who was a social worker, helped out in a variety of ways, and headed up our outreach work as outreach director, working with former residents of CSC and their families, offering assistance for education, vocational training, and emergency medical care. Gloria Deliña served as our Christian education coordinator, organizing all the Christian education activities in our homes and our outreach to the communities around CSC, where we shared the love of Christ with our neighbors.

During this time, Pete and Diane Grondahl were in Cebu as volunteers. Diane taught at Joy Academy, a school organized by Cebu missionaries. One requirement for a child studying at Joy was that one of his or her parents help teach. We wanted our daughter Jenny to attend Joy, but since Marlys and I were both working full-time with CSC, we asked if Diane could teach in her place, and it was approved by the school board. Pete did driving and assisted with some construction projects, one of which was the garage near the Cherne Home.

We were committed as a staff to not just having more kids at CSC but doing a better job of caring for them. From a small group foster home in Bulacao, CSC had been transformed into a licensed agency, one that needed to be run professionally and prayerfully. Besides caring for children, we now had assumed tons of administrativ chores in finance, HR, social work services, and child development.

Two backbones of the ministry during this time were Sandy Swanson and Mitch Ohlendorf. As child care director, Sandy's job was to ensure that we were meeting all our children's needs. She hired and trained child-care and household workers, wrote developmental reports on each child, and counseled kids who needed that service. Most of all she was Auntie Sandy to the CSC community, dispensing love, discipline, and encouragement. Her love extended beyond the walls of CSC to include former residents who had been adopted or returned to their families. Sandy's impact on CSC cannot be emphasized too strongly. She was a rock on which our childcare

Auntie Sandy gets some love.

Mitch Ohlendorf and MayMay

program was built, and her contributions were huge.

Mitch filled our need for administrative leadership during this time of growth. A graduate of Bethel College, Mitch had gone to CSC with a team from Central Baptist Church and fell in love with the kids and the ministry. He also fell in love with one of our workers. He returned to spend two summers as a volunteer before joining our staff in 1986. So he was familiar with our administrative needs when we began to expand. Much of CSC's reputation for integrity in financial management can be attributed to Mitch's work. He also supervised the construction of our new buildings, particularly the financial side of things.

1994

DURING THE YEAR WE CONTINUED GROWING INTO OUR NEW HOMES and the responsibilities that went with having more kids. Pauline Bohachek visited churches to present CSC's needs and to meet our donors. The 1994 banquet's theme was "CSC Around the World." It was amazing to reflect on how the ministry had, in just a few years, become known and respected all over the world. Through adoption, CSC had touched the lives of families in Norway, Sweden, the Netherlands, France, Germany, Australia, Belgium, Canada, and all over the United States. Our prayer had always been that wherever our children went in the world, they would bless their families, their communities, their churches, and their Lord. Although not all adoptions were fairy tales, we received reports from around the globe that our prayers were being answered for many of our former residents in their new homes. Back in Minnesota, 718 people attended the banquet at Bethel and gave an offering of $23,000. The Canadian organization had two dessert functions in British Columbia and raised $5,000 for the ministry.

John Cherne was honored by the CSC board at a volunteer appreciation dinner in May. He had tendered his resignation from the board at the February meeting. John served on the board from 1982 to 1994. He and his wife, Jackie, adopted a boy from CSC, and they both joined the board the next year. Tragically, Jackie died in 1984.

John Cherne

In 1985 John went to Cebu and, while there, met Della from the CSC staff. He returned the next year and they were married. John led the board through some difficult and exciting times. His dedication and stability through years of growth and change helped hold CSC together and grow into the organization that we know today. He is remembered for his cool-headedness when difficult decisions were needed and for his deep love for the kids we serve.

Two construction teams went to Cebu in the first half of 1994. The first was a team from several of our supporting churches. They were at CSC in late January to finish the garage the Schmidt family had begun. On June 26, we had the long-awaited dedication of the Cliff Danielson Infirmary. This building was a part of the 1991-92 construction project but was not completed then due to lack of funds. Now, more than two years later, the building was finished and ready for use. The two-story building featured a wash room on the first floor where our aunties washed clothes at least six days a week. Upstairs was the infirmary and nurses' office. We were excited about completion of that building because with the larger number of kids we were admitting, more clothes needed washing and more sick children would need the services of our medical office and infirmary.

One man from the U.S. who came to finish the infirmary was Bob Adams, a construction manager from Washington State who led work teams that went all over the world to construct buildings for Christian groups. Bob was a great guy who liked to work and who was quick with a joke or funny story. His specialty was stories of jobsite accidents, falls, impalings, and other disasters, some of which I was certain he invented just to keep everyone alert. You could hear Bob during break time saying things like, "Yeah, he dropped six stories right onto an upturned screwdriver. Took it right in the ticker."

One hot day I was helping the construction team work on the infirmary. Cement was poured into buckets, which were lifted to workers on the upstairs level. Those buckets of cement were heavy, and it was steamy hot that day. I was good for about 15 minutes before needing a break. Anticipating that, I brought several Diet Cokes, but they were gone within the first hour. I was sweating profusely and my job performance was dwindling to almost nothing. The other guys on the team were laughing pretty hard at me. They knew how to pace themselves and find shade wherever possible, especially the Filipino workers. By lunchtime I was done. It was my last time as a construction volunteer, to everyone's relief.

In August Sandy escorted our little Willy to the United States for adoption. He had achondroplasia dwarfism, as did his adoptive parents. They live in Houston, where Willy's new dad, Joe Roach, served on the Houston City Council. Sandy reported that, because of Joe's notoriety as a politician in Houston, lots of people, including members of the media, were at the airport to greet Willy, whom they would name Ross. As Sandy stepped out of the walkway, cameras began clicking and whirring, and there was lots of clapping and cheering.

Sandy would experience more fame from that escorting trip when, several years later, Oprah Winfrey did a "Where Are They Now" show that featured everyone involved in that amazing adoption story. Sandy was flown from Cebu to Chicago to appear on the show. She got to see Ross and talk about how CSC had taken him in and how the whole adoption story developed from the CSC side of things. Sandy did a great job on Oprah's show. Tragically, Joe Roach died suddenly in 2011 after an amazing life in public service in Texas and adopting children from the U.S. and Asia.

Ray and Phyllis Burke left Cebu after a four-month volunteer stint. They were great to have around and showered grandparental love on our children. We always are happy when older adults spend time with our kids because, in Philippine culture, grandparents are adored and respected. Many of our kids had some interaction with grandparents before their family situation deteriorated and they came to live at CSC, where we have no older people around. And most will have grandparents doting on them when they get to their adoptive families. Ray and Phyllis got a lot of kid hugs and lap time during their time with us.

Ray wrote a letter for the Spring 1994 newsletter recalling a deeply emotional experience involving the adoptive parents of one of our children. The baby had been found by a passerby all alone in an open field in Cebu City. He was referred to the police, who took him to the social welfare office, who referred him to us. When the couple came to get him for adoption, they wanted to see that spot where their little guy had been left. Ray was the one to drive them to that field and remembers how everyone wept when they saw the spot and thought about what had happened and what could have happened. I still cry, as I'm sure Phyllis does (Ray passed in 2021), when I remember that boy and that day with his adoptive parents.

Our support system included many different kinds of donors. Some gave once or twice a year, often during December. Others gave monthly as Foster Friends. Some donated their time as volunteers, helping with mailings in Minnesota or going to Cebu to help our staff. Some organized community fundraising events. Kids had lemonade stands while their parents or church friends organized craft or rummage sales to earn money for CSC. Others donated needed supplies. My cousin Jan Gleiter donated shoes for our kids. Jim Chalmers sent over medical supplies. Feed My Starving Children sent food packs. Ken Totushek, an adoptive parent, produced a CD of his songs focusing on children and families. He donated a portion of the profits to CSC. Still others gave books, toys, and kitchen or medical supplies.

We cared for 100 children during 1994, up 27% from 1993. The youngest child admitted was just a few hours old and the oldest, Joemar, was 18. We served over 56,000 meals during the year. Twenty-one CSC kids were adopted into families in the U.S., Sweden, Norway and New Zealand, and 25 were returned to their birth families.

Our impact in Cebu City and beyond was growing rapidly. The word about CSC was spreading all over the United States, Canada, and the rest of the world. Our 1994 income was $410,000, which came from 1,500 donors. Could there be any doubt that God was behind this ministry, which was just 15 years old but was leaping ahead with new facilities, new and faithful donors, new workers and staff, and an increasing sense of God's presence in our lives and plans?

1995

AS THE YEAR BEGAN, we found ourselves thinking more and more about the education of our children. Although we could provide excellent care while our kids were with us, including the best medical care available in the Philippines, we were sending them to poorly equipped, crowded schools where they were not given a suitable education. We dreamed of having our own school where we could meet each student at his or her point of need and ability, and prepare them for whatever would come next when they left CSC. We wanted a school that all of our children could attend, including those with special needs. Although it would not be operational for a while, we were already starting to think about curriculum development, licensing, and fundraising.

A committee of volunteers helped us in these tasks. They were led by Nancy Healy, my sister-in-law, who had done considerable work in multi-age interdisciplinary programs in the elementary grades. Other members of the group were Jill Anderson, Shari Reasoner, and my mom, Millie Healy. In June, Millie and Nancy traveled to Cebu to discuss their recommendations with the staff and Philippine board, and to put plans in motion for recruiting teachers, training, and purchasing materials and equipment.

Meanwhile, thanks to Virgil and Patty Leih, a church in Hong Kong came to know about our school dreams and pledged to help. The Leihs were friends of CSC and were in Cebu to meet their adopted son. They connected with friends from Edina, Minnesota, who were living in Hong Kong, Brian and Angela Kusunoki.

The Kusonokis were a part of Hong Kong's Union Church. Over the next months as they told their church about CSC and our desire to build a school, the congregation became interested in helping. Even though our school was still a dream, people were falling in place to help us decide what kind of school we wanted, and to help financially with the construction and purchase of land. We had our eyes on a lot near the Shelter that would allow our kids to walk to school and that was big enough for the school we were envisioning.

In January, a team from several churches in the U.S. and Canada went to Cebu to build a garage and craft area near the Cherne Home in Banawa. The building would have a garage on the main floor, with offices and an art area upstairs, as well as a small apartment for Joemar, our long-time resident who was an adult and needed a place of his own to sleep.

We were awaiting the arrival of Lynn Burke to join our staff. She had been a volunteer with CSC in 1986, and spent a year helping care for the children. She was ready to make a deeper commitment to the ministry. We were excited for this because of Lynn's great personality and love for the children. And her sense of humor and fun helped keep our spirits high.

Pauline Bohachek resigned as executive director in the fall after three years of service.

The Erickson family, from Two Harbors, Minnesota, spent their Christmas at CSC. Tim Erickson, a dentist, came to Cebu many times during the 1980s and 90s. Not only did he take good care of our children's teeth, he and Karen told their church about CSC and encouraged the church and their friends to support the ministry. Their trip to Cebu in 1985 had major repercussions for our Healy family because Tim and Karen's son Rich and our daughter Juliet got to know each other and formed a friendship that led to a romance, which led to them being married in St. Paul in 2003.

Elizabeth Healy, my sister, became our fourth executive director in November and supervised moving the office from the basement of the old Cambridge State Bank to the courthouse building across the street. As she took over, CSC was embarking on a major school project that would expand our program and budget.

Our income for 1995 was almost the same as 1994, around $425,000. We were happy for that, considering the many changes and challenges we'd faced, but we knew that the school we were planning would require additional funds for salaries, equipment, and upkeep.

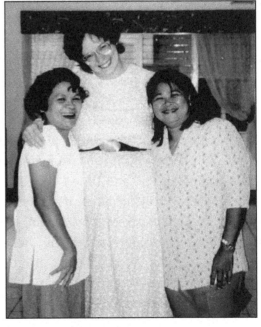

**Elizabeth Healy with
Myrna Alejado and Gloria Deliña**

1996

AS THE YEAR BEGAN, we learned that Union Church would provide the money for the land for our proposed school. Several church members were influential in this decision, including Ken and Isabel Morrison, who would become our good friends in the years to come. Ken and Isabel were active in Walk to Emmaus, a spiritual retreat ministry, and invited Marlys and me, and eventually the rest of the staff, to join them at their expense, including airfare to Hong Kong. The Walks were set up for men to go one week and women the next.

The retreat was a great experience for us. I was much in need of spiritual refreshment after some hectic years in Cebu. It was great to spend time in reflection and recharging. And I met a lot of great guys who were fellow pilgrims and who took an interest in me and CSC.

One new friend I made was Alan Wright, an architect from England who was working in Hong Kong. Alan offered to design our school building free of charge and made several trips to Cebu to supervise the construction and sourcing of building materials for a beautiful and functional school.

In July, a team of 28 members and friends of North Isanti Baptist Church in Minnesota came to Cebu to minister to the children and staff as well as the community. Organized by pastors Jonathan Larson and Jeff Chapman, the team did several construction projects, including a large rock wall and a stage and flag display. The flags represent the countries where our children of have been adopted and include the flags of Canada, to honor our sister organization, CCSSC, and Hong Kong, the country where Union Church is located and where other significant supporters reside.

We purchased a 1,500-square-meter lot for the school with the help of the Friends of CSC and Union Church. The lot was close to the CSC compound, easy walking distance for our kids.

Our joy and excitement was tempered with the death of Romulo Alejado, our Eicher Home house father, who died after a short battle with liver cancer. He and his wife, Myrna, had only been house parents for 15 months when Romulo died, and it was a big loss for CSC. Myrna stayed on as a single house parent for several months before we hired a new couple.

In reflecting on Romulo's death, we thought about other losses that CSC suffered. We thought of the four little ones who had died since 1979. We tried so hard to save them, and we marveled at their struggles to live in spite of illness and birth defects. We thought about the people for whom our two homes were named, Jackie Cherne and Arman Eicher, and how their memories had inspired our staff these many years. We thought about faithful supporters who had passed but whose gifts helped get this ministry started. And, of course, we thought about Cliff Danielson, remembering how he loved to talk about CSC and the miracles that have been our history. We thought about how happy he would have been to see CSC as it had come to be.

Romulo and Myrna Alejado

1997

DR. LISA SAAVEDRA, WHO WOULD BE OUR SCHOOL PRINCIPAL, went to Minnesota to observe multi-age classrooms and meet with our school task force to discuss recruiting volunteer teachers. Our thought was to have a faculty of both Filipino and North American teachers, with the majority being from the Philippines. We envisioned a curriculum that would be a combination of the Philippine Department of Education curriculum and one from a typical Minnesota elementary school.

While in North America, Lisa spoke at our banquet in Minnesota and one organized by our sister organization in Canada. Her words to attendees summarized our vision and the reason for our excitement for the school. She said that we are "very much aware of the disparity in educational opportunities in our country. The public schools are overwhelmed with the task of teaching many students. Poor children do not have access to a quality education. Inclusion is not a concept that has wide understanding in our country, as classroom teachers lack the time and resources to offer help to these special students." Lisa was excited about the possibilities of

Dr. Lisa Saavedra

our proposed school and was giving her enthusiasm, time, and talent to make it happen.

These discussions and planning sessions took place even as God began moving in the hearts of potential donors for the school. Union Church in Hong Kong had made a commitment, and fundraising was starting in the United States. We discovered that many people were interested, not only current donors but also new people who found something compelling about improving our children's education.

Just before Lisa departed for the U.S., we received a gift that made the fundraising component of her trip all but unnecessary. On March 18, I was working on a brochure designed to help us raise about $250,000 to construct the school building. It was a three-color brochure that we would print and mail to our CSC supporters. While I was working on the brochure, a call came to our office from the office of a friend in Manila, Dan Chalmers. The person on the phone asked to talk to me about a transfer of funds.

"Would you like us to send this in pesos or dollars?" she asked. More than a little confused, I said it would depend on the amount. She replied, "Didn't anyone tell you about this yet? We are wiring $250,000." After finding my breath and gathering some composure, my cynical mind began working. "Is that U.S. dollars, ma'am?" I croaked. The answer was yes!

When I talked to the donors, Dan and Carla Chalmers, it became clear how God had orchestrated circumstances and used people to make this happen. One person He used was Dave Jahnke, a friend of ours from Central Baptist, a missionary in Japan who visited Marlys and me in Cebu for a few days. He learned of our dreams for a school and shared that with Dan and

Carla when he passed through Manila on his way back to Japan. That's how the Chalmers knew about the school project, and God went to work from there.

"Now you can build your school," was the Chalmers' joyful proclamation when they decided to use their resources for the kids of CSC.

Things were moving fast! We broke ground in June, with a goal to have the school built and ready for the start of school in August of 1998. It was sobering and unbelievable to think what had happened in the past months. Although we were an organization without significant reserve funds and with no experience in starting a school, the following had happened:

- We had organized a task force to take our school dreams and put them into action, with a well-thought-out plan and curriculum.
- We had a person of Lisa Saavedra's caliber leading the charge in Cebu, in the community, and with the Department of Education, which would eventually need to license our school.
- We had found a piece of land almost next door to CSC that was a perfect location for the school.
- We had established a relationship with Union Church of Hong Kong, which made a significant pledge to help us purchase this land.
- We had broken ground for the eventual school building.
- We had an offer from a world-class architect working in Hong Kong to design our school.
- We had received a donation for construction costs of the school building.

Even as I write this chapter in CSC's history, I shake my head in amazement at what God did to make this happen. The faces of Virgil Leih, Brian Kusunoki, Ken and Isabel Morrison, Allen Wright, Dave Jahnke, Dan and Carla Chalmers, Lisa Saavedra, Jill Anderson, Nancy, Millie, and Elizabeth Healy, the Druckenmillers, and many others flash in my mind: another village, created by God, to make our Children of Hope School happen.

1997 was a year of growth, faithfulness, vision, and miracles. Our staff, supporters, and volunteers worked together to make it a year that will never be forgotten. Even in the midst of whirlwind activity concerning the school project, CSC kept doing what we do well and had been doing for 18 years: We took in and met the needs of children and helped them find families through adoption.

1998

CONSTRUCTION WAS THE MAIN THEME FOR 1998 as many people worked to get the school building finished in time for fall. Jerry Salgo and Mitch Ohlendorf, as project manager, were a big part of the construction efforts, making sure materials were ordered and delivered in time and that the overall standard we had set for the facilities was met.

Alan Wright, our architect, came to Cebu from Hong Kong a couple times during the construction. Alan was a perfectionist who was always finding things that were not up to snuff, and "encouraging" the project manager and engineers to do some things over to meet his and our expectations. We used to joke that Alan could spot errors or poor craftsmanship from the airport when he arrived in Cebu. As it went up we could see that the school would be amazing, everything we had hoped and prayed for.

Elizabeth Healy, a librarian by training, was in charge of setting up the library. She headed up purchasing of books and arranging the rooms. We received gifts from Union Church for the library, as well as from friends at Bethel College, Mitch Ohlendorf's and my alma mater. Many colleagues of my dad at Bethel gave money that we used for outfitting what we decided to name the Bethel Library.

With the convergence of construction completion, curriculum planning, equipment purchases, and library organization, our school was mostly finished in August, just in time for the start of the school year. It was so exciting to watch the building go up and see our hopes and dreams fulfilled. It was also a bit nerve-wracking because the pace of construction was slower than expected. Our grand opening was scheduled for August 16, and many visitors were planning to travel from North America, Hong Kong, Manila, and other parts of the Philippines. Representatives from the Department of Education would speak. Excitement was mounting as Jerry and company worked furiously to complete the work.

The night before the grand opening, I went to the construction site at about midnight, and many men were still there. I asked Jerry how things were going and he gave a thumbs up, but the gesture lacked enthusiasm. A man came into the main room and presented Jerry with a bill for some labor expenses and asked for immediate payment. Jerry said a few words to the man and then escorted him into another room. Jerry was clearly furious that someone would come after midnight on a Saturday to demand payment for something that should have been routed through our office. He was exhausted and stressed and in no mood to argue with the man. After a few choice words complete with a couple index finger jabs to the chest, the man left without a whimper. I asked Jerry what he'd said. "Uncle Paul, you don't want to know!"

But I did want to know! Very much. Jerry has kept his silence over the years in spite of regular questioning. In any case, he cleared the fellow out of there, and the work continued all night long. The last job was laying carpet squares, and the final one was put in place just as the visitors were filing into the activity room. There were undoubtedly a few little things that still needed to be done, but the school looked great, and we were so proud to show it off to the people who came and to dedicate it to the Lord and to the children who would attend there for years to come, receiving the education of their dreams while living at CSC.

I was happy my mom, Millie, my sister-in-law Nancy, and my sister, Elizabeth, could be at our grand opening because they had offered much expertise and encouragement in the planning for our school. Friends from local children's ministries attended, as well as the Association of Child Care Agencies of the Philippines and representatives from Cebu's Department of Education. Friends from Union Church of Hong Kong, which made a major donation for the main activity room, were also in attendance. The school faculty were introduced and prayed for. The featured speech was from Ron Duterte, our Cebu president and board chair:

It is our firm belief that given the opportunity to learn and prepare themselves, CSC children can take their respective places in the societies where they will find themselves later in their lives. Human talent is our most precious resource. We cannot allow any of our human potential to be wasted or neglected. And we cannot afford to shut out our CSC children from the fulfillment of hope which is shared by the rest who have the good fortune of growing up in the love and security of their families. This conviction motivates us at Children of Hope School in all that we do in giving our students quality education.

At CHS we believe that the supreme values are spiritual. The hope of the world is that character, which, built upon the solid rock, withstands triumphantly all the storms of life. We accept your best wishes and your prayers as we now open the school to our children.

We prayed prayers of thanksgiving and dedication for this fantastic facility, the children who would study there, and the teachers and administrators who would lead and guide them.

This was a big day in the history of CSC. It was a milestone in our effort to give the best care possible to the children God led to us and to announce to the world that our kids deserved the best education possible and we were starting a school to help make that possible. It reestablished the fact that CSC is, above all else, a purveyor of hope: hope for good health, hope for safety, hope for a second chance at family, and hope for an education that will open doors to opportunities previously unimaginable.

The rest of the year was spent getting used to our school and settling in to new schedules and expectations. In the space of six years the ministry had expanded in quality and quantity. It would take us time to grow into these new programs and facilities. Though the facilities were built with large gifts from amazing people, the expanded ministry meant more money would be needed for equipment and salaries of childcare workers, teachers, social workers, and administrative personnel.

In October, Craig and Jan Druckenmiller from Bozeman, Montana, visited Cebu. They had started an organization in Montana, Sacred Portion

Children's Outreach, specializing in early childhood education. They spent time with the staff and kids, and were exploring the possibility of working with our Children of Hope preschool and with early-childhood learning in our homes.

During all the hustle to get the school built and in operation, CSC continued to take in children and place them for adoption around the world. We had 25,392 kid days, up 10% from 1996. Some employees left and we hired new ones. We were fulfilling the mission that had led us to the Philippines in 1979 and that had characterized our work in Cebu for 20 years. Children's medical, emotional, social, educational, and spiritual needs were being met every day. God was being glorified. People were giving and praying and telling others about CSC. Our income for 1998 was almost $800,000, with 6,801 gifts from 1,616 different donors.

And other exciting things were happening. Our Filipino leadership was expanding. We had an excellent manager in our medical department (Warlita Manlun) and financial office (Joanna Talaid), leading our social work team (Carmelita Baya), heading up our maintenance and transportation department (Jerry Salgo), and directing our school (Cris Tabra). We had put together an impressive group of professionals: licensed social workers and teachers, registered nurses and therapists, an engineer, and a principal.

No longer were American staff alone required for decision making, financial management, and interacting with the government and other child welfare organizations. Missionary furloughs or Americans deciding to leave Cebu didn't have as strong an impact on the work as when we were getting started. Our staff was becoming a team of Americans and Filipinos working together. And we would see this process improve and expand in the coming years in response to the growth and development of our work in Cebu.

1999

THE YEAR STARTED THE COUNTDOWN to the end of the decade, and century. Y2K rumors and theories were rampant worldwide, perhaps especially in the Philippines. We didn't have the time or inclination to join that worry party. The ministry had expanded. Our Children of Hope School was in operation. We were caring for more kids in a better way. We were offering physical and occupational therapy for those with special needs. We were hiring skilled professionals in administration, counseling, therapy, nursing, and teaching. We were placing growing numbers of our children into adoptive families around the world. Our stateside organization was thriving, with new donors coming on board and generous gifts coming in to meet the requirements of a growing budget.

Here are some highlights from CSC during the last year of the 20th century:

The Sacred Portion Children's Outreach, headed by Jan and Craig Druckenmiller, agreed to work with us in preschool and early childhood education. Jan went to Cebu to begin introducing the school staff to the preschool curriculum she had developed and to start a training program on early childhood learning. This would prove to be a great partnership for the next several years and was reflective of a growing recognition by our staff that we could improve the quality of care for our children by partnering with people and organizations, both locally and internationally, who shared our commitment to Christ and to the highest quality of care and education.

Over 700 people attended the CSC banquet at Bethel College in St. Paul. The theme was "Across the Miles" and emphasized the many ways people have supported the ministry in Cebu. Banquets were also held in Seattle and Abbottsford, British Columbia, to promote the ministry and raise funds for special projects.

CSC sponsored a "think tank" for our Children of Hope School in Minnesota. Elementary school teachers who were interested in CSC met for two days to brainstorm ideas for our next school year. Aside from these Minnesota-based teachers, the event was attended by Amy Luck, who had just finished a year of teaching at CHS and was preparing to return for another year; Nancy Healy, an expert on multi-age learning who had helped develop our school curriculum; and Jan Druckenmiller, our new preschool consultant.

The CSC board passed a resolution to establish an endowment known as the Luke Fund. Luke was a CSC child who had long-term needs and who lived at CSC for almost all of his 23 years, receiving one-on-one care for his entire stay. Luke's life spoke of the need for CSC to be financially stable both today and into the future, as his needs would not diminish and he would continue to need the loving, life-giving care of CSC for years to come. The

In 1982 a baby was born in a charity ward of a small hospital in Cebu City. Luke underwent cardiac arrest during birth and was without oxygen for an extended time. Unlike many cases of charity patients, the hospital medical staff decided to resuscitate the baby, even though it was likely he had suffered massive brain damage. The baby's mother abandoned him in the hospital, and after a couple of months Luke was referred to CSC.

When we took him in, he appeared to be a healthy baby boy. We didn't know that Luke would not develop physically beyond about a year and a half, or mentally beyond a few months. Luke would never speak nor have voluntary movement of his arms or legs. We would need to feed, bathe, and change Luke for his entire life.

Luke became a fixture at CSC. For over 23 years he was an integral part of our lives and a symbol of CSC and what we are all about.

Luke was hospitalized many times and fought for his life. At least a dozen times we were sure he would die. The doctors said he wouldn't make it past 5 years old. Then they revised it to 9, then 11—certainly he wouldn't reach his teenage years.

One day Marlys called and said I should get to the hospital quickly; Luke wasn't doing well. He had been hospitalized for over a week, and his breathing was weak. I had received messages like this before, so I went to the office and took care of a few things, thinking I'd stop in and see Luke later in the day. But the Lord laid it on my heart to go see him right then, and when I entered his room his breathing was extremely labored. He looked different than I had ever seen him, and it became clear that he was dying.

I sat down next to him, kissed him, and looked into his eyes. For 23 years

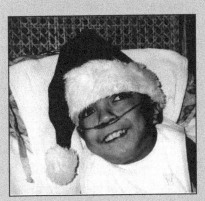

we had loved this boy. It wasn't easy to say goodbye. I said, "Luke, you can go. Go to be with Jesus, I love you." Within a couple of minutes Luke left this world. He was looking up into my face when he took his last, labored breath.

I had a strong sense of Luke being ushered into eternity. His 23 years of pain, suffering, limitations, hospitalizations, forced breathing, skin rashes, and infections were over. We would never see Luke's smile again on this side of heaven.

endowment would help with that stability, providing income through interest for our future needs.

Our sibling group of seven left for Minnesota with their adoptive parents, tying for the largest sibling group we'd ever placed.

The staff, children, and friends of CSC in Cebu celebrated 20 years of ministry with a dinner and program. It was a time of remembering the good times and great blessings over two decades and recognizing some of the people who have been a significant part of our work. In the first 20 years, so much had happened at CSC, including construction of new buildings, development of our programs and services, many new kids and workers, and placement of almost 300 children for adoption. CSC kids performed musical numbers, and there was a media presentation of CSC's history. The event was sponsored by Cebu City businesses.

When we started in 1979, we were committed to the long run, but we had no idea what would be involved in starting and building the kind of ministry we envisioned. We hadn't anticipated the financial requirements or the number of committed people that would be needed as staff, volunteers, and prayer supporters. We didn't have a master plan when we arrived in Cebu. We had no clue about licensing, budgeting, managing employees, case management, or government relations. In 20 years we had learned many things, some the hard way, some not so hard because of the people God sent to walk with us through the minefields of culture, finance, HR, childrearing, and interpersonal relationships we would encounter.

Those two decades had seen remarkable developments and progress, more than we, and some of the people close to us, could have imagined. We had overcome natural and man-made disasters, global financial crises, a political revolution in the Philippines, the death of Cliff Danielson, and for the U.S. personnel living in Cebu, the challenges of a new language and culture, and emotionally draining work that we had to learn on the fly. We had built a strong, resilient staff, a loyal and generous support base in the U.S. and Canada, state-of-the-art facilities, significant financial reserves, an innovative school program, a solid reputation in the community and with the local, regional, and national agencies that regulated us, with links to churches, other nongovernment agencies, medical providers, and missions organizations.

We were well prepared and positioned for the next century.

THE 2000s

I believe that during times when some large international
charities were cited for improprieties with funds
in crises like the ones that befell the Philippines,
people chose to give to CSC instead because
they knew us and trusted our integrity.

WE SURVIVED THE "THREAT" OF Y2K and moved into the 21st century with confidence and enthusiasm. Truly this was not our ministry any more. Of course it never had been. If God hadn't ordained and sustained CSC, it would have died an early death in the 1980s. But because a group of us from Minnesota had gotten things going and continued to direct the growth and development of CSC for more than 20 years, it had our mark on it. However, by the time our calendars rolled over to 2000 this was changing, as Filipino leaders were emerging to handle CSC's administrative, planning, and operational functions. And we American staff and the U.S. board of directors were committed to continuing that transition.

In 20 years we had worked hard to establish a program in Cebu that responded to community needs, was consistent with priorities of the Philippine government, operated with class and integrity, and provided the best care possible to the children we took in. In the coming decades these values would be tested by economic downturns, political upheaval, shifting governmental policies and priorities, and staff turnover. But our staff, board members, fundraisers, and supporters, working together, proved to be dedicated and resilient.

This section will chronicle these decades of change and accomplishment, not on a yearly basis, as previously. Rather, I will proceed by highlighting trends, stories, and milestones in CSC's more recent history, leading up to Marlys's and my retirement. Dates are necessary for context, but they are less important than people's contributions and the amazing stories of our children overcoming difficult and tragic life experiences to make remarkable and heartwarming achievements in response to our staff's love and encouragement.

At what point does an organization switch from the planting stage to being firmly planted? Certainly our mindset in the first years of CSC was that we were planting something new. There was no existing program in the Philippines like ours when we started. We didn't have a grand design for every component, but we had a general sense of what we wanted to do. Some things, like the church we started in Bulacao, just seemed to sprout without our doing much. Some things didn't prosper, like our feeding and childcare centers. Somewhere during the first 20 years we came to realize that we were an established entity in Cebu City, that we had initiated something significant and permanent, and that CSC was no longer just the crazy idea of a bunch of young Minnesotans.

As the 2000s began we were settled into our ministry and had established an important niche in the child welfare world in the Philippines. Although we had experimented with other types of programs, we had more or less centered our efforts and resources on pre-adoptive childcare services, and our work force, facilities, networks, and resources were set up for that ministry. By the early 2000s we were caring for more than 100 kids at a time between our two residential homes, Cherne and Eicher.

The Wally Johnson Teen Home

ONE OF OUR CONCERNS AS WE HIT THE 2000S was for our older children, particularly our teens and young adults. Most of our programs and services were pre-adoptive, to prepare our kids for transitioning into adoptive

Wally Johnson

homes. But what about those who were not placed? They needed educational opportunities beyond our Children of Hope School, in area high schools.

In 2002, CSC opened the Wally Johnson Home. This facility housed older teens and young adults who were not placed for adoption, and offered programs and services designed to prepare them for entering life in the Philippines, including education, skills training, and preparation for independent living. The home was named after Wally Johnson, who had taught me as a fifth grader in Sunday School at my home church of Central Baptist. His love and commitment had a big impact on my life and on hundreds of others who had him

136

for a teacher. He was an inspiration to us, and his life exemplified a commitment to Christ though tireless work with the young. Our goal was to emulate Wally and strive for the standard he set with his life. Gloria and Manny Deliña were the first house parents at the Johnson Home, and we started with just a few of our older kids from the Banawa homes. The residents were housed at Sun Valley, in the house where our CSC office was located. It was not an ideal set-up, and we hoped that someday we might find a more suitable facility for this program.

Various house parents worked in the Johnson home during the 2000s. Aside from the Deliñas, we had Jun Pellejera, our Cherne Home house father until his wife, Becky, died. After that Jun, Ondoy, and Edith Ayop took over leadership in the Johnson Home, starting in 2004, working there until this writing. The work of house parents in the Johnson Home was challenging. Most of the residents had "aged out" of adoption at CSC, and some were profoundly disappointed about not being adopted. Others had special needs that prevented them from adoptive placement. It was a difficult job to help these teens and young adults redirect their lives towards living in the Philippines through education or vocational training.

Although we did not find an alternative venue for the teen home during my time as field director, we worked to improve the program. A growing number of kids were not being adopted in the 2000s. We needed a better plan for them. God laid a burden on the heart of Ben Bonnett, who went to Cebu in 2018 as our new education director. Later, after much thought, prayer, and interaction with staff and school faculty, Ben presented us with the Bridge Program—comprehensive educational, counseling, and vocational services for children who had aged out of adoption, to better launch them into life in the Philippines.

But while we gave needed attention to our residents who were not adopted, the bulk of our time and programming went to preparing children for adoptive placement.

One consequence of focusing on pre-adoptive child care was that the responsibilities of documentation and case management would take over much of our time and attention. Our professional staff (teachers, social workers, therapists, nurses, counselors) needed to maintain records and reports on the children and their progress while at CSC. This meant much recording, writing, editing, and organizing data and observations. We had become a professional child welfare agency. Our reports were scrutinized by the Department of Social Welfare and Development, the Inter-Country Adoption Board, the Department of Education, foreign adoption agencies and embassies, and, eventually, adoptive families and their agencies.

Several new departments emerged during this time. Besides "Philippine-izing" the organization by turning over key leadership tasks and positions to our qualified Filipino professionals, we adopted new and improved ways of doing things. And as the 2000s progressed, we began thinking about the transition of leadership relating to Marlys's and my eventual retirements.

Social Work

CARMELITA BAYA, OUR FIRST SOCIAL WORKER, became the lead person in this transition during the first decade of the 2000s. She established good working relationships with Philippine government agencies, which meant dealing with the bureaucratic requirements of different offices and courts, and the competing demands of local, regional, and national agencies. She was hard working, brave, persistent, and focused on what was best for our children. If confrontation or arm twisting was needed, she did it. If a more delicate approach was called for, she handled that as well.

Carmelita traveled all over the Philippines, from northern Luzon to southern Mindanao, always representing us and our children with integrity and, when needed, intensity. She often had to motivate people to do their jobs for the sake of our kids. She talked to judges, lawyers, social workers, mayors, barangay officials, and doctors. She and our other social workers took information from our other professionals and wrote comprehensive case study reports that would be the basis for decisions about placing our children. She conferred with the local matching committee to select families for those children placed locally.

Being a social worker for a pre-adoptive childcare program is different from most types of social work, so Carmelita was learning as she went along during her first years at CSC. Eventually she became an expert, as good as any social worker in the Philippines for our type of program. Over the years she trained and supervised all our new social workers, until her eventual retirement in 2015. But what made her exceptional was her dedication and heart for the children. That she couldn't teach anyone, but she modeled it for all of us at CSC.

Carmelita Baya oversees relief supplies for victims of Typhoon Yolanda.

Carmelita's house was an extension of her CSC office. We could go there any time to bring papers for her to review or sign, to discuss referrals and issues concerning the kids, or to get her opinion on something relating to their cases. Social work was a lifestyle for her as much as a profession.

Often Carmelita went with Marlys or other nurses to get children referred to us by police, local government authorities, or private citizens. They went to squatter areas, remote mountain villages, crowded government hospital wards, and DSWD offices to gather information. They often had to make quick decisions about whether we could take in a child or sibling group, because the kids were often sick or malnourished, sometimes in a life-or-death situation.

One little boy they found in a crowded squatter area was so weak and malnourished that Marlys doubted he would live much longer without medical intervention. Although the usual protocol when finding a child is to try and find the parents or other relatives before we take custody, there just wasn't time. Carmelita found a community social worker and told her they would be taking the boy to see a doctor, giving her contact information should the mother want to know. It turned out that Carmelita and Marlys's decision and fast action saved this child's life, as the doctor determined after examining his malnourished body.

Once I accompanied Carmelita to the Eversley Sanitarium in Mandaue City, where two siblings were being referred to us. They'd been abandoned by their parents and living at Eversley for several months, though the sanitarium was not designed for children. When we got there we found the kids to be sickly and discovered that there was an older cousin living with them who had also been abandoned by her parents. When she learned that we were planning to take her two cousins, she begged Carmelita to let her come with us, too. They were all she had in the world. I was waiting in another area of the hospital, and Carmelita came and sat down. She had tears in her eyes as she told me about the older cousin and advocated strongly for us to take her, too. We did get her. I trusted Carmelita's instincts and her heart.

For many of our children, Carmelita was the best advocate they would ever have. She advocated with the staff for their admission to CSC, with judges to have them declared legally abandoned, with DSWD officials to have them declared legally available for adoption, with the National Census Office and the local civil registrar to get birth documents issued, and with anyone who stood in the way of obtaining their legal rights or best interests.

Carmelita worked for CSC for 31 years, retiring in 2016. In retirement she continued to assist us by making referrals; pulling names, addresses, and case details out of her memory; and continuing to model the compassion and professionalism that had helped CSC grow.

In 2005, Chris Secuya joined CSC to assist Carmelita with case management. Chris was a man of compassion who cared deeply about the children and their birth families. He was skilled as a counselor for families in crisis and children with behavioral problems or who needed to be placed out of CSC for any reason. Like Carmelita, he could be tough when needed, and he worked hard for our kids' best interests. Throughout the 2000s Chris did excellent work, representing CSC well and exuding kindness and love. He was scheduled to retire in 2021 but stayed on temporarily due to the pandemic and the resignation of two other social workers around the time of his scheduled departure.

On May 2, 2016 we hired Klaris Cabansal to head our social work department, replacing Carmelita and heading up our case management. Klaris was an experienced social worker who grew up in Saipan, the daughter of Filipino missionaries. Later she moved to the Philippines, where she worked for an agency that provided services to hearing-impaired adults and children. Although our work was different from what she was used to, Klaris dove right in. She learned and grew and helped CSC develop in accordance with changes dictated by the Philippine government, and as a result of our desire to improve and document our services. Klaris was a bright, highly organized, and articulate leader who established better coordination among our other departments.

In 2019 we promoted Klaris to the new position of program director. Her organizational and leadership skills were now put to better use in directing the various aspects of our ministry, from counseling to social work to medical services. She was skillful in program design and development, helping ensure that we were meeting the needs of all the children under our care, that our programs were consistent with governmental requirements, and that all our departments were working harmoniously. One of Klaris's new tasks was to develop an organizational chart listing the different jobs, departments, and responsibilities that connect employees to each other and to the leadership team. I used to tease Klaris about the charts because she had different colors for every line and function, always carefully and artistically coordinated.

When a child is admitted to CSC, the admitting social worker calls a meeting of the case management team to develop a childcare plan: medical needs, therapy, counseling, educational assessment and goal setting, birth documents and custody matters, and plans for obtaining surrender or abandonment papers.

Meetings, meetings, meetings! Sometimes it seemed like trying to become more organized and improve our communication and documentation resulted in so many meetings that we didn't have time for much else. To be honest, sometimes I felt like we had gotten away from the simple joys of taking care of kids, loving them, and helping them heal. But because we also wanted them to be adopted, all these administrative things were important. It was a tension that we would see increase during the 2000s as we continued to move ahead.

Child Care/Home Life

OUR CHILD CARE DEPARTMENT was started by Sandy Swanson in the 1980s, and she continued to lead that department until 2015. She helped hire, train, and supervise childcare workers. She supervised our first counselors hired to meet our children's psychological and behavioral needs. And Sandy wrote developmental reports for all the children and helped make the house rules for them and our workers.

In the 2000s Sandy created a team to handle the growing needs of her department. They coordinated care from the time children were admitted to CSC until they left for adoption, to return to their families, or to transfer to another childcaring facility.

Sandy retired in 2015. Losing her and Carmelita was hard for those of us who had come to depend on their knowledge, talent, hard work, and leadership. Each played a huge role in planting our ministry and helping it grow into a strong and dynamic organization, well-established and situated to make a big difference in the lives of the children who came to live with us.

During the years after Sandy's retirement, the childcare team grew in scope and function and featured the work and leadership of the following:

Jinkee Reasoner helped establish our Therapy Department and superintended its development in the 2000s. Following Sandy Swanson's retirement, Jinkee became our childcare director, supervising the childcare work force and its services. As a part of our reorganization in 2019, the Childcare Department became Home Life, and Jinkee continued to lead that crucial part of the organization.

Eunice Guinanoy was a teacher in our school in the 1990s. She left CSC for several years to pursue a career in higher education, returning in 2017 as a behavioral specialist, working with our counselors and house parents on delivering services to children struggling behaviorally. She later joined our childcare team, working with Lindsay Abong to improve our counseling services and child development reports. She was a great addition to our team, having had experience and training in special education, program development, and counseling.

When we reorganized, Eunice became director of Child Welfare Services, which included supervising the Medical Department when Marlys left CSC in 2020. Eunice matched her intelligence with dedication and love for the kids and workers to become an integral part of our team.

Lindsay Hoeft Abong worked as childcare director and led our Counseling Department, which Sandy Swanson had established. She came to CSC with experience in counseling in Minnesota and used that knowledge to expand our services in response to the need for more psychological information needed in our case management and reporting. Lindsay helped select and train our counselors to minister to the children's psychological and and emotional needs; write accurate and insightful counseling summaries; and prepare kids for their eventual adoption, return to family, or launching into the community. Lindsay met a great guy while in Cebu, and they were married in 2014. She and her husband, Marwin, a physical therapist, moved to Minnesota in 2019.

Counselors

COUNSELORS WHO WORKED AT CSC DURING THE 2000S helped CSC establish and maintain a first-rate program of individual and group counseling services. Inday Liquigan, our first counselor, left in the early 2000s for a job in Arizona. Eldie Allocod left the Homelife Department to become CSC's first human resources director. Laarni Gersua was both a teacher and counselor at CSC. Eric Abellana and Marivic Ngalan were still counselors in 2022. As our counselors became more skilled in helping our children cope with previous negative experiences, we saw many miracles. We saw healing of emotional wounds and forgiveness granted to abusers and neglecters as the Holy Spirit worked through our counselors in the hearts of our kids.

Through the leadership of Sandy Swanson, Lindsay Hoeft, and Eunice Guinanoy, our counseling became a more professional and valuable tool at CSC during the 2000s. Just as our medical services promoted physical healing for sick kids that came to live at CSC, our counseling sought to nurture emotional wellness. Our kids needed to understand what had happened to them and to forgive those who had hurt them before they could learn to accept the love offered them at CSC and, eventually, from an adoptive family.

House Parents

PART OF THE REASON FOR CSC'S GROWTH AND SUCCESS through the first two decades of the 2000s was the stability of our house parents. Patrick and Lourdes Ronquillo, our senior house parents, were with us since 1997, leading the Duterte Home. Pureza and Tarex Puncol started at the Cherne Home in 2003 and were steady and hard working throughout their ongoing service at CSC. Don and Ivy Enriquez came aboard in 2010. They were hired when we expanded to three homes after construction of the Duterte Home. So for 24 years, from 1997 to 2021, we had 53 years of combined service from those three couples.

We did have some turnover in house parents at the Johnson Home during the early 2000s. Jun Pellejera took over that job after the death of his wife, Rebecca. Jun and Becky had been house parents in the Cherne Home when she died. Jun left after a short time to work as a pastor with the Baptist Conference of the Philippines. Eventually the job went to Edyth and Undoy Ayop, who, with their two daughters, lived in the Johnson Home from 2008 until the writing of this book. Two residents during the 2000s had special needs, including Arleen, our blind resident, who finished high school and college while living in the Johnson Home.

Our house parents in Banawa have the most difficult jobs at CSC. They manage, discipline, encourage, report, love, host, and repair, and they're on duty day and night. They have over 20 workers under them and head up the care of 25-30 children, from babies to teenagers to young adults. And they all have had to deal with the challenge of parenting their own children while being substitute parents for a houseful of needy kids.

Our kids benefitted from the spiritual instruction of our house parents throughout our history, but we became more systematic and intentional about the content and regularity of this instruction during the 2000s. Others who served in leadership or administration in the Childcare/Home-life Department during the 2000s were Amy Luck, Annie del Pilar, and Charity Fuentes.

Finance

OUR FINANCIAL MANAGEMENT went through changes and improvements during the 2000s under the leadership of Mitch Ohlendorf, Joanna Aballe, and Ging Asilom. This was important because we were dealing with more money. In the early 80s, we didn't work with a budget. Money that came in was sent to us in Cebu and we spent it. In 1984 that income was $91,600. By 1990 we had a budget (Cebu and stateside) of about $300,000, and by the turn of the century we were approaching the one-million-dollar mark. This amount continued to increase in the 2000s, and our 2020 Cebu budget for the school and shelter was $1,221,400.

In addition to increased income and a growing payroll, budgeting became a more complicated and time-consuming process. We worked closely with our stateside directors to come up with budgets that reflected the needs of a growing ministry, that allowed us to increase worker and staff salaries, and that provided important reserves to assure financial security in the event of a catastrophe or a significant downturn in income.

One thing that made budgeting and financial management more difficult was currency exchange. We were dealing with three currencies: the U.S. dollar, the Canadian dollar, and the Philippine peso. All three showed volatility over the years, especially the peso. Since our income came primarily from U.S. and Canadian dollars, we had to predict what the exchange rate would be in the coming year as we made budget projections. When we first went to Cebu in 1979, the exchange rate was 7.4 pesos per U.S. dollar. By 1990 it had grown to almost 30:1. By 2001 it was around 41:1, and by 2020 it was 51:1.

We needed to have separate accounts in different banks for pesos and dollars. We needed a secure international bank for transferring dollars from the U.S. to Cebu, and a bank with the best exchange rate for converting those funds to pesos. We needed still another bank to process donations from within the Philippines and occasional government reimbursements.

One initiative that Mitch Ohlendorf and our business office took that would have many unforeseen benefits was moving our payroll to ATM disbursements. Previously, our cashier dispersed salaries from our office on paydays. Our daily wage workers, mostly childcare and household employees, were paid weekly. We needed a lot of cash for these disbursements, which made us uncomfortable and which obliged workers go to the office for their salary. Sending the money to ATM accounts was safer and more efficient. And little did we know that, years later, when many of our workers moved to Happy Homes in Talisay, a long way from the CSC office, and when we were faced with a pandemic where movement around the city was regulated by strict quarantine laws, our ATM system would be a life-saver for our ability to get salaries in the hands of our workers.

Financial management was not my strong suit. But throughout the years, particularly the 2000s, CSC had knowledgeable, honest, and well-trained people managing the funds that God provided. That was important for a variety of reasons. Many government agencies in the Philippines monitor our finances: the Securities and Exchange Commission, the Bureau of Internal Revenue, the Department of Social Welfare and Development. Also, watchdog groups in the U.S. keep an eye on us and give ratings for charities based on that management. But most important, we have a strong commitment to our donors and want to show them faithful, careful, and prayerful stewardship of the money they entrust to us. We're especially mindful of people who give sacrificially.

It starts with integrity and caution. To that we add policies meant to guide anyone who dispenses any CSC money, from the house parents who go to the market every Saturday morning to buy fruits and vegetables, taking the equivalent of $100 or less, to someone buying expensive products, such as solar panels or a new vehicle.

In the Philippines there are always opportunities to do things less than honestly or for people to line their own pockets. Someone could order from a distributor at a higher price and accept a kickback. Government agencies in the Philippines are notorious for financial shenanigans. One time shortly after a big typhoon hit Mindanao, I heard a store owner from Surigao City say he was surprised when government workers came into his store to buy relief goods and instead of bargaining him down, they talked him up, expecting a "piece of the action."

A scandal hit Cebu after Typhoon Yolanda belted the central Philippines and relief supplies started coming in, including expensive canned goods from other countries. Some government social workers were caught substituting cheaper local items for the imported ones and selling the more expensive goods, pocketing the difference.

Government offices and individuals sometimes don't issue receipts for money they collect from the public. This is a problem because we have strict policies at CSC for financial accounting, and we expect official receipts from everyone selling goods or services for our work.

There are many black market options for exchanging dollars that are shady and illegal. Once I was in Manila with a friend, Jack Hoehl, who was visiting the Philippines to get his adopted child (not from CSC). He wanted to exchange some dollars but wanted a better rate than was available at his hotel. (At the time the hotel's exchange rate was around 20 pesos to the dollar.) The licensed exchange outlets had a higher rate, 21 pesos, so we decided to go to one of them. While we were on the way, a man came up to us offering 22 pesos, which Jack liked but which made me nervous. Against my better judgment, Jack said "Okay, my friend" to the dealer, and we followed him into the small tailor's shop where he conducted his business.

In search of a few measly pesos, we walked into a dark changing room, where my friend handed over a $100 bill. The man, who would have made any carnie or street magician proud, pocketed the bill and began counting out 100-peso bills, stopping at 21. Jack said that he had been promised 22. When the dealer refused to give him another hundred, we demanded our money back. He handed us a bill and asked for his 2100 pesos back. My highly trained missionary eye saw that the C note he gave us back was not a real bill but a poorly Xeroxed version.

Jack and I moved in on the guy, who would have run for the hills or possibly brandished a knife if Jack hadn't grabbed his arm and raised his voice. (It didn't hurt that he and I both stood 6'7" next to the little guy's 5'3".) With no escape route available, and me still holding the pesos, he returned the real hundred-dollar bill. Although I could have justifiably kept the 2100 pesos because of the attempted swindle, I gave it back and we exited the tailor's shop, better and wiser people.

Some business establishments offer two prices for goods or services, one accompanied by an official receipt and one without one. The savings for opting out of the receipt can be substantial but not legal for the seller. All kinds of goods, from foodstuffs to clothing to audio or video disks and computer software, can be bought at ridiculously low prices because they're pirated.

Even large and well-established U.S. and international charities are not immune from mismanagement. It doesn't necessarily involve theft of money or property but rather taking money donated for one purpose and using it for another.

Throughout the 2000s CSC remained deeply committed to integrity and transparency in handling donations. If someone gave for something we could not buy or for a service we were not engaged in, we returned the gift or got permission to use it for something other than what the donor had designated. This commitment was tested when money came in for buildings or special projects and we needed it for general fund purchases like food, medicine, or school supplies.

When Typhoon Haiyan hit the Philippines in 2013, the devastation was incredible in some parts of the country. Fortunately, Cebu was spared, with the exception of the northern tip of the island. News of the storm and its damage flooded the international news media. Anderson Cooper of CNN spent more than a week in Tacloban City, offering live prime-time reports on the devastation. Although CSC was not known as a relief agency, people wrote checks to us because we were known and trusted and they didn't know how else to respond to what they had seen and heard about. So we were given significant amounts of money designated for Typhoon Haiyan relief, and we had no such programs and little experience. We needed to either return the money to the donors who gave for relief, or find a way to use that money as it was intended.

We initiated a modest relief effort in Leyte and northern Cebu with some of the money that came in for victims of that storm. But there was more money than we could efficiently and reliably distribute. So we partnered with a Baptist General Conference (now Converge) missionary we knew who lived and worked in Tacloban, Leyte, and who had a fairly significant relief outreach to some of the hardest hit communities. We presented him with a check on behalf of our compassionate and generous donors who had responded to the needs presented by the typhoon and chose to do it through CSC.

I believe that during times when some large international charities were cited for improprieties with funds in crises like the ones that befell the Philippines, people chose to give to CSC instead because they knew us and trusted our integrity.

Human Resources

DURING THE EARLY 2000S CSC became the employer of more and more people. Increasingly, our administrative responsibilities included human resource duties. We were hiring people to work at CSC in many different capacities, and we needed to pay them in an efficient way. This meant new rules and policies to ensure that our employment practices met requirements of the Department of Labor and Employment.

We wanted to offer wages that were fair and competitive with what other government and nongovernment agencies were paying, and within our ability to pay as a small nonprofit organization. Our workers were not unionized so did not have collective bargaining opportunities. But our commitment to providing fair salaries was consistent over the years and much appreciated by most of our workers.

Starting in the 2000s, Mitch Ohlendorf, our executive director, did much of CSC's HR work, coming up with our original salary schedule; hiring and firing practices; and policies and procedures for training, discipline, and promotion. Others involved included Joanna Talaid Aballe and, later, Ging Asilom and Angie Gingoyon, who prepared the payroll. Joel Reasoner made the duty schedules and dealt with worker discipline and performance evaluations. Peter Arneson went to Cebu to help create an employee manual and formulate policies for hiring, evaluations, job descriptions, promotion, discipline, and termination.

We were a long way from the simple handshake agreements we had with our few workers, or the days when we staff members did most of the childcare, purchasing, and financial management. As we grew we recognized the need to professionalize our operations to promote excellence in assembling and maintaining the work force needed to provide the best care possible for our children, and the best working environment possible for our employees.

When Jake Schulz joined our staff, with his wealth of administrative experience, we decided to establish a separate HR department with its own office and personnel. Jake worked with an attorney in Davao City to draft human resource policies that fit with our ministry and were consistent with requirements of the Philippine Department of Labor. We also wanted a program of human resource development that would provide workers at all levels with ongoing training in their area of service, including continuing education credits our professionals needed to secure and maintain their licenses with the Philippine government.

With all this in mind, in 2017 we hired Eldie Allocod as our first HR director. Eldie had been working for CSC as a counselor for eight years, so he knew the organization and our workers. He had the organizational and relational skills to relate with our workers and the leadership team, which he joined. Joel Reasoner was also a part of the team. He helped write policies, establish a comprehensive salary schedule, and improve our hiring and disciplinary procedures, all important aspects of improving the work of CSC as we continued to grow during the 2000s.

Joel, whose mother, Shari, was on our staff as education director, wore a number of hats at CSC over the years. He oversaw our media services,

Sheila Mae gets a lift from Joel Reasoner.

making videos and slide shows and handling our social media. Before the HR department was officially established, Joel handled scheduling of childcare workers, making sure that we had the right number of workers on duty at all times, and fielding the myriad requests for days off and preferred shifts that came from our growing workforce. I was with Joel one day and observed the number of calls he took about workers' requests, some at the last minute, which he handled with understanding and kindness.

Hiring

MOST OF OUR HIRING involved word-of-mouth advertising. The evangelical community in Cebu was fairly small, so lots of people knew when we were hiring. We sent letters to churches in Cebu City when we had an opening, and this usually resulted in many applications.

Friends referred friends or relatives to CSC for employment. For example, Angie Gingoyon, whose friend and churchmate was our financial director, was recommended as a cashier and payroll clerk. Juliet Sultan was "discovered" by one of our staff members, Gloria, when Juliet was working at a fast food establishment. Juliet served for more than 30 years as an excellent childcare worker.

We talked often about the pitfalls of nepotism in hiring, but we continued to use it. We had several mother-daughter combinations and lots of brother-sister pairs who worked for us. And there were more than a few husband-wife duos, both among our workers and our U.S. staff. The Martinez clan took the cake: 12 of them worked for us at the same time: six siblings, five of their spouses, and one daughter.

Half of the Martinez clan: Perry, Lit-Lit, Edwin, E-Boy, Dodong, Jessie

Brain Drain

DURING THE 2000S, and to some extent throughout our history, we experienced "brain drain" with our social workers and the rest of our professional staff. It wasn't exactly a revolving door, but we lost many people to employment overseas or to other local agencies that might have paid better or had less stressful job requirements. During the 2000s, as we were exerting more efforts to strengthen our Filipino staff and develop leadership, we lost many workers to this kind of attrition: teachers, social workers, nurses, and therapists. It was sometimes discouraging to train someone we really believed in and invest time in their development, only to lose them, often unexpectedly, to another organization.

We had to balance our disappointment with happiness for the opportunities that prompted the resignations, often involving a chance for our people to have "dream jobs" or fulfill lifetime hopes of working abroad. During these years we lost teachers to the United States; therapists to Australia, New Zealand, and the U.S.; social workers to opportunities in other parts of the Philippines; a counselor to the U.S.; a nurse to New Zealand; and childcare workers to Canada. In addition to these departures, we had some experienced and valuable people retire or, in the case of missionaries, resign to return to the States.

Retirements

RETIREMENTS ALSO TOOK A TOLL ON CSC during the 2000s, especially among our childcare workers. These women, who didn't have professional training and the vocational mobility provided by degrees in nursing, social work, teaching, or therapy, tended to stay with us until they reached retirement age. Their departures meant losing a ton of experience in the direct care of children and in understanding CSC and what we were trying to accomplish.

Here are just a few examples of losses that CSC experienced during the 2000s:

Bong Ganar was an excellent therapist and a great friend to our kids with special needs. He was knowledgeable, patient, and encouraging. He had a great sense of humor and was creative in developing strategies for helping our kids. He had many talents aside from his therapy work. He was good with computers, serving as our first IT guy when our network was still new, and he was an excellent song leader. I remember watching him in action at one of the camps put on by the Central Baptist Church team. He was leading a lively worship song, and the kids were really into it. At the end of the song he made a flying leap across the stage, jumping so high that I thought his head would hit the ceiling. It was a vertical jump that Michael Jordan would have been proud of! For Bong, it was just another of his many talents that blessed our ministry so richly.

But what stands out the most in my memory was the day Bong was involved in giving something to one of our kids, Jacob, which I will always remember as an amazing demonstration of love and friendship.

Jacob was born with cerebral palsy, and became increasingly rigid and spastic as he grew older. We got Jake when he was a few months old. He ended up in a wheel chair and had to be fed, bathed, and brought to the bathroom for his entire life. He was very bright and often manifested a good sense of humor. He loved to be included in as many of the activities as possible.

One highlight of Jacob's life was when Bong asked him to be his best man at his wedding. Jake had a device that supported him in the standing position so he could "stand up" for his friend's wedding, and he was able to give a speech at the reception using the DynaVox. It was a glorious day for Jake and for all of us who loved him. Because of his extreme excitement on that day, he was thrashing about as we tried to get his barong (dress shirt) on him before the ceremony. Ruth Deliña (Ohlendorf) and I worked for 20 minutes to get that shirt on. Once it was on, he looked great and was so happy that we were amazed at the gift that Bong bestowed on him. But Bong always told us that it was he, Bong, who was gifted that day. What a great symbol of what CSC was all about! We always got back more than we gave from the children we served.

Bong left us shortly after getting married, taking a job as a physical therapist in Australia. He was able to call Jacob from Australia during the last moments of Jake's life on earth, and we held the phone to Jake's ear on the hospital bed and saw his face light up at the sound of his friend's voice. For Bong, and so many of our employees, CSC was much more than just a job. It was an avenue of ministry for them to use their God-given gifts, education, and training in the lives of our children, building His kingdom through their service.

Cora Abaquita was a teacher in our Children of Hope School for the first 20 years of the school's history. She was a dedicated, focused, and talented teacher whose love for her students was always evident. She was calm, kind, encouraging, and loving. Cora didn't have bad days, at least in terms of her attitude and performance in the classroom. She got along well with the other teachers and was a source of encouragement and a great example for them, especially those who were new to our school's unique educational system.

I remember the joy on her face when she gave accounts of students' progress during our quarterly conferences. She could handle the most challenging students and never lost her faith in them and their ability to learn and overcome behavioral and attention difficulties. She always reminded us of our children's potential and the need to trust God for their education and their future. Cora's husband was a pastor, and Cora was involved in their church ministry, teaching children and supporting her husband in many ways. Cora retired in 2020.

Vivian Briones was an esteemed childcare worker for more than 35 years. She started when we were in Bulacao and was a dependable, kind, and loving "auntie" to hundreds of our children. She was soft-spoken and loving to our kids of all ages. Towards the end of her career at CSC, Vivian became sick with complications from diabetes. Sadly, our dear Vivian died in 2020, leaving a legacy of love and care. Her work lives on in other workers whom she influenced and the many children around the world who remember her affectionately.

Joanna Talaid Aballe helped lead CSC into the 21st century in terms of managing funds and meeting increased requirements of the Philippine government for financial reporting. Managing CSC's finances is complicated, considering that we work with three currencies—the U.S. dollar, the Canadian dollar, and the Philippine peso—and two governments, both with their own requirements, auditing systems and schedules, and reporting requirements, which often changed, sometimes without warning. Our yearly budgets had to anticipate an exchange rate for the year, made difficult because of the currencies' volatility.

It was challenging to be on the other side of the world from our funding organizations, needing to meet their expectations for use of funds and reporting on that usage. Joanna kept up on all those requirements and helped us establish a ministry of financial integrity that is crucial in the nonprofit world in which we operate. Joanna shared our staff's commitment to being good and faithful stewards of the money God and our supporters entrusted to us. She left CSC to take a job with the International Justice Mission in their financial office.

With the mention of these losses, it is time to revisit the words of our former school principal and board member, Elisa Saavedra. It is a hallmark of our organization that "God filled the empty slots." He filled in the organizational chart with the right people at the right times. He was never surprised by sudden departures. He was always working to provide people to help us give excellent care to our children.

Salaries

WE'VE ALWAYS WANTED TO PAY OUR EMPLOYEES fair and generous wages. Setting up a salary schedule is a complicated proposition. We were guided in this task by the Department of Labor and Employment, which established minimum wages and had requirements for fairness in disciplining and terminating employees, and standards for vacations, sick leave, retirement pay, and other employment matters. Our salary schedule was constructed to consider an employee's education, seniority, and job experience. We were committed to meeting and even exceeding minimum requirements, including sick leave, vacation pay, health insurance and retirement pay.

Buildings, Transportation, Security

WITH OUR EXPANSION IN THE 2000s came new facilities and vehicles, with the attendant need for their upkeep. We also needed increased security for our children, equipment, and facilities. Thankfully, we had **Jerry Salgo** to organize and manage these efforts. Although Jerry had been work-

ing at CSC for many years and had supervised construction in Banawa for the school and shelter, his job grew significantly in the 2000s. His leadership ability, attention to detail, and knowledge in many different areas served CSC well as we sought to maintain and protect our assets and practice the stewardship that was expected by our staff and supporters.

Jerry understood the philosophy that nonprofit organizations and Christian ministries like ours needed to live by: to be careful in stewardship of the funds entrusted to us. We always lived and worked

Jerry Salgo

with the tension between having nice things for our kids and purchasing equipment and constructing buildings that were high-quality and safe, but also being conscious of costs and always looking for the best deal possible.

Unlike many Christian and secular nonprofit organizations providing services to children, we did not settle for the cheapest equipment or facilities. And if we bought or built something, we maintained it well so it would last as long as possible. CSC's policy was simple: When something broke we fixed it. If it needed paint we painted it. We knew that, if left unattended, things like broken screens, weedy gardens, noisy plumbing, or burned out lights could soon become part of the landscape and, in time, our beautiful facilities could become rundown.

Jerry led the way in these efforts and, in the 2000s, built and managed a crew of guards, drivers, maintenance workers, carpenters, and handymen who were always busy keeping CSC running safe and looking good.

Elisio was our carpenter for 20 years, until his retirement in 2021. He could build anything and had a creative way of working. He built beds and fixed cribs. He repaired windows and was good at painting, plumbing, and basic electrical work. He could refurbish rooms, install walls and ceilings, and fix the kids' riding toys when they broke. In short, he was a wizard, a master carpenter, and a jack of all trades. And he was always kind and gentle with the children. We leaned heavily on his skill and creativity through the 2000s, and he was part of the reason that CSC had a reputation for top-notch facilities.

Bilyong, Elisio's and Jerry's assistant, was skilled in all areas of construction and maintenance. He was a hard worker who, like his bosses, was loving and respectful of CSC kids and workers. Bilyong is the brother of John Ray, a young man with osteogenesis imperfecta (brittle bone disease) whom we came to know and love in 2005. (He and his sister, Rufa Mae, who also had OI, attended our school for a few years.) Back when they lived in the mountains of southeastern Cebu, John Ray and his sister, who could not walk, were carried by Bilyong in a big basket on his back. He carried them up and down hills and across uneven and dangerous paths to bring them to school or the doctor. Bilyong was amazingly strong, and we witnessed some demonstrations of that strength of body and character in his work at CSC.

Part of Jerry Salgo's skill and stewardship involved knowing his limitations and those of his crew. He knew when to bring in outside help and when he and his crew could handle a job. Some minor automotive engine repair or body work could be done in-house, for example, and some needed a trained mechanic. The same was true with fixing broken pumps or generators or doing electrical work.

Transportation

DURING THE 2000s, CSC routinely had a fleet of eight or more vehicles. Jerry Salgo saw to it that they were regularly maintained and always had fuel. He scheduled drivers to deliver or pick up kids for medical or other appointments outside CSC, buy equipment or supplies, bring workers down the hill to where they could catch public transportation home, or be on duty for emergencies at the shelter. These drivers had a crucial role at CSC because of the cargo they were hauling—our precious kids and workers.

During the 2000s our team of drivers included Doming Condino; the Martinez boys, Edwin, E-Boy, and Dodong; Ducoy Noel; and Ike Labra. Our house fathers also handled driving duties when needed, as did Jerry Salgo and Eldie Allocod.

Staff members also helped drive. Mitch Ohlendorf, Sandy Swanson, Joel Reasoner, Roberto Atienza, Lindsay Hoeft, Marlys, and I hauled kids to activities and doctors' appointments, picked up or dropped off visitors at the airport or seaport, picked them up at their hotels and brought them to CSC, and took them on city tours. Sometimes these trips meant driving late at night or early in the morning.

Driving in Cebu can be very stressful, with narrow, congested, and accident-prone roads, liberal use of horns by most drivers, and pedestrians darting into traffic. Traffic laws are routinely ignored, and motor vehicles have to share already crowded roads with bikes, pedestrians, animals, huge trucks, jeepneys, and buses, all of which make frequent unsignaled turns and stops, plus rampant tailgating and illegal passing. Motorcycles are everywhere, zigzagging between cars and sometimes driving down the wrong side of the road or even going on sidewalks. Somebody once said that you don't have to be crazy to drive in Cebu, but it helps!

Security

AT THE BEGINNING OF THE 2000s, we used both CSC employees and agency guards to protect our property and people. By 2010 our school, offices, and shelter were all serviced by professional armed guards. This development stemmed from legitimate concerns about safety. At our office in Sun Valley we often had a significant amount of cash in our safe. At the Children of Hope School, we had computers and other expensive equipment. And the school was empty evenings, weekends, and holidays. At the shelter we had been victimized by intruders at night. Security was a necessity at CSC, but we yielded to the need reluctantly, especially having armed guards near our children and workers. At the school and shelter we had a policy of not allowing guards to carry a weapon while children were present.

In all our history, we never had any gunfire or armed intrusion at the shelter, offices, or school. Once we had a new agency guard at the office who scared us a little. One of our drivers had picked up Arlene, our blind resident, to bring her home from school and had an accident when another vehicle hit the side of our jeep. The accident was near the office/teen home, so our driver insisted that the other guys pull inside our gate so we could settle the matter. The negotiation centered on who would pay to repair our vehicle. Our guard was nearby observing the proceedings, which got more and more heated as they went along. Finally, the other party said they were leaving and we could each just fix our own vehicle. As they attempted to leave, the guard got out his firearm, pointed it at them, and ordered them to stop. Luckily, Jerry was nearby and he got the guard to holster his weapon and restored some order to the situation. Needless to say, we had a different guard on duty the next day.

As I think about it, I suppose it isn't entirely true that we never had gunfire at CSC. One night our guard at the school, Edgar, accidentally shot himself when he dropped his firearm and it went off, the bullet striking him in the thigh. The incident occurred in the middle of the night. He was able to call someone and I was informed, so I rushed to the school and brought him to the hospital. Although he was in a lot of pain from the bullet going through his leg, his damaged pride was a much more painful injury.

As time went on, guards at the shelter began inspecting the bags of people entering and leaving. Although most of our workers and visitors were totally reliable and trustworthy, we did have times when food or other commodities were pilfered. We often had new workers whom we did not know well who might have yielded to temptation and taken something. We hated to do it but felt we needed to inspect bags as a deterrent to this kind of theft, and to prevent visitors from bringing in anything that might be dangerous for our residents and workers.

A tertiary responsibility of guards was to prevent kids from running away. This didn't happen very often, but occasionally some of our newer residents would try to take off. Sometimes it was just a gesture of discontent or rebellion and didn't constitute a real desire to live elsewhere. A couple times the fleeing kid or group would get to the bottom of the hill without a plan for where to go. One former resident told us years later that he and the two boys he had "escaped" with just hung around at the corner, hoping they would be found by someone from CSC. When we got professional guards, we didn't have those situations any more.

Even though CSC was a safe place, with good food, nice places to play, a beautiful school, kind and loving caregivers, and where kids' medical needs were addressed by compassionate nurses and competent doctors, some just didn't want to stay with us. Often it was a child who had been on his or her own and wasn't used to living with rules and expectations like we had at CSC, or who had been disciplined at CSC for one reason or another. Occasionally, a child would be so worried about a sibling or birth parent left behind that s/he was not content at CSC. Although we could not keep kids against their will, we wanted to give them a chance to adjust and get into the swing of life at CSC before making a decision to leave. And we feared for their safety if they left without a place to go where there would be some level of responsible adult supervision.

Medical Care

WHEREAS MARLYS HEALY HAD HANDLED THE MEDICAL DEPARTMENT by herself in the early days of CSC, we gradually added nurses as our numbers grew and in response to increasing requirements for documentation. By the 2000s we were up to three or four nurses working with Marlys. In addition to the usual medical tasks—administering vaccines, medications, and vitamins; keeping height and weight records; taking kids to doctors and dentists; admitting them to the hospital and consulting with our pediatrician and specialists—we took on additional tasks of writing medical reports and summaries that included documenting every medical procedure, test result, medication taken, doctors visit, and illness. There was rarely a time in the 2000s when at least one nurse was not working on reports.

As we matured as an agency, our medical team became more professional, and our network of doctors and labs became more extensive. We could find the best doctors, hospitals, and medications available in the Philippines. We brought a boy to Manila for surgery and recuperation in 2013 because the doctor there was more experienced in the type of operation that he needed. Our nurses were able to enlist the help of a medical mission surgical team from the United States who were in Cebu briefly in 2018. One of the visiting doctors performed brain surgery on our boy. We even were able to consult with doctors in the U.S. who were supporters or adoptive parents, when we desired a second opinion. Doctors from the U.S. who visited CSC sometimes took a look at our kids who were sick or in need of treatment. These doctors included Allen Mork, Paul Sanders, Stuart Cox, Dale Berry, and two dentists, Tim Erickson and Matt Struve.

Bringing a child to Manila for treatment or surgery presented big challenges. Because flying the whole team there to take turns being with a child in the hospital around the clock was too expensive, it meant that one or two nurses or childcare workers needed to be there to work long shifts. And we hesitated to send large amounts of money to Manila to pay cash for hospital bills, medications, and tests. The Manila hospital we favored did not accept checks or credit cards.

Once when we knew a child would need to stay for a long stretch and the bill would be large, I called up our good friend Dan Chalmers, who lived and worked near Manila, and asked if we could transfer money into his account and let our workers get cash from him to pay the bills. He readily agreed but called me back in a couple hours and said he had second thoughts. The plan was okay, he said, except for the part about our sending him the money. He would pay the bills from the Nehemiah Project, the charity that he was a part of that had helped us in many ways over the years. We didn't need to pay him back!

CSC was receiving many referrals of children with major physical or developmental needs during these years, so it was becoming an important task of our medical team to get them evaluated by doctors before we decided to admit them. In spite of our more than 20 years of experience working with kids with all kinds of illnesses and challenges, our excellent medical facilities at CSC, and our group of competent doctors in all specialties, we were cautious about taking in children who had little or no chance for adoption. We were aware that, should we admit any referred child, we would eventually become an institution for children needing lifetime care. Because that was not our primary mission, we did the best we could to understand the medical issues that would be involved in admitting these children.

The Home Life department, our therapy team, and our counselors assisted in these evaluations, trying to determine children's developmental status and any emotional trauma or physical, emotional, or sexual abuse they had been victims of. Because our priority in admitting children was to take in those who had a reasonable chance to be adopted, any with certain medical or developmental conditions, or who had mental illnesses or had experienced traumatic abuse, were extremely unlikely to be placed. And we had to be sure we had the space, the person power, and the finances to handle them.

Our referral meetings were multi-disciplinary gatherings of our various professionals, who came with observations, doctors' or psychologists' findings, and recommendations concerning placement. We wanted to accept even the most difficult and complicated cases, and it was heartbreaking to say no to any referral. This was especially true for those of us from the "old days," when we were new, didn't have lots of experience in child development, behavioral issues, or adoption, and could more easily just go with our hearts.

Therapy

CSC'S THERAPY DEPARTMENT came of age in the 2000s, establishing comprehensive services and interventions to assist in the growth and development of children who needed physical, occupational, and speech therapy. The two biggest improvements in our therapy department were a new therapy room in the basement of the Duterte Home and the initiation of speech therapy.

In both of these, CSC was blessed to have outside assistance in the form of donations and consultancy from professionals who offered their knowledge, experience, and financial resources to our kids. Topping this list of friends who helped our Therapy Department during the 2000s was **Tara Perkins**, a speech therapist from England who worked with our therapists to improve their skills. She was a positive and infectiously enthusiastic person who loved our kids and traveled to Cebu from England often, almost always bringing wheel chairs, computers, books, and various kinds of adaptive equipment to donate to our expanding Therapy Department. While in Cebu she trained our therapists in using the equipment and assessing the children. Every encounter I had with Tara was encouraging and spiritually uplifting. Her Christian faith and commitment to her profession was a guiding light for our staff in general, and our therapists in particular.

Our new therapy headquarters in the basement of the Duterte Home was a bright, spacious, well-equipped room where our therapists could work with several children at the same time in a friendly and efficient atmosphere. It was a huge improvement over our small therapy space in the school and was consistent with the increased importance that CSC was giving to therapy ministry-wide.

Although our Therapy Department suffered from brain drain throughout our history, and especially in the 2000s, we always were able to hire excellent therapists in Cebu. This was a reflection of the quality of therapy departments in Cebu schools, such as Cebu Doctors University, Velez College, and Southwestern University.

Children of Hope School

THROUGH OUR SCHOOL'S HISTORY, most of which occurred in the 2000s, we gave attention to teacher and curriculum development. We acquired computers, books, math manipulatives, and audio visual and other equipment. Much of this was donated directly to the school or were things we could buy with grants from individuals or funding agencies, both local and international.

CHS continued to improve its educational services in line with children's needs and CSC's priorities in preparing them for the future. Because we have always sought adoption for most of our children, and because the largest share of adoptions have gone to the United States and other

English-speaking countries, we recognize the importance of our students speaking and reading English well. In the 2000s our language arts curriculum, Open Court, became the core of our school's learning program and helped our children immensely in preparing for their further education and adjustment to family life in adoption. It also exposed them to the world outside our school and helped them understand their abilities and interests in preparation for eventually choosing a vocation. The school was a major tool in building self-esteem in our CSC kids through the power of education that focused on what they could do, instead of what they could not.

Stateside Ministry

AS THE OPERATION IN CEBU EXPANDED, fundraising efforts in the United States increased to keep pace with our growing need. Our stateside directors in Minnesota during the 2000s each brought talent, enthusiasm, and creativity to the job and moved the ministry forward in efficiency, influence, and the ability to tap resources.

Just as our work in Cebu was becoming more professional, our stateside organization was becoming more skilled and businesslike. Even though many fundraising programs and strategies were retained—the CSC newsletter, the annual banquet, the Foster Friends sponsorship program— CSC's stateside leaders explored new ways of promoting the ministry and finding and servicing donors. For example, the 2000s brought us the World Wide Web, e-mail communication, and Facebook and other social media.

Elizabeth Healy and **Pauline Bohachek** each worked for a couple years as stateside directors (known then as executive directors) and helped CSC transition to having our office in Cambridge and computerizing our financial records and donor database. We were starting to get a better idea of who our donors were and what they liked about CSC.

Elizabeth, my sister, was instrumental in bringing people together to help plan our school, and used her experience as a librarian to help get our school library set up. Though neither Elizabeth or Pauline had any significant experience in fundraising before coming to work at CSC, they did a good job of communicating with our donors, informing them of developments in Cebu, and maintaining and improving our fundraising mechanisms like Foster Friends, the newsletter, our annual banquets, and our appeal mailings. Elizabeth established an appreciation dinner for our volunteers and helped make mailing days a fun time for everyone.

Matt Buley helped CSC improve the quality of our mailings, presentations, and audiovisual resources. He helped establish our Luke Fund endowment and expand our donor base. He communicated with many of our donors and nurtured larger donors with calls and visits. His trips to Cebu were successful in communicating the financial situation to our staff and workers in Cebu and building bridges of understanding and cooperation. He helped us develop and professionalize our board of directors.

Matt continued the process of shepherding CSC from a "mom and pop" fundraising operation, which had served the ministry well but needed to be modernized to meet the demands of a growing organization. He worked with the board to develop financial reserves, both stateside and in Cebu, to make us more secure and able to handle the economic instability in the world economy in those days. He led CSC in a capital campaign for construction of the Duterte Home and the infirmary building. And he helped develop our board from a "friends and family" group to a collection of people with expertise in fields like law, accounting, medicine, social work, and church leadership.

Matt was a lead advocate for legislation during the 111th U.S. Congress that kept siblings together in adoption, and worked closely with Senator Amy Klobuchar. CSC had a sibling group of nine in process for adoption to a Minnesota family who could only adopt the entire group if the legislation passed. It did indeed pass and was signed into law by President Obama in December of 2010.

Matt had a great sense of humor, and we shared many laughs. Before he started at CSC and for the first couple years of his tenure, I was president of CSC, a title I had even in Cebu. I was supposed to be the boss of those in the stateside office, including Matt. It was not a very efficient system, and I was uncomfortable making decisions and interacting with the board from 10,000 miles away. I was happy to turn over my stateside responsibilities to Matt in 2012, when he became stateside director and president of CSC.

Matt and his wife, Theresa, had special insights into the ministry because they adopted four CSC kids in 2007. Matt left CSC in 2017 to become the CEO of Hope Haven, a ministry that provides services worldwide to people with disabilities.

Tim Holmberg took over the reins of CSC in 2018 after Matt Buley's departure. Tim had served on the CSC board for several years. He was introduced to CSC when a presentation was made in his church, First Baptist of Cambridge, Minnesota. He and his wife, Barb, later adopted five CSC children, in 2004. Tim had sold his electrical contracting business but decided to delay his retirement for a time and serve CSC.

Tim had an important role during a time of major change at CSC. With the departure of Matt Buley, the retirements of Carmelita Baya and Sandy Swanson, and the impending retirement of Marlys and me, CSC needed a wise and mature leader who could convey a message of strength and solidity to our staff, workers, and supporters. Tim was that man, and he led us through some choppy waters during his five-year stint as president and stateside director. He had the confidence of the Cebu staff right from the start because he was straightforward and transparent. Tim worked well with the board and U.S. office staff.

Tim's faith and genuineness were a great encouragement to me during our last months in Cebu and in navigating the pandemic in its early manifestations. Our weekly phone calls were very important because I had no experience in managing an organization during something as difficult as a pandemic. Tim didn't either, of course, but together we worked through issues and problems.

One example was our finances during the pandemic. I felt strongly that we should be as generous as possible with our workers, even those who could not work because of family situations or health problems, or because they weren't selected to be part of the locked-in group. Tim helped me work through those important decisions by asking useful questions and expressing solidarity in striving to do the most we possibly could for our employees. He had a positive influence on Roberto Atienza and his family as they were preparing to leave for Cebu.

Kirby Stoll became our president in 2020. He had been a board member and long-time supporter of CSC. Kirby came to CSC from Northwestern University of St. Paul, where he worked in development for 19 years. He is skilled in all areas of fundraising and came to us with a deep love for CSC's ministry and a desire to help us grow. In his first days as president, Kirby led the board in planning for both the immediate and long-term future. Kirby is a man of faith and action, and he understands the science and the ministry of fundraising. He has great interpersonal skills and sees the opportunity to lead CSC as a great blessing.

Kirby was a blessing to Marlys and me as we started our terminal furlough and, eventually, our retirement in Minnesota. He met with us regularly, either in person or via Zoom, to see how we were coping with retirement, readjusting to life in the U.S. and away from Cebu, and handling all the paperwork associated with retiring: Social Security, pensions, Medicare, supplemental health care plans, etc. In addition to helping us with the transition to stateside life, he continued the great relationship with Roberto and the leadership team that Tim Holmberg had established.

TRANSITION

"Son, you are doing a good job. Bless you."

Retirement

AS EARLY AS 2016 we began thinking and talking about Marlys and my coming retirement and how to best prepare for a transition to a new leader. Among other things, the board and Cebu staff talked about the kind of person we wanted, the gifts he or she needed, and the timetable for the transition. Many questions were raised:

Within or without? Did we have the right person already in a leadership role, either in Cebu or Minnesota, who could become field director, or did we need to hire someone from outside the organization? Certainly we had a group of excellent leaders in Jerry Salgo (maintenance, security, and transportation), Eldie Allocod (HR), Ben Bonnett (education), Cris Tabra (school principal) , Ging Asilom (finance), Jinkee Reasoner (Home Life), Eunice Guinanoy (medical, therapy, and counseling), and Klaris Cabansal (program).

Did we have anyone who could inspire the confidence of our board, supporters, and Filipino staff; effectively communicate with our stateside office; write and produce promotional materials that captured CSC's vision and direction moving forward; understand the workings of the stateside organization and its relationship to the work in Cebu; and handle the challenges of leading a cross-cultural team in an increasingly complicated, regulated, and labor intensive environment?

Local person or Filipino? We had observed over the years the difficulty North Americans often had in making the cultural and lifestyle adjustments to living in Cebu. This was especially true for staff that already had children when they moved to the Philippines. There was so much change to embrace: language, food, housing , driving in Cebu traffic, cultural differences, and just the reality of being relatively rich people in a place with so much heartbreaking poverty.

Some Americans were stressed by tropical weather or political uncertainties. And some just could not handle being away from their families,

169

friends, or church mates. Obviously, having a Filipino from Cebu would eliminate those adjustment stresses.

Male or Female? As I assessed our leadership group in Cebu, it was clear that our group of leaders included and was even dominated by women. Should we consider a female field director? The great majority of our work force in Cebu were women, not only our childcare workers but our professional staff as well.

Around this time I wrote a paper entitled "CSC's Glass Ceiling: The Roles of Filipinos and North Americans in the Ministry." It addressed who should lead the work in Cebu and posed questions for the board of directors. It inspired healthy discussions by our staff and U.S. leadership. During this soul-searching, the board received an application from one of its own members, Roberto Atienza.

Roberto had been on the CSC board for several years and was pastor of a Filipino-American church in St. Paul, a church where some former CSC residents who had been adopted in Minnesota attended. Roberto was born in the Philippines but had been raised in the United States. He and his wife, Heather, who have four children, including two teenagers, had been talking and praying about the idea of becoming missionaries. Because of his background and Filipino heritage, Roberto's heart was for the Philippines. He and Heather felt God leading them to apply for this position.

The board considered his qualifications—leadership experience, communication skills, and proven love for the ministry of CSC—and decided to invite him and his family to visit CSC . They went in March of 2019 and got to see and feel the ministry first-hand. They met with the leadership team, talked in depth with the directors of each department, got to know the kids, and spoke to all the workers.

The visit went well, and we got to know Roberto. Among his qualifications for the job, one stood out for me. He is a kind person. For me that is an indispensable trait for a leader in this ministry. Loving kindness to the children and workers. Kindness to the many people who visit CSC in Cebu. Kindness to the government people we deal with on a regular basis. Kindness to the hurting and sometimes problematic birth parents of our children. Kindness and graciousness to the supporters who make CSC possible.

The board in Minnesota voted unanimously to offer the field director position to Roberto, and he and his family arrived in Cebu in September of

CSC's Field Director Roberto Atienza and a few friends

2019. The staff, led by Mari and Ben Bonnett, had found a home for them to rent that was close to CSC and comfortable for their family. They dived right into CSC life, attending birthday parties of CSC kids and hanging out at the shelter.

They also began getting to know the city, obtaining drivers licenses and visas, and meeting their neighbors and other missionaries working in the city. Since Heather was home-schooling their kids, they didn't have to adjust to a new school, but they spent a few weeks looking at churches that fit well with their family. They started attending the Banawa Bible Fellowship, and Roberto got involved almost right away, leading worship and serving as guest speaker for the church's anniversary.

Roberto and I spent many hours together talking about the ministry. We discussed the joys and challenges of CSC. He attended our leadership meetings and met with individual leaders. We reviewed our financial management and some of the problems we faced in dealing with government agencies and, sometimes, difficult workers. I held nothing back from Roberto, and he wanted and needed to know everything. It was clearly the passing of the torch of leadership from me to him.

After a couple months I had him lead some of our leadership meetings.

We had a meeting of the Philippine board, and I introduced him to some of the government people we worked with regularly and some friends of the ministry. I found Roberto to be a fast learner, very intelligent, and able to grasp principles and difficult issues easily. We enjoyed each other and our time together talking and praying. We had lunch together with our wives at our favorite restaurant, Toast, and became close very quickly. It was an answer to prayer for Marlys and me as we wound down our time in CSC and handed things off to Roberto. He was always very respectful to me and sensitive to what I was going through.

One day Roberto and I had lunch with my friend Prisco Allocod. Prisco was our pastor when we first arrived in Cebu, and he and I became close. I visited his home in Surigao twice. We traveled to a remote village in eastern Samar together in search of a birth mother of a CSC kid. He was president of CSC (Philippines) and worked with us to start the Bulacao Evangelical Free Church. We had a nice time at lunch, but then it was time to say goodbye. Prisco and his wife, Lena, had been appointed as missionaries to Japan and were scheduled to leave for Tokyo soon. I knew I wouldn't see him again for a long time, maybe never. I started to tear up after I said goodbye to my friend. Roberto understood. He had recently said goodbye to his friends in Minnesota. He knew the deep bonds that can develop with coworkers in ministry and could sense the relationship that Prisco and I shared. It was an emotional time for me and, I think, for Roberto as well. I think he could understand the feelings of loss that Marlys and I were experiencing in the days leading up to our departure from Cebu and the many goodbyes that were coming soon.

Roberto Atienza was an answer to many prayers. Our board, staff, and some of our supporters recognized the importance of getting the right person in that position. My mom, CSC's number one prayer supporter, told me later that she had been praying that God would provide someone I felt good about. She knew how difficult leaving would be for Marlys and me and how that separation would be made easier if we felt that CSC was in good hands when we left. We did. And it was.

Roberto and I took it slow and easy, thinking we would have plenty of time for the transition of leadership. We didn't know that things were about to change dramatically in the world and at CSC, things that would change our transition timetable almost completely, thrusting Roberto into more significant leadership responsibilities ahead of schedule.

Pandemic

AS MARLYS AND I WERE GETTING OUR MINDS around the idea of leaving Cebu for retirement, the world was starting to experience a widespread virus that nobody understood much about. It had apparently started in China, and the second place it appeared was the Philippines. It spread rapidly.

We were to begin our retirement in Minnesota in April of 2020, but as the virus spread the Philippine government took action to suppress that spread. Quarantines were established. Nobody could go out of their house without a quarantine pass issued by the local government unit where they lived. Seniors and children were unable to leave their homes at all. Travel in the city, throughout the province, between islands, and internationally was restricted and even stopped. People who got the virus were put in makeshift medical facilities, even against their will if necessary.

Initially, we heard that seniors would be under a 24-hour curfew. Mistakenly, we thought it meant we would be restricted from going out for one day. What it really meant was 24 hours a day, every day. We were restricted to our home and had to communicate with other staff members via phone calls, text messages, and Zoom meetings.

The leadership team was concerned about CSC's ability to get necessary personpower to the Shelter to care for the kids because some communities where our workers lived were establishing quarantines of their own. Many of the quarantines in Cebu City were established for two-week periods. We decided to put CSC on lockdown, meaning nobody could come in or go out, short of an emergency. We recruited childcare workers, nurses, teachers, and a few others to be locked in, asking if they would be willing to commit to two weeks of not leaving the grounds.

The biggest threat to CSC was the travel restriction in Cebu province. Many of our workers had moved to Talisay because of the Habitat for Humanity project that built them new houses. Unfortunately, Talisay is outside Cebu City, and coming into the city proper was restricted at various times. We could not count on our ability to get workers to Banawa. Even if they could get into the city from Talisay, there was no assurance they could get back home at the end of their duty. So we put together a group and started the lockdown. Six months later the same basic group was still locked in! And four-and-a-half months after Marlys and I were first subject to quarantine, we were still restricted to our house.

I was in a tricky situation. We were supposed to have ended our jobs in Cebu and begun our semi-retirement in Minnesota by April of 2020. Roberto Atienza, whom the board had appointed as my replacement as field director, had arrived in September of 2019. I had been able to work with him for a few months, but our time was cut short by the pandemic. The overlap was supposed to be six months, with him taking over completely when we left Cebu in April.

So I was still there after Roberto was to have taken over. I was a field director without portfolio. I had already turned over my responsibilities to Roberto, made him a signatory on bank accounts and official documents, had him chair leadership meetings and deal with personnel issues and financial decisions. So what was my role to be?

This situation could have been very awkward if it wasn't for Roberto's grace and servanthood. We were open with each other about what we thought was best for CSC. Roberto was always very respectful and kind to me, and I tried to reciprocate. He had proved to be a fast learner who did not shrink from responsibilities or difficult decisions. He sought my input and came to our house for visits while we were restricted from going out. (Because he was not a senior, he had some ability to go around the city, visit our office, and purchase food for his family.)

I could see that the leadership team liked and respected Roberto, and he was good at leading meetings and handling stressful situations. Tim Holmberg, our president at the time, encouraged Roberto and spoke with him regularly, expressing his and the board's confidence in him for what he faced in leading CSC during a pandemic. Roberto and I decided that I would be available to him as he needed. I would leave leadership to him, not only in word but in deed. I would not communicate with any of our employees about anything official without including him or at his request. Marlys and I would continue our attempt to find a flight out of Cebu. We were invited to attend the twice or thrice weekly leadership meetings (via Zoom) that were so important because the leaders could not meet face-to-face.

During this time Marlys was also turning over leadership of the medical department to Eunice Guinanoy and the nurses. Two nurses were part of the group locked in with the children. Marlys would have loved to have had the chance to introduce Roberto and Eunice to all the doctors CSC had been working with, but that wasn't possible.

The reality of our situation in Cebu was this: Neither Roberto nor I knew how to lead an organization during a pandemic! Neither of us could bank on experience in leading staff and workers who were dealing with the stresses and uncertainties that were such a part of their lives at that time. My 42 years of experience leading CSC had not prepared me for the life-and-death issues and complex problems CSC faced.

We were concerned about having the personpower to care for the kids; maintain our facilities; provide security; and offer education, medical care, and counseling. We were struggling about how to keep our kids and workers safe from the virus, and what protocols and restrictions were necessary to help ensure that safety. We needed to establish backup and contingency plans for everything, especially in the financial area. We didn't know how the pandemic would affect giving, or our ability to get the money to Cebu and access it. We had to come up with a plan for salaries during the lockdown. How much should we pay workers who agreed to be locked in? And what about those who were locked out; they needed to be paid something so they could live and feed their families, even though they were not working.

In addition to Roberto's graciousness, the situation was positively affected by the cooperative spirit and positive, Christ-like attitudes of our leadership team. Never was I so proud of the talent, creativity, and brilliance of our people as during this time of crisis. Once the lock-in dragged out from a few weeks to a few months, we needed plans on how to get workers out and bring in "fresh troops" and still maintain our quarantine protocols. Jinkee, our Homelife director, set up transition schedules and recruited workers to replace those who were going out. We had to quarantine any new workers for two weeks before they could enter the Shelter. Both those leaving and those coming needed transportation. Jerry Salgo, our transportation and facilities guru, was especially appreciated during this time. He jokingly coined the term "extractions" for getting workers in and out of the Shelter. And he set up living facilities in the school for both men and women who needed to be quarantined.

Three things worked in our favor during this time:

Children of Hope School

FIRST, WE WERE THANKFUL to have the school for a quarantine center for new workers coming in. It was both close to the Shelter and separate. It had a kitchen, three bathrooms, and individual rooms where workers could sleep during the two weeks of their quarantine. Principal Cris Tabra and Education Director Ben Bonnett were accommodating about making the school facilities available for the quarantine. As one of the locked-in workers, Cris was inside the Shelter for the first several months of the lock down. She was an amazing example of sacrificial leadership during this time. Since she was the only member of our leadership team to be locked in, she had a lot of responsibility in assessing needs and handling problems.

Because we could not use CHS facilities for schooling, we had to set up alternative classrooms at the Shelter while the school was used as a quarantine facility. Happily, Cris found her faculty to be agreeable and flexible in making this huge change. Since not all the teachers were locked in, the class structure needed to be changed. Computers were not accessible, and there could be no field trips.

Our teenagers and young adults had been attending other schools before the pandemic, and these were closed to in-person instruction after the onset of the virus. Most of these students were attending Bob Hughes Christian Academy, which uses the Accelerated Christian Education curriculum, a self-paced, self-study system. CSC provided tutors for the Bob Hughes students to help them with their homework and coordinate with the school for releasing materials and reporting on students' progress.

So, we did the best we could do for our staff, workers, and children as the pandemic unfolded in Cebu. Children of Hope School had to abide by the policies and guidelines of the Department of Education, which dictated when the school years began and ended and the standards for evaluation and promotion of the students.

Happy Homes

ANOTHER THING IN OUR FAVOR was Happy Homes, the Habitat for Humanity project where many of our workers lived. Although its location in Talisay presented complications in getting workers in and out of Cebu

City, our locked-out workers living there were much better protected from the virus than had they remained living in their pre-Habitat communities. Once we started rotating workers into Banawa, most of whom were living at Happy Homes, we didn't have to worry much about them having Covid. Although we maintained our fairly strict protocols by having incoming workers tested and quarantined in the school for two weeks before they could start their duties in the Shelter, we had little worry about them contaminating the school or spreading the virus to those under quarantine who were not from Happy Homes.

There were times when we were concerned about some behavior in Happy Homes, such as residents sometimes not wearing masks and not practicing social distancing. And, unlike their locked-in counterparts, they needed to go out from their homes to buy food, medicine, and other supplies. Also, some of our workers had husbands who were working in the community and were being exposed to the virus. So there was some vulnerability. But they were living in well-made houses that had some separation from neighbors, a relatively safe water supply, and a safe place for their kids to play.

Our Supporters

THE THIRD THING THAT WORKED IN OUR FAVOR during the dark days of the pandemic was the generosity and faithfulness of our supporters. In spite of many people being out of work in the States, CSC's income did not suffer. People continued to give and to pray for the ministry. We shouldn't have been surprised; our people came through time and time again for 43 years. But this was a time like no other, with fears and uncertainties, fueled by political differences and a contentious election in the U.S. that split the nation on the issues of Covid prevention and the economy.

But those fears did not dampen the enthusiasm of our supporters for the ministry of CSC. Because of their faithfulness, we could be aggressive in upgrading our facilities to protect our kids and workers, offer salary premiums to our locked-in workers, and pay our locked-out employees even though they could not work. And our Cebu staff didn't need to spend time and worry about our income.

Adjusting to the Pandemic

The pandemic forced us to think creatively and quickly. How could we maintain our services in the face of numerous restrictions? Roberto Atienza and the leadership team were under pressure. I often thought about how different Roberto's leadership role turned out compared to what he had been expecting. People asked him if he wished he'd never gone to Cebu. He was always resolute that he knew God had called him and his family to go to Cebu at this time in history, and he embraced the challenges that came his way. I was able to turn over a ministry that was well established; had committed, dedicated, talented leaders and workers; was financially secure; and had excellent facilities and equipment. Most of all, Roberto inherited a ministry that had found God's favor for more than 40 years, doing a work that was close to His heart.

The locked-in teachers ate and slept at Children of Hope School. We were concerned that the school was being used as a quarantine facility for workers, and we needed to keep our teachers safe. Jerry Salgo went to work on this problem and came up with a system that kept both groups separate. This involved setting up separate entrances and exits, building temporary toilets and showering facilities, and making some changes to classrooms that were used for bedrooms. We also needed an additional septic tank.

Some changes were also needed at the Sun Valley office/teen home. Residents there were locked in, but people were going in and out of the office. To minimize exposure we had the office staff work four-day weeks, and they ate and slept at Sun Valley during the week. Because our guards also were locked in, Jerry had to devise bathroom facilities outside the house and office for them to use.

Jerry's amazing team of Elisio Ewayan and Verjilio Obiedo and other maintenance workers who were locked in from the start of the pandemic showed what Filipino ingenuity, creativity, and elbow grease could accomplish under less-than-desirable circumstances. Time and again, Jerry and crew were asked to come up with a plan that involved plumbing, electrical work, carpentry, or masonry work. In addition, they had to do all the repairs at the Shelter for our pump, generator, and other appliances and equipment, since we could not bring in outside repairmen or take things out to get them fixed.

The pandemic, which we thought at first would last a few weeks, dragged on. Weeks became months and months became a year. Aside from Cris Tabra, the women who were providing much of the leadership inside were Annie Del Pilar from Home Life, and Honeylin Villar and SenSen Baya, two of our nurses. The challenge was to nurture an environment where the kids felt secure and had a daily schedule that was as much like normal as possible. They couldn't go to school, so we brought the school to them. They couldn't go to church, so we had worship services at CSC. Because of dependable vendors for food, medicine, and other goods, we never had to miss a meal, immunization, or dose of medicine. Children could have counseling sessions and programs on holidays or special occasions. Everyone got their own birthday party, just like before the pandemic. Because nurses could not bring kids to doctors' offices for checkups, they did phone consultations and only brought children in for emergencies.

Our leadership team could not go inside the Shelter but were aware of what was going on and what was needed on the inside. They set up safety protocols to protect the kids and staff. All deliveries—food, paper products, milk, rice, lumber—had to be put in a holding area for a few days and cleaned before they could be used. Delivery people had to drop off goods near the gate and let our staff complete the delivery.

If anyone had to go outside for any reason, they were quarantined for two weeks before they could re-enter. No visitors whatsoever were allowed to enter. Our Homelife Team, with help from Joel Reasoner, ordered food from trusted vendors, making sure that there was a complete and safe food supply. Eldie Allocod, our HR director, helped the driving crew by picking up the office staff and bringing them home, and handling other driving assignments.

The staff met via Zoom regularly, sometimes daily, during crucial decision times. This kind of virtual leadership and communication lasted for many months and was challenging for everyone. But we were thankful for a relatively stable Internet connection, and for smart phones and computers that allowed us to stay connected with each other and with the stateside office and with our families in Minnesota.

Never before had the Shelter part of Children's Shelter of Cebu been more evident and important. We became a shelter against the unseen invader, the threat to the health and even the life of our kids. With God's help, all of these protocols had their desired effect. Up until the publishing of this book, only about ten of our kids and a couple of workers contracted the Covid virus. God used our safeguards to put a hedge of protection around the Shelter and the people who lived and worked there.

Personally, I was blessed throughout our time in pandemic Cebu by the calm, mature, wise, and compassionate leadership of Tim Holmberg. He was exactly the kind of leader we needed to navigate those confusing, discouraging, and critical days. We could not afford to make mistakes, and Tim was there to help make sure we didn't. He asked the right questions, even the really tough ones, and was always available to discuss a problem or give an encouraging thought. Our weekly Skype calls were oases of calm and of hope for me and, later, for Roberto, as we tried to chart a path through the Corona storms.

One decision we were considering when the lockdown promised to continue concerned salaries. Roberto and I, with the leadership team, felt strongly that we needed to do two things: First, we needed to pay a premium to those who agreed to be locked in. Their shifts were longer than usual, and they could not go home to visit their families. We thought they should get time and a half at least. And we also believed that our locked-out workers should get paid even though they were unable to work. Many were the breadwinners in their families and needed a steady income to feed them. We settled on 60%. It wasn't ideal but it was as high as we felt we could go with the other financial demands of the pandemic. Labor laws in the Philippines did not require it, but we had a commitment to their health and well-being. Tim and our U.S. board were unblinkingly supportive of these salary plans. Fundraising during the pandemic was fruitful and encouraging to all of us in Cebu, and the solid-rock personality and manner of Tim helped inspire faith and hope in all of us.

During the pandemic we were in a holding pattern. Our efforts were almost exclusively geared toward keeping the children and workers safe from the virus. We could not admit new children, and adoptions virtually came to a halt. Through the first 21 months of the pandemic, only two CSC residents left for adoption. Our ability to get kids to Manila for visa work, restrictions on international travel, people's skittishness to adopt and travel, and our social workers' inability to do pre-adoptive case management all contributed to the virtual closure of adoptions for our children, some of whom had been waiting a long time.

So we had to adjust to a changing landscape. The leadership team could not meet together or go inside the Shelter. Transportation in and around the city was difficult, and government policies were constantly changing. For our staff and workers, quarantine passes were issued, but only one per household. One of our drivers, Dodong, stayed onsite during much of the pandemic, driving to buy food, medicine, and other supplies. For some reason, the government issued military passes to Ben Bonnett and Roberto, which gave them fairly unlimited mobility. When Roberto flashed his red pass at checkpoints, the soldiers saluted and waved him through. Other drivers had to wait in line, answer questions, and have their passengers show credentials for being out and about. Unfortunately, the military passes were eventually taken back, and Ben and Roberto had to rejoin civilian ranks and wait in line like everyone else.

Our concerns during the pandemic were fairly simple: We needed to get food and medicine to the Shelter and have workers at CSC to care for the children. And we needed access to our bank so we could pay bills, make payroll, and exchange dollars for pesos.

Other important issues were education, counseling, and security. We knew that our school, even if it had to be brought to the kids, would provide structure, challenge, and some manner of normalcy during this time of uncertainty and change. We were happy to have counselors locked in to help our kids and workers deal with fears and disappointments. Our workers were separated from their families and anxious about their spouses' and children's well-being. And security took on new importance since a single breach could let the virus inside CSC, where it could have spread rapidly.

On Easter Sunday, April 17, 2022, the lockdown at CSC was finally lifted. The CSC kids were thrilled that, after two years, they could finally go outside the CSC compound. There are still nationwide protocols established by the government, and revised rules made by CSC, known as Code Pearl or the "New Normal." Travelers, both domestically and internationally, must show proof of vaccination (with boosters) or a recent Covid test result. Staff are testing workers and encouraging them to get boosters.

Leaving Cebu

AS THE QUARANTINE CONTINUED, so did our "retirement." Our plan was to have a "terminal furlough" in the U.S. for one year, starting in May of 2020. But because of travel restrictions, we could not leave. Some flights had been open temporarily, but we were not clear about the quarantine situation in different countries. We knew that some airlines required a lengthy quarantine in Manila before passengers could board flights to the U.S. or other destinations, which meant checking into a hotel at your own expense and getting tested by a government agency. If you tested positive, you were subject to longer quarantine, and taking a flight back to Cebu was not an option.

Most of the available flights early in 2020 passed through South Korea, and we were told that airport health department personnel in Seoul would take our temperatures upon disembarking, and if any of us had a fever we would have had to check into an expensive hotel for at least 10 days at our own expense. Also, it wasn't clear what quarantine requirements would exist in the U.S. once we arrived there. So we waited for something less risky to open up. Jill Grasley in Minnesota worked for months to get us a flight, checking with several airlines that flew out of Cebu, to avoid the confusion and potential hassle of Manila. We waited for weeks, quarantined in our home, wondering if and when we could leave.

During this time someone remarked that we were "stuck" in the Philippines. I can honestly say that we didn't feel that way. We were certainly stuck in a pandemic and in a quarantine situation where we were not sure how things would work out. But Cebu was our home; we had lived there for 42 years and CSC was our life's work. We cared deeply about the kids, workers, and staff and didn't feel like we needed to escape. Every day that we could do something to help the kids was a good day. But our time of service in Cebu had come to a close, other people were there to lead the ministry, and we needed to leave. Still, our hearts were in Cebu, and we knew that would never change.

While waiting for a flight, we started packing up our possessions, at least the things we didn't still need for our daily lives in Cebu. We decided not to have a rummage sale because of the pandemic and because we would rather give things away to people who could really use them. We gave away books, beds, our television, storage bins, kitchen equipment, and some of Jenny's toys and things she had sewn over the years. As for what we wanted to bring to Minnesota, we had much more than we could bring on the plane, so we set aside boxes of stuff for shipping. Roberto, Jerry, and our helpers were a great help in bringing boxes and suitcases to the CSC storage area for eventual shipment. We were packing, disposing, and storing the clothes, books, important papers, and keepsakes from 42 years of our lives—a huge job. And an emotional one. It crystalized for us the reality that we were all but done in Cebu.

At the end of June we suddenly heard that there might be a flight from Cebu to Seoul in a couple of days. When a definite flight eventually opened up, we had three days to prepare. We had much to do before we could leave, and the next days were filled with packing and hauling things out of our rented house.

The leadership team planned a farewell for us at the Shelter. While we were thankful for the effort they made on our behalf, the pandemic dictated that our farewell was nothing like we had imagined it would be. We sat on the balcony of the new Gleddie Building, with the kids and workers down below. They sang for us and waved goodbye. We couldn't hug them or even go near them. One of the kids asked if he could reach up and touch our feet. At the end they sang the traditional CSC farewell song, "God Will Take Care of You," and we cried. We asked the driver to take us up to the school so we could see it one more time. Then we went back home, loaded up our bags, and headed for the airport.

Jerry Salgo had obtained the needed documents for us to pass through the several checkpoints between our home and the airport. We drove the traditional route and crossed the Mactan Bridge for the last time, each mile taking us farther from our favorite spot on Earth and the kids and staff we loved so much. The disappointment of leaving Cebu without a proper good-bye was discouraging and disheartening. Certainly, our sadness was mixed with excitement to see our family and friends in the U.S., and to see how the next chapter in our lives would read. But mostly we cried.

Trying to explain our emotions surrounding our departure from Cebu is difficult, maybe even fruitless. But I will try because those emotions are at the heart of the CSC story, and how God bestowed blessings on us and everyone who gave of their time, talent, and treasure to the care of the precious kids of CSC. Maybe the words that others have used to explain their departures, that CSC is a "very hard place to leave," were especially true for us. We pioneered the ministry and gave most of our adult lives to it. Our closest friends were in Cebu, as were people we had met as a result of our being a part of CSC. We had led the ministry through both ecstatic and tragic times. While we had made new friends in the Philippines, we had drifted away from many we were close to in the States before leaving for Cebu. We didn't have hobbies or pastimes. CSC was our life, and now we were leaving. We had established relationships with the children, staff, workers, and friends that were unlike any we had experienced before or would likely form after CSC.

We had months to prepare for the fact that we would be leaving soon, but when it happened we were floored by the emotion and significance of that farewell. We didn't know what to say to anyone. Mostly, we just cried. But perhaps those tears spoke more than words could have, showing everyone that our whole being—our thoughts, memories, and emotions—were tugging on our hearts, pulling us to not leave this community of love that God allowed us to help prosper for 42 years. Like many others who gave of their lives to the blessed children of CSC, it was never just a job for Marlys and me, and we had put everything we had, including our deepest emotions, into the ministry.

For me, leaving Cebu and walking away from CSC precipitated some doubts. Could I have given more? Could we have helped more kids or done a better job with the ones we did take in? Did our own neediness get in the way? Did we fight hard enough in our advocacy for our children? Could we have done a better job of presenting Christ to them and in preparing them for life after CSC? Were there times when we took our eyes off God and went in directions we shouldn't have?

I suppose most people face similar doubts at the end of their careers or when their lives on earth are drawing to a close. But Marlys and I walked away knowing that we had lived our lives where God wanted us, doing work that He ordained and that was and is very close to His heart.

I also asked myself what our legacy will be in Cebu and at CSC. How will we be remembered for our 42 years in the Philippines?

The pastor of the church we regularly attended in Cebu, Lowell Tallo of the Banawa Bible Fellowship, asked me to preach one Sunday during our quarantine. It was my first time to preach via Zoom. My sermon was entitled "Show a Little Kindness." As I described our coming retirement, I said I'd been thinking a lot about legacy and the assumptions some people might have. Some might point to beautiful facilities, a program recognized as among the best in the Philippines, excellent medical care, a great staff of talented people. Although these things happened during our time at CSC, I told the church that the most important thing that I aspired to for our legacy was ... kindness. If we could be remembered as kind people, and if CSC would be thought of as comprising kind people reflecting the kindness of Jesus, our careers would have been successful.

Were we kind to the staff and workers when they needed correction or discipline?

Were we kind to the children who caused serious problems?

Were we kind to the birth parents of our kids, some of whom were unkind or abusive to them?

Were we kind to visitors, even those who came at inopportune times or who were demanding and unthankful?

Were we kind to people we met on the streets or who invaded our time with requests or demands of us?

Our departure from Cebu was made easier by our belief that Roberto Atienza was the right person to lead CSC going forward. As we got to know him and observed his leadership skills, his dedication, humility, humor and work ethic, we became increasingly assured that the ministry we had dedicated many years to was in good hands. We were greatly encouraged that he is a kind man. His heart is for the children.

But we had no idea of the challenges to those abilities, gifts, and commitments that would arise as the Philippines and the whole world experienced a pandemic that would complicate every decision or action Roberto and his team would face. We all had no idea of the extraordinary leadership and teamwork that would be needed to protect our children, workers, and staff from the deadly virus that would claim millions of lives worldwide in the early days of Roberto's leadership. We knew he was an exceptional man, but our confidence in him was rooted not just in the gifts and commitment he brought to the table but also in the kind, gracious, and generous God he believed in and served, the same God that had led us from the earliest days in Bulacao throughout our thrilling history until he and his family stepped off the plane to lead CSC into the future.

From Here On

MARLYS AND I BEGAN A "TERMINAL FURLOUGH" in Minnesota starting in July, 2020, when we arrived in Minnesota. Our plans to visit churches and individuals were greatly curtailed by pandemic restrictions and precautions. We were able to attend CSC board meetings and some Cebu staff leadership meetings online. We took advantage of our big garage to host dinners for friends and CSC supporters and adoptive families. We made a video for the 2020 CSC banquet and did some devotionals for the CSC kids and workers. Just as it had been in Cebu with pandemic restrictions, it was frustrating not to be able to visit our friends, thank them for their faithful support, and encourage them to continue supporting CSC post-Healys.

In April of 2021, our retirement from CSC was official. The stateside staff of Kirby and Jill hosted a nice picnic for us in the Twin Cities, and many people came to honor us. It was bittersweet because it marked the official end of our employment with the organization we launched and that had been our employer and lifeline for 42 years.

It is difficult to know how to end this book. Our departure from Cebu and our official retirement as missionaries occurred during a pandemic, so ending it here in late 2022 leaves things hanging. How will things turn out for the children and workers who were locked in? Will things eventually get back to normal in Cebu? When?

The history of CSC does not end or even slow down with the departure of Marlys and me from Cebu. Certainly things will be different. Roberto has a different leadership style than I had. New workers and staff will view the ministry differently than its founders did, even as they bring new ideas and energy to CSC. Maybe, as in the United States, some pandemic-dictated changes regarding workplace dynamics, public health, and organizational life will not fully change back. Maybe it will never be as easy to travel internationally as it once was. Maybe there will be permanent changes to the adoption climate world-wide. Maybe CSC will need to make some significant changes in how we do things.

There are many maybes, but also many certainties. God loves CSC and will continue to bless those who bless His little ones. He has filled all the slots for our leadership team, which has the talent, wisdom, and commitment to handle the job of leading CSC into the future. Roberto Atienza is an excellent leader who has the vision and drive to help chart a course through difficult and uncertain times.

If we continue to maintain a God-honoring ministry run with integrity, both in Cebu and the United States, where funds are carefully and prayerfully used, where the focus remains on the children and their needs, and where kindness and compassion are the hallmarks of who we are and how we treat each other, CSC will have an amazing future. And if that image of Marlys sitting on the hospital bed of that sick and hurting little boy, with worry on her face and tears in her eyes, continues to embody who we are and how we feel and care, I'm sure that somebody will be writing an even better and more exciting updated history of CSC sometime in the future.

For starters, it will be up to Roberto and the staff to describe the huge super typhoon Rai (known in the Philippines as Odette), which slammed into Cebu on December 16, 2021. It was the worst typhoon to hit Cebu in all my years of experiencing and observing these storms. The death toll from Rai surpassed 375, with hundreds more injured.

CSC sustained major damage to our buildings and water system. We lost almost all of our trees, and many of our workers had significant damage to their homes. Roberto will measure the effects of this huge storm on CSC and how our organization responded to its destruction. He and his fellow leaders will write the next chapters of CSC's history as we move to an uncertain and, at the same time, certain future. It is uncertain because of the vagaries of governments, economies, and global weather. But it is also certain because we have the Lord on our side, blessing, protecting, enlightening, and strengthening those who serve his little ones.

As I write these closing words to this book, I am thinking about that future. Even as we pick up the pieces of Rai, rebuild, replant, and rejuvenate, plans are underway with our U.S. board to purchase additional property in Cebu. We are focusing on facilities for housing and training the growing number of children who will not be adopted. We want to prepare them socially, economically, educationally, and spiritually for life in the Philippines. We want to be just as good at launching our kids into Philippine society as we are, and have been, at preparing them for adoption.

Our board has handled our finances skillfully over the years, and our supporters have been so faithful and generous that we have reserves with which to purchase property. We will raise additional funds to construct new facilities in the months and years to come as we boldly move forward as God leads us into the future.

Please be a part of that future. Marlys and I will be, as long as God gives us breath.

Conclusion

IN THE MID 1980S, I WAS ESCORTING A BABY BOY named Jefferson Tagahashi to the U.S. I'd been asked to bring him with me since I was already escorting one of our children. The baby cried almost the entire trip. I'd been told I should not let other people hold the child I was escorting.

After a few hours, people seated around me on the airplane were getting annoyed. Some were really upset. "Can't you make that kid shut up?" I was exhausted because I couldn't sleep. The only way he'd stop crying was if I walked with him around the plane. I went up and down the aisles. When I needed to sit down and rest for a few minutes, he'd start crying again. Loudly.

Eventually, I needed to go to the bathroom. In the midst of my despair, a diminutive nun who was sitting behind me tapped me on the shoulder and said, "Son, you are doing a good job. Bless you." Never in my life did I need a word of encouragement like she gave.

As I look back at all the struggles and hardships of 42 years of ministry and all that we gave, sacrificed, and accomplished, I know that God is pleased. Not with everything, of course, but He sees beyond our shortcomings and failures and notes the hearts behind the actions. I believe He is pleased with the work of CSC. One day we'll see Him, and perhaps He'll reward us with the words, "Well done, good and faithful servants." But in the meantime I'll settle for the words of that nun on a Northwest Airlines flight somewhere over the Pacific Ocean. "Son, you've done a good job. Bless you."

And bless all who have contributed to CSC over the years. Bless you who gave, even when it might have hurt to do so. Bless you who believed in us and gave us encouragement along the way. Bless you who adopted one or more of our children, or gave help and cheer to those who did. Bless you who dropped a note of praise in the mail for staff members. Bless you who have shared our conviction that the suffering of little children is unacceptable. Bless all who are a part of the CSC family.

APPENDICES

Kids

CSC HAS CARED FOR HUNDREDS OF CHILDREN in our 42 years. Each of them deserves to be described, but this book is already long, so in addition to the profiles already included, here I'll note just a few CSC residents who left their mark on our organization and our hearts.

Thomas

ONE DAY IN 2018 I stood in the picnic area as we sang our traditional farewell song to Thomas and his adoptive family. Next to me was one of our childcare workers, Gina, who was weeping openly. She had given so much of herself to Thomas during his almost six years at CSC. She read to him, held him, comforted him, and prayed for him. She cared for him in the hospital and watched him on the playground. Now she was having to say goodbye and, like all of us that day, it was an emotional farewell.

In writing a book like this history of CSC, one tends to look for red-letter dates to highlight God's goodness over the years. For CSC so many of those dates have Thomas's name on them. Major surgeries in Manila and Cebu. Amazing acts of courage and recovery. Great accomplishments at school and in the Duterte Home. Hilarious statements and observations about life. And then, the answer to his and our fervent prayers—a family of his own.

What had seemed impossible a few years earlier came true in glorious fashion that day as the CSC van pulled out of our compound with Thomas and his parents waving goodbye. Thomas brought out the best in CSC. He forced our medical team to look for creative ways to get him the care he needed, even when it involved having to go to Manila for surgery on his nasal passages. He required prolonged one-on-one aftercare, which meant the house parents and Homelife staff had to make schedules that always had our very best aunties available for Thomas. His needs compelled us to provide therapy, medical consultations, and counseling.

The intelligence and depth of his questions and observations made us think carefully about how we talked to him and explained his situation. Our social workers faced many challenges in the legal aspects of his case management and needed lots of persistence and emotional endurance to get his birth documentation and other papers needed for him to be legally free for adoption. And our faithful and generous friends and supporters came through in big ways, allowing us to pay expensive medical costs and always give him the best care available in the Philippines.

We thank God for Thomas and for all those red-letter dates. I will always remember his fascination with the David and Goliath story that the aunties read to him after his surgeries. Maybe he loved that story because he realized that he was much like David. He faced many giants in his young life. He took them all on and won every time.

Jacob

JAKE CAME TO US AS A THREE-MONTH-OLD BABY, having been abandoned in the hospital shortly after his birth. The nurses noted some stiffness in his neck but attributed it to a small crib that had limited his movement. We had him assessed and learned that he had cerebral palsy and would probably never be able to walk.

Jake lived his entire life of 34 years at CSC—all of it in a crib, hospital bed, or wheelchair. His whole body was tight and spastic. In spite of his disability, he attended our Children of Hope School. He had a strong determination to learn and loved to be included in all activities. He wasn't able to form words but would laugh loudly or utter a sound of protest if he wanted something or was upset.

From an early age he received daily physical therapy for range of motion, but he remained extremely stiff. He needed someone to feed and bathe him. He was much loved at CSC. His therapists remarked about his determination and his ready smile.

When CSC received a donation of a DynaVox speech computer, Jacob was excited to have a chance to communicate. By clicking icons on the DynaVox screen, the computer would talk for Jacob. But his spasticity made it difficult for him to navigate the screen. He needed help from his caregivers to use the machine.

In the last couple of years of his life, Jacob went to colleges in Cebu City and spoke, with the aid of his CSC therapist and his speech computer. He told his life story and tried to explain his disability and the challenges he faced.

Jacob died in 2019. His body, which was twisted and contorted for most of his life, just gave out. For the last two days of his life, while lying in his hospital room, Jake would wave good-bye to his visitors. He knew that his life was almost over and he also knew that, as a child of God, he would see his friends again in heaven. A large group of CSC childcare workers, nurses, therapists, and staff were in his room when he finally took his last breath. It was just before Christmas and our friend was gone. But we were comforted by the image in our minds of him walking, running, and talking for the first time in the presence of his Lord and Savior.

Kirk

KIRK CAME TO LIVE WITH US WHEN HE WAS NINE YEARS OLD. His family history was difficult and complicated. Kirk was a bright, handsome, talented, and kind boy with tons of talent and a strong desire to succeed. He did great work in school in all subjects, and loved to sing and perform. He always had a major part in school concerts and programs.

Kirk first lived in the Cherne Home but eventually moved to the Teen Home. Upon graduation from our Children of Hope School, he attended high school at Cebu Normal University. As usual, he did exemplary work and received academic awards throughout his time there.

Kirk was able to make a trip to the United States to be trained in leading Character First groups in Cebu and promoting the program in schools. When he was a senior at CNU, Kirk won a contest for his talents and academic achievements and earned the title of Mr. High School for the City of Cebu.

Although adoption did not work out for Kirk, he was able to find family and fulfillment down another path. When an American couple working on our staff, Ben and Mari Bonnett, adopted a sibling group of six from CSC and returned to the States, they told their parents, Kathy and Larry Severson, about Kirk. In the following months they researched educational opportunities for Kirk in Minnesota, and he was accepted at Northwestern College in Roseville. However, Kirk was denied a U.S. visa, so Kathy and Larry, now with Mari's assistance, began looking for options in Canada. Because of connections with people in CSC's sister organization in Canada, they settled on Trinity Western University in Langley, British Columbia. The Seversons graciously offered to cover Kirk's tuition and living expenses, as well as his transportation to Canada. So Kirk was able to attend Trinity Western, where he got a degree in education, a major step towards realizing his dream of being a teacher.

Kirk now lives and teaches in Central Canada, far from Cebu and British Columbia and any other place he had called home. He is doing great in his new life and remains very close to people who befriended him in western Canada. Kirk has visited Cebu a couple of times to reconnect with CSC and his birth family.

Jackson

JACKSON CAME TO LIVE WITH US after having been burned severely on his shoulder, chest, and face. He spent some time in a government hospital, but they did not treat his burns. After consulting with several plastic surgeons in Cebu City, we determined it would be best for Jackson to be treated in the States. We heard about the Shriner's Children's Hospital in Galveston, Texas, which has a burn center that is internationally known and does not charge patients. They agreed to see Jackson, so we began making preparations for him and me to travel to Texas.

We needed to submit many reports, a letter of permission from the Philippine government, and certification that there would be an approved foster home to care for him after he was released by the hospital, since I wouldn't be staying in Texas with him.

Although the doctors at Shriners did good work, things started going wrong for Jackson almost right away. First, the skin graft they performed didn't "take," even though he had done everything the doctors instructed. Jackson was devastated. He would need another operation and another graft.

About this time the family that had agreed to foster him after the surgery backed out. That put us in a difficult position because someone was needed to visit him regularly in the hospital for emotional support and bring him home upon discharge until I could return from Cebu to escort him back to the Philippines.

Matt Buley and I started recruiting people from Minnesota to fly to Texas and take care of him. Shari Reasoner, Edith Bonnett, Kathy Severson, and Nora Dorsey all took their turn. When he was finally discharged, he went to stay at the Ronald McDonald house. I returned to stay with him while we waited to see how his second graft would take. The Ronald

McDonald house was a life saver for us! They provided housing for Jackson and his caregivers and good food for every meal.

While waiting to be able to leave Texas, we started trying to make airline reservations. Friends of CSC had donated over 500,000 miles, but Northwest refused to honor them for our travel. We were stuck in Houston and didn't know how we would get home. Luckily, a friend of CSC, Doug McFarland, a Northwest pilot, offered his help. He flew to Houston and escorted us back to Minnesota with his pilot's pass. He also helped us get tickets back to the Philippines.

In the meantime, one of Jackson's caregivers, Edith Bonnett, informed me that she and her husband, Dan, were interested in adopting Jackson. So I returned to Cebu with Jackson with the prayer that he would be able to return to the U.S. as an adopted child. This placement was eventually approved by the Philippine government, and the Bonnetts went to Cebu to bring him back to join their family and receive additional treatment for his burns.

Our Sibling Group of Nine

ALTHOUGH WE HAD OFTEN TAKEN IN SIBLING GROUPS large and small, and had twice placed seven together in the same adoptive family, it was a big step of faith when we admitted nine siblings in early 2007.

It took us several months to process the referral because the children were split up, living with various relatives since their mom died. It took us a while to get the necessary permissions and meet with the kids to see what their feeling were about going to live on the other side of Cebu island with people they didn't know. Eventually it was all worked out and the kids came to live at CSC.

They were a delightful group of siblings and fit in well almost right away. They ranged in age from 2 to 14. When our staff eventually began to consider adoption for the nine, we were surprised to learn that an adoption law in the U.S. had been changed by Congress. Previously, a child who was 16 could be placed in the States if he or she had younger siblings also to be adopted. The oldest of the nine was 16 and previously would have qualified. But the new law changed the qualifications, and children 16 and over could not be adopted in the U.S.—period.

So even though there was a family who wanted to adopt all nine, the adoptable group was down to eight. Everyone was crushed by this development, including the prospective adopters. It looked hopeless. The oldest child was devastated to think of being split up from her siblings. We weren't sure if we should even consider doing that.

But the family in the U.S. was not prepared to give up. They contacted their senator, Amy Klobuchar, who got interested in the case and proposed a law that would allow sibling groups like this one to stay together by raising the age limit to 18 if there are younger siblings to be placed. It seemed like a long shot, but Amy was determined to give it her best try and began to seek support for the bill. A Democrat, she went across the aisle in the Senate to find the needed votes. The prospective adoptive family went to Washington, D.C., to meet Senator Klobuchar and talk to people interested in the bill. It was eventually approved by Congress in 2015 and signed into law by President Obama. The children could go together to the family who had worked so hard and exhibited so much faith and commitment to get them all home.

Joemar

NOBODY WHO ENTERED THE GATES OF CSC in the past 37 years can forget Joemar. But nobody would want to because he is one of the greatest things about CSC and has been since he came to live with us in 1985.

Joemar is developmentally delayed and does not speak much. He can voice a few words but mostly communicates with his big smile. Since coming to live with us, Joemar has never had a bad day. Not one. In spite of natural calamities, changes in his residence, other kids not always being nice to him, a roommate dying, and many people close to him leaving CSC for retirement, furlough, adoption, or return to the States, Joemar has kept his streak of happiness and contentment alive.

Joemar came to us from the neighboring island of Negros. He lived on the streets of Bais City with his mom, who also had special needs. Aside from being malnourished, Joemar frequently was hit by motorcycles or other vehicles and had bruises all over his body. The police eventually referred him to the social welfare office, and he was placed in an orphanage run by Carmelite nuns. They had little to offer a boy with special needs and abilities like Joemar, so they told the government office that they would no longer care for him.

So Joemar was brought to Cebu and CSC, where he has grown into a fine man. He loves to help out around the house and hang out with the house father or the janitors at Children of Hope School. The smile he wore when he first entered CSC is still on his face after all these years. He has a ready laugh and can be seen walking around the grounds or arranging stuff in his room in the Duterte Home.

For the past two decades he has worked at McDonalds clearing tables, opening the door, and greeting people with a smile. At one time Joemar was given the job of opening the CSC gate, but he wasn't at all discerning about who he let in. We joked that he would smile and wave in Osama bin Laden any day of the week!

When you are looking at Joemar Llanera, you are looking at the very best of CSC. He will live out his life with us and he will bless us every day of that life. Auntie Sandy Swanson was especially close to Joemar and found it difficult to say goodbye to him when she left CSC for retirement:

> Leaving CSC is hard. One of the major reasons for that is saying goodbye to Joemar. Joe is one of those nearly perfect people in the world. He was my right-hand man in Cebu, always willing to help. He even stopped my fall down a long flight of cement steps. He loves completely and shows joy in everyday things. His smile makes any moment a better one. I miss just being in his presence. I am confident even Heaven will be a better place when Joe gets there!

Adoption

I HAVE OFTEN TOLD PEOPLE that there two kinds of orphanages in the world, and they are as different as night and day. One takes in kids and raises them until they are sufficiently educated and prepared to live on their own. The other seeks adoption. From the start, we chose to find adoptive families for our kids. The differences between these two systems are evident in every aspect of their respective programs and services.

In our system we need to document every aspect of our kids' lives: medical, developmental, social, legal. We serve meals that incorporate both Filipino and Western dishes. We give our kids the best medical care available in the Philippines. We provide an education that prepares them well for whatever type of education might come next, concentrating on having them learn English well, to make their transitions easier.

In seeking adoption for our children, we take on some problems that are unknown to the other type of orphanage. We have had to deal with the emotional issues that go along with adoption. Our children being adopted have to leave their friends, substitute family and parental figures, cultural values, language, and dietary comforts. We have learned how to counsel them about forgiving birth families and accepting adoptive families. We have had to deal with the emotional backlash that comes from not being adopted for those we cannot place.

And on top of all that, we need to document every part of our children's lives to match them for adoption, for use by their adoptive families as they seek to provide for their ongoing medical, emotional, and educational needs. Our nurses, social workers, counselors, therapists, and teachers keep detailed records of every medical test result; every medication prescribed; every illness encountered; every developmental milestone, school evaluation, or behavioral problem. A CSC child's folder contains birth or foundling documents, referral summaries, legal papers such as surrender reports, and teachers' evaluations and test results. We also keep post-placement reports concerning our children who have been placed.

In many ways, adoption has always been the heart and soul of our ministry. We learned early on that although we can do a lot of good in the lives of the children we care for, although we take good care of them and try to simulate family life in our homes, we are not a family. We believed from day one that the family is the best place for a child, and because most of our children cannot live with their birth families, we felt that getting them into adoptive homes was usually the best option.

None of our staff had any formal training in adoption, but we became expert in the field from years of practical experience and by learning from adoption professionals. Providing pre-adoptive childcare is a specialized field in child welfare work, and we established a program that does a good job of preparing children for placement. The various components of our program contribute to this preparedness.

Referrals

THE GENERAL RULE we have used when evaluating referrals is that we take in those who have a reasonable chance of being adopted. We do not specialize in long-term care, and we believe strongly that the best place for a child is in a family, so we want CSC to be a place where children can stay temporarily while waiting for a permanent placement.

Of course, there are exceptions to the rule. Sometimes the critical need for health care or protection prompts us to take in kids we know might be difficult to place. Sometimes problems arise in the case management of a child or sibling group that ends up making them unadoptable. For example, after taking in a child, we might locate the birth parent(s), but they are not willing to relinquish her. For a child to be adopted in the United States, he must be either surrendered by a birth parent or declared abandoned by the court. We have faced situations where a child's legal status changed while under our care, so our original determination of "adoptability" proved incorrect.

Another adoptability issue is the health of children needing families. When Jacob came to live with us, he was a bouncing baby boy, though just a few months old. As he grew we noticed that he seemed stiff when held and arched his back in an abnormal way. In time, our doctors diagnosed him with cerebral palsy. While having CP doesn't disqualify a child from adoption, that diagnosis makes it difficult to find adoptive families willing to accept that disability. Over the years we have placed children with CP, blindness, major hearing loss, epilepsy, developmental delay, hydrocephalus, speech delays, dwarfism, and stunted growth. When we took in these kids, we either believed they would be placeable or we learned about their disability as they grew.

The same could be said for behavioral issues. Although we have been aware of behavioral problems with some children we've admitted that existed before they came to us, often we learned of these problems while they were already at CSC. In the pre-knowledge cases, we believed the child would change in our environment of loving discipline and close monitoring. In cases where we found out about problems once the child was with us, we worked to treat that issue with counseling, discipline, and love. In extreme cases we had to transfer the child out of CSC by looking for a more appropriate child-caring agency to take him or her. Again, the litmus test for admission to CSC has been a reasonable expectation of adoptability.

Of course, our faith in accepting children with health or developmental problems has been bolstered by the reality that God has provided families for some of these children. Juliet had CP and walked with great difficulty. She could not talk and seemed to have difficulty understanding us. (We found out later that she had profound hearing loss.) But God provided a fantastic family for Juliet, where she was loved, challenged, and given every possible opportunity to reach her potential. She walks, she talks, and she has a beautiful daughter. She is just one example of our being pleasantly surprised by God's provision of just the right family for one of our children.

By placing our children for adoption, we have been able to care for more children. If we had taken in children who had little or no chance of being placed, we would eventually have become an institution filled with children who could not leave, and our services would have ended up being very different. Although our population has always included some kids who were not adopted, most of them were, which allowed us to bring in new children to replace them.

Social Work

MUCH OF WHAT OUR SOCIAL WORKERS DO concerns our children's eventual adoptive placement. First and foremost, they need to obtain birth documents. So many children in institutional care in the Philippines do not have documentation of their birth, which means, in the eyes of the government, they do not exist. When we took in a girl who had been living with her grandma under a tree in the pier area of Mandau City, we suspected that her birth had never been registered. We needed to find her birth mother, who we learned had moved to Manila. Finding her in that metropolis was daunting, and Carmelita, our social worker handling her case, put announcements in the Manila newspaper and on the radio. Eventually, the mother contacted us, and Carmelita arranged a trip to Manila to meet her and have her sign some documents. Those signatures were needed for getting the birth certificate and in relinquishing her daughter for adoption.

Counseling birth parents is a big part of what our social workers do. They need to assess their parenting capabilities and, in the case of those who have adequate resources to parent, encourage them to get their kid(s) back. This can take a long time. In cases where the birth parent does not have shelter and/or income or cannot provide a safe environment for the child(ren), our social worker will try to motivate the parent(s) to surrender them. The surrender document signing must be authenticated by a notary public and two witnesses.

If a child has been abandoned, that must be declared so by an agency of government, which requires considerable paper work. We have to show that we exhausted all efforts to find the birth parents through newspaper and radio announcements, certified by editors and station managers. These efforts are all exerted to have children who cannot live with their birth families legally qualified for adoption.

Our social workers also write case studies used in the adoption process. These reports are read by many people, from the local social welfare agency, to their counterpart in Manila, to the inter-country adoption board personnel, to foreign adoption agency workers, to embassy personnel, and, eventually, the adoptive parents. The information needs to be complete, accurate, and detailed.

Childcare

OUR CHILDCARE TEAM also has lots of paperwork to do in the adoption process. They need to document children's behavior during their time at CSC, from their social interaction to their bonding with adults and how they grow and develop. Team members keep growth statistics, have regular meetings with house parents and teachers, and write development reports that social workers use in their case studies. These development reports include summaries from counselors and teachers and highlight any behavioral problems or incidents during a child's stay with us.

From the early days, we have been committed to honesty and transparency in our record keeping and reporting. We have learned how important that is for everyone involved. An adoption worker from Wide Horizons for Children, Marylou Eshelman, who became our good friend when we placed many children through her agency, told me once that the biggest problem in adoptive placement, and a leading cause of disruptions, is surprises: adoptive families receiving a child with problems they knew nothing about. Some childcaring agencies do not disclose all the negative health and behavioral problems of their children, for fear they will not be placed if that is known. We have tried to be completely honest and reveal everything relevant to a child's placement.

This resolve is often tested. We had a pre-teen boy who had already been presented for adoption and matched with a family. We were waiting for word that his adoptive parents were coming to get him. While waiting for that call, we observed him touching one of the girls inappropriately. We talked about it as a staff. There were many ways to look at the situation: boys will be boys; nothing serious happened; we can handle this with our counselors. But all of these "solutions" were substitutes for the better course of action. We needed to tell the adoption agencies and the adoptive family. It would have been much easier to keep that to ourselves and let the family deal with any problems that might occur. But in the end, we knew that we had to tell them. And we have had other similar situations where negative behaviors in a child, things that might derail their adoption possibilities, were fully disclosed by our childcare team. It is part of who we are as an organization, and something that sets us apart from some other agencies.

Medical

SIMILARLY, WE ARE COMMITTED to transparency with the medical situations of children placed for adoption. This means that any observed health problem, any negative test result, and any diagnosis from a doctor must be included in the child's medical report, even if we don't necessarily agree with that diagnosis.

The medical care children receive at CSC is comprehensive. They receive all the immunizations required by foreign embassies. They are brought for regular medical and dental checkups. When sick, they are treated and provided with any necessary medications. They are given vitamins and are tested for tuberculosis, hepatitis, HIV, and other diseases that might affect their long-term health and well-being. We do this, first and foremost, for the sake of the children themselves, to help them be well and to know what health problems affect them. But because we are providing pre-adoptive care, we also do it to give adoption workers and prospective families all the information they need to make informed decisions.

We have received inadequate and false information about children referred to us. One government facility referred a child who was declared healthy by the center's doctor and staff. When we got him, we found that he needed immediate surgical intervention, care that required tens of thousands of dollars. We might very well have accepted the child even if we had known, but it is always better to have accurate and honest information to make informed decisions about accepting referrals and in presenting children for possible adoptive placement.

Education

OUR SCHOOL'S DISTINCTIVE CURRICULUM is designed to prepare children for what comes next in their education. English learning is important for a child's eventual placement. Accordingly, our school uses English as the medium of instruction, and much of the curriculum is consistent with what children might face when they attend school in the United States or other countries following placement.

We usually have North American teachers teaming up with our Filipino instructors, which provides another aspect of the students' preparation for what will come next. Education promotes self-esteem and confidence in our children, many of whom had never gone to school before coming to live with us.

One boy was so nervous and self-conscious when he started at our Children of Hope School that when he was introduced to the other students he sat down on the floor and tried to hide under the table. Although he was 11 years old, he had little experience in going to school, and he feared being placed with the little kids in Grade 1. But in our school he could learn in multi-age groups that allow us to meet the students at their point of need and not just lump kids together by age. This boy did great in our school, where he came to feel comfortable and accepted and where nobody teased him about not knowing how to read at his age. By the time he and his siblings were placed, he had many of the tools needed to do well in school in the United States. Our Open Court 44 curriculum is excellent for accelerated language learning, and is a great tool for our teachers in their role of helping prepare our children for adoption.

Part of our school program is music. We try to create an appreciation for music and build on children's natural abilities and interests. They can learn to sing and play the piano or another instrument. Our children will leave much behind when they leave us for adoption, but music is an international language and something they can bring with them and "plug in" when they get to their new adoptive home. They might struggle with language acquisition when they get there, but music will be something they can use right away.

Nutrition

MANY OF OUR CHILDREN come to us malnourished or undernourished, and we need to help them overcome this with a nutritious diet. Most of our meals are consistent with a Philippine diet: lots of rice, seafoods, and local vegetables. But we also serve some Western dishes to help prepare the kids for possible placement into another country. Being able to adjust to another diet is important for a child's transition into a family, and we do our best to help that happen.

Spiritual Formation

A PERSONAL RELATIONSHIP WITH JESUS is the most important thing our children can experience while with us. This relationship will provide comfort and strength in the difficult transition to a new way of life, and will pay emotional and spiritual benefits throughout their lives. While at CSC children learn about God and His son, Jesus. They are taught to pray, and they learn Bible verses and Christian songs. We have done this since we first arrived in the Philippines in 1979. We have never concentrated much on theology since our kids might go to families with different denominational affiliations than what we have as staff members, house parents, or counselors. Although most of our kids come from birth families that are staunchly Roman Catholic, they often do not know how to pray directly to God to share their problems and fears.

Learning to pray is a great tool in their lives and will prepare them for a lifetime of faith and spiritual obedience. These are eternal values that transcend everything else for our children. We want to introduce them to Jesus while at CSC. Hopefully, the seeds of faith we plant in their lives will be nurtured and will grow in their adoptive families.

Our ultimate goal for our kids in adoption is that they will bless their families, their communities, their churches, and their God. We have received lots of positive feedback from adoptive families who are thrilled that their child has been raised, at least while at CSC, in a Christian environment where God is honored and Jesus is presented as the Lord of their lives.

Lessons

WE HAVE LEARNED MUCH ABOUT ADOPTION throughout our years in the Philippines. First, we learned to value it for most of our children. Our original thinking about the ministry we would start in Cebu was more about raising the children in our home(s). But as we learned about what our children needed and lost, and what they really craved, we came to see that what they needed most, the best hope for a fairly normal development, was in an adoptive family. Our motto, which developed over time, is "Every Child Deserves a Family."

At CSC we try our best to be like a family, with substitute parental models and responsibilities and "sibling" relationships within the home. But we are not a family, and our kids can only experience that fully by joining an adoptive family. And we have learned how important family is in the Philippine culture where we work and live. Other important lessons have enriched our ministry and helped us understand how adoptive families function so we can do a better job preparing children for placement:

• It is God who builds families, not us. We have important roles, but it is God who orchestrates everything for children to come to CSC, and it is He who prepares families to commit to adopting our kids.

• A family doesn't have to look like us to be a good family. CSC children have been adopted into families who are wealthy and those of modest means, those who speak a language other than English, those who worship in churches of different denominations than are represented by our staff and workers, and those who have different views of child development and discipline than we do.

• Not every child is a good candidate for placement. This is a tough lesson. Some children have too much emotional baggage to fit into an adoptive family, no matter how skilled and dedicated the adoptive parents might be. Experiences before coming to live at CSC can compromise a child's ability to bond with new parents. Some kids who do fairly well in a large group setting like CSC will struggle in an intimate family setting where there is an expectation of reciprocal affection and openness that they cannot offer.

• We have vast differences in priorities with the agencies we work with, both locally and internationally. One example concerns our preference for Christian families, which many agencies do not share. We have been told that it is nobody's business but their own if families are Christian or even if they believe in God.

• Sometimes disruptions occur, and a second placement is needed. Mental health problems, a child's history, or unrealistic parental expectations can all undermine adoptions. Problems in the system—poor matching and preparation, incomplete disclosure about a child's needs, inadequate post-adoption support—can also contribute.

• Adoptions are not always "happy ever after" stories. Most placements are positive, but even those involve stress, adjustment difficulties, and unrealized expectations.

• CSC is an important link for adopted kids to the country of their birth and, possibly, with their birth families. We regularly host former residents when they return for a visit, assisting them in finding and meeting a birth family, when possible.

• Reunions with birth parents can be great but aren't always so. They require professional input on both sides. We make our social workers available to work with birth families to prepare them for meeting their child(ren), and try to help them understand the socioeconomic situation of the adopted child and what her feelings might be towards her past.

It is helpful if a counselor or adoption professional can prepare adoptees for the meeting, to manage their expectations and discuss how they might deal with less-than-hoped-for outcomes. Our social workers have had experiences with reunions that were emotional and healing, as well as those that didn't go well for either the child or the birth family. Sometimes the adoptive parents are part of those reunions, which contributes to the emotion of the experience.

Our longtime social worker Carmelita Baya was skilled at helping make these events as positive as possible. Once a former resident who was surrendered as a newborn and was living in the U.S. informed us that he wanted to meet his birth mother. He was then 25 years old.

Carmelita, though not giving him any promises, set out to find the birth mom, no small task considering 25 years had passed without any communication with her. She looked for birth and surrender documents, found out who had been the government social worker handling the case, discovered that she was living in England, and contacted her to see if she remembered the case. She did! She even remembered where the woman worked.

Through those leads and some more investigative work, Carmelita found a possible address for the birth mom and sent her a letter to see if she might be interested to meet her son. A few months later we were all in a large hotel lobby in Cebu City walking towards a woman and her daughter (the birth sister of the former CSC resident) for a meeting that was emotional and miraculous. (The daughter hadn't known that our guy existed until a few weeks before that day.) It was life-changing for everyone involved. They hugged, they smiled, they cried, they talked, they gave and accepted explanations and apologies, and restarted a relationship that is still active today.

Other reunions were less emotional. Or maybe the emotions were different, and forgiveness was difficult or impossible to give or receive. Maybe the birth parents' economic situation was a stumbling block for the relationship, and they could not understand how their child, now adopted, could live in luxury while they struggled to just live.

Adoption is a beautiful thing for many children and families. But it is a complicated psychosocial and legal process that involves, at least in the case of CSC adopted kids, social workers, counselors, psychologists, doctors, matching committees, house parents and other caregivers, birth parents, adoption agency workers, embassy personnel, lawyers, judges, and adoptive parents.

CSC has learned a lot in our years of preparing some of our kids for placement, and we must constantly re-evaluate our methods and priorities. International and domestic adoption laws and attitudes change regularly and sometimes dramatically. Older children, sibling groups, and kids with special needs are becoming harder to place and require better emotional preparation. The cultural situations of the receiving countries change. Attitudes towards adoption within the Philippine government change. We have needed to be aware of this changing landscape of adoption and be willing to change in response to it.

Bulacao Church

THE STAFF HAD ARRIVED IN CEBU with no intention of starting a church. But as we settled into the community in Bulacao, we felt a desire to reach out to our neighbors with Christ's love, not only by addressing their physical needs but by telling them of God's love through Jesus Christ. We did not have the language skills to preach or teach, so we decided to partner with Filipinos who had those skills and who shared our concern for the hearts in their community. Prisco Allocod, pastor of the Central Free Church, where the staff attended, expressed a desire to help and asked two of the women from his church, Gloria Navasquez and Lina Farne, to join us.

Initially, the plan was to hold weekly Bible studies at the Bulacao home. After a few months, cottage prayer meetings were also held in various homes around the community. Three families—the Martinezes, the Deliñas, and the Lims—made up the core of the group, though there were others, including Baby Go, a boy with polio named Joseph Teves, and Fredo and Minga Wenceslao.

In January of 1980, the staff and Centralites decided to start having Sunday worship services at the Bulacao home. Because Prisco and the women had responsibilities in their church in the mornings, we decided to have our service at 3 p.m. Prisco handled the preaching, the women led Sunday School for the children, and I played the guitar. Aside from neighbors in Bulacao, members from Central Free also came to offer encouragement. One reason we could initiate these efforts was that we didn't have a lot of other responsibilities. Our number of children was still small, which gave us time to devote to church-related activities.

In the coming months our group sponsored a series of evangelistic meetings featuring Rev. Gonzalo Olojan, of the Baptist Conference of the Philippines. In those days the BCP had vans equipped with a sound system and a film projector so that a movie could be shown, followed by music and preaching. One family that lived near Corpus Christi did the special music, and Rev. Olojan preached for three nights of services.

Later, a crusade featuring the Lindquist brothers, Lin and Red, from Bemidji, Minnesota, was held on the grounds of the Bulacao Elementary School. Prisco and I drove around in the CSC Fiera with a bullhorn, inviting people to the meeting. We joked that we were "old school missionaries" doing that. A large crowd came to the crusade, and those who responded were invited to attend church at Corpus Christi.

These initial efforts were undertaken without a master plan for planting a church in Bulacao. But as the group grew, it seemed like a good idea to get organized. Although we didn't feel strongly about affiliating with a denomination, others on the team did. So the church was officially founded on February 1, 1981, as the Bulacao Evangelical Free Church. At that time the church began meeting in the rented home of Manny and Gloria Deliña (nee Navasquez), who had been instrumental in helping start the church and secure its registration and affiliation with the Evangelical Free Church of the Philippines.

To be honest, I had some misgivings about the church affiliating with any denomination. Our church had been built on a foundation of kindness and compassion. We cared about each other and the community around us. In a way, the church already had established an affiliation—with Corpus Christi. And Corpus Christi did not have any denominational affiliation. I wanted our church to be free to continue with those priorities and not get drawn into denominational politics or cookie-cutter organizational or financial patterns that might undermine the spirit and community concern that was, in my opinion, the strength of the church.

As the church grew in size and maturity, the Corpus Christi staff began to withdraw from the leadership. We didn't want to impede the development of leaders from within the church, and our responsibilities with the home for children were increasing rapidly. The church had already elected officers, had called a pastor, and was very much ready to stand on its own.

Within a few years, the church outgrew the Deliña home. They applied for a loan from the EFCP and purchased a house and lot along the highway in Bulacao. They converted the home into a church with a Sunday School area downstairs and a sanctuary upstairs.

In the years after that purchase, the church grew steadily and continued to expand their facilities. They now have a large Compassion sponsorship program that serves hundreds of families throughout Bulacao. Pastor Jun Cedeño led the church into significant growth. They have a strong youth program and are involved in camping and Christian education. Several current CSC workers attend BEFC, and some are leaders in the church.

One of the most vivid and spiritually encouraging experiences I had in Cebu was when we were invited to the wake of the father of one of our workers. In the Catholic tradition in the Philippines, it is common to have nightly novenas for people who have died, often held in their home. The worker whose father died attended our church in Bulacao. We went to one of the evenings, and when we walked into their small shack there were some people from the community by the casket doing some chanting and incantations, crying and wailing. We just sat there and observed.

Outside the house a group of young people from our church were waiting their turn. They had been asked by the family to present something and were led by Edwin Martinez, CSC's driver, and one of our former Sunday School kids from the church who was now the leader of the youth group. When the wailers were done, Edwin led the group into the house, where they surrounded our worker with love and support and sang some songs and choruses of hope. Then Edwin stood up and preached a message about salvation and eternal life through faith in Christ. I was so proud of him and so thankful that God had led us to start that group in our Corpus Christi mission home back in the early 1980s, even though it had not been our original plan to do so.

In 2019 Marlys and I were invited to the 40th church anniversary of Bulacao EFC. We were excited to see a shiny new building, hear reports on their ministry in the community, and see friends who had helped us start the church and who were still active there. Some church leaders are CSC workers or former staff. At the end of the evening, Jessie Boy Martinez, the first child we helped in Bulacao in 1979, came running up and threw his arms around Marlys and cried on her shoulder. Others talked about the early days of the church and how God had blessed over the years. Some kids we had helped were now adults with kids of their own, and they recalled how Corpus Christi helped meet their physical needs and introduced them to Jesus through puppet shows or special events.

Children of Hope School

STARTING CHILDREN OF HOPE SCHOOL was different from initiating the Shelter. We had learned a lot in 18 years. In starting a home for children, we had to make assumptions and guesses about things like government regulations, costs, staffing, fundraising, and how adoption would work. We went to Cebu full of excitement and eager to get things going, but with precious little expertise and advance planning. We learned as we went, sometimes in a painful way.

With the school we had the opportunity to do things differently. Although our staff didn't have an ounce of experience in developing or running a school program, we had people within or connected to our organization who did and who were willing to pool their expertise to help us do it right:

Dr. Elisa Saavedra from our Philippine board was an educator and advisor to schools in Cebu and had served as a principal and dean at several schools. She was in the process of helping the Evangelical Free Church start a college, as well as a high school and elementary program. She had many high-level contacts with the Philippine Department of Education, which would need to license any school we might start. She became Children of Hope School's first principal and held that job for several years, helping establish and maintain excellence in our delivery of educational services to the students at CHS.

We were blessed by the contributions of Nancy Healy, my sister-in-law, an elementary school teacher in Minnesota and an expert in multi-age classrooms, and other friends of CSC who were involved in innovative education and were willing to help us put together a plan.

Jill Anderson from Minnesota was a lot of help for us in imagining a multi-age classroom and the type of training our teachers would need and the optimal curriculum that would incorporate the required material from the Philippine Department of Education and a typical U.S. public school, since most of our students would eventually go to school there.

My mom, Millie Healy, was an experienced elementary school teacher with interest and expertise in using learning stations in her classrooms. She helped us incorporate this type of learning into our curriculum and in imagining what our classrooms and school days would look like.

Jan Druckenmiller was an expert in early childhood education and, together with her husband Craig, owned and operated a childcare center and child welfare agency, Sacred Portion Children's Outreach, in Bozeman, Montana. Jan helped write an excellent preschool curriculum for our school that featured themes and incorporated structured and unstructured play activity. Jan prepared visual materials to support the themes and worked with our preschool teachers on lesson planning and classroom management. Her input was pivotal in helping us plan and establish a top-quality preschool program to prepare our children for the elementary grades, either in our school or wherever they might end up in the Philippine school system or somewhere else through adoption.

Shari Reasoner was a successful teacher in Cambridge, Minnesota, and, with her husband, Paul, a friend of the Healys and CSC. She became

Shari Reasoner

our first education director, working with principal Cris Tabra to develop the school program; train teachers; write policies and procedures; establish a budget and salary schedule; and source educational materials, books, curricula, and equipment from the United States. She also recruited teachers from the U.S. to serve in Cebu.

Shari gave much of herself to the school over 18 years of service. She flew to Cebu from Minnesota several times a year, often at her own expense. She parlayed her interest and experience in physical education into establishing a PE curriculum at Hope School and a Sportsfest program that became a regular part of the school year and a ton of fun for all the kids and teachers.

Shari's involvement with CSC and CHS had many ancillary benefits. For one thing, her son, Joel, became interested in CSC and eventually became a staff member in 2007. Shari's husband, Paul, who traveled with her to Cebu on occasion, became burdened for the needs of our workers, particularly in the area of housing. Paul and Joel came up with a plan of working with Habitat for Humanity to build homes for our workers and their families. The first phase of the project provided 63 homes in Talisay City, a neighboring city to Cebu City.

With all these people working together, we planned a dynamic school for the elementary age children of CSC and a limited number of children with special needs from the community:

- A school that would meet our kids at their point of need and ability.
- A school that would specialize in English instruction to best prepare our kids for adoption, since most of our school-age kids who were being placed were going to the United States.
- A school that would be sensitive to the difficult backgrounds of our kids and the gaps in learning they had experienced.
- A school that would incorporate technology to prepare our students for the outside world. Technological competence would help them thrive as they furthered their education outside CSC or eventually sought to join the work force somewhere in the world.
- A school with a Christian environment where faith and learning could be integrated.

Our challenge was coming up with an educational philosophy and curriculum that was in line with the needs of our kids but still acceptable to the Philippine Department of Education, which was not known for innovation or flexibility in their approach to schools and curricula. We wrestled with these issues:

Tagalog

TAGALOG IS THE NATIONAL LANGUAGE of the Philippines and, in most schools, is used as the medium of instruction for some subjects. It is an important part of the education of Filipinos and fosters nation building and community. In a country with many languages and hundreds of dialects, having a national language is important, though difficult to maintain.

We felt that because many of our kids would be adopted and not live in the Philippines, it was not productive for them to spend a lot of time learning a language they would probably never use. On the other hand, we knew that at least some of our children would not be adopted. In their case they would have difficulty in their education after CHS with no knowledge of Tagalog because it would be taught extensively in whatever school they would eventually attend. We looked into the compromise of teaching Tagalog as a language but not using it as a medium of instruction.

Inclusion

ANOTHER IMPORTANT ISSUE was how we could best meet the needs of our children with special needs. We wanted our school to be inclusive in a meaningful way, reflecting the nature of our CSC population and our commitment to taking in children with special needs.

Shari Reasoner had interest and experience in inclusion and helped us imagine the kind of accessibility and creativity we would need to fashion a school that would serve all our children. She helped us take the planning and brainstorming to the next level and make something concrete happen.

Learner-Based

TRADITIONAL SCHOOLS IN THE PHILIPPINES, whether private or public, are teacher-based or even parent-based, but rarely student-based. It is not uncommon for schools, even preschools, to have class ranks, even magna and summa cum laude honorees. Parents thrill at going on stage to pin awards on their child's gown, basking in the reflected glory of his or her achievements. Meanwhile, some students receive no award or recognition of effort or attitude.

Students are taught that respect for the teacher involves accepting what he or she says as the incontrovertible truth, not to be questioned. Often creative and critical thinking loses out to rote memorization. Children are often branded as limited or dull because their needs or learning styles differ from the norms. And because of huge class sizes in Philippine public schools, teachers are forced to teach to the center of the class, with little time for those with learning challenges or disabilities, or those with exceptional aptitude. Our CSC kids were rarely in the middle, so were not well served.

Ernesto had cerebral palsy. He could not walk, use a pencil in the accepted manner, or participate in games or other recreational activities. His teacher had little or no training in inclusion or special education. Ernie was bright and read well and could learn what was being taught in the classroom. On test day, however, the teacher would distribute the test papers and collect them exactly when the time was up. Ernesto knew the answers to the questions in all the subjects, but he could not write them down legibly or within the prescribed time. He was given an "F" and subject to ridicule from his classmates, even though he was as bright as many of them. The teacher simply could not, or would not, make accommodations for his special needs. We wanted our school to be a place where Ernie and others with special needs could experience achievement and success instead of frustration and humiliation.

At our school, every child receives an award of some kind. All types of achievement are recognized, from Most Energetic, to Most Helpful, Most Improved, Most Loving or Most Cooperative, as well as Best in Math, Science, Writing, etc.

CSC vis-a-vis the School

DUE TO PHILIPPINE LAWS AND POLICIES, our school would need to be a separate entity with its own board, facilities, budget, and organizational structure. Even so, we wanted the school to be subservient to the Shelter in terms of scope, curriculum, and population. In short, we wanted the school to always be organized to serve the needs of the Shelter in educating our kids and preparing them for the future. We had children from many different backgrounds, with needs that dictated some nontraditional, innovative, and creative learning opportunities. We didn't want the school to develop a life of its own, conforming to the traditional Philippine style of one-size-fits-all education, or innovate in ways that weren't directly related to the backgrounds, situations, and learning styles of CSC kids.

Throughout its history our school has fulfilled that mission of serving CSC and our kids. It has helped prepare them for adoption. It has helped open their minds to the world around them. It has reinforced the work of our counselors, house parents, and staff in building self-esteem and self-confidence by putting tools in their hands, promoting life-long learning, and teaching the English language, which is important for them whether they are adopted or remain in the Philippines. Our school has helped our children discover talents and express themselves through music, drama, and art—and learn about cooperation, teamwork and diversity.

Brain Drain

ONE UNANTICIPATED DEVELOPMENT at the school was turnover of faculty from year to year. We spent a lot of time and effort training teachers in our style of education, which was different than how they were trained and had taught prior to coming to our school. So we had time and money invested in these teachers. But the opportunity for much better salaries in the United States and other countries lured a number of our faculty away.

Our salaries were competitive or better than other private schools, but we could not come close to offering what was offered in California, Illinois, or other states or countries. So each year we had new slots to fill and more training to initiate. It was disappointing and frustrating for the school leadership and the CSC staff. But we learned the truth of Lisa Saavedra's well-known principle for ministry: God always fills the slots. And so he has done throughout the history of Children of Hope School.

Curriculum

RATHER THAN A CURRICULUM used by many Christian schools, we chose to teach from a hybrid curriculum we developed by combining the Philippine DepEd curriculum with one from a typical Minnesota elementary school. We believed we could adopt a Christian point of view without teaching theological content. We wanted to promote discussion and interaction and even wrestling with Christian faith and moral absolutes instead of simply memorizing them to be recited on test papers.

We have been reminded that other kids from Christian homes who attend Christian schools have just one set of parents with one belief system. They come from similar denominations with similar doctrinal statements. They want school to promote their beliefs and not present content from another point of view.

Our Children of Hope teachers are Christians with vibrant faith and a desire to model it for their students. They have devotional times together. They pray for their students and for each other. The Spirit of God is always evident in Children of Hope School, even though our students aren't educated with a "Christian curriculum." This has been an ongoing discussion over the years: How can we effectively integrate faith and learning?

U.S. Teachers

Ben and Mari Bonnett went twice to serve at CSC. Mari had heard about CSC at her church, Berean Baptist, and was at a presentation that Marlys and I gave there. Their first stint was from 2003-05 as teachers. Like our other school staff, they were flexible and dedicated in dealing with our children. Although he had no experience as a band director, Ben was willing to take that on when we needed someone. He put together a band using donated instruments. The CHS band's highlight was their performance at our 25th anniversary celebration in 2004, though they had other opportunities to perform. Shortly before the Bonnetts returned to Minnesota, they adopted a sibling group of six from CSC. A few years later, they adopted two more boys who were from Cebu. They also had two biological kids, bringing their family to an even dozen.

In 2017, Ben took on the job of education director at Children of Hope School. The Bonnetts went to Cebu to start this second assignment 12 years after they left CSC the first time. Accompanying them were their son, Josh, and their two younger daughters, Rylin and Johanna. Ben led the school through some challenging transitions, working closely with principal Cris Tabra. The school was the beneficiary of several sizeable donations for the purchase of books, curriculum, and equipment. When another similar donation came through, Ben, in a gesture of kindness and inclusion, gifted the other departments from that money so that they, too, could buy needed equipment or pursue staff development opportunities. During Ben's tenure as education director, many improvements were made to the facility, including some major renovations when the building was needed as a quarantine center during the pandemic.

In response to our changing population at CSC, with more of our residents aging out of adoption and our need to launch them for life in the Philippines, Ben authored a program called Bridge, which involves education and counseling but also vocational and job preparedness training and life skills.

One highlight of Ben's time as education director was the celebration of the school's 20th anniversary in 2018. Ben and staff planned a weekend of activities, including a gala banquet that featured videos, games, and testimonials around the theme of Stories of Hope.

Carla Sjolund was a trailblazer, serving on our initial team when the school opened in 1998. She helped us forge cooperation between our Filipino and U.S. teachers, a challenge because our local teachers were trained differently than those from the U.S., and a spirit of compromise and flexibility was needed. Also, the multi-age system we adopted was new and challenging for everyone on the faculty.

Amy Luck was also a charter faculty member. She had heard about CSC when I spoke in her church in Kulm, North Dakota, and became interested in the opportunity to use her training as a teacher in our school. She stayed at CHS for a total of 15 years, developing our preschool program into an integral part of the school. She had a big heart for students with special needs, integrating them into her classroom in creative ways that helped us fulfill our goal of providing excellent education for all CSC kids.

Amy gradually took on additional responsibilities at CSC, serving on our Child Development team and writing developmental reports for our younger children. Amy eventually married a pastor, Marcel Pacada, and they moved back to North Dakota, where she is teaching in Fargo.

Tammy Vosika grew up hearing about CSC in her home church, North Isanti Baptist. She and her family were part of a mission team that went to Cebu in 1996. (As a result of that trip, Tammy's parents adopted four brothers from CSC.) Although she took a teaching job in Texas, she never forgot about CSC and later expressed an interest in our school to Shari Reasoner. I was in Texas for a few days, having escorted one of our kids to the Masonic Burn Hospital in Galveston. I made a quick flight to Houston, where I met Tammy and we talked about the possibility of her joining our team in Cebu. This eventually happened, and Tammy went to Cebu with a one-year commitment that kept getting extended and eventually developed into a wonderful eight-year time of service.

Tammy was an excellent teacher who loved her students and spent time with them outside of class. She completed her teaching in Cebu in 2013, when she returned to Cambridge, Minnesota, and resumed her teaching career. Tammy, married and the mother of twins, lives in Fargo, North Dakota, where she maintains her friendship with Amy Luck Pacada.

Nora Dorsey served for five years (1999–2004) at Children of Hope School. She loved to teach science and challenged students with creative experiments and projects. Nora learned about CSC through Sandy Swanson, whom she got to know at Camp Shamineau.

I need to add a story about Nora, although it doesn't have to do with Children of Hope School. Nora had already finished her time in Cebu and was substitute teaching in Minnesota. I had brought Jackson, one of our CSC kids, to Galveston, Texas, for treatment. We arranged for a family from Galveston to foster him while he was in the hospital and for a couple weeks after his release. For reasons known only to them, the couple bailed out after a day or two, and we were in a difficult situation of needing people to care for Jackson and bring him from the Ronald McDonald House to his appointments. Several people we thought might be able to go there from Minnesota couldn't. I was scheduled to go back to Cebu, so we were getting a little desperate. Nora Dorsey stepped in and saved the day! She went to Texas and took over Jackson's care until he could be discharged and return to Minnesota. I will always be grateful for that act of kindness.

Alan and Rachel Lecher taught music in our school in 2000-2001. They helped establish a music program by giving instruction in piano, voice, and band, putting to use instruments that had been donated to the school. CHS gave several performances while the Lechers were in Cebu.

We have always felt that music is an important part of our program because it is an international language. If our kids can learn to play an instrument or read music, they'll be able to use that wherever they go in life, whether they are adopted in the U.S. or other countries, or stay in the Philippines. We have seen that musical ability builds self-esteem. One highlight of Alan and Rachel's time in Cebu was when the band performed "25 or 6 to 4" with the assistance of my fabulous garage band, the Trash. We rocked!

Dawn Miller heard about CSC the spring of her senior year at St. Olaf College in Northfield, Minnesota. She was attending my brother Will's church, and one Sunday my sister, Elizabeth, went there to speak about CSC. It was an impactful day for Dawn and resulted in her making three trips to Cebu. The first was in 2001, when she was there for three months helping with individualized instruction for students having difficulty. The second trip was for six months during 2005-2006, again working in Children of Hope School. The third was a much shorter visit, for two weeks in 2007. Dawn was great to have in Cebu. She was willing to do anything needed at the school and got along well with everyone.

When **Michelle Peterson** came to teach at the Children of Hope School, it was her fourth trip to Cebu. In 1998, when she was 16 years old, and again in 2000, she went to CSC with a team from Constance Free Church Youth Ministries. She made another trip with a friend from church, Sherri Stumpf, in 2007, and went again for a year of teaching in 2009-2010. In 2011 Michelle made another trip on her own to see all her friends at CSC. Michelle was a dedicated teacher whose love and concern for her students was evident. She continued her teaching career in Minnesota after her time at CHS.

Bjork and Lindsay Ostrom, from Cambridge, Minnesota, served on our staff for a year in 2012-2013. They brought talent and enthusiasm. Lindsay taught in CHS and Bjork helped out in the office while they both continued to work on their successful food blog, Pinch of Yum.

Filipino Teachers

Cora Abaquita was on our initial faculty at CHS. An excellent teacher who cared deeply about her students, she encouraged them, prayed for them, and challenged them. Teachers presented quarterly progress reports on their students to the house parents and staff, and Cora's were always upbeat, positive, and celebratory as she focused on the improvement and abilities of her class. She never seemed to get discouraged by behavioral challenges and maintained a belief in her students' abilities and excitement for all their accomplishments. Cora retired in 2020.

Cris Tabra has been a shining star at Children of Hope School from the start. She taught in the preschool and the primary grades, and proved to be an excellent instructor for our emerging readers. She was a big help to Lisa Saavedra in managing our relationship with DepEd and integrating our language arts curriculum into the school program. She was bright and articulate and set a tone of professionalism with our teachers, leading by example in teaching technique and classroom management.

Cris became our school principal in 2008, exhibiting exceptional leadership in curriculum and professional development, upgrading our facilities, and sourcing educational opportunities for students who graduated from CHS. She worked well with our two education directors, Shari Reasoner and Ben Bonnett, as well as CSC staff members and the leadership team.

During the pandemic, Cris showed her colors by developing a system whereby children could continue their education even during the quarantine at CSC. She was willing to be locked in to supervise that school effort, being away from her family for months. As our only leader on the inside, she was a key person in setting up schedules and reporting to the field director and medical team about needs and problems on the inside. We will never know all the problems she solved and fires she put out during her time while locked in, but we know that God used her in significant ways in that role.

Cris was gracious in putting CSC's needs first by allowing the school to be used as a quarantine center for workers who needed 14 days of quarantine before being allowed in the shelter. She worked with Jerry Salgoon making changes to the school facilities, adding bathrooms, and providing sleeping and eating facilities that promoted safety and privacy for our quarantined employees.

There have been many more Filipino teachers who have made our school strong over the years. Because of the high turnover of local teachers, they are too many to name. But their contributions have been great ones as they loved and taught our kids for the first 23 years of the school's history, and continue to do so into the future.

Outreach

CHILDREN OF HOPE SCHOOL occasionally served the community by enrolling students who were not residents of CSC, including kids with special needs such as cerebral palsy, Down syndrome, and other maladies that made it hard or impossible for them to study in other schools in Cebu.

Rufa Mae and John Ray were examples of these children. Both suffered with osteogenesis imperfecta, a genetic bone disorder that is present at birth. It is also known as brittle bone disease. Children born with OI may have soft bones that fracture easily, bones that are not formed normally, and other problems. Neither Rufa Mae nor John Ray could walk, so they needed wheelchairs for mobility.

These children lived with their family in the mountainous region of southern Cebu. They had been visiting an aunt in Cebu City when they came to the attention of one of our staff members who invited them to talk to me about the possibility of attending Hope School. They had not been able to attend school where they lived because of the hilly terrain, which made it impossible to navigate with their wheelchairs. John Ray's brother,

Billong, would carry them on his back in a large basket, up and down the mountain. It was very dangerous travel because any bump could cause fracturing of their bones. Our school administrators were willing to enroll them, so they began attending Hope School, a life-changing opportunity that started a relationship between CSC and the Obiedo family that has grown and expanded and blessed everyone concerned.

John and Rufa did well in school and enjoyed the facilities of our school and its wheelchair accessibility. They both loved music and participated in the school band and dramatic productions. Eventually, three of their sisters and their older brother took jobs at CSC, cementing their family's relationship with us and opening up the world to these two precious people through education.

John Ray graduated in 2009. Sadly, Rufa died of pneumonia in 2010.

Field Trips

FIELD TRIPS WERE A WAY to expand our students' horizons by bringing education outside the walls of the school to include local, regional, and national learning opportunities. Our students were brought to animal reserves, zoos, marine sanctuaries, and the seats of government. In 2009, the older students flew to Manila to visit museums, theme parks, and historical sites, while the younger kids went to the neighboring island of Bohol. They visited the Chocolate Hills, a group of more than a thousand, unusual, conical hills scattered within a 50-square-mile area, explored some underground caves, and saw the tarsiers, the smallest primates in the world.

One day when I was in Manila for meetings with ICAB, the taxi took me through Makati, the financial center of Metro Manila. We passed by a monument depicting the assassination of Ninoy Aquino, an opponent of Ferdinand Marcos, the dictatorial leader of the Philippines from 1965-1986. I was struck by the fact that most of our CSC kids and CHS students would grow up and leave for adoption abroad without ever getting to see many of the important historical and cultural centers of the Philippines, as most of these are in Manila.

The geography of the Philippines makes it all but impossible for many Filipinos to travel to Manila or other historical places. So unless we provided opportunities for our students to not only learn about them in the classroom but visit these sites on field trips from Hope School, they would grow up not seeing important sites of the Philippines. So our field trips were an important educational tool for our students.

Ancillary Uses

IT WAS GREAT TO HAVE A PLACE for large-group gatherings. Over the years the school was used for workers' meetings, seminars, worship services, rallies, memorial services, and even a few weddings. Our daughter Nelia got married to Neil Collins in the grassy area behind the school in 2001. When our treasured friend Ron Duterte died in 2005, we had a memorial service for him at the school attended by staff, kids, other friends of Ron, and members of his family. Every Christmas Eve we had a party that included the arrival of Santa, hijinks, and the opening of gifts.

The longer that CSC exists the more it is clear just how important the establishment of CHS was and how it contributed, as much as any part of our program, to our success in caring for children and helping prepare them for whatever will come next in their lives. It is aptly named, because the precious education they receive there helps provide hope by establishing a firm educational foundation on which to build as they grow up and pursue additional schooling and training, in the Philippines or wherever they will live their lives.

Furlough

"FURLOUGH" IS A TERM THAT'S NOT USED MUCH anymore for missionaries. "Home assignment" is usually used to describe the time that missionaries spend in their home country between terms of service. Most missionaries accrue one year of furlough for four years of service. For our family, furloughs varied from seven months to almost two years. Our first term of service was four years, but others have been longer and shorter.

In the early years, when we were only receiving an honorarium for our work, we could not live in the United States during furlough without additional income. For our first few furloughs, Marlys worked as a medical assistant at the Fridley Medical Center, where she was employed before we went to Cebu. It was a good place to work because she knew many people there, and she got to keep her hands in the medical field and learn new things to help her in her work with CSC as medical director.

CSC staff spent their time on furlough helping the stateside office with promotion and fundraising. On weekends we visited supporting churches. Most of our churches are in Minnesota and neighboring states, but sometimes we traveled to Washington, California, Colorado, Nebraska, or Connecticut. We also traveled to visit adoptive families, which was always a lot of fun. Some furloughed staff used the time to further their education. For example, Sandy Swanson, who had studied early childhood development prior to working with CSC, earned a B.A. in psychology from Northwestern College.

It was both enjoyable and difficult to be on furlough. We missed Cebu and the kids, and were torn between thinking and worrying about how things were going there and trying to do our stateside work. And there was a lot of adjusting to do for us Americans who had been gone from the States for extended periods. There was new lingo to learn, and we had to accept the fact that although we had exciting stories to tell about our adventures in the Philippines, some people we thought would be interested, were not.

During our first furlough in 1982, the ministry was still finding its way in Cebu, so two people being gone created difficulties for the remaining staff. It helped that Kathy and Joe Grafft went to Cebu for a year to help. Sandy Swanson, Kathy and Sned Flora, and the Graffts did a great job handling everything, establishing a precedent of flexibility and grace that has characterized our staff throughout our history.

Setting up household in Minnesota for a year or part of a year was tricky. Before Marlys and I had our own kids, it was easier. But after we adopted our three girls, furloughs had to coincide with U.S. school schedules. We needed housing, transportation, and furniture—and later, cell phones and Internet connections. There were so many things we didn't know. One time I was in a drug store shortly after arriving in Minnesota for furlough, and I accidentally handed the cashier Philippine currency. She looked at me and said, "Oh man, I'm vegging out!" Maybe we can shorten our furlough, I thought.

Our first furlough with our girls was in 1992, and we lived in a trailer in Ham Lake. Five people in a small trailer was interesting. We had a lot to learn about the sociology of trailer courts. One day we were sitting in our living room when a policeman barged in without knocking. He asked if we were all right. I said, "Yes, we're fine." He left and went next door, and we saw him hauling our handcuffed neighbor away in his police car.

Little things could be annoying. Things most Americans take for granted were challenging for us. Cell phone plans required a two-year subscription, and our furloughs were usually a year or less. Computer and technology language was often confusing. Coming from a tropical climate in the Philippines, we had to readjust to the cold and snow in Minnesota. The grocery stores offered options for foods we hadn't been able to buy in Cebu. Traffic laws were different, so we had to constantly remind ourselves that turn signaling was needed and common courtesy on the road was expected. Gestures were different. Raising your eyebrows to indicate assent or agreement is common in the Philippines but unknown in the States. And, unlike Filipinos, Americans expect you to be on time for appointments and speaking engagements. We missed the friendliness of Filipinos and their special brand of hospitality.

Housing on furlough was a mixed bag. Marlys and I lived in six different places over our career. Mitch and Ruth Ohlendorf stayed with family in Washington or rented a place in Minnesota. Sandy Swanson lived with her mom while on furloughs, as did Lindsay Hoeft Abong. Joel and Jinkee Reasoner stayed with Joel's parents in Cambridge. Amy Luck stayed with her mom in Kulm, North Dakota.

Finding a place to rent could be difficult because of lease requirements. Marlys and I were given furniture and purchased other items we had to put in storage when our furlough was over. None of our stuff was valuable. A few times people offered free space in their attic or shed for our things, but usually we rented storage space. Often we had our belongings in different places with different arrangements. To this day I wonder if we forgot to get something in someone's attic and it's still there waiting for us. We've told people that we have the most expensive furniture in America, factoring in the storage costs over the decades.

Staff members doing presentations on furlough have encountered humorous situations. Marlys and I had the wrong starting time in mind one Sunday for a presentation at a Lutheran church in central Minnesota. We discovered our mistake on the way to the church and called ahead to alert the pastor that we would be late. Nobody answered the phone. (We learned later that the pastor was not there that Sunday and had left matters in the hands of a layman.) We drove as fast as we could and got there at least 30 minutes after I was supposed to speak. Leaving Marlys to set up the display, I walked in the side door and took a seat, to the obvious relief of the song leader, who figured I must be the speaker, and called out, "The fifth stanza as the last." Having long since supplemented the morning's liturgy with additional songs, he had been sweating at the thought of having to preach himself or find a way to fill up the rest of the hour.

Some churches had us give a greeting in the worship service and then meet with one or more Sunday School classes. Other churches wanted me to preach. Some church visits were exhausting. One church that required a long trip from Saint Paul, were we lived, had me preach in two services and handle the combined Sunday School hour in between. Then, after the second service, I met with the Missions Committee before having lunch with the pastor. Then I made the long trip home. But it was great to be with people who loved CSC and wanted to hear as much as possible from us.

On a rainy spring morning I was in a church that had been supporting CSC for quite a few years. I was the speaker that morning, and although the pastor had said he would be there, he wasn't involved in the service or sitting in the congregation. When it was time to introduce me, he came from the side door and went slowly to the pulpit. And there, just before I was to speak, he tendered his resignation as pastor in an emotional announcement. Then he introduced me!

In Kulm, North Dakota, I was scheduled to speak in two churches on Sunday morning. The first service was in the Congregational church just down the block from my second assignment at Kulm Baptist. The first service ran late, and the reception line at the back of the church moved agonizingly slowly as many members were elderly, some in walkers. I was nervous because it was already 11:40, so I scooped up my display table items and ran to the Baptist church, dropped my stuff with an usher who promised to set up a table for me, and went in the side entrance. Nobody told me what to do so I walked in, went across the stage, and sat down right as the choir finished their version of "Speed Away, Speed Away." I was sweating, my two college friends who were in the congregation were laughing, and I was already being introduced to preach.

Some of the travel was monotonous or risky. Some of the vehicles we drove weren't the best. Sometimes the speaking arrangements weren't what I was expecting. Occasionally we got lost and didn't think we'd make it in time. But once we were actually there, once we stood up to speak, something happened. It was all good. It was an honor to be ambassadors of CSC, representing the kids. There was something about the needs of those children that captivated people and enlivened us. Undoubtedly there were times when I wasn't all that great a speaker or when the slide projector didn't work, but there was never a time when making a presentation was drudgery. Whether it was an Awana Club with 15 kids or a large church worship service, it was always a blast.

In North America, furloughed staff members had the pleasure of addressing church groups in California, Oregon, Washington, Colorado, Nebraska, Missouri, Minnesota, North Dakota, South Dakota, Iowa, Wisconsin, Ohio, Kentucky, Tennessee, Florida, Virginia, Connecticut, Massachusetts, Maine, New York, and Vancouver, British Columbia. In Asia we were able to present at churches in Hong Kong and Japan and, of course, the Philippines.

The finances involved in traveling and making presentations during furloughs were sometimes awkward and confusing. Some churches that invited us to speak reimbursed us for gas to get there; others did not. Some took an offering for CSC after our presentation or let us make a collection at the back of the church. Some didn't. Some arranged for lodging in a church member's home or at a local motel. Often we were on our own to find a room.

One church in Wisconsin always put us up in a nice hotel or resort, or in a lakeside cottage owned by one of their families. It really made a big difference, if we had a long drive to get to the church, that we could get a good night's sleep before making presentations the next day.

Once a CSC supporter, a high school teacher in Coon Rapids, Minnesota, and a good friend of Cliff Danielson, asked me to speak at his school's Honor Society Awards night. A strong Christian, he thought it would be good for the students to see how Marlys and I had chosen to spend our lives. Because it was a public school, he told me that I needed to be careful about how I talked about Christianity but that I should feel free to mention my admiration of Jesus and how his life had impacted mine.

After the program he sidled up to me and handed me an envelope with a check inside for my honorarium. I didn't look inside the envelope until I got into my car to drive home. I was flabbergasted to see the amount of the check: $250. I could not believe it! In the 15 years I had been representing CSC to churches, I had never received anything remotely approaching that amount. I was high and called up my brother Dave to tell him of my windfall. He was less excited than me. He told me that, although he hated to pop my balloon, I should know that "out in the real world," as he put it, "that's what speakers get paid for traveling and giving up an evening of their time to speak to a group." Not in my world!

One great thing about furlough was getting to see our families after a long separation. People often talk about the sacrifices missionaries make to leave house and home and go to another country. For Marlys and me, the only significant sacrifice we felt we made involved being away from our families. We missed many birthdays, anniversaries, graduations, weddings, and reunions.

One year we were in Minnesota for the wedding of my niece and were excited to attend. As the lovely bride walked down the aisle with my brother, I realized that I didn't really know her. She had grown up, graduated from high school, and gone to college without my being around. I had missed out on most of her life, and here she was walking down the aisle to be married. How fortunate we felt to be there for that big day in our family's life, but there was sadness to think of all that we missed.

I have often reflected on the sacrifices our parents made to have us on the other side of the world. When I saw my 94-year-old mom when we arrived in Minnesota to begin our retirement, she said many times that she was so glad she lived long enough to see us again. CSC owes so much to the parents of our staff who endured that separation with faith and strength.

Marlys's dad, Cliff, had a host of medical problems as he got older and would have loved Marlys to be around to care for him. Amy Luck's mom suffered from Type 1 diabetes and would have benefitted greatly by having her daughter there to provide care. Sandy's mom was a widow for much of the time she was in Cebu. Sandy's family is very close, and it was hard for them to have her so far away. Lindsay Abong was in Cebu when one of her grandparents died and her mom was dealing with cancer. But all of these parents put their personal dreams aside and allowed their children to answer the call of God without hindering us or making us feel guilty.

A sermon that I preached occasionally on furlough was about Zebedee, the father of two of Jesus' disciples, James and John. I reflected on his life and how it was greatly affected when Jesus arrived in their home. Zebedee worked with his boys in the fishing business. They were a team. He undoubtedly had hopes and expectations that they would take over the business eventually. In fact, Zebedee's financial future likely depended on them doing so. We don't read anything about Zebedee standing in the way, questioning, or complaining about their decision to drop their nets and follow Jesus. But Zebedee's grace and obedience came with a big price.

And there was a big cost to pay for us to be in Cebu, far from loved ones. So it was especially sweet to have furlough time with them every several years. One of the things that missionaries get to be skilled at is saying goodbye. And hello!

Disappointments and Challenges

ANY HISTORY OF CSC that doesn't include conflicts, failures, heartaches, tragedies, and frustrations would not be honest or accurate. There have been lots of difficult days. Our success as an organization has had a lot to do with our ability to bounce back from these negative experiences, learn from them, and move ahead with what we were called to do.

As noted earlier, our fundraising efforts started in a disappointing, even disastrous way, with our ill-fated, ill-advised, ill-timed BJ Thomas concert, a failure that set our plans to go to Cebu back by months. But it didn't stop us. We were young, determined, maybe even hard-headed.

Further disappointments were to come. When we arrived in Cebu to start the ministry in May of 1979, a person we had been with in Cebu was nowhere to be found, having left for the United States, unbeknownst to us. We were back to square one. Even worse, this person returned to Cebu and filed a case against us with the Immigration Office seeking to have us deported.

National Disasters

NATURAL AND MAN-MADE DISASTERS presented difficulties and frustrations over the years. About one fourth of our house in Bulacao burned in 1981, which forced us to move out for a few months as it was being repaired. Several storms hit our island over the years, the worst being Typhoon Nitang, in 1984. Although our house wasn't damaged, we were without phones and electricity for more than a month. And some of our workers lost their homes to the high winds and torrential rains. When super Typhoon Haiyan, known in the Philippines as Yolanda, hit in 2013, it was the most powerful tropical cyclone ever recorded. It packed winds of 190 mph, claimed thousands of lives, and destroyed homes on several islands, most notably Leyte. Cebu was affected greatly by Yolanda, particularly in the north part of the island.

It seemed like every year at least one major typhoon hit the Philippines. The national weather service (PAGASA) classified storms as Signal 1-5, with 5 being the worst. When it started to get windy, we made sure to listen to the radio to find out which signal was forecast for Cebu City and what to prepare for.

Typhoon winds can be incredibly strong. Yolanda's were almost 200 mph. Coconut trees, with their slender, textured trunks, resemble windshield wipers as they bend back and forth in the wind. The winds make a howling noise that can be frightening for the children and for Americanos not used to such storms.

During Typhoon Ruping in 1990, Mitch Ohlendorf went outside to secure some items in our yard and was barely able to walk back to the house. The wind literally blew him off his feet. Inside, we closed all the jalousie windows, but still the rain poured in. We ran around the house trying to mop up the invading waters. We were thankful we had a solid house with a well-built roof, and that our CSC children were safe and secure during these periodic typhoons. Another missionary described God's hand of protection reaching down to the missionary homes, where nobody lost their roof. But many of our workers lost their roofs during the storm. I thought that it was probably less about the favored status of missionaries and more about the quality of structures that they could afford to build or rent.

In October of 2012, a 7.2 impact earthquake hit the central Philippines, with the epicenter in Bohol, a neighboring island to Cebu. Some damage was wrought in Cebu, an unsettling experience for our kids and staff. I was in the States at the time, so Mitch Ohlendorf was responsible for seeing that everyone was safe and doing a safety check on our facilities with Jerry Salgo and engineers. We experienced several other lesser quakes over the years, so we were always concerned about the possibility of a more serious earthquake and underwent disaster preparedness training for our staff in how to respond to that type of event.

Man-Made Disasters

MAN-MADE DISASTERS WERE HARDER TO FORECAST. Political unrest spawned demonstrations and massive unrest in the Philippines on several occasions during our history. Although Cebu itself was relatively peaceful, this unrest affected the whole country.

The most dramatic example was in 1986, when the regime of Ferdinand Marcos was toppled as a result of a "People Power" revolution that took place largely in Manila. Following the murder of opposition leader Benigno Aquino and an election that many considered fraudulent, thousands of Filipinos took to the streets in marches and rallies that were nonviolent but inspired the loyalty of the Philippine military and eventually brought down Marcos. Cebuanos watched closely as these events transpired in Manila, classes were suspended, and smaller demonstrations were held in support of People Power.

Some political unrest included anti-American sentiment, which presented difficulties for our American staff. Leftist groups decried what they considered American tampering in Philippine politics and the existence of several U.S. military bases that they wanted closed. Although we were far from supporting any American imperialistic activities in the Philippines, we sometimes worried about being targeted by leftist groups. Mostly, though, we just continued with our work and trusted God to protect us and our ministry from any outside interference.

It is helpful to understand Philippine geography and its impact on natural and man-made disasters to better understand how these affect the country and people like us attempting to live there. The Philippines is made up of more than 7,000 islands, divided into several regions with various subcultures and language groups. There are 120–175 distinct languages in the Philippines, 13 of which have at least a million speakers. There are additional dialects, as well. For example, our language, Visayan, has many dialects, and regional variations exist in Bohol, Leyte, northern Mindanao, and other surrounding islands. The trained ear can even differentiate various forms of Cebuano used around the island of Cebu itself. And there are other distinct languages on surrounding islands.

Undoubtedly the Philippines is a linguist's paradise. I have always been interested in the way language shapes culture and how the geography of the Philippines shapes national politics and affects development. Certainly the idea of what is a Filipino is affected by these variations. The project of nation-building is made more difficult because Filipinos come from such different geographical, cultural, and linguistic regions. Although the government came up with a national language, Filipino, it is widely considered a form of Tagalog, the language of Manila, which is the center of government and commerce. There is certainly some reluctance among Filipinos outside Manila to embrace Filipino as the national language. Many of our CSC workers speak Cebuano primarily but also know Filipino because it is taught in the schools and is featured in television programs that originate in Manila and in movies distributed nationwide. Some know one or more other languages.

But it is geography, not necessarily language, that challenges Philippine nationhood. Isolation is created when people live on different islands not spanned by land transportation. When we first moved to Cebu, we met an elderly woman who was the grandmother of Gloria Navasquez Deliña, a friend of our staff who eventually joined our team. Her grandma was in her 90s, which is extremely old for a Filipino. She lived in the place of her birth, an area called CarCar, about 50 kilometers south of Cebu City. I was shocked to learn from her that she had never been to the city. It might just as well have been a world away. But her experience indicates how separated some people are, or feel they are, in an archipelago, and how the government dealings can seem distant or even foreign to people living in provincial areas. We often felt that way living in Cebu when so much of the action was in Manila.

When the tanks were rolling down EDSA highway during the height of the People Power revolution in 1986, the international news media were all over the story. Friends of ours in the States who didn't understand the geography of the Philippines saw the action in Manila, a one-hour flight or 24-hour boat trip from Cebu, and were worried about our safety. Someone called and asked how I was holding up in the midst of all this. I responded, "Not well. I couldn't make a putt today on the back nine." While the tanks were rolling in Manila, I was having a round of golf.

So the question of what it means to be a Filipino is not always simple to answer when people are separated by oceans and languages. And the English language can further complicate the situation. English is widely used in business and government and is the medium of instruction in schools, together with Tagalog. So the ability to speak English is a symbol of being well-educated. But the poor, who do not have the opportunity to enroll in high-quality elementary and high schools, or to pursue higher education, might struggle with the English language. Thus, language differences among English, Tagalog, Filipino, Cebuano, etc. often separate Filipinos.

Cultural Differences

LIFE CAN BE DIFFICULT WHEN LIVING IN ANOTHER CULTURE, far from the place one knows best. We learned a lot about cultural differences, especially early during our time in Cebu. Some of these differences were language-based, some a matter of personal taste or relationship norms.

In trying to settle a conflict that existed when we first arrived in Cebu, I talked with the person with whom we were in disagreement. He had just returned from the U.S. after having been gone from Cebu for several months. He seemed different to me from the time I had known him when he visited us in Minnesota. I said, "I feel like I don't know you any more." He was offended by that statement. I came to learn later that he took my statement to mean that we were disavowing any knowledge of him, considering him *persona non grata* for what he had done.

One time a woman came to our house in Bulacao around supper time. She was Mrs. Mamerta Sy, a member of our Philippine board and a friend of the ministry. She helped us a lot in our early days. We purchased lumber from her store in CarCar on occasion. Since we were about to eat, we invited her to join us, but she declined, saying that she had to go. But she didn't go. So we brought the food out and the kids and staff started to eat. Finally she left, but we heard later that she had been shocked that we didn't offer her supper. We thought we had, but in Philippine culture you have to offer several times, and if the person still declines but doesn't leave you bring them a plate of food. Only then have you graciously invited them to eat.

I've told about when Arnold, one of our babies, died. When we went to the Shelter to tell the house parents, workers, and children about Arnold's passing, everyone was surprised and saddened by the news, but the question the workers asked was, "Who is with Arnold?" For Marlys and me, after seeing that Arnold was taken to the hospital morgue, we hadn't hesitated to leave the body there to go and tell people and make arrangements. For them, our leaving him was cold, bordering on heartless. Several workers went immediately to the hospital to be with the body. They took turns keeping a vigil there and also at the funeral home when the body was brought there.

I often felt like the cultural differences between our American staff and our Filipino workers created a wall between us, which was frustrating and sometimes hampered the smooth operation of our work. Clearly, it was our responsibility to make adjustments in our adopted home, but in spite of good intentions, we often made cultural gaffes that caused hard feelings and confusion. We didn't want to be the "ugly Americans," insisting on our way of doing things, but some of us might have come across that way to the Filipinos. An older missionary we knew was in that category. He had a "little brown brother" approach to the people he worked with. For him, compromise consisted of the Filipinos coming over to his way of thinking. He was seemingly incapable of budging.

What made cultural differences more intense for us as Americans was that because most of our CSC children were going to be adopted and almost all of them would be going to homes in the West, we felt we needed to prepare them by introducing elements of Western culture to them at CSC. This influenced areas of our program such as medical care, education, discipline, and language. Some of what we tried to teach the kids was foreign to our Filipino workers. We also had the situation of our children learning English at our school, a language some of our workers could not speak or understand well. We had to constantly walk a tightrope between East and West in our work and private lives while living in Cebu.

The tourist or casual observer might assume that Filipinos and Americans are much alike because of our joint use of English and American influence in clothing, fast food, government structure, architecture, and economic institutions. Philippine national newspapers are in English, as are some television news programs. American shows are broadcast, and our movies are shown in Philippine cinemas. But differences between the two countries are significant in terms of worldview, relationships, spirituality, child-rearing, family dynamics. and organizational planning.

Sometimes we were lulled to sleep by the seeming similarities, and the differences hit us like a slap in the face. But I can say without hesitation that in my experience as an American living in Cebu, the Filipinos in my world were kind, gracious, and long-suffering with me and the other Americans working at or visiting CSC. Still, culture was a complicated body of water to navigate, and we didn't always do it without taking on water.

Language Learning

LANGUAGE LEARNING WAS OFTEN FRUSTRATING, necessary but difficult, and sometimes embarrassing or hilarious. In our early days, Marlys and Kathy studied with Mrs. Liberty Jesalva, wife of the pastor of Bible Baptist Church. I had a tutor named Dina, who was recommended by Pastor Lucas. Good language tutors for the Cebuano language are hard to come by. Whereas Tagalog is studied in Philippine schools, Cebuano is mostly spoken and only sometimes written. So people in Cebu can tell you if you say something wrong but usually not why. Three stories show the embarrassment of saying or understanding something incorrectly:

One day I was riding on the back of a friend's motorcycle in a town in western Cebu. Along the ocean I saw a sign that read, AYAW PAG LABAY SA INYONG MGA ILO NGADTO SA DAGAT. My translation was, "DON'T THROW YOUR ORPHANS INTO THE OCEAN." Technically, I was correct and my righteous indignation at the thought of people needing a directive to refrain from throwing homeless children into the bay was understandable. My friend driving the motorcycle laughed when I asked about it, explaining that the word *ilo* has two meanings: orphans and used toilet paper. When spoken, there is a difference in stress and intonation that is clearly discernable, especially to native language speakers, but identical when written. I was aware of the first meaning but not the second. I'll bet my friend Sammy is still laughing over that gaffe, even 42 years later.

Another time I was in a restaurant in uptown Cebu City and called the waiter over to order. I asked for lamuk (mosquito) when I should have said manuk (chicken). To make matters worse, I told him I wanted only a quarter lamuk because I wasn't very hungry. The waiter hurried to the kitchen, and I could hear people laughing good and hard at my expense. I didn't blame him and was happy that, for the most part, Filipinos were kind and long-suffering about my attempts to speak their language.

One day we were having a bowling tournament for our workers, and I was about to leave my house for the bowling alley. Nang Teddy, the lady who was washing clothes in our house, wanted to know if I had any dirty clothes that needed washing. She used the word *boling-on* for dirty clothes, but I thought she was asking about going bowling. Since she wasn't a CSC employee, she would not have been included in the outing, so I was trying to explain, but she wasn't interested in bowling, just doing her job. It took us about 10 minutes to sort that one out.

One thing that made learning Cebuano difficult for me was its use of the passive voice. Filipinos, in all their languages, often use a passive construction. For example, where we would say "June threw the ball," the Cebuano way would be to say "the ball was thrown by June." Americans describing events focus on the doer of the action, making him or her the subject of the sentence. As English speakers, we are shaping our world, doing things, and making events happen. For the Filipino, there are things happening to people and objects quite apart from their initiating or controlling them. So learning to speak properly meant first learning to think another way.

When I look back at my career in Cebu, one thing I would do differently would be to study Tagalog. In our early days in the Philippines, I could not have predicted that I would eventually spend a lot of time in Manila attending meetings or seminars, or matching our kids for adoption at the DSWD or ICAB. Whereas English is the official language of commerce and government, Tagalog is also widely used, and I spent a lot of time not knowing what was being said. A spoken sentence might include Tagalog and English words woven together skillfully but, for me, indecipherably. The longer I was in Cebu the harder it got to find time for language study, but I wish I would have prioritized it and developed proficiency in Tagalog.

I also wish my use of Cebuano had been better. I was moderately skilled in the local language but could have been a much more effective leader if I had taken the time to further develop my language skills. Perhaps I would have had to do so if English wasn't used widely in the Philippines. But I would have been a more effective leader if I had been more fluent in the Cebuano and Tagalog languages. I think that other U.S. staff had similar regrets, particularly in regard to the language of Cebu.

Government Relations

IT IS SAFE TO SAY that relations with the Philippine government caused some of the most stressful times for me and the ministry of CSC, especially in the early years. Although our friend, attorney, and CSC (Philippines) President Ron Duterte helped in these areas and shielded us from some of the hassles and potential misunderstandings, they still existed and caused a lot of stress. As the leader of CSC for its first 41 years, most of that hassle fell on my shoulders. Sometimes it became pretty intense, especially when it affected our ability to do what we felt was needed for the proper care of our children.

One difficulty was that, living in a province, far from the center of government, we were subject to national laws and policies but also governed by regional and city laws, which were not always consistent with the national government. We had to satisfy licensing requirements both nationally and locally, and both required significant paperwork. Domestic adoption cases were handled locally, whereas international placements were processed and regulated in Manila. The paperwork for getting passports for our children who were to be placed internationally came from Manila but had to be submitted in Cebu.

Our school calendar could be changed unexpectedly at the last moment if the president decided to declare a national holiday. This might include Muslim holidays celebrated nationwide even though there was no significant Muslim population in Cebu.

In our early days, immigration paperwork for all the American staff had to be approved in Manila. This later changed to Cebu, but all immigration policies came from the capital city. The Philippines is Manila-centric. Most policies flow from there to the rest of the country. Often, Manila people see things differently than we do in the south.

We also suffered at times from the seemingly inherent conflict between government and nongovernment agencies and their perspective on matters relating to the care and placement of our children. We always sensed some distrust of what we were trying to do at CSC. In spite of having the required licenses and accreditations, we were subject to inspections, new policies enforcement, and program audits from the regional and national agencies we were under. This sometimes made for difficult and stressful meetings and complicated relationships, particularly with the DSWD and ICAB.

Some conflicts were about whether to keep children at CSC and eventually place them for adoption, or return them to their birth families. If we believed that the child(ren) would be safe with their birth families and not be exploited or maltreated, we would gladly agree to return them. But often our social worker's assessment of the birth family differed from the government's findings. Case conferences were called and emotional confrontations sometimes occurred.

After years of dealing with the social welfare organizations of the Philippine government, we eventually had to add the Department of Education to our list of supervising agencies. We started our Children of Hope School in 1998 and had to meet DepEd requirements to obtain a license. Again, there were sometimes significant differences of opinion and philosophy between us and the government agency over us. We were pioneering a new style of education that wasn't entirely understood or embraced by DepEd. Because most CSC students would leave the Philippines for adoption, we felt a need to prepare them for whatever kind of education would come next when they were adopted. We didn't think that learning Tagalog was worth the time and effort. We believed that more time learning American and world history would better prepare them for what their lives would look like post-CSC.

However, we had some children at CSC who would not leave and who would attend Philippine schools, where Tagalog and Philippine history and culture studies would benefit them greatly. We needed a licensing arrangement with DepEd that would allow us to give a good overview of the Philippines to our kids while at the same time preparing them for their future. These needs sometimes created conflict and difficulties for our school administrators and teachers.

Philippine government is a huge bureaucracy that employs around 1.4 million Filipinos. One characteristic of any bureaucracy is the amount of paperwork needed to fuel it. For CSC, this means a staggering number of reports, statistical summaries, social case studies, case inventories, financial statements, and other legal and operational paperwork. Our social workers, accountants, school administrators, teachers, and therapists spend a lot of time feeding the bureaucracy by submitting these reports.

Aside from the big three—the Department of Social Welfare and Development, the Department of Education, and the Inter-Country Adoption Board—we are required to submit paperwork to the Security and Exchange Commission, the Bureau of Internal Revenue, the Department of Labor and Employment, the Office of the City Mayor, the Fire Department, the City Sanitation Office, city building inspectors, Social

Security, PagIbig (government housing organization), the Department of Health, Bureau of Immigration, Department of Justice (for court cases involving our kids), and the Department of Foreign Affairs (passports for our kids to be adopted).

Sometimes we felt almost strangled by the bureaucratic system because of overlapping authority, changing and unclear requirements, and just the huge number of hours required to keep our heads above water. Thank heavens for the great workers in all our departments who kept track of all the requirements, deadlines, and changes over the years.

Corruption

WHEN DEALING WITH GOVERNMENT AGENCIES, corruption is a recurring problem. Corruption exists in any bureaucracy and has long been a problem and a deterrent to development in the Philippines.

Sometimes the lines were blurred between going by the rules and enabling corruption. When we had to process our immigration papers in Manila, I would go to the Bureau of Immigration to get all of our staff passports stamped with extensions. The BOI was a crowded and noisy place, and simple transactions could involve hours of waiting in line. It was possible for our papers to go from the bottom of the pile to the top by including cash with the paperwork, but I never was comfortable doing that.

However, there were men waiting just outside the BOI door who identified themselves as "fixers." They would process your papers at the various desks inside and you would pay them an undocumented "facilitation fee." The fixers were apparently acceptable to the authorities because they were always there.

One portly gentleman would scurry over to me when he saw me approaching the immigration office. His name was Ernesto, and he was a good guy who saved me hundreds of hours waiting over the years. He had an almost unbelievable appetite for food. As soon as we agreed on a price for his services, Ernesto asked for a cash advance so he could stock up on snacks. I never asked him how he got things done inside, and he never offered that information to me. Eventually, the government cracked down on fixers at the immigration office, and I'm pretty sure Ernesto was out of work. Perhaps I should have forgone Ernesto and taken the high road. I hope he's okay wherever he is.

Similar "fixer" systems or other ways of getting around the otherwise poky bureaucratic system existed at many other government agencies at various times: Cebu City Hall, the National Bureau of Investigation, the court system, the Department of Motor Vehicles, the Bureau of Fire Prevention, and others.

Health Problems

WE HAVE HAD TO DEAL WITH SICKNESS AND DEATH AT CSC. Watching our kids battle sickness and disease is always emotionally draining. We have had children with tuberculosis, hepatitis, Potts disease, cerebral palsy, heart abnormalities, stunted growth, hydrocephalus, parasites, tumors, club feet, deformities of the hands, severe malnutrition, brain damage, respiratory illness, and others.

Countless times I sat with Marlys and other staff in hospital rooms watching our kids get intubated, having their stomachs pumped, prepping for surgery, thrashing with pain, or slipping away and entering the presence of our Lord and Savior. My most recurrent image of CSC is Marlys sitting on the side of a child's bed with tears in her eyes, talking with a nurse or doctor and worrying and praying deep into the night.

We had several children die over the years: Sonny, Micah, Nilo, Luke, Ronny, Jacob, Arnold, Darvie, Samantha. With the exception of Ronny, all of them had been very sick before they died, so it was not a big shock. But losing a child was emotional and discouraging for our staff and workers. In spite of having the best care available in Cebu—with the best doctors, medicines, and facilities—there were times when we just could not save a child. Watching them deteriorate and eventually slip away was the hardest thing we had to endure.

Two of our house parents died while working at CSC. Becky Pellajera was the house mother in the Cherne Home. She got sick and died quite suddenly in 2001 after a short hospitalization. It was late morning when she died, and we wanted to tell the kids during their school lunch break. I told the teachers first, then the staff and workers. I asked the teachers to come to the Cherne Home to be with the kids when I told them. It was an emotional time, and when I was done the kids were crying and the teachers were counseling and hand-holding. Becky's husband, Jun, soon arrived and talked to the kids, and there was more crying. She had been much loved by the children and workers, and it was a shock and a great loss when she left us.

Romulo Alejado was the house father in the Eicher Home. His wife, Myrna, was his partner as house mother. He was sick with liver cancer for a few months before finally passing away. He was sent home from the hospital a few days earlier and got very sick in their apartment, so we decided to bring him back to Cebu Doctors Hospital. It was raining hard that night when we drove down the hill from CSC, the jeep slipping and sliding on the road, and we couldn't see more than a few feet ahead of us. We somehow made it to the hospital, but dear Romulo passed away a few hours later, surrounded by his wife, daughter Gigi, friends, and some of the CSC family.

Gloria Navasquez Deliña died in 2018 after a long illness. She had been retired for a long time and for the last few years was confined to a wheel-chair. Gloria was a CSC staff member for more than 25 years. She worked in childcare, was a house parent in the Sun Valley Home with her husband, Manny, and did outreach work for CSC. When CSC operated a childcare center in the downtown area, the Magbalantay Center, she was on the team. She was great at teaching children about Jesus.

Several former residents have died in the States after having been adopted. That always came as a shock to us. Maybe we had a notion that our adopted kids would always be safe once they got to their families in other countries. Although we realized the unrealistic nature of that assumption, we were usually taken by surprise when news came about a former resident passing away. If he or she had been ill, we likely wouldn't have been aware of it. And sometimes the death was sudden, the result of a tragedy like a fire, car crash, or hiking accident.

Staff Problems

CSC HAS BEEN BLESSED WITH TREMENDOUS PEOPLE at all levels of the ministry, from childcare workers to professional staff to departmental leaders. There have been acts of heroism, self-sacrifice, ingenuity, and going far above the call of duty. Filipinos and Americans have given their time and talent to provide loving services and care for our children.

Of course, when people are involved there will be problems. For one thing, our type of work seems to attract needy people. Usually they can find appropriate ways to meet those needs in their families and in their work at CSC. But sometimes those needs were so significant that they made their work difficult or even impossible. Some can be related to the culture of poverty, where the pressures of insufficient money, indebtedness, natural disasters, or expensive medical issues pose distractions that are hard to ignore. Many of our workers are the sole breadwinner in their family and, in spite of a relatively good salary and benefits at CSC, have a hard time making ends meet. And there have been staff and workers whose own emotional needs have made it difficult for them to minister effectively to the needs of our kids

Sometimes cultural roadblocks affected staff members or workers. How we care for and discipline our children at CSC is often very different from how our workers handle their own children or how they were raised by their parents. Once we discovered that a childcare worker was telling scary stories at night in an attempt to frighten the kids into quieting down at bedtime. In her family and community, that was acceptable behavior modification. In spite of CSC rules, some staff and workers played favorites among the children. Again, that may be what they observed and experienced growing up, and it might be acceptable practice in their homes, but was very much against our philosophy at CSC.

My most difficult jobs during my time of leadership in Cebu were when we had to terminate a worker. It was always emotional and sometimes contentious. Even if we could carefully document the offenses or shortcomings of the person being let go and actions we took to correct the problem with written warnings and other measures, we still were summoned to labor court on occasion.

Many of our workers come from extreme poverty. Some of their extended families were living hand-to-mouth, and our employee was expected to help the rest of the family financially. That made it difficult for them to save money or even stay solvent. Because many people don't have health or life insurance, one illness or death can bankrupt the entire family. It's common for people to borrow money from neighborhood usuries at exorbitant interest rates. So in spite of the fact that our workers are paid a good wage, with health care benefits for their immediate families, the cultural mandate of helping parents and extended family when called upon means that sometimes our workers struggled with indebtedness, which could affect their job performance.

As leaders, we had to walk the line between helping workers who were in financial trouble, versus enabling them in borrowing beyond their means. CSC provided financial relief to our employees in the form of salary loans, grants, and gifts. It was a part of running an organization in a developing country, where the culture of poverty exerts a big influence on people and indebtedness is rampant.

There were also times when U.S. personnel needed to be let go or counseled off the field. A ministry like CSC is not for everyone, and the strain of living in a different culture—away from family, friends, and church members—can be too much for some to handle. Some were affected emotionally by the abject poverty in the Philippines and felt guilty for the relative level of wealth they enjoyed compared to those suffering in squatter areas. Some had difficulty processing the abuse that some of our CSC kids experienced before coming to us, or the negative behaviors at CSC resulting from that abuse. Some were emotionally crushed when we had to transfer children out of CSC for behavior that threatened the well-being of other kids. And some, by personality, were just not cut out for living and working in Cebu or at CSC.

Some staff members, who might not have had the enthusiastic support of their families, particularly their parents, felt an emotional pull when they were on staff and eventually yielded to pressure and went home to be near their families. Some parents would write about family problems in great detail, with every letter peppered with language like "since you left," "when you get back," "sorry to burden you with this, but," or "I don't know how much longer she will live . . . ."

Sometimes it was the best for everyone if these staff members went back to the States because it was difficult for them to function with family pressure, or to be involved in a ministry that could not meet their own emotional needs.

It was always difficult to lose staff members, no matter the reason. But it bothered me most when parents exerted negative pressure on their son or daughter, either when they were considering joining our staff or once they were in Cebu. Parents might assert that they had been praying for their child ever since he or she was born, praying that God would use their child for His glory. But their hope and trust in God didn't seem to extend to that child going to work on the other side of the world. However, most parents of our staff were supportive and didn't let their personal desires affect their son or daughter in a negative way. My dad used to joke that when I decided to go to Cebu, they bought me a one-way ticket.

One thing we older staff had to remind ourselves of was that people who came after might not have our commitment to spend their working lives in Cebu. As family situations changed or problems were encountered, we career missionaries found a way for things to work. I don't intend this as an indictment of anyone else's attitude or commitment. Everyone is different. But when Marlys and I left Cebu after being there 42 years, I can honestly say that was the way we imagined it would be for us from the start. Not the pandemic part, of course, but after having finished our working lives with CSC in Cebu.

Adoption

THE AREA OF GOVERNMENT RELATIONS that has consistently caused the most stress and heartache is adoption. Adoption is a complicated social process that involves a lot of science and a lot of faith. The science often involves conflicting opinions on which children should be eligible for placement and what types of families should be approved and matched with kids. To say the least, the people making final decisions about placing our CSC kids often have had very different views on these issues than we have.

One example is the religious faith of a potential adoptive family. We value Christian families for our children, but government adoption workers handling our cases often had a different idea of what it means to be a Christian family than we did. We believed it was not entirely a matter of where they went to church or what was the national religion of the country where they lived.

Some home studies don't mention a family's faith or how their beliefs influence their family life. We were more comfortable with families who articulated their faith in their reports, who shared our core beliefs and would continue the influence of Christian faith that characterized our teaching and modeling at CSC. We tried to keep an open mind about families that worshipped in churches different from what we were used to. And we were also aware that not all Christian families are good families and not all good families are cut out to be adoptive families.

Matching a child for adoption with a family is a huge responsibility. It felt like the biggest decision anybody other than the child would make for his or her life. I sometimes felt like I was playing God, saying this child should go to that couple over another one. Sometimes several applicants had similar family configurations, financial resources, and emotional support systems. Who was I or anyone else to decide which family was better?

Imagine waiting outside the matching conference room where the decision will be made about placing a child you love deeply. You've chosen a family from the roster of approved families that the government adoption office gave you. Maybe they had recommendations for which family they thought was best. You read many home studies from families interested in a child or children of the age and gender of your child. You wrote a summary of the family you preferred, with the reasons you believed they were the best family available. You presented the child's legal papers: birth or foundling certificate, decree of abandonment or surrender document, child study report, medical summary, developmental and psychological reports, and school records.

You sit and wait to be called into the room where the committee has made the big decision. That person wasn't always me. Mitch Ohlendorf did that work when I was on furlough. Carmelita Baya, our social worker, did much of the local and inter-regional matching, as did Klaris Cabansal, our social work director in later years. In the late 1980s and early 1990s, Sandy Swanson also went to Manila to select families for our children.

Sometimes I left the government adoption office in Manila feeling upset and defeated after a matching session when my choice of family was not approved or my assessment of a couple's parenting capacity was attacked. I walked from the adoption office to catch a cab feeling down, then facing at least an hour taxi ride to the domestic airport, an hour flight to Cebu, another hour cab ride home from the airport, and finally the difficult task of informing the rest of the staff that our child would be going to a family that was not our first (or sometimes even second) choice.

It certainly would have been too much to handle if I hadn't believed that God was working through me and the other people involved in matching a child, and that He was much wiser than me. I prayed for God's enlightenment and I believed He gave it because I knew that He loves our children much more than I did. Whereas I was limited to information on a home study report or even my intuition, God knew the hearts of all the applicants as well as the needs of the child.

Adoption was the source of other frustrations, too. It was always difficult for our staff to watch a child grow up with a strong desire to be adopted and then not see that happen. Because our program has always sought and valued adoption for most of our kids, they got to see other children leave with their adoptive parents. But their time never came. It was heartbreaking to answer their inquiries about when they would have a mom and dad, knowing as we did that it was becoming more and more unlikely as time went by.

Forced Departures

PERHAPS THE MOST DIFFICULT THING we had to do at CSC was remove a child from our care. Usually such situations involved behavior that put other kids or our workers in danger. Although we knew we had to do it, it always made us feel bad, as if we had failed that child. More than one child exhibited behavior resulting from sexual curiosity that required immediate intervention. This was necessary because we always had young, vulnerable children at CSC that needed our protection.

The problem with removing children was finding a place to put them. Most had no family. They were living at CSC precisely because no family was in a position to care for them. Other childcaring agencies were reluctant to take in children who had exhibited negative behavior. Some of our kids came from the streets, and we couldn't send them back there. It was a terrible dilemma for our staff.

On a few occasions we were able to place kids with faith-based centers such as Christ for Asia, Sonshine Corner, SOS Center, or Mercy in Action. Other times we were forced to release them to programs we were not too excited about. On rare occasions, when there were no other options, we had to find a distant relative who would take the child.

Once we had a girl who lived with us for a couple of years but whose behavior became dangerous and unmanageable. We worked for months to find an alternative place for her. What made things more difficult was that, aside from her general behavior, she manifested signs of mental illness. No center in Cebu would even consider taking her in. Our social worker, Carmelita, went all over Cebu and other islands trying to find a suitable place for her. We prayed and brainstormed and prayed some more.

Because of her age, mental illness, and aggressive behavior, we finally realized that we had only one choice: the government-run Elsie Gotches Village in Alabang, outside of Manila. We had heard about the place, and the descriptions were grim. Children and adults with mental illnesses lived together in crowded conditions with little therapy or rehabilitation services.

Mitch and I went to visit Gotches and found that these accounts were largely true. It was a depressing place. I'm sure the people who worked there did the best they could with limited budgets and facilities, but in spite of those efforts it was a sad and dreary environment. We prayed extra hard that another option would develop for our girl. But things were getting worse for her at CSC, and I was feeling a lot of pressure to move her out.

I made a few phone calls and learned that Elsie Gotches was not accepting referrals at that time. Desperate, I made a quick trip to Manila to talk with one of my good friends in the DSWD, Lulu Balanon, who had recently been promoted to undersecretary. It was December 23 and I was able to see her in the early afternoon. She could tell that the case was urgent and emotional for me and said she would help. She got on the phone and worked it out for our girl to be admitted to Gotches after Christmas.

Although I was relieved that we finally had a placement, there was no joy whatsoever in my heart as I returned to Cebu. The decision to place her at Elsie Gotches was easily the most difficult one I made in my time at CSC. As I write this my heart is still breaking over that decision. It brought us all face to face with our limitations as a childcaring agency, and the limitations of the entire child welfare system in the Philippines.

At CSC we had cared for children with all kinds of medical and psychological problems. We had taken in children who simply did not know how to behave or to accept love or affection. We had experienced success in helping most of these kids improve. But this little girl had exposed our shortcomings and forced us to make a decision we wanted so badly to avoid—to send her to a place where we didn't want her to go. I have had many moments of heartache and regret over that decision. I can sometimes see her face or hear her voice or see how she looked when she left CSC for the airport to go to Gotches.

Other difficult decisions involved saying no to referrals of kids who desperately needed the care CSC could provide. We knew they would not be able to receive care elsewhere for what they needed. We knew the decisions of whether to take them in could have life-and-death outcomes.

But there was a limit to how many children we could care for. We had to consider the workload of our aunties and house parents. It would not have been fair to them or the other children to stretch ourselves too thin. We also had to consider our financial situation. Taking in a sick child from the hospital might mean hundreds of thousands of pesos in medical expenses. Saying no was part of our commitment to quality. But in honesty, it was a commitment that we did not always honor. There were times when our hearts warred with our minds and the minds took the loss.

Our social worker, Carmelita Baya, knew all about this. It was her job to field the referrals made to CSC and to advocate for the referred child. As such, her recommendation would almost always be for admission. She also knew the heart/mind warfare at work in these decisions and that if we actually saw the child(ren) referred, it would be much harder for us to say no. One morning I entered my office to find five kids sitting on my desk, with Carmelita standing nearby with a smile on her face. "Say no to them if you can, Uncle Paul," she seemed to be saying.

We had a cross-stitched picture, made by Marie Hagfors, of owls in a tree that said "We Always Have Room For One More." The picture surely represented the hearts of our staff as we handled those difficult decisions. But the owls didn't have to consider financial and manpower limitations and the impact a new admission would have on our whole CSC tree.

Staff-Board Relations

CSC HAS BEEN BLESSED WITH EXCELLENT BOARD MEMBERS on both sides of the ocean. Inevitably, some communication problems or differences of opinion between the board and Cebu staff occurred, but these have been managed well because both parties valued harmony and kept their eyes and hearts on the needs of the children.

Our board volunteers have given of their time and talent to move the ministry forward. They have dealt with board governance issues, and have set up excellent principles for fundraising and financial and personnel management. They have ensured that CSC meets U.S. governmental requirements and private watchdog agency standards for board function and financial integrity. CSC received the highest rating (4 stars) from the highly regarded Charity Navigators for how we run our organization.

COVID Pandemic

AS THIS BOOK IS BEING FINISHED, we are still in the midst of a global pandemic. One of the first nations to get the corona virus outside of China was the Philippines. As the virus spread nationally and in Cebu, there was an immediate impact on CSC. It was a stressful time for everyone. In addition to protocols set up for CSC during this time, our workers and staff have had to follow regulations in their own families and communities. Our leadership team met at least twice weekly via Zoom to manage the ministry and see that the children were safe and doing well.

I have discussed those protocols in another section of this book. Indeed, an entire book could be written about what has been undertaken by our staff in Cebu during the pandemic. But suffice it to say that this has been the biggest challenge and difficulty in CSC's history. Our concerns have gone further than just keeping the virus out of Banawa. We have been concerned about the physical and emotional health of all our workers, whether those who were locked in with the children or those who were locked out. We needed to set up a system for compensating all our workers, whether they could work or not, and to give a bonus to those willing to be locked in and separated from their families.

Our professionals have had to work from home for the most part. We haven't been able to accept referrals of new kids or process cases for inter-country or local adoption. Only two CSC residents were matched and placed for adoption during the first year of pandemic protocols. Thanks to a group of teachers willing to be locked in, we were able to have regular school classes, but we could not use our school building because it was needed as a quarantine facility for workers rotating into the shelter. Life at CSC was put in a big holding pattern, trying to protect against the virus while waiting for things to return to normal and all parts of our ministry to resume.

Our new field director, Roberto Atienza, was still new to Cebu and his leadership role when the pandemic hit, so he was thrust immediately into crisis management. Because city-wide quarantines were ordered in March of 2020, his wife and children were not able to leave their compound. Roberto and the other leaders were not able to go inside CSC facilities in Banawa. They were only able to meet via Zoom.

The normal administrative functions of purchasing, payroll, banking, HR, and report filing were difficult or impossible. Every several days the local government announced new quarantine guidelines for the city and province, and the national government made changes in its policies concerning travel, both within the Philippines and internationally. As a leadership group, all we could do was take these things one day at a time. Uncertainty about the future added to our stress.

A Faithful God

ALTHOUGH THERE HAVE BEEN MANY DIFFICULT DAYS in our history and we have had to deal with disasters, disappointments, and hardships, we have been blessed throughout this journey by the loving arms of Jesus that protected us. He has healed bodies, given strength and comfort, mended relationships, shown us the light of hope, and kept us on the right path.

One night in the early 1990s I was heading in the middle of the night to a town in the mountains of southern Cebu, where I had to deal with a crisis involving two of our workers. An incident had occurred that needed to be dealt with immediately. My trusted driver Juantoy was driving me, and the road was dangerous, with steep slopes on either side and not much light to guide us. I was worried about the confrontational meeting awaiting me and was concerned about whether we would even get there safe and sound. I wondered, as I had at other times, why things could get so complicated and thrust me into situations where I found no joy and for which I had no experience.

Nothing in my more-than-30-years of life had prepared me for what was happening that night. My attraction to going to Cebu and helping start the ministry was the children—playing with them, watching them grow, teaching them, and enjoying time with them. Not this. I often said during my 41 years in Cebu that the easy and joyful part of the ministry was the kids. Not so much the adults!

God didn't choose to reach down and remove all the problems, difficulties, and disappointments that came our way. But he gave strength, wisdom, and endurance. He helped me realize that caring for children sometimes involves handling difficult people and relationships, and dealing with situations like the one that had me out on that bumpy road in the middle of the night.

God has been faithful and good. He provided the right insights, the right amount of courage and resolve exactly when they were needed. He got us through that awful night and every difficult time that CSC faced throughout our amazing history.

Fundraising

CSC DID INDEED EMERGE FROM THE ASHES of the B.J. Thomas concert. From that dismal start in raising funds, we have grown into an organization with a budget well over $2,000,000. Indeed, the B.J. Thomas concert was not our only fundraising failure. We have tried other programs and approaches that simply didn't work. We have sent letters that weren't carefully planned and God-honoring. And there have undoubtedly been times when we have plowed ahead without committing our plans to God before acting. But we have consistently strived to do things in a positive, honest way, with integrity and humility. We have endeavored to give God the glory for the money that comes in. And for some reason, God has chosen to bless these efforts. We praise him for the lessons He has taught us over the years.

Fundraising Is a Ministry

THE FIRST THING WE NEEDED TO LEARN was that fundraising is a ministry and not a "necessary evil." As we raise funds for the ministry, we open people up to be blessed. Those who have raised funds for CSC have learned that God blesses those who bless His little ones. So providing opportunities for people to bless those precious children in Cebu opens them up to receive bountiful blessings from God. In that regard, we are doing people a favor by telling them about CSC and asking them to consider supporting us financially.

The Bible is clear about the responsibility of Christians to help orphans (James 1:28). But many Americans don't know any orphans they can help. By providing a ministry to orphans, we are giving them the chance to fulfill a biblical mandate and receive the blessings of obedience.

A story on TV news during the 1990s told of a child abandoned in western Wisconsin. The child was left in a public area and was found by someone out for a walk. The child was eventually turned over to human services and a search was initiated for the parents. In the coming days the television station received thousands of calls, letters, and e-mails asking for information about the baby. Many asked if they could adopt the child. The story had touched the hearts of American people, both believers and nonbelievers.

In some ways, nothing is as pitiful as an orphan. Perhaps that is why God makes special mention of them, along with widows, as being the responsibility of believers. But we see so few of them in our daily lives. Ministries like CSC provide faces and specific stories and opportunities to alleviate the plight of orphans. So we learned early on that our fundraising efforts should not be looked upon as an annoyance or something we must endure to do the ministry. It *is* a ministry—a channel of blessings.

Friend-raising over Fundraising

IN 2003, BETTY BARNETT WROTE A LANDMARK BOOK for missionaries and missions organizations called *Friend Raising: Building a Missionary Support Team That Lasts*. It was written to people who are often squeamish about raising money, no matter how noble and effective their ministries might be. The book focuses on "the principles of lasting support raising, such as intimacy in relationships, interdependence, mutual sharing, bearing each other's burdens, generosity, good communication, and prayer with promises."

The world is full of fundraising gimmicks and hype, even among Christian organizations, which sometimes don't look much different from the secular world's way of doing things. Betty's book helped us think about adopting and maintaining an approach based on relationships: friend-raising rather than simply fundraising. What can we do as an organization to make friends with people who share our values and priorities, to nurture and grow those relationships and to build each other up?

We have sometimes failed at this, thinking too much about the amount of money we need to raise and how to convince new people to give and old friends to give more. We do this because we want good things for the kids in Cebu. But we do the most good for CSC and them when we think more about friend-raising.

CSC has hundreds of good friends who came to know about us, liked us, and got involved in the things we believe are important. In many cases our efforts at building relationships with friends have paid dividends by fostering good feelings, loyalty, and generosity. If we strictly do fundraising, we might accomplish short-term goals for income, but the people who give might be "one and done," having responded to an emotional appeal but not sticking around for the long term.

Integrity Is Everything

A RESOLVE TOWARDS INTEGRITY IN FUNDRAISING is often tested. This has been the case for CSC, even when we were working very hard to raise only a few dollars. In the aftermath of the B.J. Thomas concert, we were faced with a stack of bills and no money to pay them. We embarked on some fundraising projects, such as selling candy and donuts, and speaking to churches and civic organizations. Our dilemma was that although we were ultimately planning to use the funds we raised to feed, clothe, and house homeless children in Cebu, part of our immediate need was to pay debts associated with the concert. Not only that, but after the concert was paid off, our next need was to get our staff over to Cebu. Only then would we be able to feed the hungry and do the other things reflected in the verses from Matthew 25 we were using to promote the DelAdlawan Foundation.

In all this we tried to be honest with people and explain our predicament. Many were sympathetic and appreciated our frankness.

But integrity is a garment that needs to be refitted and worn at all times, especially in financial matters. It means always using gifts for the purpose they were intended for. Although we might be greatly in need of money for our general fund, for the everyday care of our children—for gas, food, medicine, school supplies, utilities, and salaries—if someone designates a gift for a new bicycle, we need to us it for that purpose, or get expressed permission to use it for something else. Lacking that, the money should be returned.

Gifts and Givers

HERE WAS ANOTHER EARLY LESSON learned in fundraising: Every gift is important, and every giver needs to be thanked. We were grateful that people were willing to give with no existing ministry to see and evaluate.

We were quick to thank them. And we have tried to maintain that thankfulness throughout our history, even as our financial needs have increased.

We have always strived to send out a receipt and a thank you letter within a week for every donation received, and we try to write a personal note on as many of these letters as possible. Our intent in the early days was to show people we were thankful recipients of their loving gifts, but also that we were trying our best to be efficient in our financial dealings.

As we grew and our financial needs increased, we wanted to show that we weren't too big to appreciate each and every gift. People have a variety of capacities to give. The story of the "widow's mite" in Luke 21 has instructed us. We need to let God be the judge of capacity and generosity, and to set a tone of thankfulness as an organization.

A Widow's Prayer

SOME OF OUR SUPPORTERS SEND IN NOTES WITH THEIR CHECKS. A common theme to these notes is, "I wish I could give more. I send a prayer with this gift that God would multiply it for His glory." And God does exactly that.

When we receive bigger donations from people with a larger capacity to give, we have found that they appreciate hearing of the "widow's prayer" and that they are an answer to those prayers. When Dan and Carla Chalmers were able to make a sizeable gift for construction of our Children of Hope School, their check had the invisible signatures of many of our faithful, praying givers who brought CSC's needs to the throne of grace.

The Personal Touch

MAINTAINING A PERSONAL TOUCH has always been a value at CSC and has meant avoiding some fundraising methods. For instance, we decided not to use outside agencies to raise funds for us.

One evening in the early 1980s, Marlys, Cliff, and I drove to southern Minnesota to speak in a small church. We parked our car and hauled in armloads of newsletters and brochures, a slide projector with trays of slides, and items for the display table. During our presentation we heard sounds and voices from the church basement. After the service, as we were putting our paraphernalia back in the trunk of Cliff's car, we saw a man walking towards us, carrying only a briefcase. We greeted him and asked if he was a church member. He replied that he was not from there but had been doing a presentation in the church basement to the Missions Committee about a Christian camp. It turned out that it was a camp where Marlys had been a counselor and Cliff had served as camp pastor. We asked the man if he knew the camp director, mentioning him by name. He admitted, somewhat sheepishly, that he had never actually been to the camp, but his organization had been engaged to raise funds for it.

I recall thinking, "God, please keep us off that path." Although there is nothing ethically wrong with outsourcing fundraising, we saw, and see, it as an impersonal way of communicating our needs and presenting opportunities for giving. Also, there is a good chance of misinformation by entrusting the promotion of a ministry to someone who knows very little about it. Plus, a percentage of all money that comes in goes to the hired company and not to the ministry's needs, which is the intent of most donors.

This "personal touch" at CSC has extended beyond fundraising to include those who work in the stateside office. The organization has made it a policy that those who represent CSC to our supporters and the public in general should visit Cebu and experience the ministry first-hand.

Mailings

ONE OF OUR FIRST TASKS as a fledgling organization was to generate interest through a mailing list. Today we have a list of 5,000 names, but in our early days we struggled to come up with the minimum needed to do a nonprofit mailing. Cliff Danielson started with families and close friends of our staff, and churches where he knew the pastor or someone involved with missions. That was it.

Many organizations routinely buy mailing lists from other organizations. Although that approach can be lucrative, we consider it inconsistent with who we are and the things we hold dear, such as maintaining personal touch. At various times we have had to recommit ourselves to that principle, and God has chosen not to bless appeals that cast a wide net rather than focusing on reaching people who want to hear about CSC.

Because we have not purchased mailing lists, CSC's list has grown primarily through presentations, where those who showed an interest were encouraged to sign up for mailings. Later, people who responded to our website or Facebook page, or those who attended our banquets, were included on the mailing list, unless they indicated that they did not wish to receive mail.

Our first list was kept on index cards, and mailing labels were typed on Cliff Danielson's manual typewriter. From there he moved to an electric typewriter and later, with the help of CSC board member Warren Hagfors, to a computerized database and printed labels.

One question we've faced all along is how much mail people should receive from CSC. How much is too much? We've learned that people differ in how they answer that question. For some, any mail is too much. Some can accept that we need to send receipts and perhaps newsletters but don't want anything that involves "asking for money."

We have wrestled with this issue because we want people to know what's going on at CSC and what the needs are. In pre-Internet, mail was about the only way for that to happen.

We decided to send newsletters and prayer/appeal letters to everyone on our mailing list, as well as a receipt letter for each gift, thanking our supporters for their donations. We have tried to be sensitive to those who want less mail than this and have provided ways for them to communicate that with our office. Once we started accepting online donations and producing an e-newsletter, we offered the option of going paperless by getting receipts electronically as well.

In addition to determining what mail to send, we needed to decide how much we would spend on mailings. We wanted our letters, brochures, and newsletters to look good, but we didn't want to spend more than we needed or to give the recipients the impression of being wasteful or pretentious. We believed in our early days, as we do today, that people support CSC because they like what we do in Cebu. They like that we send as much money as possible to Cebu to meet children's needs. If they want to support a ministry with fancy promotional materials, they have other opportunities to do so.

Along the way we came up with a way to describe our attempt to strike a balance between beautiful and inexpensive: simple elegance. By doing as much as possible in-house, we could produce promotional materials that effectively informed people about our work while remaining consistent with our values and mission.

Our Niche

TO BE SUCCESSFUL IN FRIEND- AND FUNDRAISING, CSC has needed to understand our niche: who we are and who our supporters are. First of all, we are a Christian organization. People not in step with that will find some of what we do confusing or even offensive. Also, our size might not be appealing to those who resonate better with a bigger operation, reaching more people in a more impressive way.

Rod Henry, a good friend of CSC's and former missionary in Cebu, understood smallness in ministry. Asked to go to Cebu and train Filipino pastors, he prepared materials for the group he envisioned training, using his education at Fuller Theological Seminary. He arrived in Cebu with tremendous enthusiasm, ready for the task ahead, and rented a large house in Paradise Village with lots of room for the pastors to stay and be trained. He had sent letters to the pastors who signed up for the training, telling them the schedule and when to show up at his house. To his dismay, only a few showed up.

In interviewing the men, he discovered that not all were Christians, so not all were ready for his training. At the end of the screening, he was left with three pastors to train. He said something to me that made a big impression: "God had called me to a ministry small beyond my wildest dream."

We could relate. We had left Minnesota with big plans. I imagined hundreds of orphans with uniforms and knee socks moving in ordered fashion around the grounds, the staff holding clipboards and tooting whistles, maintaining strict order of their smiling, well-scrubbed charges. This vision was assaulted with the reality that things were not going to be what we expected. Instead of hundreds of children, our first months on the job would involve only one child. We knew what Rod was talking about. We were destined to be a small ministry with unimpressive numbers of children served, a modest budget, and limited appeal in the marketplace.

CSC appeals to those who like the feel of a small, personal ministry where they can have an impact on the lives of small groups of children. While our smallness undoubtedly discourages some from giving support, others are attracted to us because of that size.

We learned other lessons early on about how various groups of people view a ministry like CSC's. I was visiting a large supporting church in California in the late 1980s. A family who lived about 30 miles from the church had expressed an interest in adopting one of the large sibling groups living at CSC at the time. I wanted to talk with them about the children and "size them up." The problem was, I didn't have a car to make the trip to their house in South Pasadena. The pastor of the church made an announcement in the morning service that I needed a car for a couple days and asked anyone with a spare vehicle to let him know. A family agreed to bring their spare car to the evening service, and I was given the keys to a shiny Mercedes Benz 540 convertible.

"It's yours as long as you need it," they told me. After all, it was their spare car!

I headed very carefully for South Pasadena in the Mercedes. I pulled up in front of a large mansion and was greeted by the man of the house wearing a smoking jacket and holding a glass of champagne. Two hours later I was escorted to my car, feeling self-conscious about being seen driving a Mercedes. The incongruity of an orphanage director driving that kind of car loomed huge in my mind. When we got to the curb, I made some kind of lame apology for the car. It wasn't mine. I was just borrowing it from someone in the church. Blah, blah, blah. The man didn't seem the least bit aware of any discrepancy. In fact, he told me that "in my world, we expect fundraisers to drive cars like this." I thought to myself, "In my world, I couldn't raise a penny from anyone if I pulled up in this car."

Both of us were right. And the experience dramatized the different priorities in Christian ministry. Our supporters, mostly middle-class evangelical Christians, expect the people they support to live simply and without flash. In the world of wealth, on the other hand, the mantra is "success breeds success," so a fundraiser driving a Mercedes bespeaks a successful organization that warrants consideration for further financial assistance.

Several early CSC banquets were held at an upscale hotel in the south suburbs of Minneapolis. It was a very nice place with plenty of parking and great food. But the cost was in line with the hotel's swankiness. Although CSC got sponsors to underwrite the evening's costs, some in the organization were not comfortable with the venue. There seemed to be a disconnect between raising money for hungry, homeless children in the Philippines, and spending that kind of money to feed our supporters. Eventually we found a less expensive location.

CSC's ministry has been successful because we have been committed to honoring God in how we raise funds and manage our resources, by being thankful for every gift, and by understanding who we are as an organization. To be sure, we have not always lived up to this high standard, but we've tried to keep our eyes on God for enlightenment and discernment.

Presentations

MOST OF OUR PRESENTATIONS over the years have been in churches: Sunday School classes, missions committees, Vacation Bible School groups, AWANA Club, small groups, or filling the pulpit for worship services. We have used storytelling, slide shows, videos, games, sermons, question and answer times, and Skype calls to share the message of CSC. Our access to churches has varied, from a couple minutes in the worship service to an hour in Sunday School and everything in between. Churches have varied from a handful of members to more than a thousand.

In the United States, we have had the pleasure of addressing church groups in California, Oregon, Washington, Colorado, Nebraska, Missouri, Minnesota, North Dakota, South Dakota, Iowa, Wisconsin, Ohio, Kentucky, Tennessee, Florida, Virginia, Connecticut, Massachusetts, Maine, and New York. In Asia we presented in churches in Hong Kong and Japan and, of course, the Philippines.

Other opportunities have been with civic organizations, such as the Lions, Kiwanis, Rotary, and Inner Wheel Clubs; senior citizens and womens associations; prayer groups; employee groups; and sports clubs. I once spoke to a group of hockey players in Edina, Minnesota, just after they'd come off the ice. Another time I presented CSC to the employees of a post office branch in Saint Paul, having been invited by a friend of CSC, Mike Rowe, who was a mail carrier.

In addition to groups large and small, there have been hundreds, if not thousands, of presentations made in homes, coffee shops, and restaurants as our staff has taken advantage of any opportunity to share the ministry of CSC with a willing listener, potential supporter, or prospective volunteer, staff member, or adoptive couple.

Sometimes, getting to where we were going was challenging—for example, visiting churches in North Dakota and northern Minnesota during the winter. On one trip to Warroad, Minnesota, blowing snow coming off

Red Lake made it almost impossible to proceed. Heavy rains and gale-force winds near Wahpeton, North Dakota. Fog in Colorado. Ice storms in central Minnesota. And yet, while getting there was often difficult, I have never had a less-than-enjoyable experience standing in front of a church group with an opportunity to share CSC.

Some travel was monotonous or risky. Some of the vehicles we drove weren't the best. Sometimes the speaking arrangements weren't what I was expecting. Occasionally we got lost and didn't think we'd make it in time. But once we were actually there, once we stood up to speak, something happened. It was all good. It was an honor to be ambassadors of CSC, representing the kids. There was something about the needs of children that captivated people and enlivened us. Undoubtedly there were times when I wasn't all that effective or the slide projector didn't work, but there was never a time when making a presentation was drudgery. Whether it was an Awana Club with 15 kids or a large church worship service, it was always a blast.

We have always tried to be honest and balanced in presenting the ministry and the situations we encounter in the Philippines. When I was preparing for my first furlough, I got some good advice from Bob Carey, a veteran Free Church missionary in Cebu. Bob said that when he made a presentation he always imagined that there was a Filipino in the front row. He thought that doing so would help him present the Philippines in an appropriate way. As our missionaries and stateside staff have talked about the social problems in the country and the types of family situations that lead to children being malnourished, maltreated or neglected, it has been important also to talk about the beauty of the Philippines and the positive aspects of the people and the culture. This has helped us avoid painting an unfair picture of the country in order to advance the cause of CSC.

Presenters have encountered some challenging situations. Arriving for a luncheon session with a seniors group at a large Twin Cities church, I was informed that another missionary would talk before me and the lunch would follow. (It's not a good situation to be the second presenter at a luncheon with stomachs starting to grumble as you take the dais.) The first presenter was a member of the church and had just completed a tour as a volunteer on a ship that visited ports around the world to distribute Bibles, sell Christian literature, and present programs with international themes for churches in those cities. (It's also not a good situation to share the program with a son or daughter of the church, who doesn't have to trot out credentials.)

The first speaker went well over the allotted time, and the smells drifting out of the kitchen were having a distracting effect on the audience. He ended his presentation with a well-told story of the ship crew's last day in a country in Southeast Asia. He described thousands of people having made decisions for Christ during their stay, many weeping and gnashing their teeth as the ship pulled out of harbor. As the ship was leaving but before it was out of reach of the crowd, the speaker heard the cry of someone on shore, yelling, "One more Bible, brother. Just one more, please." He ran to the ship's bookstore, grabbed a New Testament, hurriedly put a rubber band around it, and threw a high, tight spiral towards shore. It sailed through the tropical air, much farther than he could have imagined, and right into the hands of the man who requested it. This sure-handed young man later became an evangelist known as the Billy Graham of his country, parlaying that New Testament reception into the salvation of untold thousands, according to missionary number one.

"And now we'll hear from our second missionary, who has a ministry with children in the Philippines."

Making presentations to children could be unpredictable and humorous. At a church in Maine, we were telling a group of youngsters about the children at CSC. During the question time one little boy asked which operating system our kids were using. When we told him they didn't have any computers, he was incredulous. Why weren't we providing them with such basic needs? I tried to explain that food, clothing, shelter, and medicines were basic needs that we were providing. The poor little guy didn't understand how we could be so heartless!

But children have been great audiences for CSC presentations. They are compassionate and inquisitive. They don't understand why kids have to suffer. And I believe their prayers are powerful for their honesty, purity, and lack of pretention. They are always interested in the ages of the kids, to see if there are some their same age. And they want to know what grades they are in and what they learn in school.

One of the most successful ongoing fundraising efforts among children has been at the First Baptist Church of Sturgeon Bay, Wisconsin, under the leadership of Pastor Cory Dahl. Cory and the Vacation Bible School leaders at FBC have been very intentional about sharing the ministry of CSC with the kids and motivating them for daily offerings. The FBC crew raised thousands of dollars each year when CSC was the sponsored ministry. They sent letters to parents, pitted the girls against the boys, and used visual aids to chart the progress of giving each day. The children were always excited to make a difference in the lives of CSC kids, and they loved seeing pictures and hearing stories. Children from FBC have been willing to give of their own money and even do extra chores at home or in their neighborhoods in order to bring more money for the offering at Bible School.

Audiovisual Materials

AUDIOVISUALS HAVE SPICED UP our presentations since the beginning. Larry Hansen was the architect of many of these shows. The first ones were slide shows with background music and narration, the latter often provided by Jerry Healy. CSC bought a slide projector with a cassette tape player that would automatically advance the slides. This method was used for hundreds of presentations.

One night Larry and Jerry were putting the finishing touches on a slide show for the CSC banquet. When they wrapped things up it was well into the night, and they loaded the equipment into Larry's car. Larry pulled onto University Avenue, forgetting that the carousel of slides was on top of his car. The tray fell onto the street and slides spilled everywhere, necessitating some hurried retrieval.

Working with Larry was always enjoyable, though sometimes nerve-wracking. He is a man of amazing creative gifts, and he never charged CSC for his work. That has amounted to tens of thousands of dollars of donated services and has meant that we always had first-rate media presentations to update and encourage our supporters. Larry Hansen has had much to do with the success of CSC's fundraising, and he and I developed a friendship and creative collaboration that has spanned five decades.

For one of our trips to Canada, I borrowed a Dove machine from Larry. You could use two trays of slides, and the Dove would dissolve slides from alternating trays. It had a cassette tape device that automatically alternated the slides. When it worked. There were three programs on consecutive nights in British Columbia, and the Dove machine didn't work for any of them. The first night was a total disaster. Before the second night I was able to get a joy stick contraption that allowed me to manually alternate and dissolve the slides. When it worked. It sometimes jammed so that the slides didn't correspond to the narration. That wasn't a big deal until near the end of the show, when the narration described services that CSC's staff was providing for pregnant mothers. But instead of a mother, a slide of a Canadian board member, Phil Enerson, came on the screen and would not go away no matter how I manipulated that joy stick. The audience roared at Phil's (and my) expense.

Things weren't so funny in 1998 when a video that Larry and I had spent many hours putting together would not play at the Minnesota banquet. Try as Larry might, the projector would not work. He brought in a backup unit, but that didn't work either.

Eventually, slide shows gave way to videos, and Larry had the interest and ability to make that transition. The CSC staff sent him video footage and he edited it into a show. That was an exciting development for CSC, and although the initial efforts were crude by later standards, they were an improvement on the still images of the slide shows and gave our supporters a better sense of what was happening in Cebu.

In the late 1990s, Larry handed video production over to his talented son Chris, an experienced editor and cameraman who shared his dad's love for CSC and willingness to work for free. Chris's handiwork has graced the screen at many of our banquets and has been shown in churches, schools, and homes all around the world. In years when Chris was unable to help out, Larry came out of retirement and did the video editing. In 2013, Larry and his other son, David, went to Cebu to shoot and edit the banquet video "Through the Eyes of a Child."

The CSC News

THE *CSC NEWS* HAS BEEN OUR OFFICIAL PUBLICATION since the very beginning. The editors, printer, layout, and length have changed over the years, but the newsletter was and is the primary source of news for CSC.

In 1978, I typed, cut, and pasted together a newsletter introducing the ministry. I had it printed at Insty-Prints, and it was mailed out to whomever we could think of. Those early mailings did not include return envelopes. and we did not have nearly enough recipients for the postal bulk mailing. But it was a good first effort and easy to improve upon. Since then we have mailed out hundreds of issues of the *CSC News*.

The following editors have served the *News*:

> Dave and Nancy Healy
> Dave and Nancy Healy and Lorene Roste
> Nancy Healy and Elizabeth Healy
> John Cherne
> Grace Sandness
> Paul Healy and Pauline Bohachek
> Paul Healy
> Jill Grasley

Regular features of the *News* have included Prayer Requests, Kids' Korner (originally put together by then-board-chair Kathy Johnson, later taken over by Sandy Swanson), listings of memorials and honoraria, and news stories about the ministry. In the early days, Cliff's column, Cliff's Notes, often highlighted presentations he'd made and donations CSC had received. Other fairly regular features were financial reports and "Comings and Goings" (news about friends visiting Cebu and staff going home for furloughs or returning to Cebu). Volunteers have always been used to fold, address, and mail the newsletters. Originally, faithful friends from Constance Free Church did the mailings, but things shifted to Cambridge after we moved our office there.

While some of the first editions were typeset, Dave and Nancy Healy introduced desktop publishing for newsletter production during their time as editors. Getting the copy and pictures from Cebu was often the most difficult part of the editor's job, especially in pre-Internet days. The earliest newsletters were sent six times a year, then quarterly, and eventually three times a year. With the advent of the CSC website, the newsletter could be downloaded by those who preferred to read it electronically, thanks to the programming skills of Chris Hansen.

Guilt?

ONE CONSISTENT PRINCIPLE AT CSC has been to avoid using guilt as a motivator in our newsletters, prayer letters, videos, websites, or any other promotional items. Undoubtedly, readers and viewers have experienced guilt when confronted by the needs of homeless and hungry children displayed in our media, and the disparity between lifestyles of the wealthy and the poor. But we have tried to avoid building that emotion into what we produce and distribute. We have attempted to honestly present the needs we address in Cebu but let the Holy Spirit impress those on people's hearts.

And our practice of imagining a Filipino sitting in the front row during a church presentation has also applied to that imaginary person reading our mail or looking at our website. Rather than relying on guilt, we try to present honest and balanced information designed to inform, educate, and inspire. God has richly blessed our efforts to promote the ministry of CSC and has reminded us to avoid manipulative means in raising funds.

The CSC Banquet

CSC'S ANNUAL BANQUET, held most years since 1980, has been a successful event throughout our history. It has had two major purposes: a gathering of those who love the ministry, and a fundraiser. From modest beginnings, the banquet was attracting 800 people by the 1990s. We have never sold tickets to the event, but freewill offerings have been a great blessing to our fundraising. By 2010 our banquet offerings were consistently over $100,000. Since the late 1980s, banquets have mostly been held in the Bethel University gym. In 2019 and 2020, they were cancelled due to the Covid pandemic.

CSC banquets have almost always had featured speakers; since 2000 these have been primarily former CSC residents. They have been a popular part of our programs, allowing our supporters to see the impact CSC has had on their lives, their families, churches, and communities. Speakers have included Ed Henry, Kirk Pilapil, Angie Otsubo, Arlie Ausich, Erna Ahlmann, Ronald Dee, Janice Dreiling, Cherry Stoltenberg, Rosalyn Robb, Weston Babelay, Amanda Polzin, Josiah and Sam Schiffer, MaLou Rodriguez, Janice Glader, and Allen Morgan.

Other speakers have graced the dais at CSC banquets. Harry Schmidt, the Canadian businessman whose family foundation built homes for us in Banawa, spoke of his involvement with CSC. The doctors who operated on Ann Clark, Robert Winter and John Lonstein, gave a report on the surgeries. Four men who made significant contributions to our work gave short speeches: Ron Duterte, long-time friend and president of CSC in the

Philippines; Ken Morrison, friend, supporter, and a leader in the Hong Kong Union Church that helped with the cost of our Children of Hope School; Dennis Beausejour, an executive with Proctor and Gamble who made a major gift towards construction of the school; and Tim Erickson, a dentist who provided dental care for CSC children.

Other speakers were author Bernard Palmer and some of our Filipino workers, including Jerry Salgo, Elisa Saavedra, Gloria Deliña, and Joanna Talaid. In 2011, Senator Amy Klobuchar spoke about the process by which she introduced legislation to change federal adoption laws in support of placing our sibling group of nine children, who were also featured at that banquet.

One popular feature of the banquets has been reporting the evening's offering. Al Sannerud, who served as CSC's treasurer in the early decades, supervised the totaling of gifts with the help of his Lake Accounting staff. No banquet was complete without Al lumbering to the mike to announce the total. Al passed away in 2022, leaving behind a lifetime of service to the community and to organizations like CSC.

Every banquet has included media presentations to give attenders visual representations of the ministry and its progress. These have included Larry Hansen's slide shows, Chris and Larry's videos, video greetings produced in Cebu, and pictures of building construction. One video was a fake "feed" from Cebu. Jerry Healy, the banquet emcee, talked to the staff as if they were coming through a satellite connection, though it was just a video they made. This got a lot of laughs and fooled almost nobody.

One year we served breakfast in place of the usual dinner fare because the video that evening featured the kids in Cebu coming down the stairs to have breakfast. Other program highlights have been a flag procession, cakes to honor CSC birthdays, testimonies of people who visited Cebu, recognizing staff members for ending their service, live Skype connections with Cebu, introductions of new staff members, updates from staff and board members, and impromptu songs and "stall tactics" when the offering counting took longer than expected. One year we decorated the gym to resemble a Philippine barrio fiesta, with streamers and lanterns, and a group doing cultural dances.

Jerry Healy was the capable and humorous emcee for more than 20 annual banquets. He gave way to son Will, who took the baton for six years.

Other emcees have included Dana Olson, Chuck Sorlie, Jared Gustafson, and Randy Stroman. Special music for the banquets has been provided by an eclectic group of musicians: the Reedy Family Singers, Over and Back, the Central Baptist choir, Joanna Talaid, Andrew Merkouris, Greg Dirnberger, the Golden Strings, Roger Anderson, Alan and Rachel Lecher, Sam Butler and family, Janice Dreiling, Angela Erickson, the Abrahamson sisters, Sue Garrison, and various groups featuring former CSC residents.

Volunteers have made significant contributions to the banquets: making centerpieces, arranging flowers and balloons, setting tables, handling the seating, taking the offering, and coordinating with Bethel for all the arrangements.

With the exception of one year when we experimented with multiple dessert evenings, the gatherings have included a meal. Costs for the food have been underwritten by generous supporters who sponsor tables at the banquet. Though the initial events were held in churches or hotel ballrooms, the banquet has been held at Bethel University since 1985, except for 2020 and 2021, when the Covid pandemic forced us to cancel.

The CSC banquet has developed into a much-loved and anticipated yearly institution. Many of our supporters don't want to miss the annual affair, and feel comfortable inviting friends to attend. Some have attended every one of the banquets.

Foster Friends

DURING THE LATE 1980s, the CSC board was brainstorming about fundraising. They agreed that we needed more income but that having additional events was time-consuming and labor-intensive. The idea of having a sponsorship program was brought up and discussed extensively. One characteristic of the CSC family, as we had come to think of our support system, was that people loved to hear stories about individual children. The more personalized we could make our promotion of the ministry, the better. So giving our supporters the opportunity to support a particular child seemed to make sense.

Betty Sannerud, wife of Al and a board member at the time, was one of the strongest supporters of that idea, in spite of significant administrative challenges that would be posed by such a program. There would be many components to a sponsorship program: choosing the children, assigning them to sponsors, gathering information for updates, and getting that information from Cebu to Minnesota. The board looked at other organizations' sponsorship programs for ideas.

Out of these discussions emerged CSC's sponsorship program. Lynn Burke, on our staff at the time the program was being planned, won a ministry-wide contest by coming up with the name Foster Friends. (Lynn submitted several entries, including Be A Real Friend, the acronym of which just didn't seem to work for the judges.) From modest beginnings, the Foster Friends program has grown to include 50 of our children and has been the most consistent part of our income for the past 30 years. While other sources have experienced downturns and fluidity, Foster Friends has been solid and consistent. From a suggested monthly donation of $20 a month at the outset of the program, sponsors were giving $30 a month by 2012. By 2015 we had 640 sponsors.

Foster Friends differs from sponsorship programs for organizations such as World Vision and Compassion, in that we have more than one sponsor per child. We have been careful to make that known to sponsors, explaining that costs for providing residential care to our children—which includes childcare, social work services, education, and complete medical care—cannot be covered with one sponsorship amount. We have explained it this way: CSC sponsors provide an "extended family of support" to a particular child.

Foster Friends sponsors have been a blessing to our children in many ways. Their support allows us to provide the best care possible for the kids under our care. Some sponsors have sent gifts for birthdays and Christmas, or have written encouraging letters to their sponsored child(ren). Our children who are old enough to write send letters to their sponsors about twice a year, and that has been an avenue of blessing on all sides. Foster Friends sponsors include individuals, families, civic organizations, and church groups. Some sponsor more than one child. From the start, our sponsors have known that CSC works hard to find adoptive homes for our children, so "their child" might end up in a family, which necessitates matching them with another child. We have found that our sponsors are thrilled by this, as they share our passion for seeing children get into permanent homes.

The CSC Website

IN THE 1980S I ATTENDED A CONFERENCE IN NASHVILLE with people from Christian organizations across the United States. One breakout session I attended was about the Internet, including the use of websites. In those days the idea of having a ministry website was new, and many were just getting their feet wet in this novel avenue of promotion. The seminar leader asked which organizations had a website, and of the 50 people in the room about 20 raised their hands. Then he asked which of those who raised their hands had a website made by someone 18 years old or younger. At least half of that group raised their hands again. Including me.

CSC's first website was made by a teenager—Matt Healy, my nephew. He was just learning about the Web in high school, but that put him way ahead of any of us. It was a simple site, but it worked. I have no idea what kind of traffic it attracted, if any. We didn't know what to put there or how to use it. Years later, Larry Hansen made us a new one, with palm trees and cool little coconuts that served as navigational buttons. We put all the information we thought anyone could ever want about CSC on that site.

In 2006 Chris Hansen replaced his dad's site with a shiny new one, with lots of bells and whistles. We could put lots of pictures and video there, and he developed a utility whereby people could make donations on the site. Another feature he added was a way for people to register for the banquet online. Most important, he made the site in such a way that we could easily update it with fresh information and media. In 2010 Chris updated that site with new features like an online market for CSC tee shirts and a place for staff to blog.

Another milestone for CSC's promotion was when we added an e-newsletter option for our supporters who wanted to go paperless. Conceivably, a supporter could get the *CSC News* online, make donations through our website, and receive e-mail receipts. These developments were part of a larger emphasis: to attract younger donors to CSC, people who are computer and Internet savvy and who might not otherwise give to us.

Social Media

WITH THE RISE OF SOCIAL MEDIA, CSC considered if and how we might join the party. For several years we had been interested in attracting younger supporters to the ministry, and this avenue seemed like a natural one to help accomplish that. Bjork Ostrom, who spent a year in Cebu, is an expert on social media for business and ministry promotion, having worked for Youth Frontiers and, with his wife Lindsay, on their family business, Pinch of Yum. He helped CSC develop a Facebook presence that has been an online destination for many of our supporters and has attracted new people to CSC.

Fundraisers

MANY PEOPLE HAVE ENGAGED IN FUNDRAISING ACTIVITIES FOR CSC. Our stateside directors have been at the forefront of these efforts, planning and carrying out activities, writing letters, making phone calls, having lunch or coffee with prospective donors, and making presentations in churches.

Many other people have contributed to fundraising at CSC, pitching in ways large and small. Some made presentations in their home, church, or civic organization, when it would have been logistically difficult for a CSC staff person to do so. Some did fundraising projects in their communities, such as food or lemonade stands, walk-a-thons, craft and bake sales, auctions, art sales, planned famines, rummage sales, concerts, or golf tournaments. One CSC supporter who was a faculty advisor for his school's Honor Society got his club to support CSC. A group in Hong Kong had our children do art projects and auctioned them off to wealthy businessmen in their city. A CSC board member organized a multi-artist craft sale at a Twin Cities church. Kids encouraged their classmates to give money. Others distributed coin banks to places of business in their communities.

The Science of Fundraising

THERE IS CERTAINLY SOME "SCIENCE" TO FUNDRAISING. But our history has been one of unpredictable, unscientific outcomes where God blessed our efforts even when we didn't understand that science or chose to go against prevailing practices. People we never dreamed were in a position to give a large gift, did. When we questioned the value of mailing newsletters, someone might read an article or a description of a child and respond with a donation. A person who had never heard of CSC did an Internet search of Philippine orphanages, ended up at our website, and decided to become a donor.

In the early days of the ministry, Cliff and I did a luncheon presentation at a Twin Cities church. We showed a few slides and told the story of how we got started. We've done hundreds of these presentations. Sometimes we were able to take an offering, sometimes not. From a "scientific" point of view, it probably didn't make sense for us to invest our time in efforts that didn't have any guaranteed outcome. But we've learned that God is the orchestrator of events and makes good things happen out of seemingly unproductive efforts. In one way or another, He blesses. One of the men who was at that luncheon was impressed with what he heard but was not in a position to help financially at that time. Later, when his new company became successful, he remembered CSC and made a very large gift, fulfilling a promise he made to God to be faithful as He blessed his labors.

In the mid-1990s I went to Hong Kong for a Walk to Emmaus retreat. Friends of ours in Hong Kong offered to sponsor me and, eventually, each of our staff members to participate in the retreat. For me, this would be an opportunity to retreat from my often-hectic life in Cebu and reflect on God's grace in my life. But I didn't want to go. I had so much work to do. I had images of men's retreats I'd heard about, complete with sweaty hug gauntlets and health-and-wealth stories by successful businessmen.

A few days before the Walk I was in Manila, having done adoption matching at the Department of Social Welfare and Development. I was sound asleep at the Christian and Missionary Alliance guest house, and was planning to leave later that morning for Cebu. I had decided not to attend the Walk. There was a knock at my door—a missionary friend, Roger Tompkins, who'd just arrived from Hong Kong, having attended Walk to Emmaus on the weekend before I was scheduled to attend. He gushed about the retreat, telling me how great it was and how God had spoken to him in a powerful way. No hug gauntlets. He would not stop talking, even though it was early in the morning. He had no idea I had been invited to attend the next Walk. I took this encounter as being God's way of getting me to Hong Kong. Roger Tompkins was his mouthpiece.

The Walk to Emmaus was attended primarily by expatriates like me, guys from the U.S., Canada, and Europe who were working in Hong Kong or other places in SE Asia. I met the men who were leading the Walk and others who were pilgrims like myself. Amazingly, we formed friendships that lasted beyond the retreat. Though I didn't make any presentation about CSC, I got to know men who were leaders in business in Hong Kong and throughout the world.

And here is an amazing, unscientific, God-inspired outcome of that retreat. In addition to all that I learned, the relationships I made there resulted in the following:

- An architect, Alan Wright, offered to design our proposed school building free of charge. He made numerous trips to Cebu, did the drawings, helped supervise the construction, and eventually did the same for our infirmary and Duterte Home buildings.

- A member of the Hong Kong Union Church of got excited about his church getting involved with CSC in a deeper way. This church eventually paid for the land for outfitting the activity room of Children of Hope School.

- An executive of FedEx Corporation became a major donor of CSC, giving faithfully and generously to the ministry.

We would never have strategized this. Our fundraising plans would not have targeted these men for gifts. In and of ourselves, we had no way of penetrating corporations or getting the ear of executives. Instead, God used Roger Tompkins to help get me to Hong Kong, and He did the rest.

From the late 1970s, when I was pecking out a quarterly newsletter on a manual typewriter, to the present day when Internet sites need to be updated almost daily with fresh information and media, CSC has strived to put out accurate, well-written, and entertaining information in printed and electronic forms, and, through presentations, to get people interested and excited about the ministry in Cebu.

Many talented people have helped us along the way—writing, editing, and laying out our newsletters; helping us learn how to do effective mailings; writing scripts; shooting and editing video; building a first-rate website and social media sites; and helping us put on a successful banquet. All these efforts have helped us to fulfill our mission in Cebu: to provide high-quality services to homeless Filipino children. Our fundraising efforts have always been firmly rooted in the needs of these children.

Some "raindrops have fallen on our heads" along the way; not everything we tried has been successful or God-honoring. But we have strived to remember that nothing we do can be done for its own sake or to aggrandize people or the things they create. It's all for the kids. And God has taken our efforts and talents and passion and blessed them richly, helping us raise hundreds of thousands of dollars for food, clothing, shelter, education, and medical care. And these same fundraising efforts have been a blessing to those who have been inspired to give, helping them be the kind of loving, compassionate, and generous people that God wants them to be.

People

THE CONTRIBUTIONS OF PEOPLE TO THIS MINISTRY have been amazing and humbling. Along with financial resources, God has provided the human resources that have allowed CSC to thrive. These resources include workers and staff in Cebu, volunteers, financial and prayer supporters, and people who had an encouraging word along the way. We have learned important lessons from God's provision of the people needed to accomplish the task He laid before us.

The Right People at the Right Time

I WILL NEVER FORGET what former Children of Hope School principal Dr. Elisa Saavedra said about staffing. At a time when we had some unexpected departures from our school faculty, she told me, "Paul, God always fills the slots." Indeed. That has been true throughout the history of CHS and CSC. He has provided people at the right time, in the right capacity, to accomplish a needed task or fill a needed role. Some have come along to fill major roles, like Ron Duterte, Sandy Swanson, or Kathy Flora. More common are those who have only been there for a brief time to do something specific and timely. Some did only one thing, but that thing was powerful and transformational.

Joe Lincoln made a major donation to help us get started, then virtually disappeared. We lost track of Joe in the early 1980s, making me wonder if he might have been an angel. But he danced across the stage of CSC, and without him we might not ever have gotten started. He wasn't called to be a staff member, a volunteer, or even a long-term donor. His calling was to make that gift at that time.

Mae Ness was a friend of Cliff Danielson and a relative of some CSC supporters. During the early 1980s, when we were contemplating automating our address list and financial information, our board treasurer made us aware of software that would be of great help in this process. But it was very expensive. Mae made a totally unexpected donation of $6,000 to pay for the software. The result was that we were able to track giving and be more creative in our mailings and receipting, and move our organization ahead in a big way.

Rebecca Deliña was the first person we met in Cebu in 1979. She was a remarkable woman who lived her life for others. As a city government nutrition worker, she went around the community with a baby scale, weighing children to determine whether they were malnourished so she could educate their parents about nutrition and help with emergency food assistance. She walked all over the neighborhoods surrounding her home, dispensing hope and good will. She was happy to meet us and learn about our desire to help children.

Rebecca was a Christian woman with a gentle, Christ-like spirit. And because she cared about the children she served, she was frustrated with the family problems that often resulted in malnutrition. She wanted to spread the Good News to the people she worked with in Bulacao. Rebecca had a practical view of the gospel. She saw how changed hearts resulted in stronger families. Men who formerly were drunkards or who gambled or used drugs, wasting money that should have been used to buy food or milk for their children, could be transformed into responsible husbands and fathers through the power of the Holy Spirit. In some cases that was the only hope for saving the malnourished kids she saw every day. Certainly Rebecca believed in salvation and eternal life as rewards for faith in Christ, but she also saw the benefits of changed priorities, restored relationships, and healthy lifestyles.

Rebecca had a big influence on me and the rest of our staff and workers. She worked for CSC for a time, mainly doing night shifts or hospital duty. And she was a mainstay in the Bulacao Church that was started in the Corpus Christi Home. Rebecca continued to do outreach work in Bulacao well into her 80s and until her death in 2020, and often referred children to CSC who needed our services.

Paul and Luanne Binsfield served in the Philippines as short-term missionaries and, while there, adopted three of our children. When their term of service was up, they returned to their home in Wisconsin. Paul had formerly owned a small trucking business, but changes in the industry while they were gone rendered that business untenable. Paul was forced to look for a job and eventually became a bus driver for Greyhound. He did well there and was eventually given an award as Driver of the Year. With the award went a fairly large sum of money. Within a few days that amount was given to CSC. In spite of their financial struggles as a family readjusting to life and its many challenges in the States, Paul and Luanne decided that the award money was a windfall from God, and they wanted to bless the CSC children with it, something they might never be able to do again.

Many others come to mind. **Tom Johnson** was the Minnesota Twins pitcher who bailed us out after the B.J. Thomas fiasco. **Ron and Jerry Swanson** purchased the first vehicle we had in Cebu. **Variety Clubs International** heard about us and donated a new air-conditioned van. **Brian Kusunoki** moved from Minnesota to Hong Kong, where he got involved at the Union Church. When he told the church about CSC, they became interested and eventually gave a large donation for our school project, paying for outfitting our main room. **Arvid Olson** shared about CSC with **Harry Schmidt**, a philanthropist in British Columbia, who eventually built our homes in Banawa. **Dan and Carla Chalmers** heard about our desire to build a school from **Dave Jahnke**, a friend of CSC and a member of Central Baptist, my home church. They decided to provide the money for construction of that facility.

The amazing thing about CSC is that there have been hundreds of such people who have come into our lives at just the right time to make a gift, render a service, or say a prayer on our behalf.

It Takes a Village to Raise a Child

THIS OLD AFRICAN PROVERB has garnered some controversy since it was used by Hilary Clinton in a book she wrote about her vision for the children of America. A conservative response to her use of the proverb was, "No, it doesn't take a village to raise a child; it takes a family." The reality at CSC is that both are true. We provide a "village" of support around our children to meet their many needs. CSC is, indeed, a village where their physical, medical, emotional, social, and spiritual needs are addressed by a vast team of workers. But we know that what we can provide is second best to a family, so we do our best to find adoptive families for the children for whom that is appropriate.

Our village includes workers with many talents and areas of expertise. We employ childcare workers, house parents, counselors, occupational and physical therapists, nurses, tutors, teachers, and social workers to care for our children. But our village also includes support staff such as cooks, cleaners, guards, drivers, maintenance workers, laundresses, bookkeepers, accountants, and administrators and their assistants. Providing residential care to children is labor intensive, particularly if the "village" is committed to a high quality of care. As of 2021 we had 120 employees in Cebu

In 2005 we had a staff development seminar to help our workers understand the whole program of childcare that CSC provides. It's easy for individual workers to be caught up in what they do but fail to appreciate the other tasks that make up CSC's total program. I had the group imagine that a 10-year-old boy, Juan dela Cruz, would soon be coming to live at CSC, and then had someone from each department tell how they would minister to Juan.

A childcare worker talked about how she would help him get to know the routine of the home and make sure he had clothes and school uniforms when he needed them. The house parents said they would monitor his behavior and emotional well-being. The counselor said he would work to establish a positive relationship with the boy and get him to talk about his past and things that affected him before coming to CSC. A teacher talked about assessing Juan to determine his level of learning and to place him in the right classes at Children of Hope School, and how she would try to individualize instruction for his ability level and learning style. The social worker explained her role in processing the referral, gathering information and documentation, and writing the necessary reports for the child's eventual adoptive placement. A nurse talked about the intake physical, immunizations, and medical and lab reports that would be accomplished for Juan while he was at CSC. Even the maintenance and office staffs had a chance to describe their work and how it would contribute to Juan's care. It was an eye-opening experience for all of us to see the scope of our services and the number of people who are a part of the village of support that we offer the children who come to live at CSC.

A Sense of Calling

FOR THOSE OF US ON THE STAFF, the importance of calling cannot be overemphasized. Although the nature of that calling differs greatly from person to person, it is vital for people to have a sense that working for CSC in Cebu is God's will for our lives. It is not simply a matter of coincidence or convenience.

This sense of purpose and calling is important as staff members face the difficulties of living and working in the Philippines. There is often loneliness for family, cultural estrangement, difficulty in communicating with or understanding Filipinos, and the emotional weightiness of dealing with the tragic circumstances of children's lives. When facing all this it is of great value to know that God wants us to be in Cebu.

I have described this calling as being like a mattress. We often fall down from the pressures of life, but the mattress allows us to bounce back up and keep going. I have wondered how anyone could thrive in a ministry like ours without the firm assurance that God's calling had been at work in getting him or her to CSC and that He was a constant support through the inevitable difficult times.

We want that same sense of calling to hold true for everyone connected with CSC, as a worker or volunteer. It will certainly be different for every person, and we realize that many of our workers look at the ministry differently than we do on the staff. Many of our workers see it as, first and foremost, a job. We don't want to hold them to the same view we have because we enjoy many advantages—privilege, education, economic security—they don't have. For instance, most staff members could leave CSC at any time and expect to get another job to feed ourselves and our families. Our workers don't have the same assurance, so their needs and perspective are different.

But even though our life's circumstances vary greatly, we want all our workers to feel like God brought them to CSC. He shaped their lives and used circumstances to make it possible for them to be a part of this great ministry. We want them to see their work as ministry, not just a job. Sometimes that takes effort on our part, but we can rely on God to help impress that on each worker's heart.

We have an employee who has been washing clothes for 31 years. Her name is Lena, and she has been a great worker—steady, faithful, dedicated.

She never comes late to work or complains. She just keeps on washing diapers, bedding, and clothes. Sometimes it gets really hot in the wash room, but she doesn't let it get her down. She is an inspiration to the staff, and a good example to the other workers and the children. We don't know exactly what is in her heart, but we suspect she finds contentment in being a part of CSC and understands how important it is to have clean clothes and diapers for the children. Surely God takes Lena's hands and makes them His, scrubbing and wringing and folding for His glory.

Little Becomes Much

THE FIRST "THEME SONG" WE HAD was "Ordinary People," by Mom Winans. Marlys' friend Stacy recorded the song for us and we used it in 1978, before we went to Cebu. It captured the way we felt about ourselves being ordinary folks whom God called and made exceptional with his hand on our lives:

> Just ordinary people.
> God uses ordinary people.
> He chooses people just like me and you
> Who are willing to do as He commands.
>
> God uses people that will give Him all
> No matter how small your all may seem to you.
> Because little becomes much
> As you place it in the Master's hand.

How true for the people of CSC! Our history has not been primarily one of wealthy and experienced people making CSC successful, but rather simple folks with commitment, vision, and obedience joining hands with the Master's hand, and then doing amazing things. It's the ultimate recipe for success. Even people who have been able to make large donations to the ministry are those who came from backgrounds similar to ours, share our values, and appreciate the simple principles on which CSC was founded and has operated for 42 years.

God has used amazing people at CSC.

Cebu Staff

Marlys Healy, nee Danielson, is CSC's founder and served as medical director from the beginning. She graduated from Anoka High School in Minnesota in 1973 and later attended Anoka Technical College, graduating as a medical assistant in 1974, when she began working at Fridley Medical Center. She worked there in pediatrics and emergency care until leaving for Cebu in 1979.

Marlys's medical experience and her compassionate heart served her well in meeting the medical needs of CSC's children. For years she was the sole medical person on the CSC staff but later entrusted that task to other nurses. Initially, nurses joined our staff to fill in for Marlys while she was on furlough, but in time the medical department expanded to include Filipino nurses. Eventually the team included four nurses in addition to Marlys.

As medical director, Marlys developed relationships with doctors, clinics, labs, and hospitals. CSC has used doctors representing 28 specialties, from pediatrics to neurosurgery. Marlys initiated the system of keeping comprehensive medical records for all our children, as well as preparing the medical reports required by agencies that license and accredit CSC and the Philippine Inter-Country Adoption Board. She trained her team to do these reports and to see that all the needed immunizations and tests are given.

Marlys spent thousands of hours in hospitals and clinics with our children, including doctors' waiting rooms, emergency rooms, and labs. In the early days, she often stayed in the hospital with children because "watchers" are required for hospital patients in the Philippines.

Not all of our children's medical needs have been treatable in Cebu. Marlys arranged for care in Manila and the United States for kids with exceptional needs.

Marlys' other duties included household upkeep and attending to visitors. Her commitment to keeping the houses clean and well-maintained has been a hallmark of CSC's ministry. When repairs were needed she saw that they got done. When Harry and Marlene Schmidt, whose family foundation built our homes in Banawa, came to the 25th anniversary celebration, they were thrilled with the condition of our facilities, which were by then more than 12 years old. This was a tribute to Marlys, other staff who supervised their upkeep, and the workers who did the cleaning, painting, and repairs. CSC's commitment to be good stewards of the property God provided has been an important value, and that commitment started with Marlys.

Marlys' city tours are famous around the world among friends who have visited Cebu. She brought people on shopping trips to buy native handicrafts, to historical and tourist sites, and to areas of the city where our children come from. Many adoptive parents who have gone to pick up their children have seen where their kids were born and grew up, thanks to Marlys' city tours. Tours routinely included the downtown area of Colon, Carbon Market, including the Freedom Park basket market, the pier area, Fort San Pedro, City Hospital, and one of the large, public cemeteries where some of our children are buried. These tours have given our visitors a balanced view of both the beauty of the Philippines and the difficult situations many of its residents face.

Sometimes Marlys' role as medical director included attending to visitors who became sick, helping them navigate the medical system in Cebu, seeing doctors, getting lab tests, and purchasing medications to get them on the road to health before heading home.

Marlys traveled to Europe twice to escort children and visit former residents in their homes. On the first trip she went to Germany and Norway, and on the second trip she visited Norway, where we have many adopted children. The Norwegian adoption agency, Adopjusmforum, hosted her and paid for her travel within the country.

The ministry of CSC began in Marlys' heart in 1978. Since then that same heart has beat strongly and steadily for the children under our care, and for adopted children she has visited around the world.

Paul Healy was born in Haywarden, Iowa, but grew up in Saint Paul. His parents were both educators, his dad teaching at Bethel College and his mother in several Saint Paul public elementary schools. He attended Murray High School, graduating in 1972, and went on to study at Bethel College, where he graduated in 1977. Paul played football, basketball, and baseball in high school and basketball at Bethel. He was interested in writing, and served as the editor of the Bethel *Clarion* in 1976.

Paul married Marlys Danielson in 1978 and was part of the initial team that went to Cebu to start the ministry. He was field director from the outset, helping establish the organization in Cebu and its relationship with various branches of the Philippine government that regulate and oversee the work: the Department of Social Welfare and Development, Cebu city government, the Inter-Country Adoption Board, the Departments of Health and Education, and the local government units of Cebu City.

Paul served on the first Task Force on Child Care and Placement in Manila, from 1986 to 1989, helping the government establish a new adoption program following the fall of the Marcos empire, and helping establish CSC as an important player in that new system. Paul helped organize a provincial task force in Cebu as well, and sat on the specialists group that administered local matching.

In addition to his role as field director, Paul served as president of CSC until 2006. He helped develop the organization's fundraising and promotion including the CSC website, planned banquets, wrote many of the promotional materials, and edited the CSC newsletter. During furloughs he visited and spoke at churches throughout America, often with Marlys and sometimes their three daughters. He served on the CSC board and headed up the long-range planning committee's work reorganizing the board and the stateside ministry.

Kathy Norlien Flora was one of the pioneering missionaries of CSC, going to Cebu to start the work in 1979. She married Sned Flora in November of 1979.

Kathy was born in Minneapolis and lived in Blaine, Minnesota, for 15 years before her family moved to the Constance area. She graduated from Anoka High School in 1971, spent a year at Miltonvale Weslyan College in Kansas, and then transferred to Anoka Ramsey Junior College.

During this time Kathy worked at various jobs, ending up in the bookkeeping department at Old Dutch. She began to feel discontented with this job, having a desire to do God's work. In 1978 she was involved in a car accident and could not work for five months. After the accident she moved back home. Before long she left Old Dutch and went to be a counselor at Camp Shamineau. She thought about going back to school and was seeking God's direction for her life..

In February of 1978, Kathy's friend Marlys Danielson invited her on the now-famous investigative trip to the Philippines. Kathy had known Marlys for more than a year, having met her at Constance Free Church, and the two had taken several vacations together. This trip, however, proved to be more than just another vacation, for by the time it was over, Kathy had decided to return to Cebu some day and help begin a ministry to children. This was no small decision for a young woman who, as a little girl, had told God: "I'll do anything, but please don't make me be a missionary!"

One of the first people Kathy met in Cebu was Sned Flora, one of two Filipinos to join the staff at the beginning. Watching Sned's marvelous way with children and working with him in the team's many activities, Kathy became quite impressed. One thing led to another, and a few months later they were married.

Kathy and Sned continued on the staff until 1984, when they moved to Minnesota, where they served on the CSC board for several years. Kathy returned to school, got her nursing degree, and then worked in the medical field in the Twin Cities.

Kathy Flora was a pioneer missionary. Her enthusiasm and drive helped the first staff establish a ministry out of nothing, and persevere through the difficult early days in Cebu.

Sned Flora was part of the initial CSC staff in Cebu. Together with Della Longakit, he was a godsend for our American staff, helping us navigate the language and culture when all of that was very new to us. Sned was gifted in working with children, though he didn't have much prior experience doing that.

Sned was born in Larena, Siquijor, an island south of Cebu. He was valedictorian of his high school class and moved to Cebu to study electrical engineering at the Cebu Institute of Technology. During that time Sned became involved in the Chi Alpha Student Center, run by the Evangelical Free Church of the Philippines. There he started hearing about the "orphanage project" and met Jeff Snyder, our first missionary to Cebu. He also met Della, and they became the Filipinos we selected to be a part of our staff.

When Sned and Kathy left CSC and moved to Minnesota, he took a job with the Ryerson Company, a metal/steel fabrication company.

God used Sned in a powerful way to help get the ministry going. He was patient with us Americans as we were trying to learn the culture and language and establish relationships with people and institutions. I loved working with Sned and appreciated his gifts and his sense of humor. He was great in our puppet shows, working as a front man, often restating our mispronounced Cebuano words in an attempt to make the performances at least somewhat understandable to the kids.

For one puppet show our theme was accepting others. One puppet was dark brown, and the other puppets were making fun of him. My puppet was one of these, and I was using a word, *ngit-ngit*, which is hard for Americans to pronounce. Even if I had been able to wrap my tongue around it, it was the wrong word. I kept saying it, and Sned started laughing. He told me later that our attempts at Cebuano "tickled his ears," and that day, unlike many others, he hadn't been able to keep from laughing. The kids probably thought it was all part of the show.

Sandy Swanson was one of our original staff members. Sandy grew up on a farm. After moving several times when she was young, her family ended up in the Constance, Minnesota, area. Sandy and Marlys were childhood friends, and both attended the same church. In their high school years they traveled together to Florida, Colorado, and the Canary Islands. When Sandy was 17, she, Marlys, and Lois, Marlys's older sister, were in a devastating car accident in northern Minnesota. Sandy broke her leg and had to use crutches for over a year. Lois died a few months after the accident.

During high school, Sandy had several jobs: picking vegetables, washing dishes, and babysitting. She graduated from Anoka High School in 1971 and attended Anoka Technical College, taking courses in child development. After graduation she worked in a childcare center and during summers was a counselor at Camp Shamineau in Motley, Minnesota. Eventually she worked there as a full-time staff member.

Sandy's experiences in child development, counseling, and administration were to serve her well when she left Shamineau in 1979 to join the staff in Cebu. She was our childcare director (later changed to child development director) for all her time in Cebu, until her retirement in 2015. She helped train our childcare workers, house parents, and counselors, made schedules, helped handle discipline problems, and was "Auntie Sandy" to hundreds of CSC kids over the years.

Sandy was part of the pioneering spirit that helped CSC get started, and her work helped enable the later growth we experienced. She gave so much of herself, investing her life in the lives of the children that God brought into her life at CSC. Sandy was house mother of the Eicher Home for several years before our move to Banawa. On one of her furloughs, Sandy went back to school and got a psychology degree from Northwestern College in Saint Paul.

Sandy's contribution to CSC's success is incalculable. Her dedication was always amazing and inspiring. If ever I gave her a job, she did it well and on time. She was fair with the children and workers, and had an understanding ear when workers shared their personal problems with her. Her sense of humor served her well, as she had to deal with many complicated problems over the years. Her faith in God was a great example to everyone she came in contact with. And her sacrifices on behalf of the children are something we will not fully appreciate until we get to heaven.

Mitch Ohlendorf attended Central Baptist Church in Saint Paul, my home church. He was an accounting major at Bethel College. When I was in Minnesota escorting Edgar for brain surgery, I talked with Greg Dirnberger, who worked with Central's college students, about the possibility of a team from the church going to Cebu. Greg was intrigued and shared the idea with his group, and Mitch expressed an interest in being part of that trip.

Mitch liked our ministry and volunteered to come for the summer of 1984 to work on the staff as temporary financial director. That went well, so he appied to join the staff permanently and left for Cebu after he graduated from Bethel in 1985. Mitch gave 32 years of his life to the children of CSC. He served as executive director for most of those years, and was the acting field director in Cebu when I was away. He and his wife, Ruth, also had a stint as house parents.

Perhaps Mitch's biggest contribution to the ministry was his leadership in our various building projects. Although he had no training in construction work, he was a fast learner and had great organizational skills and attention to detail. He worked with his brother-in-law, Jerry Salgo, an engineer; the architects who designed our buildings; and our benefactors and financiers to put up first-class buildings for CSC and the children who live there.

Ruth Deliña Ohlendorf, Rebecca Deliña's daughter, grew up in Bulacao, where CSC began. Ruth started working at CSC as a teenager. After finishing high school, she took up social work at the University of Southern Philippines. She met Mitch in 1983 and they were married in 1986.

For the next 30 years Ruth served CSC in a variety of capacities, most notably as the head of CSC's outreach program. She worked in our feeding programs in the early 90s and served on our child development team before retiring, with Mitch, in October of 2016. Ruth, together with her mother, Rebecca, was instrumental in getting us established in Bulacao, and her advocacy for our former residents' needs did much to help them in their lives post-CSC. Her kind heart and friendly personality made them feel loved and appreciated, and helped CSC remember to support them and provide opportunities for them to be healthy and finish their schooling if they desired to.

Jeff Snyder was the first staff member to go to Cebu, in 1979. He was still a teenager when he started with CSC, but he had a vibrant faith and a desire to be useful. He prepared the way for the rest of us to join him in Cebu. Jeff's family was not enamored of him being on the other side of the world, and Jeff felt pressure to return home, which he did in 1982. After leaving CSC, Jeff went to seminary and engaged in church ministry.

Shari Reasoner served as CSC's education director for 10 years. She was a major force in getting our Children of Hope School started, and helped it grow and develop and become increasingly more responsive to students' educational needs.

Shari saw the school through growing pains, licensing, frequent changes in personnel, and shifting priorities of the Philippine Department of Education. She recruited U.S. teachers to complement our Filipino teachers. She was a mentor to Cris Tabra, who became our principal in 2008. They were a dynamic team of innovators, constantly tweaking the facilities, organization, and curriculum to improve CHS. Shari went to Cebu at least quarterly to work with the teaching staff. Shari secured donations of equipment, curricula, books, and musical instruments. She used her background in physical education to develop a PE program at CHS, and other teachers created our now annual Sportsfest, a highlight of the year for our kids.

Shari also found school placements for students who had graduated from CHS but were not yet adopted and needed to attend high school outside of CSC. That involved visiting schools, talking with principals and teachers, and seeing that our kids took the necessary placement and entrance exams. Shari worked to help our teachers develop their classroom management and evaluation skills. Each quarter the school has student evaluations attended by house parents and staff.

Della Longakit Cherne was a part of our original staff. She is from Cebu and met Marlys during the Aubrey McGann crusades. Della was working at the Montelbello Hotel, where the team that Marlys was a part of stayed, and a friendship was born.

When Marlys went back to Cebu with Kathy and me, Della took time off work to show us around. One of the most important things she did was introduce us to Ron Duterte, who was the Cebu City vice mayor at the time, as well as a prominent attorney. When we went to Cebu to start the ministry, Della quit her job and joined the staff. She also introduced Jeff Snyder to Sned Flora, who eventually joined us.

Living communally and working among the poor was something very new to Della (and all of us), but she handled it well and made a meaningful contribution to the ministry. She did a lot of our cooking and helped us in the community by translating for us. She was very loving with the kids we were taking in, though she didn't have much experience working with children or caring for babies. Having Della on our staff was a big help in our getting established in Bulacao.

Lynn Greene was a blessing to CSC and a joy to know as a friend and co-worker. Her relatives told us when we were first getting to know her that "when Lynn arrives, then, and only then, does the party begin!"

She initially went to Cebu in 1985 to visit her uncle and aunt, Ray and Phyllis Burke, who were serving as managers of the Baptist General Conference guest home in Cebu and who had become good friends of the CSC staff. Lynn got to know and love the ministry and decided to join our staff for a year in 1986. She could not get CSC out of her heart, so she returned in 1995 and served for three more years. She did some administrative chores in the office, handled CSC's brand-new child sponsorship program, took pictures for the CSC newsletter and other promotional materials, and helped Sandy Swanson with childcare duties. She had a great sense of humor that all of us on the staff benefitted from, and was a kind and loving auntie to the children.

I have often said that Lynn has been on the longest furlough in missionary history, since she never officially resigned from the field. Her extended furlough has now reached over 30 years (and counting) as she scours the Guinness Book of World Records for authentication of her self-proclaimed world record. Part of the authentication problem is the definition of "furlough," since Lynn hasn't done any church presentations or other furlough activities, nor is she prepared to return to Cebu if asked to do so.

Lynn visited CSC several times after her "retirement." She and Sandy

Swanson became close friends while Lynn was in Cebu, a friendship that continues to this day.

Tammy Vosika served as a teacher in our Children of Hope School from 2005 to 2013. She was an excellent teacher whose love for her students and all the CSC kids was very evident. Her parents, Beth and Darrell, adopted four brothers from CSC, and her home church in Cambridge, Minnesota, has been a long-time supporter of the ministry.

Tammy was teaching in Texas before joining CHS. Her initial commitment was for one year, but she kept extending until her tenure reached eight years, when she went back to Minnesota to continue her career as an elementary school teacher. One of Tammy's accomplishments was developing and teaching an American Studies class, a short course in American history and culture to prepare our kids who were joining adoptive families in the United States.

Amy Luck was a charter member of the Children of Hope School faculty. She started teaching at CHS when the school opened in 1998 and taught for two school years, returning to the U.S. in 2000 to teach in Moorhead, Minnesota.

Amy was a hard-working teacher who was willing to accept any challenge. Our school was new and had a different system and curriculum, so our teachers needed to be flexible and able to learn on the fly. Amy excelled at both of those and helped us establish our school as an excellent place of learning for all our kids, regardless of special needs, learning difficulties, or behavioral challenges.

Amy returned to Cebu in 2003 to join our child development team. She married a Filipino pastor, Marcel Pacada, in 2012 and continued on our staff until 2016. Amy and Marcel live in North Dakota with their two daughters.

Lindsay Hoeft went to Cebu in 2011 to join or staff. A marriage and family counselor by profession, Lindsay helped start our counseling department, hiring, training, and supervising counselors to work with our older children. Because our counselors had little experience in that field, she offered training in counseling sessions and record keeping, and how to write counseling reports used for adoption matching.

Our counseling department is now an integral part of our services to our children, and Lindsay's skill and drive in getting that started have touched the lives of many CSC kids, especially those with emotional and psychological problems resulting from abuse or neglect before coming to live at CSC. Lindsay also headed up our child development team for several years. She helped professionalize our delivery of services to the children and how we chart and report their progress while at CSC. While in Cebu, Lindsay met one of our physical therapists, Marwin Abong, and they were married and moved to Minnesota in 2019. They live and work near Willmar, Minnesota.

Joel Reasoner grew up knowing about CSC because his parents, Shari and Paul, were close to the ministry. Joel went to Hope College in Michigan, where he excelled in cross country and track. After graduation he worked for Habitat for Humanity before joining our staff in 2007.

Joel has worn a number of hats at CSC, most recently as media manager, producing pictures and videos for our promotional materials and events. He is especially skilled at making videos that capture the emotion and spirit of CSC.

Joel helped establish our Human Resources Department and wrote some of our employee policy manuals. He has also handled scheduling. He is kind and compassionate with our workers, helping them with both personal and job-related problems. Joel was also involved in mentoring our older boys. He and his dad, Paul, were the driving force behind the Habitat for Humanity Happy Homes program that built 60 homes for our workers in 2018. Joel is married to **Jinkee**, our Home Life director, whom he met after he started at CSC. They have two young boys.

Ben and Mari Bonnett served twice at CSC. Mari heard about CSC at her church, Berean Baptist, and was at a presentation Marlys and I gave there. The Bonnett's first stint was from 2003 to 2005 as teachers in our school. Like our other school staff, they were flexible and dedicated. Although he had no experience as a band director, Ben was willing to take that on when we needed someone. He put together a band using instruments donated to the school. The CHS band's highlight was their performance at CSC's 25th anniversary celebration in 2004, though they had other opportunities to perform.

In 2017 Ben applied for the job of education director in our Children of Hope School. He and Mari started their second assignment 12 years after they left CSC the first time. Accompanying them were their son, Josh, and daughters, Rylin and Johanna. Ben led the school through some challenging transitions, working closely with school principal Cris Tabra. The school was the beneficiary of several sizeable donations for the purchase of books, curriculum, and equipment. When another similar donation came through, Ben, in a gesture of kindness and inclusion, gifted the other staff and their departments from that money so that they, too, could buy needed equipment or avail of development opportunities. During Ben's tenure as education director, many improvements were made to the school, including some major renovations when the building was needed as a quarantine center during the pandemic.

In response to our changing population at CSC, with more of our residents aging out of adoption and our need to prepare or "launch" them for life in the Philippines, Ben authored a program called Bridge to help with this transition. It involves education, counseling, vocational preparedness, and life skills.

One highlight of Ben's time as education director was our celebration of the school's 20th anniversary in 2018. Ben and staff planned a weekend of activities, including a gala banquet that featured videos, games, and testimonials around the theme "Stories of Hope."

Short-Term Staff

SOME PEOPLE JOINED OUR STAFF for short-term assignments, giving several months or a few years of their lives to the ministry in Cebu.

As mentioned above, **Joe and Kathy Grafft** were our first short-termers, serving for a year in 1982 while Marlys and I were on our first furlough.

Nora Dorsey served for five years (1999-2004) at Children of Hope School as a teacher. She loved to teach science and challenged the students with creative experiments and projects. Nora found out about CSC through Sandy Swanson, whom she got to know at Camp Shamineau.

Andrew Merkouris, from Cambridge, Minnesota, spent seven months in Cebu in 2009 doing computer work and scanning and organizing our office files. He also used his musical and athletic skills to entertain the kids and staff. In a wrestling extravaganza, he took on local strongman the Big Show to the delight of teachers and students at CHS. Andrew's parents, Tim and Rene, adopted 11 children from CSC in 2010 and 2011.

Alan and Rachel Lecher taught music in our school in 2000 and 2001.

Dawn Miller heard about CSC the spring of her senior year at St. Olaf College in Northfield, Minnesota. She was attending my brother Will's church, and one Sunday my sister Elizabeth went there to speak about CSC. It was an impactful day for Dawn and resulted in her making three trips to Cebu. The first was in 2001 for three months helping in the school doing individualized instruction with students who were having difficulty. The second trip was for six months during 2005-2006, again working in Children of Hope School. The third was a two-week visit in 2007. Dawn was great to have in Cebu. She was willing to do anything that was needed in the school and got along well with everyone.

When **Michelle Peterson** went to Cebu to teach at the Children of Hope School, it was her fourth trip to Cebu. In 1998, when she was 16 years old, and again in 2000, she came with a team from Constance Free Church youth ministries. She made another trip with a friend from church, Sherri Stumpf, in 2007, and went again for a year of teaching in 2009-2010. In 2011, Michelle made another trip on her own to see all her friends at CSC. Michelle was a dedicated teacher whose love and concern for her students was very evident. She became a close friend with fellow teacher Tammy Vosika. Michelle continued her teaching career in Minnesota after her year at CHS.

Bjork and Lindsay Ostrom, from Cambridge, Minnesota, served on our staff for a year in 2012-2013. They brought talent and enthusiasm to the work. Lindsay taught in our school and Bjork helped out in the office while they both continued to work on their amazingly successful food blog, Pinch of Yum.

Grace Anderson Ohlendorf, from Saint Paul, learned about CSC through her church, Central Baptist, and went to Cebu for a year starting in August, 2014. She served on our childcare team, working with toddlers and helping write child development reports. She married Andrew Ohlendorf when she returned to the U.S.

Amber Swanson is a niece of Sandy Swanson so grew up knowing a lot about CSC. She spent several months in Cebu in 2018 helping in the office, especially organizing our pictures. She scanned thousands of images; got others from hard drives, CDs, and thumb drives; and found others on the CSC network and the cloud. Her work was a big help in preparing this book and for historical documentation.

Jake Schulz spent a year working on our staff as deputy field director, starting in the Fall of 2015. He and his wife, Pam, and their three kids, Carter, Isaac and Maddy, belonged to First Baptist Church in Sturgeon Bay, WI, a long-standing supporting church of CSC. They heard about CSC at church and felt led by God to be a part of our ministry. Jake had worked in the business world and was able to help CSC improve our financial and accounting systems. He helped us develop a Human Resources Department and hire Eldie Allocod as our HR director. He helped write a new workers policies manual and other HR documents, and reviewed our hiring and compensation system. Jake and Pam enjoyed hanging out with the older CSC kids and would have them in their home for devotionals and fun nights. Jake is a good example of how God brought a person to us who had specific skills that we needed at the time to help improve the ministry. And although he wasn't able to stay in Cebu long-term, he made an impact that will last for years to come.

Pete and Diane Grondahl were in Cebu from 1993 to 1996. Pete served as a driver and repairman while Diane taught at Joy Christian Academy, a missionary kids school where our daughter Jenny went to school. The rule at JCA was that parents needed to help teach or provide a teacher, so Diane fulfilled our obligation, since Marlys and I were both heavily engaged at CSC. Pete's former employer, Betty Hardle, was a CSC board member, business owner, and generous supporter of the ministry.

Peter and Megan Arneson were in Cebu from December, 2014, to December, 2015. His dad, Paul, went to Bethel when I did and was involved in leadership in several international ministries. Peter worked in the office helping Joel Reasoner with HR matters, including helping write our operations manual and working on our salary plan. Megan had been to CSC previously as a part of a Central Baptist Church team. She helped our social workers with paperwork and accompanied them on their field work. Peter joined the CSC Board in Minnesota in 2020.

Stateside Staff

Cliff Danielson was CSC's first stateside director and initiated our fundraising program. He worked tirelessly to introduce people and organizations to the ministry through personal contacts and presentations. Not incidentally, he was the father of CSC's founder, Marlys Healy.

Cliff was born in Saint Paul and attended Minnehaha Academy and

Bethel College and Seminary. He served in the Navy during World War II, returning to the States to marry Eleanore Sandquist, with whom he had three children: Roger, Lois, and Marlys. Cliff served as youth pastor at Bethany Baptist in Saint Paul. Later he was ordained by the Evangelical Free Church and became the pastor of Constance Evangelical Free Church, remaining there for 25 years. During that time his daughter, Lois, was killed in a car accident, and his wife, Eleanore, died of leukemia.

In January of 1978, Cliff joined the Aubrey McGann Evangelistic Association as crusade director. In that capacity he traveled extensively throughout the United States and the Far East. Marlys joined him on one of these tours, to Cebu City, Philippines, and it was then that she developed a burden for the homeless children they saw there. So the DelAdlawan Foundation was formed, and in April, 1979, Cliff was appointed its executive director.

Cliff loved the ministry of CSC and the children in Cebu. He was always telling people about the work, and visited Cebu several times. He made countless presentations in churches, civic organizations, homes, coffee shops, and places of business during his tenure. He pioneered the CSC banquet, and was proud of how that event grew in attendance and offering.

Cliff served the organization enthusiastically until his health declined in 1990. He died of congestive heart failure in 1993. Until that day Cliff remained intensely proud of his daughter and the ministry that she and others pioneered.

Dennis Eicher volunteered to serve as interim executive director while CSC was between stateside leaders. His willingness to take on this responsibility, in addition to the demands of running his business and serving on the CSC board, spoke of his deep commitment to the ministry and desire to use his leadership ability to further our efforts.

Gary Bawden became CSC's second executive director when Cliff had to resign for health reasons. Gary was working for Midwest Challenge at the time, and continued to do so as he assumed responsibilities for CSC's fundraising. Well-versed in mail solicitations, Gary helped CSC automate our systems and improve the quality of our letters and promotional materials. He introduced donation software that helped us record and track giving and systematize our receipting process.

Pauline Bohachek served as our executive director when we moved the CSC office to Cambridge and were going through some big changes in our office systems and fundraising program. She helped us get established in the Cambridge area and organized a team of volunteers to help with mailings. She was a pastor's wife, serving with her husband, Bob, at the Hillman Baptist Church near Mora, Minnesota.

Elizabeth Healy, my sister, followed Pauline as executive director. She had been working as an executive assistant for the Minnesota Baptist Conference before coming to CSC. She was a skilled writer and creative thinker who made improvements in the quality of our printed materials and presentations to churches. She did a great job with our CSC banquets, and helped upgrade the technology in our office. She initiated volunteer appreciation functions to honor our loyal helpers, and visited Cebu to see the children she loved so much.

Matt Buley joined CSC as stateside director in 2004. He came to us from Hospitality House, a Christian outreach to youth and their families in Minneapolis, where he worked in development. Matt had experience as a fundraiser, understood how Christian organizations work, and sought to honor God in and through our stateside ministry.

CSC's stateside responsibilities of communicating about the work in Cebu and raising funds for the ministry were growing rapidly when Matt got started at CSC, and he ushered in a new era of success. He helped the board through a time of self-evaluation and governance policy review, while bolstering our fundraising programs: Foster Friends, mail appeals, newsletters, church relations, presentations, and the CSC banquet, and he helped get our endowment, the Luke Fund, started. He worked closely with the board on long-range planning and staff relations, as well as an improved salary and benefits package for our Cebu staff.

For me, having Matt at CSC was a great blessing. I enjoyed brainstorming with him about the future of the ministry and how we could work together to promote the work. He was respectful of the past while excited about trying new things and challenging the board to consider new approaches to board governance and financial management.

One of the things I will remember most about Matt's time at CSC was his trips to Cebu. We always spent a lot of time in meetings with staff and workers, but he always took time to hang out with the kids and get to know them better. He never lost sight of who we are and what our priorities are. For our meetings, he never failed to have an ice breaker to start things off, which bought him a lot of grief from the staff.

Matt was instrumental in helping CSC turn the corner towards becoming a stronger and more efficient and effective ministry. In 2012, I was so happy to turn the president's duties over to Matt. Doing that job from Cebu didn't make much sense, and Matt had the ability and experience to handle those tasks and lead the organization where it needed to go. Matt completed his service to God and the children of Cebu in 2017. He and his wife, Theresa, adopted four children from CSC in 2007.

Jill Grasley, who was hired in 2013 as development director, became interim stateside director in 2017. She came to CSC from a background in adoption work, having served as a case worker at Crossroads Adoption Services (now Evolve Family Services).

Jill has established and maintained strong relationships with our donors while working on new initiatives to increase our base of support. She has spent many hours on the phone with donors, keeping in touch and thanking them for their gifts. She has traveled several times to Cebu to witness the ministry first-hand, and worked hard with Matt Buley to establish a good working relationship with the staff and workers. Jill's dedication and commitment has served CSC well for almost 10 years, especially during the time of transition after Matt Buley left.

Tim Holmberg joined CSC as president in 2018, after selling his successful electrical contracting company. He and his wife had adopted five of our CSC kids in 2004. He served on our board for several years before accepting the leadership position, so he knew a lot about the ministry.

Tim became president during a time of significant change at CSC, and set as one his top goals the smooth transition to a new field director, with Marlys and my pending retirement. Tim was the leader we needed during that period of change. He helped improve the board's stewardship of our financial resources and gave guidance and encouragement to the Cebu staff as we dealt with the early days of the Covid pandemic.

Supporting our stateside leaders has been a succession of administrative assistants who have processed donations, sent out receipt letters, supervised the volunteer teams for our mailings, maintained our computer records and mailing list, and performed a host of other clerical tasks so important in an organization like ours.

Kathy Hagfors started at CSC when we moved our office to Cambridge, where she lived. Kathy's husband, Gordy, is a brother to Warren Hagfors, who was a long-time friend of CSC and who volunteered during the 1980s. Kathy knew just about everyone in Cambridge and had a friendly and welcoming presence on the phone and with visitors to our office.

Brenda Leaf was also from the Cambridge area and worked in our office in the old courthouse. She remained with CSC when we moved to Shoreview, continuing to do excellent work. Brenda had many talents and would do any task to move the ministry forward. Her husband, Les, was a CSC volunteer, helping with a wide variety of jobs, from carpentry to moving to making props for the annual banquets.

Roger Anderson worked for CSC for several years, starting in 1998. He and his wife adopted four kids from CSC in 2003. Roger lived near Cambridge and was a member of Elim Isanti Baptist Church, which was a long-time supporting church of the ministry.

Board of Directors

MANY PEOPLE HAVE SERVED ON THE CSC BOARD—too many to name. Their donations of time and talent helped move the ministry from a largely "mom and pop" operation to a well-run, financially secure, God-honoring organization that is known for integrity in how we care for children and raise the funds to do it.

Board members have hired personnel, set budgets, encouraged staff, managed our relationships with U.S. government agencies, set policies for fundraising and the use of our endowment, and performed many governance matters in relation to our membership in watchdog agencies such as ECFA and Charity Navigator. They have been pastors, lawyers, accountants, financial managers, teachers, social workers, retired missionaries, homemakers, businesspersons, doctors, and adoptive parents.

In the early years, our board consisted mainly of our Cebu staff's families and personal friends. Sandy Swanson's brother, Greg, was on the board for several years, as were my parents, Millie and Jerry, brother Dave, sister Elizabeth, and sister-in-law, Nancy. Mitch Ohlendorf's brother Chris served for a couple of years. Those were the days before CSC had financial reserves or proven fundraising success. Some board meetings in those days involved discussing how CSC could manage that month's money transfer to Cebu.

Many prayers went up from those loving friends, who were truly pioneers, like our missionaries. Many board members visited Cebu to offer encouragement to the staff and learn more about the program of caring for homeless children that they were helping support.

CSC board chairpersons included Jerry Healy, Kathy Johnson, John Cherne, Randy Stroman, Kirby Stoll, Dennis Eicher, Heidi Erickson, and Carolyn Anderson.

Volunteers

VOLUNTEERS HAVE BEEN AN IMPORTANT PART of CSC's history. They have donated their talents and time in many capacities and for various lengths of time, both in Minnesota and Cebu.

U.S. Volunteers

Among the most significant volunteer involvement has been the mailing crews that folded and addressed letters and newsletters. The original group met at Constance Free Church when our office was in Ham Lake. When we moved to Cambridge, volunteers were recruited from that area and did their work at First Baptist Church or at the CSC office. When there was a lot of mail, the group numbered up to 25 people. As with other volunteer contributions, the mailers saved CSC thousands of dollars, in this case in mail preparation costs.

Other stateside volunteers have donated time in computer networking, photography, audio/visual production, graphic art, carpentry, moving, banquet planning, performing at banquets, secretarial support, committee work, emceeing and narration, website design, and programing.

Cebu Volunteers

We have also enjoyed labors of love from hundreds of volunteers in Cebu, helping with construction, teaching, arts and crafts, training, recreation, camping, and taking kids on outings.

Tara Perkins, a speech therapist from England, has made frequent trips to Cebu to do training and testing. She has brought technical equipment, computers, and mobility aids for our kids. She makes the most of every minute she is at CSC, and her time in Cebu is a flurry of activity. We were always excited when it was time for Tara to come to Cebu again.

Bob Adams, from Washington State, led a number of construction teams that worked on our garage, washhouse, and infirmary buildings.

Tim and Karen Erickson went every other year to Cebu to do dental work for our kids. This amounted to thousands of dollars in savings for CSC and, of course, quality dental care from loving people. Part of providing residential care to our kids was getting them into the infirmary. This sometimes meant doing some sweet talking or even chasing, or recruiting someone else to do the chasing!

When the Ericksons retired from dental duty at CSC, they found a replacement in **Matt Struve**, a dentist from Lindstrom, Minnesota, who attended the same church as Tim and Karen's son and daughter-in-law. He is also an excellent dentist and very kind and loving to the kids. Tim and Karen, and Matt and his wife, **Jamie**, worked long hours every day and evening when they were at CSC so they could see every child.

Several times we had volunteers from Denmark who helped in our school, doing tutoring or special activities with the students. They were sent from the Rise Above Foundation, run by our friends **Flemming and Elisabet Hansen**, who recruited and provided housing for the volunteers.

Our Fabulous Workers

WE HAVE EMPLOYED HUNDREDS of talented and dedicated Filipino workers to minister to our kids in a variety of ways. Our childcare workers, cooks, cleaners, and house parents have the most hands-on impact with the children on a daily basis.

House Parents

House parents serve as substitute parents for the kids in each house, providing spiritual guidance, discipline, and lots of love and affection. They also manage the workers in their home, making schedules and monitoring their performance. I have always felt that our house parents have the most difficult jobs at CSC, living right with the children and being totally immersed in their lives and problems. In spite of that, we have not had significant turnover with our house parents over the years.

Romulo and Myrna Alejado were friends of ours from Central Free Church whom we hired to be our Eicher Home house parents in 1995.

Romulo got sick with liver cancer and died in August of 1996. Myrna stayed on at the Eicher Home until 1997, when she transferred to the Children of Hope School and helped out in the preschool department until she retired in 2011.

Carlo and Elma Paña. As was the case with several of our house fathers, Carlo was a pastor before working at CSC. Elma was very good at teaching the kids songs and developing in them a love for singing and for Jesus. She was an excellent story teller. They started as house parents in Sun Valley before the new houses were opened in 1992. They transferred to Banawa and worked with CSC until 2001. Sadly, Carlo and Elma both died of Covid in 2021.

Gloria and Manny Deliña were house parents in the Cherne Home when it was still in Sun Valley, from 1986 to 1987. They continued on at CSC in different capacities, and both ended their work in 1997.

Jun and Becky Pellejera were house parents in the Cherne Home from 1999 until 2001, when Becky died suddenly. Jun transferred to the newly opened Teen Home (now Johnson Home) and was the house father there until 2004.

Bernie and Grace Masong were the Cherne Home house parents from 2001 to 2003.

Dondon and Ivy Enriquez had been working in church outreach in Bulacao, where CSC got started. They have been the Eicher Home house parents since 2010.

Pureza and Tarex Puncol became the Cherne Home house parents in 2003. Pureza had been working as a childcare leader for 16 years before becoming house mother at Cherne. Tarex was a pastor before joining CSC.

Patrick and Lourdes Ronquillo have the longest tenure of our house parents, having served since 1997. They started in the Eicher Home and moved to the Duterte Home when it opened. Before joining CSC, they worked at a children's home in Manila.

Sandy Swanson and **Mitch and Ruth Ohlendorf** also had stints as house parents during their years of service.

Childcare Workers

Our childcare workers have served the children well over the years, assisting house parents in supervising kids in the home. They have always worked on a shift basis, including overnight shifts in the nurseries. They feed the children, supervise them on the playground, dispense medicine, feed the babies and serve food in the homes, enforce house rules, and perform many other duties in caring for our children.

Some childcare workers have been with us for as long as 40 years, most of our history. CSC's reputation as a place of excellence in caring for children starts with our hands-on childcare workers. They have a lot of positive influence on the children, and there is significant bonding that goes on between them. Many tears are shed when our kids leave for adoption, and there is great happiness when a former resident comes back for a visit.

Some of our workers live in Bulacao because that is where we started the ministry. When we moved to Banawa in 1992, they all continued, commuting the 10 miles to their new work place. Most of our childcare workers had not had formal education or experience in childcare, so they have learned it through CSC's training. Our most skilled childcare workers are promoted to leaders, with additional responsibilities, especially reporting to the house parents, dispensing medicines, and settling disputes among the kids when the house parents are not around.

One duty of our childcare workers has been caring for kids when they are isolated in our infirmary or admitted to the hospital. We assign our best workers to those shifts. It can be stressful when the kids are really sick. In the Philippines, "watchers," as they are called, are responsible in the hospital for bathing and changing a child, watching the IV container to make sure it doesn't run out, monitoring and recording food and liquid intake, and keeping a record of their temperatures and reporting to the medical staff any changes. It can be a big responsibility, especially if the child is very sick or recovering from a major surgery.

Visitors to CSC often comment on the loving nature of our childcare workers and how diligent and hard-working they are. What they don't know is that most of our workers have children of their own. After a long shift at CSC, they return home to cook, clean, wash clothes, and parent their own kids. One difficulty they, and CSC, face is that we have different standards for behavior, cleanliness, and discipline than what our workers might have in their homes. They must shift their thinking and reacting when on duty at CSC.

Household Workers

Our household workers should be considered among the unsung heroes of CSC for their tiring labor behind the scenes every day, rain or shine. They clean, cook, and wash clothes—and diapers. Our kids live in clean homes, eat nutritious food, and have clean clothes to wear every day. When they get up on school days, the aunties have their school uniforms cleaned and ready to go in their rooms. During a power outage, all washing must be done by hand. Our workers do this, and everything, without complaint.

Cooks show their love to CSC kids by preparing tasty and nutritious meals three times a day. We usually have two shifts of cooks in each house. The first shift starts early in the morning with preparations for breakfast, then lunch. The second shift starts around lunch time with serving and cleanup, followed by supper preparations. Between meals the kids get snacks. Sometimes house mothers pitch in with the cooking, especially if there are visitors or a birthday party.

A highlight of every mealtime is when the kids, after one gives the meal prayer, say in unison, "Thank you Jesus. Thank you Aunties and Uncles. Thank you Auntie Helen (or whoever was the cook for that meal)."

Menus at CSC usually start with rice. Rice, rice, rice, almost every meal, every day. We go through 12 sacks of rice—600 pounds—every month. Our cooks prepare a lot of seafood, as well as stir fries, pork and chicken, noodles, spaghetti, Chinese noodle dishes, Filipino eggrolls (lumpia), and native fruits like mangoes, papaya, bananas, and watermelon.

Maintenance and Security

Keeping our facilities clean and safe and our equipment and vehicles running properly is vitally important. Until the 1990s, CSC employees guarded our homes and property around the clock. Mateo Martinez was one of our first guards.

Later, CSC began hiring professional guards through an agency. Security is a big expense but is essential. We have experienced theft by intruders and people trying to sneak into our compound during the night. Our Banawa compound is on a semi-isolated road that is not brightly lit. Since building our homes there we have always provided transportation down the hill to workers who go off duty after dark. And all persons and vehicles wanting to enter our property must pass a security check.

We wish we did not have to implement so many security procedures or have armed guards around our property 24/7. It detracts from the homey, family atmosphere we would like to provide. But we have had to face the realities of the place where we live and work.

U.S. staff have lived in different communities over the years. Now, most of them live in gated, limited-access neighborhoods, for security reasons. Our first home in Saint Jude Acres in Bulacao was very exposed, and we had frequent thefts of property, sometimes in broad daylight. So whether we like it or not, security is important to protect our children, staff, and property.

Our maintenance men keep the grounds clean, along with electric fans, roofs, ceilings, and driveways. Our grounds always look good and are impressive to visitors. Most important, cleaning and maintaining our buildings keeps them safe for the children and insures that our facilities will last a long time. We have always tried to be good stewards of the property we have been given.

Office Workers

Clerical and administrative tasks are important to our daily operations. Clerical staff type and file reports and submit required paperwork to government agencies: the Department of Labor, Social Security, the Security and Exchange Commission, the Department of Foreign Affairs, the Bureau of Immigration, the Land Transportation Office, and others. Staff also handle papers and transactions for banking, insurance, and rent. They receive payments and issue receipts, and receive and send mail and parcels.

Because our office workers are the primary contact with our other staff and our vendors, they are important for CSC's efficient and friendly operations. **Layla Tabornal, Dada Labadan,** and **Vanessa Prieto** have worked as administrative assistants in our office. **Angie Gingoyan** became our cashier and payroll clerk in 2013. **Maribel Rizon** worked for several years with our blind resident, Arlene Lozada, helping get her to and from school and helping her with her school work. After that Maribel moved to our financial office, handling our accounts payable.

Managing CSC's funds with integrity is something we have always taken very seriously. Financial accountability has been maintained with excellent staff. For many years, **Mitch Ohlendorf** was our financial director. He helped establish policies and procedures to protect our money. But we have also had a number of Filipinos managing finances for CSC.

Joanna Talaid Aballe worked in our financial office from 1991 to 2013. For several of those years she was our office manager. A CPA and a lawyer, Joanna was extremely valuable to CSC. She prepared financial statements, submitted reports to our stateside office, and worked with the financial director on designing and implementing policies for all financial matters. As a lawyer, she also prepared legal documents for court cases involving our kids, such as abandonment hearings. Joanna was a bright, talented, and hard-working member of our team, and a strong Christian who led by example. She left CSC in 2013 to work with an NGO in child welfare. It was a big blow to lose her.

Ging Asilom started her career at CSC as our cashier. In those days we did a cash payroll every week for our daily wage workers. So we kept a lot of cash on hand, and Ging had to count it and put in envelopes for the workers every Friday. Later we instituted a new system whereby our employees are all paid via ATMs. Eventually Ging was promoted to financial director, which entails doing all the banking and submitting financial reports regarding CSC's total budget. Ging makes detailed and accurate reports, is cautious with the Lord's money that is entrusted to us, and is a good team member.

CSC's history of integrity in managing our money is a tribute to strong and unwavering financial policies, to a system of checks and balances initiated by our staff in coordination with our stateside board, and to the people of integrity who make financial decisions. I take no credit for any of this. Those things were not my strengths, so I was always happy to have people like Joanna Aballe, Ging Asilom, and Mitch Ohlendorf to handle those tasks.

Human Resources

In 2017, HR became a CSC department, though we had been hiring employees and managing their performance, compensation, and benefits since 1980. HR tasks were being done by the financial office as well as individual departments. **Jake Schulz,** who served as deputy field director from 2016 to 2017, helped initiate HR as an official department, with the responsibility of hiring and terminating employees, managing salaries and benefits, overseeing staff and worker development, and administering discipline for workers who violate rules and regulations. With more than 120 employees, HR had become a necessary part of CSC's ministry. **Eldie Allocod** became our first HR director in 2017.

Social Workers

Social work is what we are all about at CSC. We are a social welfare institution doing case management for a group of dependent children. We're required to be licensed and accredited by the Department of Social Welfare and Development, and to have a certain number of licensed social workers based on our number of cases.

Our social workers helped establish CSC with the governing authorities and remain in good standing by the quality of reports we submit to them. Our social workers' main tasks are gatekeeping, reporting, and case management. They handle referrals from government social welfare agencies, set up treatment plans for each child admitted, write case study reports, handle all legal matters and necessary documents, and see that the appropriate services are being performed and documented.

Because we are a pre-adoptive organization, we need to submit paperwork to the government concerning the legal, social, medical, and emotional preparedness of our kids to be adopted. So our social workers write a lot! And the nature of the system means they often have to re-write what they have already done to satisfy the bureaucracy.

Consider a typical case. The social worker files an intake report that outlines the circumstances of a child being referred to us. This report goes to the social work director, who might ask for revisions or additional information. Next it goes to the field director, who considers whether the referred child is within the category we are licensed to care for, as well as financial issues relating to the child's ongoing care. He might ask for additional revisions to the intake report. Then a referral meeting is called with appropriate staff: medical, counseling, home life, school (if the child is school-age), therapy, finance, and, of course, social work. This panel might have questions for our social worker handling the case, which might necessitate finding out more information about the child's background or current functioning, and then rewriting the intake report again.

If the child is admitted, CSC's departments go to work to meet his needs. He is assessed by the school principal to determine where he should be placed. A therapy schedule is planned if he needs it. Eventually, he will need psychological tests by an outside psychometrician. The nurses will bring him to the appropriate doctor(s) and will order a battery of lab tests. One of our counselors will begin seeing him regularly to see how he is processing all that has happened to him before and since coming to CSC.

Our Home Life team will start writing developmental reports, with help from the house parents. Paperwork from these tests and sessions will eventually pass to the social worker so she can write the case study report that will be the basis of deciding whether the child will be adopted. The case study will go through internal screening with the program director and field director. Again, this report could get sent back for changes. Then it goes to the regional office of the DSWD for review. It could, and often does, come back from there for more revisions. Then it goes to the national office of DSWD in Manila for their scrutiny. Almost always, it comes back to us for another re-write, in spite of all the eyes that have already looked at it. Finally, it goes to the Inter Country Adoption Board's social worker for review. And, you guessed it, it might come back for additional changes. Once it passes that persons' desk, the child is scheduled for matching.

An inexperienced social worker might consider this the end of the process, but we have learned better. The placement committee could also ask for clarification and changes to the child study document. Once that is done to their satisfaction and the matching is finished, it goes to the ICAB board for final approval. But they can and often do ask for changes, or they might suspend the placement altogether for reasons that may or may not be explained to us.

Our social workers need to develop thick skins and lots of determination to keep going in the face of this governmental juggernaut. We often ask ourselves whether the bureaucracy is a good thing that helps protect a child's best interests, or is it mostly a jungle that contributes to frustration and unnecessary delays for a child's eventual placement?

Our place in the jungle is not to question or rebel against the system but to do our part as best we can. I am thankful beyond words for our social workers, who hang in there and suppress their irritation over the process and the picking apart of their work by people who never even met the child being presented nor had any experience in the pre-adoptive case management work we do.

Our first social worker was **Carmelita Baya,** who worked for CSC for more than 33 years. She was a dedicated, knowledgeable, persistent advocate for our kids. If ever there was a person who went into a field of endeavor for which she was well fitted, it was Carmelita. She stood up to governmental desk jockeys, social workers, hospital personnel, police, abusers, whoever stood in the way of her doing the best for her client child. Someone described her as "small but terrible," the terrible part meaning fearless, devoted, and tenacious. But she could also be personable, gracious, and encouraging. In short, she was an amazing social worker and helped establish us as a respected and successful agency. I cannot count the times she and I had contentious meetings with people whom we felt were standing in the way of our child's best interests being served. Those meetings were never fun, but I always marveled at Carmelita's moxie, poise, and emotional endurance. Untold numbers of CSC kids have a loving family today because of her good work.

On occasion, Carmelita headed up CSC's relief efforts following typhoons or fires. We never solicited aid for victims, but well-meaning CSC supporters often heard about a disaster somewhere near us and donated money to help. So we became reluctant relief workers. Carmelita did a great job analyzing who among our contacts needed help and devising a distribution plan that made sense for CSC to tackle.

Klaris Cabansal was hired in 2016, when Carmelita retired. Klaris came to us from an agency that worked with deaf clients in Bohol and Leyte. She was a huge help in our transitioning to new ways of handling referrals and doing case management, in line with the government's shifting priorities, policies, and standards. She helped us through a major re-accreditation process with the DSWD in 2018.

Klaris brought a wealth of talent to CSC in organization and documentation, and assumed the work of matching our children for inter-country adoption as I was moving towards retirement. She reorganized the social work department around new policies and procedures, and planned and led the move of the social work office from Sun Valley to our new Gleddie Building in Banawa in 2019. In 2020 she was promoted to program director, and now supervises all the programs and services that CSC provides to the children we take in.

Cris Secuya started working at CSC in 2005, after having served with World Vision as a social worker. Cris is well-organized, thoughtful, and compassionate. Since he did not have a background in pre-adoptive case management, he had to learn the kind of issues and challenges our social workers face. Cris is very involved in his church, the Minglanilla Assembly of God, where he has worked with youth and young adults. His sister, Veronica, is one of our most experienced childcare leaders. They were recommended to us by Pastor Lucas, who was their pastor for several years.

Loida Ares was another valuable social worker in the 1990s who helped us establish our reputation for quality in case management and documentation. **Ruth Ohlendorf** did a great job establishing our outreach program, delivering services to former CSC residents who returned to their birth families but needed help with education and medical care.

Counselors

CSC has become increasingly effective as we professionalized our counseling department. Our first official counselor was **Inday Lequigan**, who started at CSC when we opened the Children of Hope School. Her office was in the school, and she served mainly as a guidance counselor, handling behavioral matters. Her counseling was mostly in response to how such matters affected a student's ability to learn. Later Inday moved to the Shelter, where she had clinical counseling sessions with many of our older children. She explored their past experiences, family relationships, and feelings about what had happened to them before and after coming to live at CSC.

Eventually we hired an additional counselor who handled the boys while Inday worked with the girls. Since then we have always had two counselors. But other people participate in counseling our children, too. The house parents, as substitute parental models, handle many issues in the homes that require interventions and spiritual counseling.

Our counselors have had a big role in helping our kids prepare for the future by dealing with their past. Their reports are used to help evaluate a child's readiness for adoptive placement. Counselors have many opportunities to share Christ with kids struggling with anger and hatred over things that happened to them. Counselors emphasize the need for forgiveness and for having Jesus in their lives and to trust Him for their future.

From 2011 to 2019, **Lindsay Hoeft Abong** instituted changes and improvements in the counseling department. Our counselors under Lindsay during those years included **Laarni Gersua, Eric Aballana,** and **Meravic Nalang,** as well as **Eldie Allocod,** who counseled the boys from 2010 to 2017.

In 2020, as CSC responded to the retirements of Sandy Swanson and Carmelita Baya and prepared for the departure of Lindsay Abong and Marlys and my retirements, some reorganization was made. We organized our programs and services under Program Director Klaris Cabansal. We also added a position of director of child welfare services, filled by **Eunice Saavedra.** She supervises the medical and therapy departments, which had been led by Marlys, and the counseling office, which had been overseen by Lindsay. Eunice started at CSC as our behavioral specialist. She is bright, talented, and flexible—able to handle any challenge put before her.

During the several years preceding my retirement, CSC made significant strides in developing Filipinos to lead the ministry. In the earlier days, much of the leadership was in the hands of U.S. staff. In time, all the major leadership positions at CSC were assumed by Filipinos. We were slow to make that transition, and I regret not having promoted people like Eldie, Ging, Klaris, Eunice, Jinkee, and Jerry sooner. This includes other talented people: Joanna Talaid Aballe and Cris Tabra. We were learning on the job about how to run a ministry that was also a social welfare organization and a multi-million-peso business. We made mistakes along the way, and I feel like this was one of them. But eventually we started recognizing the amazing talents of people within our employ, and putting them in positions of leadership.

Visitors

VISITORS FLOCKED TO CSC FROM THE VERY BEGINNING. Most have been a blessing to the staff and children. Some came to learn. Some brought gifts. Some were former residents who came to reconnect. Some were CSC supporters who wanted to see the work for themselves. Some were friends or family of staff or representatives from the stateside board or office. Although some visitors presented challenges and stretched our patience, we tried our best to give all a warm welcome. Filipinos are gracious, friendly, and welcoming people, so we learned a lot about hospitality from them. They always helped us make sure our visitors and guests were treated like kings and queens.

Visitors fall into several categories: "once or twice" visitors, recurring guests, adoptive families, and teams. Some "one timers" came from Manila or other parts of the Philippines. We also had international visitors from Hong Kong, Australia, New Zealand, Singapore, Taiwan, China, Japan, South Korea, India, Malaysia, Canada, the United States, England, Scotland, France, Germany, Spain, Germany, Belgium, the Netherlands, Norway, Finland, Sweden, Italy, Switzerland, and Denmark. Although a small facility, CSC is known and appreciated around the world.

Some of these people were adoptive parents coming for their child(ren) or were representatives from adoption agencies in the countries where our children went. Some were family members of staff. Others had heard about CSC or discovered us online and wanted to see what we were all about.

Hosting visitors was often as simple as showing them around CSC, but might also have included conducting city tours; serving them meals; providing or finding lodging; helping them with ongoing transportation or side trips to other parts of Cebu or neighboring islands; picking them up or delivering them to the airport, bus station, or boat dock; getting medical help when they got sick or sunburned, stung by sea urchins, suffered sunstroke or various tropical bugs; and many other services and courtesies.

We had some interesting and mysterious visitors over the years. One guy who said he was from the U.S. Embassy in Manila asked us lots of questions and answered our queries so vaguely that we were sure he was not who he said he was. We decided that he was with the CIA. People have shown up at our gate unannounced, wanting to have someone show them around. For security purposes we have to be careful with such people, even if they name-drop someone on our staff.

Most visitors are interested in CSC, asking questions and offering compliments about our work. Some, however, feel a need to lecture us about what they've seen on trips to other countries. One guy talked about Haiti so much we were thrilled when his visit was over! And although most visitors are gracious and appreciative, some have been difficult and demanding.

At times we've wondered whether the investment of time and effort in hosting visitors was worth it. But there have been times we were unknowingly entertaining a future donor during those visits. Some ended up getting excited about the ministry and made significant contributions after seeing our place and interacting with staff, workers, and kids. Some didn't, but we felt like we were educating them about God's Kingdom work and what can be accomplished with faith, trust, and dedication. And for the most part, we enjoy "showing off" CSC because most people understand how God has made great things happen for our ministry. This is especially true when hosting supporters of CSC, who often say how blessed they are to see first-hand what they had been hearing and praying about.

Filipinos also enjoy seeing CSC. Local people often comment that CSC is the best-kept secret in Cebu. They've never heard about us and are amazed that such an impressive place exists right under their noses. One well-to-do doctor commented that our Children of Hope School was nicer than where he or his children had studied. "Can I send my kids here?" he asked. My answer could have been, "Yes you can, if you abandon or surrender them!"

For some of our visitors, it seems incongruous that such beautiful, well-maintained, and generously equipped facilities are for the exclusive use of orphans, many of whom have special needs. Perhaps they are acquainted with orphanages, children's homes, or special needs schools that don't have nice facilities or equipment, or are overcrowded and undermaintained. In the Philippines, there is often a "you get what you pay for" reality in terms of housing and education. But our kids, who can pay nothing, are living in beautiful houses and attending a showcase school with first-rate facilities and equipment. My response to those who are confused by this inverted value system is that we believe our children deserve the very best we can offer, not the least.

Marlys was the guest relations person at CSC, but everyone on the staff has an important role in showing people around and taking good care of them. Many different people drive to and from the airport, often late at night or early morning. For groups we often need two or more vehicles, one for passengers and additional vans or jeeps for luggage. Among our Filipino employees, the ones who've made the most airport runs are Jerry Salgo, Edwin Martinez, Juanito Parnes, Patrick Ronquillo, and Ondoy Ayop.

It's always important to get to the airport on time, which is difficult when traffic is heavy or there are stops for accidents, road repair, or inexplicable detours. Often those trips are hurried and tense. Sometimes visitors have tight layovers in Manila or other places, so missing their flight in Cebu might cause huge problems for the rest of their trip.

One evening we were having supper in our home with Greg Swanson, Sandy's brother, who was supposed to leave later that night for Manila and, eventually, the U.S. We got a call during dessert that his flight had been canceled and he would need to get to the airport right away to get an alternate flight that would allow him to make his connection. Greg said his good-byes, and we hopped in my car and headed for the Mactan Airport. It was a wild and stressful ride where more was risked than should have been, especially on the bridge, where traffic was backed up and tempers were running hot. I will confess that, at one point, when I noticed that the car ahead of us was stopped with engine trouble, I pulled onto the sidewalk in what Greg has referred to as a "lunatic right turn" to pass the stalled vehicle. We arrived at the airport several minutes late, but they hustled Greg through ticketing and security and onto the plane that had been waiting just for him. He collapsed in his seat, avoiding the glances of his fellow passengers, who weren't happy with the delay.

Former Residents

Visits from former residents have been a great blessing to our staff and workers, and to the former residents themselves. We always roll out the red carpet for them and, when necessary, drop what we are doing to show them how glad we are to see them.

One CSC banquet included a video of reunions with former residents, which we described as "leaving the light on." We want former residents and their families to know that, though they have new homes in places far away, and though they might not have any family in the Philippines, CSC is there for them. We are their primary link with the place of their birth, and we remember them fondly.

Recurring Visitors

Marv Hadenfeldt, a college friend of mine, lives in Anchorage, Alaska, and works as an educational aide in an elementary school. Since 2005 he has visited Cebu every March to spend a week at CSC. An accomplished puppeteer, he and his sidekick, Lokoy, entertain the CSC kids and provide many hours of laughter and mirth. At our 40th anniversary celebration in 2019, Marv and Lokoy helped me with a News/Fake News game. Marv is also a skilled piano player who was a member of the 50s singing group I was a part of at Bethel College, Priest and the Scribes.

We met **Marylou Eshelman,** an adoption worker at Wide Horizons in Massachusetts, when one of our kids was adopted by a WH family, and a friendship was started that lasted for decades. She visited CSC whenever she was in the Philippines representing her agency. We learned so much from her about adoption from the side of families and receiving agencies. Marylou is a person of integrity who works for children's best interests.

Once Marylou was in Cebu at the same time that I was in Manila matching some of our kids for adoption. She had brought a donation to CSC from Wide Horizons, but she waited to give it until I returned from Manila so there wouldn't be any sense of obligation to match with one of her WH families, or for there to be any appearance of impropriety. I always appreciated her integrity and knowledge of inter-country adoption. I was a visitor in the Eshelman home in Boston several times, and she organized get-togethers with families who had adopted our children.

Dennis and Sharon Eicher visited CSC many times, often bringing along friends and fellow parishioners. Dennis was a CSC board member, and he and Sharon adopted three brothers from CSC in 1989. They also adopted two children, now adults, from Hong Kong.

The Eichers were always encouraging to the CSC staff, and we looked forward to their almost yearly visits and the new people we met through them. Dennis and Sharon are generous supporters of CSC and other charities, such as the Philippine Society for Orphan Disorders, an organization concerned with the needs of individuals with rare diseases. They have also been a huge blessing to people throughout the Philippines who suffer from osteogenesis imperfecta (brittle bone disease).

The Eichers were generous to our family, treating us to stay with them at the Plantation Bay beach resort when they visited Cebu and bringing us and the rest of the staff out to dinner at their favorite restaurants. They always sponsored a big dinner at the Shelter for the kids and staff featuring lechon (roast pig) and other Cebu delicacies. Sometimes, when they brought friends from Minnesota, we hired a Philippine dance troupe to entertain everyone.

The Eichers have been a big influence on Marlys and me, with their lives of generosity and other-centeredness and the choices they've made to share what they have to help the less fortunate. They have chosen a lifestyle of giving that has blessed many people around the world. CSC has benefited greatly from their generosity and love.

Howard and Marilynn Plucar served CSC by facilitating seminars and retreats for our staff and workers. They worked for the Evangelical Free Church (Reach Global) Mission, traveling to Asia to minister to EFC missionaries, and have visited CSC often. They lived in Cebu for several years.

The Plucars helped us realize the importance of what we do and the need for spiritual rest and refreshment. Howard played Santa for the CSC kids several times and was a big hit. One year we had Santa arrive on a carriage the staff had decorated. The horse got spooked when the kids started yelling and took off across the lawn. The kids laughed and thought it was part of the show, but we were pretty worried until the horse calmed down and the gifts could be unloaded. Another time Santa was exposed as a fake by a detective and the police came, handcuffed him, and led him away. Luckily the real Santa arrived shortly thereafter with the gifts. Howard always played his role masterfully.

Sherri Stumpf learned about CSC at Constance Free Church, where she was a member. She went to Cebu on a team from Constance and fell in love with the ministry. She always brought gifts when she visited and even "adopted" a family in the community, helping several of them go to school. She always had a gift for our daughter Jenny, too.

Jim Chalmers is a brother of Dan, the benefactor who, with his wife Carla, launched our Children of Hope School. Jim has donated medical and other equipment to CSC. He recruits nurses from Cebu to work in Minnesota and other places. His trips to Cebu often include visits to CSC, and he has brought clients and colleagues with him. Jim is well known and respected within the Filipino community in the Twin Cities.

Ken and Isabel Morrison live in Hong Kong and attend the Union Church. Ken is originally from Scotland. Through the church they learned about CSC and helped in bringing some of our staff to Hong Kong to attend Walk to Emmaus retreats. Union Church made a large contribution to our school building project. Ken and Isabel had a lot to do with that gift and have visited CSC several times. Ken performed for the CSC family with the

Trash Band on the Flag Stage, singing "Jumping Jack Flash" in his Scottish attire. He spoke at our 1998 CSC banquet.

Teams

Central Baptist Touch a Life teams have gone to Cebu every other year since 2002 to do various projects: landscaping, painting, wallpapering, and building a conference room and carport at the CSC office. Since 2006 Central teams have run an off-site camp for our kids, involving crafts, singing, Bible lessons, games, swimming, and good food.

Many of the Central teams were led by Ben Baltes, a close friend of Marlys and me and the Ohlendorfs. Along with Ben, several Centralites who joined these teams went many times to Cebu: Alice Magnuson, Sharon Nelson, Todd Erickson, Mark Kulla, and Chuck Sorlie. In all, 46 people from Central were a part of a team.

Chuck Sorlie did much of the planning for activities with the children, and was a rousing song leader and inspirational Bible teacher. His energy was boundless! The teams had a favorite game where the kids twirled around on a baseball bat, then ran and tagged off to the next in line. They never tired of watching video of dizzy kids running and falling over. The camps, run by Central teams and reinforced with CSC staff and workers, were a lot of fun for everyone and provided the kids a chance to get off site and interact with different people while learning about God in new and exciting ways. The teams were well-organized and brought craft projects, games, wacky songs, and money to buy food, snacks, and drinks. Mitch Ohlendorf, with help from Jerry Salgo and others on the staff, did a lot of the planning from our end.

Several Central teams took side trips after the camp ended, meeting other missionaries their church supported and seeing the sights in Bohol, Leyte, and Corregidor, as well as doing some whale-watching in southern Cebu. They have made presentations in various churches, helping spread good will for CSC. One team member, Sid Teske, an accomplished clown, performed in area schools. The teams often sponsored our kids on an outing to the beach or water park. In 2020, the Central team trip had to be canceled due to the Covid virus, and the children were very disappointed.

For me personally, I was encouraged that my home church thought enough of our ministry to invest in these people coming over every other year. The kids were able to go off site to experience things they would never have had the opportunity to do otherwise. Jesus Christ was presented in new and creative ways by new people. And the fun that the kids had will, for many of them, be remembered for lifetimes.

The **North Isanti Baptist** team, which went to Cebu in 1996, was the largest we ever hosted, with 28 participants. They were truly a work team, doing projects around the grounds, including the construction of a huge rock wall on which we adorned our flag display. The flags that fly there represent the countries where CSC kids have been adopted. Huge rocks were used for the wall, and we were amazed at the strength and endurance of the team members, especially Joyce Greenberg.

Another large team from Cambridge, this one from **First Baptist Church**, also went to CSC to do a variety of projects and activities with the kids. The FBC team included high schoolers and adults, and they taught the kids lots of songs and games.

A team from **Berean Baptist** in Burnsville, Minnesota, led by my Bethel buddy Greg Dirnberger, taught our kids a musical written by one of their team members, entitled Prophets, Parables and Praise. Kids from Berean had performed the play in their church, so they were experienced in producing it when they got to Cebu. It was a lot of fun for everyone.

Special Friends

Marilyn Manuel has worked in child welfare in the Philippines since the mid-1970s. I met her when she was working for the government as a specialist in the Bureau of Child Welfare in Manila. Marlys and I had a discouraging meeting with her boss, Mrs. Eufemio, who was very negative about us starting a children's home in Cebu. We left that meeting with broken spirits because we had hoped the Social Welfare Department would embrace what we were planning and be our partners. Our exit from her bosses office was noted by Marilyn, who called us over and talked with us for a few minutes. Another worker there was **Lyra del Castillo**. They tried to encourage us, telling us "that is just her way" and not to be put off.

Thus started a 40-year friendship with those two women. I learned so much about child welfare and adoption from them. They were generous with their knowledge and were always advocates for CSC in Manila. In the mid-1980s we served together on the National Task Force on Child Care and Placement, and saw each other often at various agencies in Manila. Marilyn worked for Kaisahang Buhay Foundation, affiliated with Holt International, which used to do many adoptions from the Philippines. Lyra worked for an international adoption agency that had an office in the Philippines and, later, as a professor of social work at the prestigious University of the Philippines. Both women served on the Philippine Inter-Country Adoption Board, the central authority for all international adoptions of Filipino children. These bright and dedicated women showed me that you can be highly professional in your work and still have a heart of compassion and kindness for the children you are serving. Their careers were a testimony to that and a great influence on me and CSC.

Minnie Dacanay was another child welfare professional who worked in Manila and took CSC under her wing. She understood adoption from both sides of the ocean, having worked in Eugene, Oregon, with Holt. She was passionate but knew how to work within the Philippines system. Many times she "talked me down" from being confrontational with government adoption agencies, regular sources of frustration, and gave me advice on how to deal with those problems in a better way. Minnie's Christian faith was always evident in my dealings with her, and she understood our convictions about the kind of families we wanted for our children.

Lourdes Balanon was the head of inter-country adoption in the Philippines for many years, starting in the early 1980s. She had a distinguished career in the Department of Social Welfare and Development, where she retired as an undersecretary. Lourdes visited Minnesota once when Marlys and I were on furlough. She came to Cebu several times to meet with us concerning complicated adoption cases involving our children and was consistently a strong advocate for them.

Missionary Friends

From our earliest days in Cebu, we benefited from the friendship of other missionaries. Although most of them were involved in ministries very different from ours, we were able to receive and share advice on how to live in the Philippines, as well as gain insights into Philippine culture.

The Baptist General Conference Mission operated a guest home in Cebu for their missionaries and other guests. CSC visitors often stayed there, so we got to know the managers who lived there: couples who usually stayed one or two years. Many visited the Shelter, and several served as Santa Claus at CSC Christmas parties.

Ray and Phyllis Burke were guest house managers three different times. They are from Olympia, Washington, and were very interested in our work. When the Corpus Christi gang went to the beach, they often came along, helping supervise the kids in the water or serving food. Ray loved to take pictures, and, even in the day of cameras with film, shot hundreds of pictures. Ray and Phyllis volunteered at CSC for a couple months in 1990, and we became good friends with them.

Two couples who served the Evangelical Free Church as managers of their mission home in Guadalupe Heights, Cebu City, became close to us, and both ended up having significant impact on our work.

George and Virginia Foutz, from the Seattle area, went to Cebu in 1980. After visiting the Shelter and getting to know us and the children, they expressed an interest in adopting three of the older children. Several months and a host of miracles later, this adoption did occur.

George was an old Navy man and had many stories about his time on Navy ships. One day the CSC gang was going to the beach, and the Foutzes went along, as they often did. George found an old rowboat and headed out for a ride. After a while he started heading in a direction that wasn't where he wanted to go, and, in spite of furious rowing, he couldn't get turned around, due to a strong undertow. We all laughed as the old salty seadog headed out to sea. He came back to shore way down the beach and walked back sheepishly as some of the staff sang "Anchors Aweigh."

George was the first Santa Claus for the CSC kids in Bulacao. The tattoo on his arm gave him away to most of the them, but one little girl wanted to be sure so she reached up and pulled his beard down and said, "Yeah, its Lolo George."

Warren and Marie Hagfors went to Cebu in 1985 to manage the Free Church Mission Home. Warren had a background in computers and worked for many years for Minnegasco, the Twin Cities gas company. Marie was skilled at crafts and cross-stitched many pictures that are displayed in our homes. The Hagfors were frequent visitors and became known as Lolo (grandpa) Warren and Lola (grandma) Marie.

Warren had a big impact on CSC by teaching me about computers. The Hagfors gave CSC a portable Compaq computer, and I learned to do word processing and basic programing, which served the ministry well in the years to come. Warren was a patient teacher, and he and Marie were good friends to us.

When they returned to Minnesota, Warren served on the board of directors. In 1990 the Hagfors did a short-term stint with CSC. Warren helped out in the office while Marie held babies. The Hagfors stayed with Marlys and me in our Happy Valley home.

One night we got a call from the house parents of the Cherne Home (then in Sun Valley) that there was a big fire nearby. Warren and I got in the car to drive the short distance to the Cherne Home but discovered that the road was closed for fire trucks. We brought the car back to my house and headed out on foot. As we ran down the street we heard explosions from the direction of the Cherne Home. We ran as fast as we could, which wasn't all that fast, and we were huffing and puffing. I worried that if there was an ambulance on the way to the fire, it might stop and attend to us instead of the fire victims!

When we got to the home we helped get the kids and staff loaded into the CSC jeep. The house father, Carlo Paña, was so rattled that he couldn't drive, so Warren got behind the wheel and drove the jeep to the Eicher Home while I helped get valuables out of the home in case the fire spread to where we were. Luckily it didn't, and everyone was safe, though Warren and I were stiff for a few days, recovering from our mad dash.

Years later, the Hagfors' daughter, Pat Hoeft, who had visited them when they were in Cebu City, donated medical laboratory equipment to CSC. Pat is a medical doctor in Willmar, Minnesota, and a long-time CSC supporter. Her daughter, Lindsay, a marriage and family counselor, joined our staff in 2011. Our long and fulfilling relationship with Warren and Marie and their extended family was a source of blessing to CSC and to our family over the years. Warren passed away in 2017 and Marie in 2018.

Rod and Camille Henry were among the best friends we made during our time in Cebu. They went to Cebu in 1982 to work with their denomination's churches. Specifically, Rod was sent to train pastors, none of whom had attended seminary. The Henrys were friendly and outgoing, especially Rod, who has a great sense of humor and who made an instant connection with me and the rest of the staff. We met the Henrys at a missionary get-together and reconnected soon afterward to joke about how little we had enjoyed the meeting.

The Henrys became regular attenders of the Saturday night potlucks at the Bulacao home. It was common to sit around long after eating to tell stories and laugh, and share the progress of our respective ministries and pray for each other. Rod had a humorous and self-effacing way of relating his ministry challenges.

Rod and Camille's two young children, Eric and Tanya, enjoyed playing with the Corpus Christi kids. They all fell in love with one of the babies, Eddie, and began the legal process to adopt him. Eddie was the first baby ever placed as a foster child with us, and came to live at Corpus Christi when he was one day old. He became the first child ever adopted, too, and it was a bittersweet day when the Henrys came to get him, with smiles and tears all around. It was the first of many thousands of tears that were to be shed in the days to come, as much-loved children left with their families.

I traveled with Rod to the province of Zamboanga, on the southern island of Mindanao, to visit one of Rod's pastor trainees. When we arrived in the town of Molave, near where the pastor lived, we found that the local hospital doubled as a hotel. We asked for an air-conditioned room and were surprised how cold it was and were shivering as we prepared for bed. At some point we learned that our room was also the hospital morgue. We were learning lessons about life in the Philippines, though few would provide the years of laughs of that experience in the Molave Morgue Motel.

Rod returned from a furlough in California with plans to write a book about spirit world beliefs in the Philippines. I helped him on this project by editing his manuscripts, giving encouragement and insights, and helping him organize his thoughts. The book, *Filipino Spirit World: A Challenge to the Church,* was published by OMF Literature in 1986.

Wes Hagen was a good friend to us throughout his 13 years in Cebu. A 65-year-old bachelor who volunteered with the Free Church mission, Wes arrived in Cebu in early 1979, just a few months ahead of us. He was a friendly, eccentric guy who loved to eat ice cream and chocolate and serve the EFC missionaries. He was always driving his mission's yellow jeep around Cebu and was a regular visitor to the Corpus Christi home in Bulacao. Wes loved to sing, and it never took much persuading for him to break into his version of "Too-ra-loo-ra-loo-ra" or "Mona Lisa."

When the Bulacao home burned in 1981, the staff and children moved into the home Wes was renting in Happy Valley while our house was being repaired. This was a huge stretch for Wes, who had zero experience with kids and wasn't used to babies crying in his vicinity. He referred to all the kids as "twinks." "Does that twink every stop crying?"

Wes was our friend for many years, even after he left the Philippines for his retirement in Minneapolis. Wes passed away in 2015.

Louise Lynip was an amazing woman who modeled dedication and perseverance in doing work similar to that of CSC in the southern Philippines. Louise was from Rochester, New York, and arrived in the Philippines as a missionary in 1940. When the Japanese invaded the country, Louise escaped into the jungle on the island of Mindanao.

After the war she established an orphanage, and cared for homeless children for 64 years until she passed away in 2006, at the age of 94. She was the founder of Bethany Christian Home and cared for hundreds of children there in the mountains of Talakag, Bukidnon. I had the pleasure of visiting Louise and her staff often, and was captivated by her stories and her dedication to the children of that province. I served on Bethany's board for several years in the 1990s. Louise and I served together on the National Task Force on Child Care and Placement from 1986 to 1990.

Grandma Bertha Holt was a one-time, but memorable, visitor from Eugene, Oregon. Grandma was a pioneer in international adoption and, together with her husband, Harry, founded Holt International Children's Services in 1956. She was inducted into the National Women's Hall of Fame in 2002 and was known around the world. She died in 2000 but was still traveling the world in her 90s, and visited Cebu as a 90-year-old ambassador of adoption.

We had a dinner to honor her when she was in Cebu. She spent a night in our home and visited CSC to see the children. She literally had callouses on her knees from her daily prayer sessions on behalf of children around the world. When Marlys was showing Grandma around our house and they got to the kitchen, she asked if it would be okay to brush her teeth in the kitchen sink. Marlys said sure, so Bertha pulled out her false teeth and a toothbrush and started brushing. What an awesome house guest!

Giving attention to visitors has helped us communicate the central truth of God's goodness to CSC and the children we serve. People have been blessed to hear our story of how God provided the amazing buildings of CSC, as well as the people who do the work and the resources to provide the level of care that we have become known for over the years. It's the story of how God can multiply the loaves and fishes we bring to him and make amazing things happen for many people. And it is good for people to see how He uses simple and even "unqualified" people to do his work. We always tried to tell people that the message of CSC is that God blesses those who bless his little ones.

Thousands of people have joined forces over four decades to make this ministry thrive. They have given time, talent, treasure, encouragement, prayers, advice, knowledge, blood, sweat, and tears to establish and maintain the Children's Shelter of Cebu, and to make it a special place on earth. Some showed their love by writing out a check, saying a prayer with their kids at the breakfast table, telling a friend, serving on the staff, washing clothes, cooking, changing diapers, teaching, balancing books, serving on committees or boards, answering phones, setting banquet tables, folding newsletters, adopting a child, visiting the Shelter or school, being a link in the prayer chain, making a video, or opening up their home to Marlys and me or other staff during our travels.

These people, together with our many supporters, are the village that has surrounded, protected, inspired, and raised our CSC children for these 43 years. They came to us from many walks of life, with various interests and gifts. What unifies them and makes them collectively such an effective village of support is their heart for the children. Some served in Minnesota. Some served in Cebu, some in other places. Some visited. Some pioneered. Some reinforced. All mattered and contributed to the success of this dream that became the amazing reality we call Children's Shelter of Cebu.

A danger of this kind summary of significant people, which relies heavily on my memory, is that someone's contribution to CSC—as a worker, staff member, short-termer, volunteer, or visitor—might be missed. I ask forgiveness for these unintentional omissions. So many different people have had an impact that it is difficult, maybe even foolhardy, to attempt to list them all.

Medical

FOR ALL OF OUR HISTORY our children's medical care has been the largest budget item and the biggest challenge to our staff. The first child we took in, Mary Ann, had medical needs that required surgery in the United States. Kids who followed her presented us with illnesses, diseases, and complications ranging from simple skin diseases to tuberculosis, hepatitis, and major conditions like meningocele, cerebral palsy, and birth deformities.

We have cared for children who were so malnourished that our pediatrician told us they would not live. We have provided hospitalization and surgery for hundreds of kids and thousands of doctors' visits, lab tests, and emergency room admissions.

One reason we've had so many challenging medical situations is that CSC has always been willing to admit children who were sick or in need of medical interventions. In some cases we were the only childcaring agency in Cebu or surrounding islands that would consider admitting a particular child. And we were committed to providing high-quality care no matter the medical challenges a child might face. We have brought children to Manila and even to the U.S. for consultations and surgery.

For years Marlys was the sole medical person at CSC. She established close relationships with doctors and hospital personnel. Her advocacy for our kids saved lives and helped assure the best of care. She trained our house parents and childcare workers to dispense medicines, take temperatures, and perform other basic medical care functions. She made thousands of trips to Cebu Doctors, Chong Hua, Perpetual Succor, Southern Islands, Velez, Miller, Community, Saint Vincent, and Cebu City hospitals, as well as the T.B. Pavilion, the Cebu Skin Clinic, Puericulture Center, and a host of medical laboratories and dental clinics.

After the early months when we all pitched in for hospital duty, Marlys—and eventually her team of nurses, house parents, and childcare workers—brought stool and other specimens to the labs day and night. She spent thousands of hours waiting for doctors in their offices or calling them on the phone. She was on duty 24/7 for the children. She purchased medicines at pharmacies all over the city and solicited donations of medicines, medical equipment, and medical services. She sought second and third opinions and even consulted with doctor friends in the U.S. about especially complicated cases. Because of her interventions on behalf of our children and their respect for her work, many doctors did not charge CSC for consultations, hospital visits, or even surgeries. Marlys negotiated for charge accounts and discounts at hospitals and labs. She accompanied many kids to Manila for their U.S. visa medical examinations and embassy visits, and trained childcare leaders and other staff to do that task.

Once in the 1980s when an epidemic went through our homes, many children needed to be hospitalized at the same time. When a child is hospitalized in Cebu, it is necessary to have a "watcher" stay with that patient to do some things we would expect a nurse to do in the US: check on IV fluid bags, take temperatures, bathe the patient, and purchase needed medicines that the hospital pharmacy might not have. So, for each hospitalized child, three watchers were needed to do eight hour shifts every day.

During that epidemic we had at least a dozen kids in the hospital. We were able to have two or three kids in a room, but we were still way understaffed for all the watchers needed. Marlys called former employees and missionary friends to help us out, and many responded positively. Keith Williams, a Southern Baptist missionary friend, and I had overnight duty with three babies. To say the least, we were not blessed with nursing skills, and we couldn't hold all three at once when they were crying at the same time. Frequent diaper changes were required, and when we ran out of diapers I had to go out of the hospital in search of a pharmacy that was open, leaving poor Keith alone with three crying, wet, and soiled babies. Somehow Keith was busy the next time Marlys called.

In 1996, when Marlys and I were anticipating a furlough, we started looking for a nurse who could join our staff for a year. One day we met a young lady, Rebecca Domingiano, married to a Filipino who was just starting medical school at Cebu Doctors Hospital Medical School. They had recently arrived in Cebu from California. She was an American nurse and could not work in a hospital but was interested in finding a medical job while her husband was studying. The right person at the right time! Rebecca became our nurse not only for our furlough year but for the next four years. She was a huge help to CSC.

Also hired as a nurse in 1996 was Warlita Manlon, who had been working as a childcare leader in our nursery. She worked for CSC for the next 20 years, serving as head nurse until her retirement in 2015. Warlita was more than just a great nurse. Being spiritually mature, she became like a mom to our other nurses and many of our childcare workers, helping them with family problems and sharing the message of God's love.

One reason we could honor our commitment to provide the best medical care for our kids is that we have had excellent doctors in Cebu. Some were trained in the U.S. or other countries. Some medical technology in Cebu might be lacking compared to Western countries, but the quality of doctors compares favorably with any country. We've had several favorite doctors:

Dr. Jesusito Zubiri is a world-class plastic surgeon who has done many cleft lip and palate surgeries for our children. He is a Christian man who has done emergency and cosmetic surgeries on our kids all the years we've been in Cebu. He has never charged CSC a single cent. He's still practicing and recently did an operation on one of our children. His son is also a plastic surgeon who is skilled and generous. Dr. Zubiri is a committed Christian who uses his considerable gifts to change the lives of our kids through cosmetic and restorative surgery. Whether it's surgery to correct a clubfoot, fix a cleft lip or palate, bring healing after a terrible burn, or any of a number of other operations, Dr. Zubiri was ready and willing to help. Sometimes people asked about a child needing plastic surgery or cleft palate repair, if we considered waiting for the surgery and letting the child have the operation when he or she got to the states for adoption. We told them why we didn't wait: We had one of the best surgeons in the world right here in Cebu!

Dr. Doris Obra is a pulmonologist who has seen hundreds of our kids. Upper-respiratory infections are common among our children, as well as tuberculosis. Dr. Obra has diagnosed tuberculosis in many of our kids and some of our workers and has prescribed treatment to get them on the road to recovery and protect other children and workers. Although one of the top doctors in the Philippines, she has never charged CSC. Ever. She has been especially important to us because all our children who are adopted in the U.S. must meet the Center for Disease Control requirement of a chest x-ray, done at St. Lukes Medical Center in Manila. Dr. Obra's medical reports and documentation of treatment in Cebu have been helpful for our kids in the visa process and much appreciated by families who have adopted them.

Dr. Jorge Oñate has been our pediatrician for our entire history. He has seen all our kids for pre-admission check-ups, well-baby checks, routine physicals, and hospital and office visits. He made medical reports used in the adoption process and made referrals when specialists were needed. He is a kind and gentle man who has always had a calming presence when our kids were sick and suffering. We could call him at any hour if there was an emergency.

I will never forget the morning when one of our kids died. Dr. Oñate had stood by us for many years of caring for him, with frequent hospitalizations, sometimes in the emergency room. He was in the room just after the boy passed away and was emotional when he offered us comfort and the assurance that we had done everything possible for him. Dr. Oñate always admired Marlys, Warlita, and the other nurses and workers who brought children with special needs and health challenges to see him or attended those kids in the hospital, and he admired our commitment to offering them the very best care possible in Cebu.

Jorge Oñate has been part of that "best care possible." He has been a solid partner in our ministry for 41 years, and we thank God for bringing this kind, experienced, and talented man into our lives. Dr. Oñate was given a Ronnie Award at our 40th Anniversary celebration for his contributions to the ministry. The award is given in honor of Ronald Duterte, our former CSC president in Cebu who had such a huge impact on our ministry.

Other doctors providing specialized services to our kids have included Melvina Baclayon (gastroenterology), Grace Ediza (pediatrics), Margaret Modequillo (neurology), Peter Paul Segura (ENT), and Leopoldo Jao (orthopedics). All in all, we have used the skills of doctors in 25 specialties. Add to this list the hundreds of technicians, residents, and emergency room doctors whose names we never knew or have forgotten, who examined, treated, comforted, stitched, x-rayed, and prescribed medicines for CSC kids at hospitals all over Cebu City.

We also have great nurses in Cebu, and CSC has been blessed by their contributions to the health of our children. In addition to Warlita and Rebecca, our Medical Department has benefitted from the work of dedicated and talented nurses to serve our children: Sen-Sen Baya, PrengPreng Arcenas, Arlyn Verdeflor, Honeylyn Villar, Angelie Baya, and Jocelyn Baya. When you walk into the nurses' office in our infirmary, you can feel the love that flows from them to the children of CSC. Whether a nurse is examining a child, taking height and weight readings for his or her chart, updating a medical record, giving an immunization, calling doctors or labs for results, or holding a sick baby, the Frankie Wright Infirmary has always been a place that dispenses love and hope along with medical treatment. Many of our kids had never visited a doctor, lab, or hospital before coming to CSC, so it's often a little frightening for them to go to these places. But our nurses helped alleviate those fears with loving smiles, reassuring words, or a hand to hold.

CSC's intervention in the lives of Filipino children has been transformational. I can honestly say that we never once had to deny any CSC child the best medical care possible in the Philippines. They got the best because they deserved the best and because our faithful God and generous donors made the best possible. CSC's medical care has saved many lives, relieved many others of pain or discomfort, provided restorative and plastic surgery, and put hundreds of others on previously uncharted roads to physical well-being. Lots of love has been expressed and received through CSC's medical services.

I will never forget the day when one of our children came home from an extended stay in the hospital. Many CSC aunties and nurses had stayed with him. He had been really sick but had recovered enough to go home, and CSC was home. The van pulled in and went down the driveway towards the Duterte Home. All the kids went running to see him. All the nurses went down from their offices in the Infirmary to greet him, joined by aunties and house parents. The whole CSC family was there, forming a gauntlet for him to walk down on his way to his house. We gave him the best of medical care, and now we were giving him the best of welcomes. There were lots of hugs and tears and smiles. And as we were celebrating, one of the nurses was carrying a sick baby into the van to head to the doctor's office. Such was the cycle of life in the CSC Medical Department.

Many of our children who are now in adoptive families or have families of their own will never know the extent of the medical care they received at CSC. They won't know about the aunties or nurses who sat on the edge of their beds in the hospital, mopping their feverish brows while saying a prayer, reading them a book, or singing a lullaby. They won't know about the midnight trips to the pharmacy or the lab, the hours spent waiting at doctors' offices, or the days of worry and stress endured while nursing them back to health. And they probably won't know the price that was paid by everyone at CSC to keep them healthy. Not only is there the financial price for doctors' visits, hospitalization, medicine, lab tests, and salaries for our nurses and childcare leaders, but there is a lot of emotion, effort, and faith that is spent, too. And it has always been money, time, sweat, and tears well spent for the precious kids at CSC.

Institutions

THE TERM *INSTITUTION* can be used for people, events, activities, and traditions that have become regular, and seemingly indispensable, parts of life for CSC. For instance, we could say that the CSC annual banquet and newsletter are institutions that have existed for many years and are very much a part of the fabric of the stateside ministry. And we could bestow institutional status on Joemar, who has been around CSC for more than 30 years and has entertained and influenced thousands of people who have lived at CSC and worked for and visited us. Here are some other CSC institutions:

Christmas Activities

THE CHILDREN OF HOPE **Christmas pageant** kicks off the season. Costumes, songs, decorations, spoken pieces, and laughter combine for festive and heart-warming presentations that encapsulate the message of Christmas and showcase our students' talents.

Our **workers' Christmas party** is a chance to honor the work they do and give them a fun night of good food, laughs, presentations, games, more laughs, awards, music, and still more laughs. Cash and grocery gifts are given; a nice dinner is served; and a program is presented that features musical, dramatic, and dance numbers by the different homes or departments of CSC, and the awarding of door prizes. Workers dress up fancily for the party, which is planned by a committee of their peers. The staff and some former employees are on duty with the children that night so all our workers can attend. At the end of the night the older children distribute notes of thanks and love to the workers, who give so much of themselves to CSC throughout the year.

The **outreach party** has been going on every Christmas since the mid-1980s. It is for former residents of CSC who went back to live with their birth families, and their parents and siblings. Some of these former residents are being helped by our CSC outreach program with medical care, education, and other expenses. The outreach Christmas party brings them all together with our Social Work Department and the staff. It is a time of reunion, wild games, gift giving, and a presentation of the gospel through the Christmas story. Attendees look forward to this party all year long. Santa or one of his assistants/imposters makes an appearance each year to distribute gifts purchased by our social workers.

At our annual **progressive dinner** the kids are divided into four or five jeep loads and taken to staff members' homes for different meal courses. Each home provides an appetizer, salad, soup, or main course and a part of the Christmas story. Then everyone heads back to the Shelter for a dessert featuring cinnamon rolls topped with green frosting to complete the meal.

Junel's Box is an activity whereby our children can give money saved from their allowances to benefit a poor family in the community. It's named after one of our former kids, Larry Junel, who, in spite of having lived in abject poverty for most of his life, wanted to help children he heard about in school who didn't have money for shoes. We have a decorated box for the kids' cash donations, and this money is used to buy food, personal care items, building supplies, and home furnishings for a family selected by our social workers. Some older kids help with shopping, and all the kids and staff pile into jeeps and go to sing and give gifts to the family.

Christmas Eve is when the CSC kids get their gifts from Santa. We have had a long lineup of great Santas, usually someone who is visiting at Christmas time, or a missionary friend. We have invented lots of creative ways for Santa to make his entrance, always trying to keep the kids guessing.

Santa has arrived in a horse carriage, on top of a jeep, in an ambulance, a fire truck, and even an armored car. Ambulance attendants carried a sickly Santa in on a stretcher one year, with a nurse monitoring his heartbeat. When Howard Plucar was serving as Saint Nick, police came, handcuffed him, and took him off to jail for being a fake Santa. Luckily the "real" Santa arrived with the awaited gifts before the kids could get stressed.

After his big entry, Santa goes into the school to distribute gifts the staff have purchased and wrapped for each child, calling them up one by one to sit on his lap. Bedtimes are relaxed so the kids can play or model their gifts and watch the fireworks that are always a feature of Christmas Eve in Cebu City.

Christmas Day dinner is served in the late afternoon. After we eat there is a depiction of the Christmas nativity with live animals. This was something I instituted to honor Ron Eckert, a former pastor of Mitch Ohlendorf's and mine who used to get live animals for the church pageant at Central Baptist Church. The Christmas dinner at CSC has always consisted of baked ham, mashed potatoes, rice (to placate those for whom dinner isn't dinner without rice), green bean casserole, fruit, and Christmas cookies made by the staff and kids.

There are almost always **visitors at Christmas** because CSC is a fun place to be for the holiday season. We usually choose our Santa for the year from among our visitors so the kids won't easily recognize him. Often, Christmas visitors bring presents for the children. One year we heard from Holt International that a group from their offices in Oregon would be visiting and would bring money to pay for a gift for each child. We were supposed to buy the gifts in advance of their coming so the group could watch the kids open them.

We were eating supper on the evening of their arrival, having totally forgotten that they were coming that night for a meal and gift giving. We saw them drive past the Shelter and head up to the school, where they thought the party would be held. We panicked! We hadn't prepared food or bought gifts. Our staff huddled and agreed that one vehicle would go to Pizza Hut and get food while another would take the staff women and house parents to buy a gift for each child. It ended up being the most amazing feat of fast thinking, faster action, and amazing teamwork I've ever seen.

I went to the school and brought the group to the Shelter, where we gave them an extended tour of the houses and infirmary. We had a time of questions and answers. We stalled and stalled some more. We had a sing-along. We had the visitors introduce themselves, which took up so much time that we had the children introduce themselves, too. When the pizzas arrived, we quickly set the picnic table and started supper. "Who wants more?" we kept asking. Soon they didn't want any more. Our guests started getting their cameras ready to get shots of the kids opening their gifts. What gifts?

After seemingly an eternity, the guard reported that the CSC van had just passed by on the way to the school, so we rounded up the kids and the Holtians and headed up for gift opening. Afterwards, one visitor commented that they were impressed with the thoughtfulness of the gifts we had purchased on their behalf!

Holiday Activities

EITHER AT THE SCHOOL OR THE SHELTER, staff and teachers always have **special activities** for the kids on holidays such as July 4 (Philippine American Friendship Day), Easter, United Nations Day, Philippine Heroes Day, New Year's Eve, and Thanksgiving Day. Even though Thanksgiving is not an official Philippine holiday, the kids enjoy celebrating with us. We have an annual turkey drawing contest for the kids; the winner gets to have turkey dinner with the staff on Thanksgiving night at the home of a staff family. Often on Thanksgiving Day a live turkey appears at school, to the delight of the kids—and teachers! The kids and adults then have a turkey calling contest, usually won, in recent years, by Eicher Home house parent Uncle DonDon.

On July 4 the staff parade into the school wearing patriot hats and playing "Stars and Stripes Forever" while tossing candy to the kids. On New Year's Eve just about every household in Cebu blows off fireworks of all kinds, so the older CSC kids stay up and watch and have a snack just after midnight.

Adoption Institutions

TELLINGS ARE WHEN WE INFORM THE OLDER CHILDREN they will be adopted. These meetings involve staff, house parents, and the kid(s) to be "told," and are always happy and emotional times for everyone. We present the kids with picture books from their families-to-be, show them on a map where they will be living, and say a prayer of thanksgiving and praise to God for answered prayers for a family. One of the staff, often Joel Reasoner in later years, videotapes the tellings to give to the adoptive parents, together with pictures of their child's time at CSC.

Skype calls take place between adoptive parents and older CSC child(ren) a few months before departure. Kids get to know their new parents a little before meeting them in person. Often the kids are shy at first, so there's a lot of silence. But eventually everyone warm ups and some conversations start. Some kids want to take the camera around so the parents can meet their friends or house parents. Some sing a song or tell about their favorite things. They have a lot of questions. One adoptive couple from Australia took their phone outside and showed their kids a kangaroo near their gate. Often the whole family, including grandparents and other relatives, is there for the Skype.

Most **arrivals** on international flights arrive in Cebu either late at night or mid-morning. Someone from CSC meets the flight. Those arriving at night proceed to their hotels, to be picked up in the morning to meet their child(ren). Those arriving in the morning go straight to Banawa.

It's always an exciting time at CSC. The kids who will be meeting their new parents get dressed up. A greeting on the greenboard is written by Uncle Patrick. Lunch is ready. Emotions peak as the van pulls into CSC and proceeds to the picnic area, where the meeting takes place. Sometimes parents-to- be start opening the door before the van stops, wanting to run to their new child(ren).

City tours were led by Marlys for every adoptive family who came to Cebu. It was a chance for them to see the city where their child(ren) came from. Highlights included Fort San Pedro, built by the Spanish in 1565 and the oldest fort in the Philippines; Cebu City Hall; Cebu Harbor; and, for the kids who came from Cebu City, the place where they were born or lived prior to coming to us.

Meetings with staff give adoptive parents an opportunity to learn as much as possible about their child(ren) while they were at CSC. Typically, parents have separate meetings with the house parents, social workers, teachers, counselors, and medical team.

Farewells are emotional occasions, when a child or sibling group is about to leave with their new family. Everyone gathers at the picnic area, where there is a prayer for the family, a chance for the adoptive parents to share their feelings, and a traditional song by all the children: "God Will Take Care of You":

> Be not dismayed whate'er betide
> God will take care of you
> Beneath His wings of love abide
> God will take care of you.
> God will take care of you
> Through every day, o'er all the way
> He will take care of you,
> God will take care of you.

This time is often especially poignant for older children being adopted, some of whom stood and sang that song many times for other kids leaving. Now it's finally their time. If you could sit through that and not shed a tear . . . well you probably aren't reading this book in the first place!

Aside from adoptive families, it became our practice to have farewell observances for visitors returning home and staff going on furlough or retiring. These farewells were often emotional, with lots of hugs and tears.

Someone once said that CSC is a difficult place to leave. Our kids, workers, and staff have had a lot of experience greeting and then saying goodbye to people.

Welcome Lunches

THOUSANDS OF VISITORS TO CSC have been given a welcome lunch in one of the homes, attended by staff, house parents, and kids from the house where the luncheon is held. The menu has stayed the same for years: egg salad or chicken salad sandwiches, chips, roast chicken, and mangos. In addition to being served good food, visitors are given a greeting by the field director and introductions of staff members in attendance. Although most of these lunches are planned well in advance, sometimes visitors arrive unannounced at mealtime, and the house parents and staff have to scramble to get a meal ready and call people to attend on short notice.

Birthday Parties

EACH CSC CHILD HAS THEIR OWN BIRTHDAY PARTY, though with more than one birthday on the same day, we combine parties. These are attended by the staff and kids at the home where the celebrant lives, along with any visitors who are on hand. The kids choose the menu for their party, and most have spaghetti, lumpia (Philippine eggrolls), roast chicken, or pancit (rice noodles with chopped vegetables and meat). There's always a birthday cake and ice cream, followed by opening gifts, with the other kids and aunties crowded around to ooh and ahh. Our kids are always excited to celebrate their birthday. And, although it means our staff has to go out 70 or more nights a year, we all enjoy being a part of these institutions in CSC community life.

Humor

IS THERE A RECIPE FOR SUCCESS IN CHILDREN'S MINISTRY? Certainly there are some necessary ingredients: a calling, reliance on God, integrity, stable finances, and loads of patience and compassion. Might I suggest something else?

For some it might be a subtle component while for others it's the main ingredient. I'm talking about humor and laughter. For me, injecting humor into the ministry of CSC was easy but very important. I recognize that not everyone finds humor to be either of these. Humor came easily to me because of my upbringing; my dad was the funniest person I've ever known. Humor and laughter were always a part of our family life. We could see the funny side of people and events.

I think one healthy byproduct of humor is that through it we learn to laugh at events and people, including ourselves. Mark Twain said that "humor is the great thing, the saving thing after all. The minute it crops up, all our hardnesses yield, all our irritations and resentments flit away, and a sunny spirit takes their place." I believe Twain was right. Humor is a life skill and we all need it. We have always strived for a "sunny spirit" at CSC.

At many tense meetings over the years, anger and contentiousness were defused by the injection of humor into the proceedings. Humor and laughter and fun go together with kids. Humor is infectious, and an element of our success at CSC is that humor and fun started with the adults— staff, workers, and leaders—and spread to the kids.

I learned this lesson from Chuck Sorlie, former youth minister at Central Baptist Church in St. Paul, who brought teams to CSC to do off-site camps. Chuck is energetic and fun and skilled at getting kids excited about camp activities. His song leading and story telling are legendary at Central and CSC, and he told me once that if the leaders are having fun, the kids will follow. Some of his games and songs were funny and even goofy, but always fun for our kids.

CSC is a place of fun and laughter. Many visitors to CSC have commented that "your kids look so happy." It's true. They looked happy because they were happy. Even though most of them had difficult life experiences— abuse, neglect, sickness, malnutrition, abandonment, fear, and lack of hope—things changed when they got to CSC. All their problems did not simply go away, but their load was lightened and their childhood was restored, complete with fun, happiness, and laughter. Perhaps, aside from learning about the love and salvation of Jesus Christ, the best gift we can give our kids when they leave CSC is the gift of humor.

I am aware that some people found my sense of humor irreverent. Certainly it was not always politically correct by U.S. standards. Sometimes my stunts might have been funny to Americans but not Filipinos, or vice versa. And I'm sure that sometimes it wasn't funny by any standard or to any group.

Once I brought a group of friends to the Cebu Bible Training Institute in Naga, Cebu, for a fun night with the students. Our friends, the Henrys, did the music, and the rest was skits and humor. One stunt was to smear a shaving cream pie in the face of a guy named Ray, who was reading a lengthy poem by Lord Byron. Good, clean, slapstick humor. Even better, though unplanned, was that Ray's toupee almost fell off. To say it went over like a lead balloon would be overstating the response to that gag.

I am forever thankful to my co-workers and all the kids and visitors who endured—usually with grace, patience, and tolerance—my attempts at humor. I always thought they were worth the effort, and I hope we succeeded more times than we failed.

Here are some funny events at CSC:

We had uproarious Christmas Eve skits with wild antics and bizarre, twisting plots involving fake Santas, naughty elves, and surprise endings. A couple times I was asked to give my version of the Christmas standard "Walking in My Winter Underwear." For some reason the requests stopped coming in.

We had rock and roll parody concerts featuring Mitch Ohlendorf, Joemar, myself, and some friends of CSC known as the Trash Band, featuring songs like "Rogainne" and "The YumYum Tree." The group existed in one form or another for more than 30 years. Some non-CSC members were Jonathan and Jerome Sarmiento, Kenneth Aballe, Martz Padilla, Eric Larson, Francis Gershua, and pastor Lowell Tallo.

Joel Reasoner rode a water buffalo and had his head shaved as a result of the kids winning the Reading Challenge, and they threw me in the swimming pool with my clothes on for another contest incentive. Including adults in the humor made it all the funnier for our kids.

Marv Hadenfeldt, a friend and frequent visitor, came to CSC every year with his hilarious puppet Lokoy.

At one point we had three Jacobs living in the Duterte Home. Uncle Patrick, the house father, at Jacob Collamat's birthday party made a joke by having a rousing introduction and a grand entry for Jacob, but for the wrong one. Twice. When the right Jacob was finally wheeled into the dining room in his wheel chair, he and all the kids were laughing uproariously.

Ginda, who also is in a wheel chair, loved to try and trip Auntie Tammy Vosika. When Tammy walked by, Ginda raised her leg at just the right time.

Tammy went into an exaggerated fall and Ginda roared.

Perhaps these incidents are in the category of "you had to have been there to appreciate it" humor. Undoubtedly. But I wish everyone reading this could have been there sometimes to participate in our unique style of fun that made everyone smile and savor the moment in our community of love and laughter.

Laughter and fun even extended to Luke, our little guy with CP and major brain damage, who needed one-on-one care 24/7 for his whole life and who never was able to walk or talk or move his arms or legs voluntarily. He was usually in pain and a grimace could often be seen on his face. But I will never forget one of our childcare workers, Auntie Gaga, who was usually assigned to care for Luke. She talked to him, laughing and teasing and tickling until, against all odds, Luke broke out in a huge, radiant, bright, magical, laughing smile. It wasn't just his mouth that smiled; his whole body was part of it. It lit up the room and every heart in it.

Perhaps that smile is the best metaphor for the ministry of CSC. In a world of fear and hurt, when things were tough and hope was hard to find, when physical or emotional pain just wouldn't go away, when frowns and tears would be an appropriate and expected response to life, Luke smiled. He laughed. He responded. And praise to God that someone was there to see it, to absorb and reflect it, and, in so doing, give meaning and purpose to his life. And for the rest of us, Luke's smile reminded us that our problems seem insignificant when we challenge them with a smile that comes from a joyful heart.

Stories

Amateur Social Workers

IN 1984, A MISSIONARY COUPLE serving in Cebu City expressed an interest in adopting three of our children. One had been living in Cebu but came from another island, Samar. Those were the days before CSC had its own social worker, so I was handling some of those duties.

For this girl to be eligible for adoption, her birth mother had to be found, and she needed to sign a surrender document if she was unable or unwilling to parent her. I had never traveled to Samar before and didn't speak Waray, the language of that province. I asked my good friend Pastor

Prisco Allocod if he would go with me in search of the mother, not knowing where this task would take us and how much time it would involve. We had the name of a small town on the island of Samar, but that was the only information to help us. We were young and motivated but hopelessly unprepared—two amateur social workers heading for the field and an adventure they could not have imagined.

Our travel to a remote part of eastern Samar began with a plane ride from Cebu to Tacloban, Leyte. That was to be one of seven different modes of transportation we would take in the next few days. Prisco didn't speak Waray either but could converse in Tagalog, which enabled us to get basic information along the way.

From Tacloban we took a bus across the island to eastern Samar. We didn't know it at the time but learned later that this trek took us through dangerous areas controlled by communist rebels, not the safest place for an American to be traveling in those days. From the town of Borongan we rode a jeepney south along the eastern seaboard of Samar. (We were going to a place so remote that people who lived on the same island didn't know where it was.) Soon we came to a bridge that had been destroyed in a recent typhoon, so we had to take a barge to the opposite side of the river. From there we took another jeepney as far as it would go.

Now the roads were getting rough, so we switched to riding on the back of two motorcycles. We ended up in the town of Giporlos, far from any city. It was mid-afternoon when we got there, but we learned that the village where we needed to go could only be reached by a banca, a narrow motorized boat with runners used by fisherman in the Philippines.

We found a social worker in Giporlos who was willing to accompany us, so we climbed aboard and headed towards Giguso, not knowing if and how we would be able to find the woman we were seeking. The water was rough and the small boat's motor stopped a few times, causing us to bounce around in the ocean. Prisco was half my weight and the social worker quite a bit less than his, so distributing the weight safely in the boat was impossible. Each time the boat operator was able to get the motor going again, and after two hours we arrived in the remote village of Giguso. We went ashore and rested on some big rocks along the coastline.

The social worker went ahead and made inquiries, not wanting the American to have to wander around the village. She was sure that no American had been to this place in many years. A half hour later she returned and informed us that she had found the mother, but that we needed to talk first with some of the village leaders. When we arrived at the home of the barangay captain, the elected leader of that place, we learned that no American had been in their village since World War II. He pointed out the place where an American navy ship had anchored.

As we walked towards the mother's house, a curious crowd began following us. Word spread ahead of them so that when we got there the mother already knew we were looking for her. She was frightened and unable to talk or walk very well because she was suffering from cerebral palsy. Informed that the group was looking for her to discuss the situation of her daughter in Cebu, she was shocked and worried.

Prisco and I learned that the girl had been brought by her grandma to Cebu to live with an aunt. The mother didn't know that the girl had been neglected and abused while in Cebu, and that the government had eventually intervened and placed the child with Corpus Christi. She was happy and surprised to learn that the girl was being cared for by Americans. She told us, through a family member who could understand her speech, that she was unable to provide for her daughter and that she hoped her daughter could be adopted into a family where she would be safe and loved. She said that she would sign a surrender document.

The social worker informed us that the signature would need to be notarized but that the nearest notary public was in the town where we had come from. So we brought the mother and the grandmother to the banca boat and headed back to Giporlos. As we motored away from the village I noticed that the mother was crying. When I pointed it out to the social worker, she said the woman had never been on a boat before and had never left the village. This was a huge stretch for her, fueled by her desire to make a better way for her daughter, whom she would probably never see again.

Although it was now late at night and very dark on the ocean, the boat operator found his way back to Giporlos, though not without some frightening moments for the exhausted American and his boatload of companions. When we got to the town's harbor, we hopped on a tricycle (a motorcycle and sidecar) and headed for the home of the only notary public within miles. We learned that there was a ship leaving for Tacloban in one hour, and that was just about the only way to get out of there that night.

When we arrived, we found that the notary had already gone to bed, and when his maid informed him that visitors were downstairs and needed documents notarized, he said to tell us to come back the next day. We had no place to stay, so I asked Prisco to tell the maid to inform the notary that we were up against a major time crunch and really needed him to notarize the documents right away. "Impossible," said the notary public; he was already in bed.

Prisco and I had a brief meeting and I did some soul searching (for about 15 seconds) before sending Prisco back to talk to the maid with an offer we felt would be an incentive for the honorable notary to notarize the document post haste. The maid came back with a counter offer and, a few minutes later, the papers were headed upstairs for the notarization.

With notarized papers in hand, we sent the mother back to her island in the banca and headed out. We took a motorized trike to the pier and ran onto the gangplank just as it was being pulled in. When the ship arrived in Tacloban, we hustled into a taxi and headed for the airport. It was tight but we made the flight and laughed most of the way back to Cebu.

Hey, we thought, this social worker job is fun!

Rock Video

FOR A NUMBER OF YEARS I would make a slide show or video for the adopted kids party in Minnesota, held each year in conjunction with the CSC banquet. These were often humorous productions, perhaps a little silly.

One year I got the idea of doing a rock video with some CSC kids and staff. It featured a song popular at the time, "Come on Over, Baby," and involved dancing and lip syncing. The day we made it at the school, we had to blast the music so the kids could hear it for their dance movements. Ruth Ohlendorf and Lynn Burke helped with the choreography.

We shot it after school, and things were wild and noisy when two visitors arrived at the Shelter. It was Rollie and Esther Reasoner, grandparents of Joel and mother and father-in-law of Shari, our education director. They were retired missionaries from Japan visiting CSC for the first time. Marlys had greeted them at the Shelter and decided to bring them up to see the school, not knowing about the rock video. She was horrified when they came through the gate to see all the kids doing a big dance number to loud pop music blasted from speakers pointed right at the senior missionaries! Thankfully, the couple was understanding and continued to be supporters of CSC. Maybe they even liked the video!

A Baserunning Blooper

IN THE 1990S WE HAD A BASEBALL TEAM AT CSC, and for the younger kids a tee-ball team. Both teams were the Twins. The kids loved to play, and Mitch and I, with help from Ben Bonnett, enjoyed coaching. The other kids in the league were from families of expatriate American parents and wealthy Filipino families.

Our kids had never played baseball before, but we practiced a lot, trying to give them a picture of the sport, teach some of the rules, and develop basic skills of throwing, catching, and hitting.

We thought we had done a pretty good job of preparing the team for our first game. In the second inning, one of our kids, Lito, stepped to the plate to the cheers of the substantial CSC rooting section. He gripped the bat, peered at the pitcher, and, when the pitch arrived, took a huge swing and connected with a hot line drive into the outfield. "Run!" we screamed.

Lito took off running towards first base. When he got to the bag he made a hard, acute left and headed for third base! In all our coaching, while we had concentrated on things like what to do if you are in a rundown, tagging up on a fly ball, being sure to touch the base before advancing, cutoff throws, and how and when to bunt, we had made some basic assumptions we should not have made. We failed to teach base sequencing. We all had a good laugh about that play. Even Lito!

A Seafood Science Lesson

(Warning to those with weak stomachs: This might inspire a gag reflex. Or worse. Check with your doctor before reading.)

MY BROTHER WILL AND HIS FAMILY WERE IN CEBU FOR A VISIT IN 2004. The church he was pastoring at the time, Emmaus, in Northfield, Minnesota, had paid for all of them to visit Cebu, and I was excited to see them. We had a great time showing them around Cebu and CSC.

One day I brought Will to a fashionable hotel for supper. Though he was in exotic Southeast Asia, he cautiously ordered a burger. I went with the seafood buffet—just about every kind of seafood you could imagine. Let's just say that I consumed much of that variety. That night my stomach felt a little queasy, and by morning I was expelling much of the ocean's bounty I had consumed the night before. I was really sick.

I know that millions of people have gotten sick while in a country like the Philippines, so it was no big deal, even though I ended up in the hospital for three days with food poisoning and amoebic dysentery. But I learned something from that experience that most people, even students of science like physicists or gastroenterologists, do not know and haven't even considered. Here it is: A calamari ring that flies out of your nose will spin in a counter-clockwise manner from the right nostril if you are above the equator. I proved that several times within an hour, as well as the left nostril corollary.

Some have told me that I should have written my findings up in a scientific journal for the betterment of mankind, but I didn't. (Unless I experimented below the equator, my findings would be suspect.) But if even one person is helped by my including it here, I will be happy.

Cabulan Island Drama

ONE DAY I FOUND MYSELF ON A SMALL BOAT with a group of friends, heading for Cabulan, a small island off Bohol. The boat belonged to World Vision, and we were going to visit Romulo and Myrna Alejado, who ran a World Vision program sponsored by their church. CSC often did children's outreach programs in those days, before we had lots of kids to care for.

The weather turned windy as we headed for Cabulan, and water washed over us with each big wave. One in our group was wearing a toupee, and each time a wave hit he had to hold it on with one hand and grip the side of the boat with the other. We thought we might lose him and the hairpiece over the side.

It was scary for me, and I could sense some apprehension even among the Filipinos, some of whom were experienced boaters. The man from World Vision who was driving the boat seemed concerned as well. He was worried about taking on water and about how he would land the boat on the rocky shore once, and if, we made it to Cabulan.

We did eventually arrive, and the islanders shook their heads and told us they were sure we wouldn't come that day because of the weather. We were invited to lunch, but nobody had the stomach for eating after that trip. We toured the island and invited people to come to the service that night at the community stage.

That night there was a nice crowd. We figured there would be since there was nothing else for people to do there, and word had spread over the island that there was a higante (giant) amerikano to be seen.

After the perfunctory songs and introductions by the Alejados, we did a skit for the kids. We called them up on the stage to watch. It was a story about two friends who got into a fight. They were eventually to reconcile and there was some spiritual application coming.

But when the fight began the kids all panicked. They jumped off the stage and ran away as fast as they could. They thought the fight was real! Our drama troupe had done such a realistic job that we caused a near riot. These kids had rarely, if ever, seen a dramatic production like this one. Many had never watched television or seen a movie. They were fishermen's kids on a remote island, largely ignorant of dramatic device.

The kids were called back to the stage, and Romulo explained that it was just a story and not real. He suggested we start again, and we did. When we came to the fight part, even though we toned it down, the kids panicked again! They jumped off the stage and headed for home. That was the end of the night's program! We had risked our lives and our companion's hairpiece for a couple of near riots.

Encouragement

WHAT KEPT US GOING FOR THE PAST 43 YEARS? What was our source of encouragement? Aside from our sense of calling and purpose, what helped us keep our eyes on the road and avoid the pitfalls of negativism and defeatism? Perhaps it would be instructive to start with the negative, looking at where our encouragement did not come from.

I've described the time at the beginning of our ministry in Cebu when Marlys and I visited a DSWD official in Manila who led the Bureau of Child Welfare. During our meeting she let us know in no uncertain terms that our proposed program in Cebu for homeless children was not needed and we should come up with another plan or go home. Although that rebuke had a harshness that we didn't ever experience again, it was, in a general sense, an extreme example of an attitude of distrust and lack of cooperation that we saw in most of the government agencies we encountered.

I can honestly say that I do not remember more than a couple of times in 43 years of working in Cebu that we received a compliment or a word of encouragement from any branch of government in Cebu or Manila. That simply is not how the system works there. The attitude of government was often that they were above us, that we operated only with their permission, and their role was to oversee and formulate policies, standards, and requirements such as permits, licenses, and accreditations—not to hand out words of thanks and encouragement.

Aside from recognizing me when my retirement was announced at the Global Consultation in Manila in 2018, I cannot remember a single time that an executive director of ICAB or a regional director of the DSWD, Department of Education, or Ministry of Health gave a word of thanks or appreciation to CSC for its work on behalf of homeless Filipino children. And that lack of encouragement did not only involve upper-echelon government people. It extended down through the ranks to social workers and direct service workers and even to barangay officials in the communities where we worked.

Perhaps it's like that in other countries as well, but in the Philippines there is often a contentious relationship between government and non-government agencies that can be felt in many aspects of their relationships. Even as we amassed a track record of long-term excellence in Cebu, encouragement was, for the most part, not forthcoming.

When our friend Ron Duterte was vice mayor of Cebu City, CSC was nominated for an Award of Excellence by city government. We got a certificate from the city at an awards dinner held at Plaza de Independencia. But Ron had made that award happen. He was both the nominator and the decision maker. The mayor and city council members did not even know where CSC was or who was running it. After Ron's time in office, until the present, a time frame of more than 35 years, CSC never received any award or nomination. The only recognition we received was a yearly official receipt for the fees we paid for our permit to operate.

It's true that government needs to uphold standards, guard against poor management, and offer protection for children in childcare agencies. We were always respectful of that reality, and we always followed the rules in our subservient relationships with government. But I have never understood the value gained by withholding encouragement and thanks from those who are doing a good job, sometimes in very difficult situations.

CSC was not just an asset to the children who lived with us or to the child welfare community in the Philippines. We employed more than 120 workers, giving opportunities for them to educate their own children and change their standards of living for generations to come. We pumped more than $40M into the economy, benefitting food venders, medical clinics, doctors, utilities companies, banks, and commercial establishments. We had facilities that were second to none in the entire country.

I remember when a man came to us to do an accreditation visit for the government. He had never been to CSC before, and he took an extended tour of our facilities. After seeing our residences, school, playground, infirmary, nurseries, offices, and therapy room, he didn't say a single word until he pulled out a tape measure and told us that our bunk beds were inches too high off the floor and out of compliance with some code we were previously unaware of.

During the pandemic, the Department of Labor and Employment wanted to cite us for some kind of labor law infraction, calling in Roberto Atienza to answer for CSC. In the course of their discussion, Roberto mentioned that CSC had around 130 employees, and more than 70% of them were being paid even though they were not working. Flabbergasted, the DOLE official didn't know what to say since our doing so was not a requirement of an employer, and was not being done by any other business or charity that he knew about.

So, the reality was that if we had needed a lot of stroking or back-patting from the community or government, we were in the wrong line of work in the Philippines. Luckily, we got considerable compliments and encouragement from other sources. Visitors raved about our facilities and our work with children. Supporters built us up by telling us they were happy with our financial integrity and the careful and prayerful way we stewarded our buildings and grounds. Adoptive families told us how happy they were for the blessings of adopting from CSC or how grateful they were for the way we hosted them during their time in Cebu. Non-government people all over the Philippines who heard about CSC or visited our campus gave us doses of positivity and support for our work. And the biggest source of encouragement came from our faithful supporters, who showed solidarity with our mission by giving faithfully and generously for 43 years. Some wrote positive notes, letters, and e-mails to us.

Although some adoptions of children from CSC did not go well, most had positive outcomes and were the source of joy and encouragement to our staff and workers. Marlys and I and other staff members had the pleasure of visiting former residents in their adoptive families or hosting them in Cebu when they came for a visit. Lots of tears of joy were shed in seeing how their lives were influenced by our work and the opportunity we gave them to be adopted. The chance to help in building families was the ultimate reward and encouragement to all of us.

Happy Homes

FOR MANY YEARS THE CSC STAFF had been concerned about our workers' quality of life. Although we were paying them a competitive wage with decent benefits, many were struggling financially and lived in substandard housing. Few were able to own their own home. Most were unable to save money. It was not uncommon for workers whose homes were on rented land or who were squatting on private property to lose their homes to fires, typhoons, or floods, or to have to relocate to another location. For many Filipinos, home ownership was something they would never be able to experience, no matter how they might dream of it.

One day in 2010, Joel Reasoner and his dad, Paul, had a conversation when Joel shared his concerns about the living condition of CSC's Filipino employees. Joel said that although they were part of the extraordinary care given to children at CSC, they themselves were often living in very difficult housing situations. Joel had worked at Habitat for Humanity in west central Minnesota and was very aware of how important housing is for quality of life. Paul was already involved with HFH-MN and had been raising funds for HFH projects. They decided to see if HFH in Cebu would be able to build houses for some CSC employees.

In the coming months, the Reasoners initiated negotiations with HFH in the Philippines, both on the Cebu and national levels, who agreed to work with us on building homes for our workers. This was complicated because of the different organizations involved, and there were frustrating delays in the process. HFH originally offered to purchase land for the project but later backed off and asked Paul Reasoner to raise those funds.

Paul and Joel negotiated for the project to be an "institutional build," which meant the houses would only be for CSC employees. They also made an agreement with HFH that Paul would raise money to be applied to the individual mortgages of our workers to make them more affordable. Further negotiations were made with the government mortgage agency, PAGIBIG, to handle the mortgages. CSC offered to help workers repay their mortgages through salary deductions.

In the end, Paul raised a significant amount of money for purchase of a lot and for gifts to each family for construction of their homes. The development needed to be in general proximity to CSC so the workers could get to work easily.

Needless to say, our workers who qualified for a new home were extremely excited when they were told about the project and got to see plans. They formed a homeowners association called CSC Happy Homes and started to dream about having a home of their own in a new community. They were in for a long wait, however.

In 2013 two natural disasters hit Cebu and the surrounding areas: a major earthquake and Typhoon Haiyan. As a result, HFH-Philippines put a halt to projects like ours, which were a typical model where the beneficiaries of the homes provided hours of "sweat equity," working on their homes as a down payment, and then took out a mortgage for the cost of the home. They shifted their focus to relief projects, building homes for those who lost theirs in one of these tragedies. There were other delays in the project due to changes in the staff of HFH-Cebu and confusion as to what would actually be funded by Habitat and what needed to be provided by CSC and the Reasoners.

A parcel of land was eventually located for construction of the homes. HFH and the Reasoners had settled on 60 houses to be built for CSC workers and three for local families who would be displaced by the development. The lot, 6,754 square meters, was located in the city of Talisay, about 20 kilometers from CSC. It was finally purchased in early January of 2015, thanks to generous donors in the U.S., including two gifts of $100,000. Paul Reasoner was proving to be not only a visionary but a skilled fundraiser and a patient negotiator.

January 22, 2015, was the ground-breaking ceremony. Jan Plimpton, HFH-MN executive director, and a strong supporter of the CSC Happy Homes project, came to Cebu for the ceremony. She joined the Reasoners, a large group of HFH people from Manila and Cebu, CSC staff, and the eventual home owners for a joyful celebration of what was to happen on that site. Paul Reasoner remembers at the end of the ceremony when two CSC workers, with tears of joy in their eyes, asked if they could start clearing rocks from the land right away.

Paul Reasoner had another grand surprise for the already excited beneficiaries. He announced that he had raised $20,000 for a vehicle that would be donated to the Home Owners Association when the project was completed. It would be used to transport CSC employees back and forth between the Happy Homes community and CSC.

All of 2015 and 2016 were taken up with HFH trying to get the title for the lot transferred from the original owners into HFH's name. This was a time of wrangling about lost documents and changing personnel in charge of the title transfer. It was a frustrating time for everyone, especially Paul, who had to answer questions from donors about the project's progress.

In 2017, the deed was finally transferred and construction on the Talisay site began. In mid-August, HFH changed contractors and staff in the main office in Manila, as well as in Cebu. The new COO from HFH-Philippines, Lili Fuentes, visited the site several times and, eventually, the construction work began picking up. Around this time four teams of Japanese university students began helping on the build.

On August 17, 2017, raffles were held for each of the CSC employees in the group of 60 who would receive homes based on a selection process by a committee of HFH and CSC representatives. Lots were drawn to determine which home each would get. This took place at the Children of Hope School and was a time of great excitement and rejoicing.

CSC employees who were receiving HFH houses were required to put in 250 hours of sweat equity on their home. Shari Reasoner went to Cebu in the fall of 2017 for five weeks to work on the site, moving rocks and dirt to prepare the lots for footings. She donated her hours to some employees who, for health reasons, had trouble completing their 250 hours of sweat equity.

In June of 2018, Shari and Paul were in Cebu visiting the project. The homes were mostly completed, but several things were badly needed: a security wall to keep people out of the construction area, and some major drainage work. Paul raised additional funds in Minnesota to pay for these projects to keep things moving along in Talisay. CSC paid for the Dizons, a couple who had worked on construction of the infirmary and Duterte Home in Banawa, to spearhead these projects.

The Turnover Ceremony was held on October 28, 2018, at the Talisay property. All 63 homes had been completed. The week before the turnover was a whirlwind of activity to get water connected, temporary electricity supplied by a generator, and a host of other last-minute things. At this time officers of CSC Happy Homes were elected and the community was born.

As this book is being completed, about half of the beneficiaries are ready to start their mortgages with PAGIBIG. This long delay has been due in part to COVID but also because of the time it is taking to get individual lot titles into the names of each beneficiary. This process has not been finalized, and HFH-Philippines is waiting until all beneficiaries have the necessary paperwork completed to start their mortgages so the titles can be transferred all at once.

Aside from the Reasoners, who initiated this amazing project and saw it through to completion, kudos should be given to Jerry Salgo, CSC's director of maintenance, transportation, and security. Although Joel Reasoner was the main liaison with HFH throughout the project, Jerry served as a liaison with the construction teams and HFH administrators; did actual plumbing, construction, and electrical work on the units when the builders had done substandard work or had refused to do work we felt was necessary; and fielded questions and complaints from homeowners when there were problems with their units.

It is difficult to grasp the extent of the blessing that CSC Happy Homes has been for our workers who were able to get a new home. Although to the Western eye they might seem small, they are not seen that way by the homeowners. They are solidly built and provide protection from the elements. The houses are situated on streets where children can run and play safely. There is a spirit of camaraderie and community that has increased the quality of life for everyone in Happy Homes, not only for today but for generations to come.

Snapshots

WE HAVE AMASSED A TON OF PICTURES during 42 years. And tons more have been taken by people who visited us. Todd Erickson and Chuck Sorlie from Central Baptist probably have more photos than everyone else combined.

CSC makes for great pictures. The kids have been willing subjects, and the staff and workers have been gracious and kind. Who knows how many hundreds of thousands of pictures exist on CDs, hard drives, camera cards, and other devices around the world? I'm happy they exist, and Marlys and I will certainly feast on them throughout our retirement years.

But I long for the photographs that don't exist, the snapshots that are stored only in my mind or in the minds of other staff or workers. Nobody was there nor was anyone prepared to take those shots. They don't exist physically but they are still a part of CSC's story. I want them recorded, the best I can, through the words I write. They have been reviewed countless times in the photo albums of my memory, where they are more vivid and captivating than my words can ever be. But I don't want these mental snapshots to die when we are gone. Let me open the album and share some of these pictures as I close out this history of CSC.

I made it to the hospital as Luke was taking his last breaths. Labored and agonized breaths. I had held him many times during his 23 years. I was used to hearing him rasp and struggle, but this was somehow different. The angels were clearly on the way, as Marlys had recognized when she called and told me to go to the hospital as soon as I could. I looked into his eyes, wondering, as I always had, whether he could see me or how much of his situation he could grasp. I wanted so much for his suffering to be over. The aunties in the room with him said they thought he had been waiting for me. I don't know. Maybe that was true on some level. I know he recognized my voice and maybe my touch.

I told him, "Go to Jesus, Luke. I love you. Go dance with Jesus." His breathing seemed to ease a bit. I looked into his eyes and I saw . . . eternity. I saw heaven in a way no written description could ever capture. Not 23 years of suffering, but a forever of well-being. That snapshot of eternity in his eyes was vivid for me as they closed for the last time. How I want Aunties Gaga, Veronica, and others in the Cherne Home to know about that picture. They held him, kissed him, fed him, cleaned and changed him, and sang to him, their reward an occasional big smile. That picture is my assurance that Luke is waiting for all of us beyond the sunset in a place where there is no crying, pain, or disability.

J.L. was going to school for the first time in his life. His path to CSC had led him through difficulties and agonies we could only imagine, including seeing his twin brother die in a government hospital and suffering abuse from his cruel father. Being at CSC meant safety from abuse, quality medical care, friendships, good food and plenty of it.

And school. Children of Hope School. When the Chalmers family chose that name for the school they helped build, it was just this kind of student that I think they imagined. Kids who are admitted to CSC can begin school as soon as they are physically able. When J.L. entered school for the first time, he looked at the classrooms, books, and computers, raised his arms, spun around, and exclaimed, "I can't believe I'm in school!" That look of ecstasy produced a mental picture that tells the story of hope, thanksgiving, and joy that is the basis for our school.

Before coming to CSC, J.L. had given up on the possibility of ever going to school. Education is a privilege in the Philippines, not an entitlement. For the poor and disadvantaged it is often unattainable. And those who are able to attend endure class sizes of as many as 80, with few books or other educational materials. Many go to school having had no breakfast and lack the energy to concentrate. Many drop out.

I think of my own approach to school as a kid, taking for granted a comfortable and safe classroom, with plentiful books and recreational facilities. So often American kids don't appreciate the opportunities they have to study and learn. J.L.'s exaltative moment spoke of newfound hope in life that comes from educational opportunity. It was a gift, given by CSC to kids like him, because of the generosity of people like Dan and Carla Chalmers and other CSC supporters. I love that picture of the celebration of hope. And I can call it up any time I want!

AnnAnn was leaving Cebu for Minnesota, where she would have surgeries to her back and neck. She had walked into our lives when we were brand new to Cebu, needing lots of medical and emotional care. CSC was a place of stability in her life, and now she was leaving for an uncertain future. She walked bravely with her escorts toward the airport gate, holding her small bag. Where did that bravery come from?

That mental picture of AnnAnn walking away is really a picture of many, many kids who came into our lives for a time and then left us, going to other people who would love them and who could provide for them more completely than we could. When I see that picture in my mind, it reminds me of the many tears that came with adoption at CSC. We sang our goodbye song, said a prayer, and then watched as our precious, dearly loved child climbed into the van and drove out of our lives.

I was sitting with Jackson in a waiting room at the Shriners Childrens

Burns Hospital in Galveston, Texas. Jackson came to CSC with major burn scarring on his shoulder, chest, and back. We'd been able to get him in at Shriners and were waiting to see a doctor to learn what the decision would be about surgery and grafting. We waited and waited, way past our appointment time. Jackson got up to watch a couple of burn victim kids playing a game of pool. We were getting hungry and frustrated.

In the midst of our annoyance a boy, maybe seven or eight years old, walked into the waiting room and went over near Jackson. He was covered from head to toe with bandages. There were two holes in the wrappings for his eyes, another for his nose, and a small slit for his mouth. Probably 95% of his body was covered with third-degree burns. I looked at him for a long time, standing by Jackson, and a picture was snapped in my mind that still exists.

Of all the children in the waiting room, Jackson's condition was the least serious. Jackson stared at the little guy as I did. Suddenly I felt guilty for my annoyance at having to wait. I looked at the two boys standing near each other, and my heart filled with hope that Jackson would realize that his own situation, though painful and tragic, paled in comparison to what others had suffered and would continue to suffer for the rest of their lives. And not only Jackson but all our CSC kids. I wanted so much for empathy and compassion to enrich their hearts and lives. I wanted CSC to be a place where kids could see those qualities modeled by our staff and workers, and learn to have thankful hearts for what they have instead of what they lost.

And here is the image that visits me more than all the rest. I wish everyone in America could see it and know the backstory. I have written about Junel, the boy I went to get in Leyte. He had been living with his auntie, who had children of her own. Her kids got to eat first, and if there was any left, and there usually wasn't much or any, Junel got to eat. He wasn't allowed to sit at the table. He sat in the corner, third-degree malnourished, with a white film over part of his eyes from vitamin deficiency, hoping against hope that one of his cousins would leave something for him to eat. When he got to us he was shocked to discover that there was a place at the table for him and he could eat as much as he wanted. He wasn't second-string any more.

After his first meal with us, he looked into our kitchen. The picture in my head is of Junel standing by the kitchen door watching an auntie taking

351

leftover food from plates and scraping it into the garbage pail. He asked me what she was doing. Where was that food going? I told him it was going in the garbage. Maybe it would be given to the pigs. He was incredulous. I understood immediately what he was wondering, the source of his confusion. That discarded food was his. Though not enough to properly nourish him, it had kept him alive in his auntie's house. Someone needed that food.

How to explain the notion of excess or waste to a boy who had previously only known scarcity and deprivation? There were no words. And for me, just a picture. One that will stay in my mind as long as I live.